LIBRARY

Tel: 01244 375444 Ext: 3301

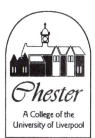

Chester

A College of the
University of Liverpool

This book is to be returned on or before the
last date stamped below. Overdue charges
will be incurred by the late return of books.

Family and Friends in Eighteenth-Century England

Household, Kinship, and Patronage

This is a book about the history of the family in eighteenth-century England. Naomi Tadmor provides a new interpretation of concepts of household, family, and kinship starting from her analysis of contemporary language (in the diaries of Thomas Turner; in conduct treatises by Samuel Richardson and Eliza Haywood; and in three novels, Richardson's *Pamela* and *Clarissa* and Haywood's *The History of Miss Betsy Thoughtless* and other sources). Naomi Tadmor emphasises the importance of the household in constructing notions of the family in the eighteenth century. She uncovers a vibrant language of kinship which recasts our understanding of kinship ties in the period. She also shows how strong ties of 'friendship' formed vital social, economic, and political networks among kin and non-kin. *Family and Friends in Eighteenth-Century England* makes a substantial contribution to eighteenth-century history, and will be of value to all historians and literary scholars of the period.

NAOMI TADMOR is a Fellow of New Hall, Cambridge. Her research is focused on the history of the family, and history and literature. She has published articles in *Past and Present*, *Social History*, and *Continuity and Change*, and was co-editor of *The Practice and Representation of Reading in England* (Cambridge, 1996).

Family and Friends in Eighteenth-Century England

Household, Kinship, and Patronage

Naomi Tadmor

New Hall, Cambridge

CAMBRIDGE
UNIVERSITY PRESS

PUBLISHED BY THE PRESS SYNDICATE OF THE UNIVERSITY OF CAMBRIDGE
The Pitt Building, Trumpington Street, Cambridge, United Kingdom

CAMBRIDGE UNIVERSITY PRESS
The Edinburgh Building, Cambridge CB2 2RU, UK
40 West 20th Street, New York, NY 10011– 4211, USA
30 Stamford Road, Oakleigh, VIC 3166, Australia
Ruiz de Alarcón 13, 28014 Madrid, Spain
Dock House, The Waterfront, Cape Town 8001, South Africa

http://www.cambridge.org

© Naomi Tadmor 2001

First published 2001

Printed in the United Kingdom at the University Press, Cambridge

Typeset in Plantin 10/12 pt [VN]

A catalogue record for this book is available from the British Library

Library of Congress cataloging in publication data

ISBN 0 521 77147 1 hardback

Contents

Acknowledgements

I would like to express my warmest thanks to my former research supervisor, Keith Wrightson, who not only directed my PhD but continued to read my drafts until this book finally emerged. Special thanks are also due to Adam Fox who read the entire typescript. I am grateful for the comments made by the anonymous readers at Cambridge University Press. Separate chapters have benefited lately from the criticism of Jean La Fontaine, Paul Ginsborg, Miri Rubin, and Amanda Vickery. Lizzy Emerson helped me to prepare the typescript for production and Vic Gatrell helped to find a picture for the cover. I have drawn on the expertise of Jonathan Herring on the subject of family law, and Barbara Bodenhorn on kinship. Stephen Bending, Christine Carpenter, Penelope Corfield, Larry Epstein, Robert Ferguson, Anne Goldgar, Joanna Innes, Lisa Jardine, Peter Laslett, Neil McKendrick, Linda Pollock, Richard Smith, James Raven, Zvi Razi, Moshe Sluhovsky, Richard Wall, and Jay Winter have all read parts of my work over the years and given me the benefit of their advice. So did the late Bob Scribner and the late Lawrence Stone. Michael Heyd, my teacher at the Hebrew University who first encouraged my interest in eighteenth-century history, continued to discuss with me my research long after I left Jerusalem. Other scholars in Jerusalem who contributed to the development of this project are Alon Kadish, Elihu Katz, Violet Khazoum, and Emmanuel Sivan.

Thanks are due not only to people but also to institutions. My undergraduate and graduate studies were assisted in various ways by the Departments of History, English Literature, and Communication at the Hebrew University. The Foreign and Commonwealth Office and Pembroke College, Cambridge, provided me with a research studentship. Gonville and Caius College supported generously my post-doctoral research. I am very grateful to the Fellows and students of New Hall for their great encouragement over the recent years.

Roger Davey and Christopher Whittick at the East Sussex Record Office, and librarians and archivists in Yale University Library gave me much help and expert advice. David Vaisey was extremely generous in letting me consult his transcripts of Thomas Turner's diary at the Bodleian Library.

The bulk of chapter 1 and some parts of the introduction and chapter 2 originally appeared in an article entitled 'The Concept of the Household-Family in Eighteenth-Century England' in *Past and Present* 151 (1996), 111–40, and are reprinted here with kind permission (World Copyright: The Past and Present Society, 175 Banbury Road, Oxford, England). Extracts from Thomas Turner's diary and related documents appear by kind permission of Yale University Library.

My greatest debts of gratitude are to my parents, Hayim and Miriam Tadmor, for nurturing me in this project, and to my husband and friend David Feldman for his endless support and scholarly insight. I dedicate this book to my parents.

A note on the text

All italics are mine, unless stated otherwise.

Abbreviations

BL Add. MS	British Library Additional Manuscript
CKS	Centre for Kentish Studies
ESRO	East Sussex Record Office
N&Q	*Notes and Queries*
OED	*Oxford English Dictionary*
P&P	*Past and Present*
SAC	*Sussex Archaeological Collections*
SCM	*Sussex County Magazine*
SNQ	*Sussex Notes and Queries*

Introduction

After decades of academic research on the history of the family in early modern England, scholars and students are both enlightened and perplexed. We now have a very considerable body of knowledge at our command. A field once dominated by ill-informed myths about family life in the past has been enriched with well-researched facts and many well-founded interpretations. Thus, for example, we now possess invaluable data on the demography of the family. We know the mean age at marriage of different populations, the average duration of marriage, rates of re-marriage, and the extent of non-marrying populations. We know how many children families in the past were likely to have, how many were born out of wedlock, and how many were likely to die before they reached maturity.[1] Beyond these facts and figures, we know much about conventions of courtship and marriage, as well as the history of marital breakdown.[2] We are aware of different life-cycle stages, from childhood

[1] See especially E. A. Wrigley and R. S. Schofield, *The Population History of England, 1541–1871: A Reconstruction* (Cambridge, 1989; 1st edn 1981); P. Laslett, *The World We Have Lost* (New York, 1965); P. Laslett, *Family Life and Illicit Love in Earlier Generations: Essays in Historical Sociology* (Cambridge, 1977); P. Laslett and R. Wall (eds.), *Household and Family in Past Time: Comparative Studies in the Size and Structure of the Domestic Group Over the Last Three Centuries in England, France, Serbia, Japan and Colonial North America* (Cambridge, 1972).

[2] The following represents a very small selection of works in this area: A. Macfarlane, *The Family Life of Ralph Josselin: A Seventeenth-Century Clergyman* (Cambridge, 1970); D. Levine, *Family Formation in an Age of Nascent Capitalism* (New York, 1977); R. B. Outhwaite (ed.), *Marriage and Society: Studies in the Social History of Marriage* (London, 1981); K. Wrightson, *English Society, 1580–1680* (London, 1982), chs. 2–4; R. Houlbrooke, *The English Family, 1450–1700* (London, 1984); M. Ingram, *Church Courts, Sex and Marriage in England, 1570–1640* (Cambridge, 1987); D. O'Hara, 'Ruled by my friends: aspects of marriage in the diocese of Canterbury *c.* 1540–1570', *Continuity and Change* 6 (1991), 9–41; R. B. Outhwaite, *Clandestine Marriage in England, 1500–1850* (London, 1995); D. Cressy, *Birth, Marriage and Death: Ritual, Religion and the Life Cycle in Tudor and Stuart England* (Oxford, 1997), esp. chs. 10–16. On separation and divorce see, for example, L. Stone, *Road to Divorce: England 1530–1987* (Oxford, 1992); L. Stone, *Broken Lives: Marriage and Divorce in England 1660–1875* (Oxford, 1995).

and adolescence to the experience of old age.³ We know about differences between town and country, rich and poor, east and west, north and south. Indeed, we have many studies that inform us about the experience of particular localities.⁴ We also know much about the different experiences of women and men in the past, and about the laws and customs that bred and nurtured these experiences.⁵

³ For childhood and adolescence, see, for example, R. Wall, 'The age at leaving home', *Journal of Family History* 3 (1978), 181–202; A. Kussmaul, *Servants in Husbandry in Early Modern England* (New Haven and London, 1981); J. H. Plumb, 'The new world of children in eighteenth-century England', in N. McKendrick, J. Brewer, and J. H. Plumb (eds.), *The Birth of a Consumer Society: The Commercialization of Eighteenth-Century England* (London, 1982), pp. 286–315; L. Pollock, *Forgotten Children: Parent–Child Relations from 1500–1900* (Cambridge, 1983); K. Thomas, 'Children in early modern England', in G. Avery and J. Briggs (eds.), *Children and their Books: A Celebration of the Work of Iona and Peter Opie* (Oxford, 1989), pp. 45–77; I. K. Ben-Amos, *Adolescence and Youth in Early Modern England* (New Haven and London, 1994); P. Griffiths, *Youth and Authority: Formative Experiences in England, 1560–1640* (Oxford, 1996). For old age, see, for example, P. Laslett, 'The history of aging and the aged', in Laslett, *Family Life and Illicit Love*, pp. 174–213; K. Thomas, 'Age and authority in early modern England', *Proceedings of the British Academy* 62 (1976), 205–48; R. M. Smith and M. Pelling (eds.), *Life, Death and the Elderly: Historical Perspectives* (London, 1994), chs. 3–4; S. Ottaway, 'Providing for the elderly in eighteenth-century England', *Continuity and Change* 13 (1998), 391–418; R. Houlbrooke, *Death, Religion and the Family in England, 1480–1750* (Oxford, 1998). See also Cressy, *Birth, Marriage and Death*, chs. 1–8, 17–20.
⁴ Important details about family life can be found, for example, in D. G. Hey, *An English Rural Community: Myddle under the Tudors and the Stuarts* (Leicester, 1974), esp. pp. 126–84, 198–218; K. Wrightson and D. Levine, *Poverty and Piety in an English Village: Terling, 1525–1700* (Oxford, 1995; 1st edn 1979), esp. chs. 3–4; N. Goose, 'Household size and structure in early Stuart Cambridge', *Social History* 5 (1980), 347–85; C. Howell, *Land, Family and Inheritance in Transition: Kibworth Harcourt* (Cambridge, 1983), esp. pp. 198–208, 237–69; J. Boulton, *Neighbourhood and Society: A London Suburb in the Seventeenth Century* (Cambridge, 1987), esp. pp. 120–37, 247–61; G. Nair, *Highley: The Development of a Community 1550–1880* (Oxford, 1988), esp. pp. 104–27; D. Levine and K. Wrightson, *The Making of an Industrial Society: Whickham 1560–1765* (Oxford, 1991), esp. pp. 308–44.
⁵ For example, K. Thomas, 'The double standard', *Journal of the History of Ideas* 20 (1959), 195–216; G. J. Schochet, *Patriarchalism in Political Thought* (Oxford, 1973); P. Crawford, 'Attitudes to menstruation in seventeenth-century England', *P&P* 91 (1981), 47–73; L. Charles and L. Duffin (eds.), *Women and Work in Pre-Industrial England* (London, 1985); J. A. Sharpe, *Defamation and Sexual Slander in Early Modern England* (York, 1980); V. Brodsky Elliot, 'Widows in late Elizabethan London: remarriage, economic opportunity and family orientation', in L. Bonfield and R. M. Smith (eds.), *The World We Have Gained: Essays Presented to Peter Laslett on his 70th Birthday* (Oxford, 1986), pp. 122–54; S. Amussen, *An Ordered Society: Gender and Class in Early Modern England* (Oxford, 1988); L. Pollock, '"Teach her to live under obedience": the making of women in the upper ranks of early modern England', *Continuity and Change* 4 (1989), 231–58; B. Hill, *Women, Work and Sexual Politics in Eighteenth-Century England* (London, 1989); P. Earle, 'The female labour market in London in the late seventeenth and early eighteenth centuries', *Economic History Review* 42 (1989), 328–53; V. Fildes (ed.), *Women as Mothers in Pre-Industrial England: Essays in Memory of Dorothy McLaren* (London, 1990); P. Sharpe, 'Literally spinsters: a new interpretation of local economy and demography in Colyton in the seventeenth and eighteenth centuries', *Economic History Review* 44 (1991), 46–65; A. J. Vickery, 'Golden age to separate spheres? A review of the categories and chronology of

This impressive accumulation of facts and interpretations attests to the productivity of historians of the family. The implications of this knowledge, however, reverberate well beyond the boundaries of this particular field. Over the last decades, findings about norms and customs of family life have informed research in many other areas, from the development of the agricultural economy and industrial change to practices of local government and state control; from the study of religious life and political thought to the study of popular culture.[6]

Yet if we seek to ascertain some comprehensive process of development in the history of the English family, we find ourselves at a loss. Some attempts to produce general syntheses are so categorically conflicting – and some are also so categorically sweeping – that over the years they have had the effect of deadening constructive debate in the field. Initially, the main point of disagreement centred on whether the history of family structures, relationships, and sentiments in early modern England was marked mainly by processes of change, or by enduring patterns of continuity. For instance, historians debated whether small households, populated mostly by nuclear families, with close sentimental ties among the family members and considerable independence from broad networks of kin, were the product of developmental processes leading to modernity, or whether these were enduring structures, typical of English society from at least the early modern period until today. Clearly, such vast questions invite disagreement. But for some years these questions generated extremely heated debates. Some scholars strongly emphasised continuity,

English women's history', *Historical Journal* 36 (1993), 383–414; A. L. Erickson, *Women and Property in Early Modern England* (New York, 1993); A. Fletcher, *Gender, Sex and Subordination in England, 1500–1800* (New Haven and London, 1995); A. Laurence, *Women in England, 1500–1760: A Social History* (London, 1994); L. Gowing, *Domestic Dangers: Women, Words and Sex in Early Modern London* (Oxford, 1996); H. Barker and E. Chalus (eds.), *Gender in Eighteenth-Century England: Roles, Representations, Responsibilities* (London, 1997); L. Pollock, 'Rethinking patriarchy and the family in seventeenth-century England', *Journal of Family History* 23 (1998), 3–27; A. J. Vickery, *The Gentleman's Daughter: Women's Life in Georgian England* (New Haven and London, 1998); R. B. Shoemaker, *Gender in English Society, 1650–1850: The Emergence of Separate Spheres* (London, 1998).

[6] This is but a selection of some broad studies which also contain arguments about the family: K. D. M. Snell, *Annals of the Labouring Poor: Social Change and Agrarian England, 1660–1900* (Cambridge, 1985); J. C. D. Clark, *English Society, 1688–1832: Ideology, Social Structure and Political Practice during the Ancien Regime* (Cambridge, 1985); E. A. Wrigley, *People, Cities and Wealth: The Transformation of Traditional Society* (Oxford, 1987); P. Collinson, *The Birthpangs of Protestant England: Religious and Cultural Change in the Sixteenth and Seventeenth Centuries* (Basingstoke, 1988); P. Earle, *The Making of the English Middle Class: Business, Society and Family Life in London, 1660–1730* (London, 1989); A. Kussmaul, *A General View of the Rural Economy of England, 1538–1840* (Cambridge, 1990); D. E. Underdown, *Fire From Heaven: The Life of an English Town in the Seventeenth Century* (London, 1992).

others highlighted change.[7] Most notably, Lawrence Stone described great shifts in the history of the family from the decline of the late medieval 'open lineage family' to the emergence in the middle of the seventeenth century of the 'closed domesticated nuclear family', and its subsequent development.[8] Edward Shorter, Randolph Trumbach, and John Gillis, for example, have also identified some similar processes of discontinuity, although their chronological and thematic emphases differ.[9] On the other side of the historiographical field, there emerged a powerful school that emphasised continuity in familial structures and familial sentiments. Works by Laslett, Macfarlane, Wrigley, Schofield, Wrightson, Levine, Pollock, and Houlbrooke, for example, all emphasise in various ways the enduring characteristics of the English family, complemented by enduring patterns of family sentiments.[10]

The sparks that initially flew from these scholarly encounters grew dim by the late 1980s. By now the debates have virtually reached a standstill. In many ways, the 'continuity' school has emerged triumphant, as the importance of nuclear family life in early modern England seemed firmly established by the early 1980s.[11] The idea that the period from 1500 to 1800 witnessed great developmental changes in the history of the family, however, did not entirely lose its appeal. Stone, for instance, continued to

---

[7] See Wrightson's overview of the field in K. Wrightson, 'The family in early modern England: continuity and change', in S. Taylor, R. Connors, and C. Jones (eds.), *Hanoverian Britain and Empire: Essays in Memory of Philip Lawson* (Woodbridge, 1998), pp. 1–22. I would like to thank Keith Wrightson again for giving me the unpublished draft of his chapter.

[8] L. Stone, *The Family, Sex and Marriage in England 1500–1800* (Harmondsworth, 1977).

[9] E. Shorter, *The Making of the Modern Family* (London, 1976); R. Trumbach, *The Rise of the Egalitarian Family: Aristocratic Kinship and Domestic Relations in Eighteenth-Century England* (New York and London, 1978); J. R. Gillis, *For Better or Worse: British Marriages, 1600 to the Present* (New York and Oxford, 1985). For European studies which also emphasise discontinuities, see, for example, P. Ariès, *Centuries of Childhood* (Paris, 1960), trans. R. Baldick (London, 1962); J.-L. Flandrin, *Families in Former Times: Kinship, Household and Sexuality* (Paris, 1976), trans. R. Southern (Cambridge, 1979); M. Mitterauer and R. Sieder, *The European Family: Patriarchy to Partnership from the Middle Ages to the Present* (Munich, 1977), trans. K. Osterveen and M. Horzinger (Oxford, 1982).

[10] It is important to note that arguments in favour of long-term continuities in family structures and sentiments had been made before the publication of Stone's thesis; however, the historiographical debate about continuity and change sharpened following Stone's intervention.

[11] By the early 1980s this new history of the early modern family had been instated in leading syntheses, most notably Wrightson, *English Society*, chs. 3–4; Houlbrooke, *The English Family*. The question of the nuclear family is discussed in detail in ch. 1. Note also that the compelling suggestion has been made that, far from eroding kinship ties and bringing about the rise of the nuclear family, the onset of industrialisation has created some complex kinship and household structures in local communities: M. Anderson, *Family Structure in Nineteenth-Century Lancashire* (Cambridge, 1971); Nair, *Highley*, esp. p. 255.

develop his arguments in subsequent publications, and in fields outside history, such as literary criticism, his work continued to be used as a standard reference on the history of the family and marriage.[12] There also remained unanswered questions about historical difference and change that could not be addressed successfully within the existing polarised approaches.[13] A specific area in which there were conflicting findings that could not be accommodated easily within existing frameworks was the history of kinship.[14] Important work on the history of the family thus continued to be produced, but evidently the field now attracted less scholarly interest. After a formative period of intensive research, the history of the family has been hit twice. If some broad interpretations of familial change proved unconvincing, some of the greatest achievements in the field – the assessment of central enduring patterns of familial experience – appear now as pyrrhic victories. For, once established, these patterns of long-term continuity have ceased to excite interest. Thus, on the one hand, heated debates have led to an impasse, while on the other

[12] Stone, *Road to Divorce*; Stone, *Broken Lives*. See, for instance, references to Stone in N. Armstrong, *Desire and Domestic Fiction: A Political History of the Novel* (New York and Oxford, 1989), p. 41; J. P. Zomchick, *Family and the Law in Eighteenth-Century Fiction: The Public Conscience in the Private Sphere* (Cambridge, 1993), pp. 19, 41, 133. The continuing allure of the developmental chronology of the history of the family is probably also sustained by the fact that some processes of change noted in the historiography of women in the seventeenth and eighteenth centuries are also based on developmental approaches. See Vickery's critique of such chronologies 'Golden age to separate spheres?'.

[13] On the question of accommodating difference see Wrightson, 'The family in early modern England'.

[14] Whereas some traced the rise of the nuclear family and the erosion of extended kinship ties in early modern England, others emphasised the enduring importance of the nuclear family and the looseness and limitations of extended kinship ties, and others highlighted the abiding importance of kinship in early modern England. See, for example, some debates on kinship in D. Cressy, 'Kinship and kin interaction in early modern England', *P&P* 113 (1986), 38–69, and references to earlier works there; D. Cressy, *Coming Over: Migration and Communication between England and New England in the Seventeenth Century* (Cambridge, 1987), esp. ch. 11; Levine and Wrightson, *Whickham*, esp. pp. 329–44; D. Rollison, *The Local Origins of Modern Society: Gloucestershire, 1500–1800* (London, 1992), esp. chs. 4–5; C. Phythian-Adams (ed.), *Societies, Cultures and Kinship, 1580–1850* (Leicester, 1993); K. Wrightson, 'Postscript: Terling revisited', in Wrightson and Levine, *Poverty and Piety* (1995), pp. 187–97; J. A. Johnston, 'Family, kin and community in eight Lincolnshire parishes, 1567–1800', *Rural History* 6 (1995), 179–92; M. Hunt, *The Middling Sort: Commerce, Gender and the Family in England, 1680–1780* (Berkeley and Los Angeles, 1996); Cressy, *Birth, Marriage and Death*; B. Reay, 'Kinship and neighbourhood in nineteenth-century rural England: the myth of the autonomous nuclear family', *Journal of Family History* 21 (1996), 87–104; R. Grassby, 'Love, property and kinship: the courtship of Philip Williams, Levant merchant 1617–50', *Economic History Review* 113 (1998), 335–50: I am grateful to David Cressy for directing my attention to this article; L. Davidoff, M. Doolittle, J. Fink and K. Holden, *The Family Story: Blood, Contract and Intimacy, 1830–1960* (London and New York, 1999), esp. pp. 77–83. See further discussion below, ch. 4.

hand it might appear that to a large extent the history of the family has done its job.

How can we emerge from this stalemate? One way forward, this book suggests, is to examine and indeed re-cast some of the terms of the debate. Particularly problematic, I believe, are some of the terms and categories borrowed from the social sciences, which have influenced the conceptualisation of the history of the family.

The history of the family has developed in the past decades within a very close dialogue with the social sciences. For many of the pioneers of the history of the family, the fusion of demography, economics, sociology, anthropology, psychology, and history opened new and exciting horizons for research. The use of certain terms and categories borrowed from the social sciences, however, has also had some problematic effects. In fact, the merit of some categories and their systematic application was questioned at early stages in some debates in the field, but often with little effect. For instance, some scholars noted that the category of 'the nuclear family' was too static and narrow in view of life-course changes,[15] too unrepresentative in view of the complex kinship relationships that could exist in families mainly due to death and remarriage,[16] and often hard to reconstruct with any certainty due to limitations in the sources.[17] Nor was

[15] See T. K. Hareven, 'The family life cycle in historical perspective: a proposal for a developmental approach', in J. Cuisenier and M. Segalen (eds.), *The Family Life Cycle in European Societies* (The Hague, 1977), pp. 339–52, and the critique on pp. 339, 342–3; T. K. Hareven, 'Cycles, courses, and cohorts: reflection on the theoretical and methodological approaches to the historical study of family development', *Journal of Social History* 12 (1978), 97–109. See also discussion and further references in T. K. Hareven (ed.), *Transitions: The Family and the Life Course in Historical Perspective* (New York, 1978); T. K. Hareven, *Family Time and Industrial Time* (Cambridge, 1982), e.g. pp. 5–8; G. H. Elder, Jr, 'Family and lives: some development in life-course studies', in T. K. Hareven and A. Plakans (eds.), *Family History at the Crossroads: A Journal of Family History Reader* (Princeton, 1987), pp. 179–99, and criticism by M. Segalen in *ibid.*, pp. 213–15. But it is important to emphasise that there are studies that highlight both life-course changes and the basic pattern of the nuclear family, e.g. P. Laslett, 'Le cycle familial et le processus de socialization: caractéristiques du schéma occidental considéré dans le temps', in Cuisenier and Segalen (eds.), *The Family Life Cycle*, pp. 317–38; K. Wrightson, 'Kinship in an English village: Terling, Essex, 1500–1700', in R. M. Smith (ed.), *Land, Kinship and Life Cycle* (Cambridge, 1984), pp. 313–32; Levine and Wrightson, *Whickham*, p. 337.
[16] See especially M. Chaytor, 'Household and kinship in Ryton in the late sixteenth and early seventeenth centuries', *History Workshop Journal* 10 (1980), 25–60, and esp. p. 38. See K. Wrightson, 'Household and kinship in sixteenth-century England', *History Workshop Journal* 12 (1981), 151–8, and esp. p. 151. Wrightson agrees with Chaytor on the point that apparently nuclear family households could in fact contain complex family structures, and comments on the importance of Chaytor's stress on this neglected aspect.
[17] For instance, Berkner discusses the difficulties in reconstructing household and family units from listings that do not include details about age, exact relationships, or the wife's maiden name. Relationships within households, he suggests, may perhaps have been different or more complex than an analysis by surnames indicates: L. K. Berkner, 'The

it always clear whether the unit referred to by historians as 'the nuclear family' was the elementary kinship unit in the anthropological sense, the functional and affective unit in the sociological or psychological sense, the domestic unit in the demographic sense – or various combinations of all of these.[18] The utility of the concept of 'the extended family' was also questioned; indeed, as we shall see, historians differed significantly in the ways in which they charted familial 'extension'.[19] But despite these critical reservations, 'the nuclear family' and 'the extended family' and 'extended' kinship ties remained among the most used terms within debates on the history of the family.

In addition, some terms and concepts borrowed from the social sciences have proved problematic because of the assumptions embedded within them. Many social concepts and categories have themselves been predicated upon historically specific notions about what the family is – or ought to be – as well as upon developmental notions about the history of the family. For example, until the 1960s it was taken as given in diverse sociological traditions that the nuclear family, with its specific structures and relationships, was particularly typical of the industrialised, urban, and individualistic societies of modern times, whereas more complex and extended family forms were typical of 'traditional' and pre-industrial societies.[20]

use and misuse of census data for the historical analysis of family structure', *Journal of Interdisciplinary History* 5 (1975), 721–38, and esp. pp. 724–5. See also L. K. Berkner, 'The stem family and the developmental cycle of the peasant household: an eighteenth-century Austrian example', *American Historical Review* 77 (1972), 398–418. Wrigley points out that family reconstitution studies yield no direct evidence about members of co-resident families who join them in ways other than birth or marriage, or leave them in ways other than marriage or death: see E. A. Wrigley, 'Reflections on the history of the family', *Daedalus* 106 (1977), 75.

[18] See, for example, R. McC. Netting, R. R. Wilk, and E. J. Arnould (eds.), *Households: Comparative and Historical Studies of the Domestic Group* (Berkeley and Los Angeles, 1984), Introduction, and R. R. Wilk and R. McC. Netting, 'Households: changing forms and functions', in *ibid.*, esp. pp. 3–4, on functional and morphological definitions of household and family.

[19] See especially J. Goody, 'The evolution of the family', in Laslett and Wall (eds.), *Household and Family in Past Time*, pp. 103–24, and further discussion in ch. 4, below.

[20] See, for example, the following critiques and references therein: Hareven, *Family Time and Industrial Time*, pp. 1–3; T. K. Hareven, 'The history of the family and the complexity of social change', *American Historical Review* 91 (1991), esp. pp. 95–6; Wrightson, 'The family in early modern England', esp. pp. 2–3; M. Anderson, 'What is new about the modern family?', Occasional Papers of the Office of Population Censuses & Surveys, *The Family* 31 (1983), reprinted in M. Drake (ed.), *Time, Family and Community: Perspectives on Family and Community History* (Oxford, 1993), pp. 67–90, and esp. pp. 67–73; M. Segalen, *Historical Anthropology of the Family*, trans. J. C. Whitehouse and S. Matthews (Cambridge, 1986), esp. pp. 73–5. For some sociological accounts see, for example, T. Parsons, 'The kinship system of the contemporary United States', in T. Parsons, *Essays in Social Theory* (rev. edn, New York, 1949; first published in *American Anthropologist*, 1943), pp. 177–98; T. Parsons, 'The social structure of the family', in R. N. Anshen (ed.),

When pioneering social historians set out to investigate the history of the English family, they sometimes wished to test and challenge specifically developmental notions such as these. As Laslett explains, for example, he wished to test 'Whiggish' notions of historical progress which herald the European nuclear family as a symptom of modernisation, as opposed to 'traditional' or 'primitive' kinship-oriented systems.[21] But, paradoxically, as these historians continued to rely heavily on terms and methods borrowed from the social sciences, and to apply them with polemical ardour, the old developmental categories were perpetuated. As a result, discussions in the history of the family continued to be construed in classical oppositional terms, which seemed to imply movement away from one polarity and towards another.[22] The nuclear family and various

The Family: Its Function and Destiny (New York, 1959; 1st edn 1949), pp. 241–74; T. Parsons and R. F. Bales, *Family, Socialization and Interaction Process* (London, 1968; 1st edn 1956); W. Goode, *World Revolution and Family Patterns* (London, 1963), esp. chs. I–II; W. F. Ogburn, 'Social change and the family', in R. F. Winch and L. W. Goodman (eds.), *Selected Studies in Marriage and the Family* (3rd edn, New York, 1968; 1st edn 1953), pp. 58–63; W. Goode, 'The role of the family and industrialization', in *ibid.*, pp. 64–70, and see also and compare R. F. Winch and R. L. Blumberg, 'Social complexity and familial organization', in *ibid.*, pp. 70–92, and references there. Note, however, that the nuclear family has also been recognised as a universal human grouping, either as the sole prevailing form of the family or as the basic unit from which more complex familial forms are compounded: e.g. G. P. Murdock, *Social Structure* (New York, 1949), esp. p. 2. See also, e.g., S. M. Greenfield, 'Industrialization and the family in sociological theory', *American Journal of Sociology* 67 (1961), 312–22. Some of the terms of these debates can probably be traced to the legacy of a set of developmental assumptions, current in nineteenth- and early twentieth-century social thought and manifested in various ways in works by some of the 'founding fathers' of social thought, such as Maine, Morgan, Engels, Toennies, Weber, and Durkheim. I have discussed these ideas in 'Privacy, sentiment and the family', unpublished paper, delivered at the Anglo-American Conference, Institute of Historical Research, London, 1–3 July 1993; 'The structural transformation of the private sphere', unpublished paper, circulated in 'Feminism and the Enlightenment: Colloquium on women and the civilizing process', 8 May 1999, The King's Manor, University of York.

[21] See P. Laslett's illuminating essay on 'The character of familial history, its limitations and the conditions for its proper pursuit', in Hareven and Plakans (eds.), *Family History at the Crossroads*, pp. 263–84, and esp. pp. 267–72, on 'Proceeding forwards in time and avoiding the use of "modernization"', and 'Reading history backwards and changes in family composition over time', and various references there to other works by Laslett. The effect of Laslett's findings on social thought, and particularly its challenge of a functional interpretation, are discussed in *The International Encyclopedia of the Social Sciences*, 18 vols. (New York, 1968), s.v. 'family', pp. 310–11. Laslett and Wall also wished to test the Marxist model in which the fragmentation of the family is an important stage in the emergence of industrial capitalism. Others, such as Stone, debated Marxian views and Parsonian functionalism while offering alternative developmental interpretations. The testing of developmental approaches has thus triggered extremely important research, but different interpretations: Laslett, *The World We Have Lost*; Laslett and Wall (eds.), *Household and Family in Past Time*; Stone, *The Family, Sex and Marriage*. See also Ariès, *Centuries of Childhood*; references to Macfarlane, n. 23, below; J. Goody, *The Development of the Family and Marriage in Europe* (Cambridge, 1983), esp. pp. 6–33.

[22] I am using here Wrightson's formulation, as explained and discussed in 'The family in early modern England', esp. pp. 12–13.

patterns associated with it thus continued to be studied in opposition to complex and extended family forms. Considerations of individual choice were still compared and contrasted to various familial strategies. Warm and affective family relations were still seen as opposed to formal, ritualised, authoritarian, or instrumental family relations. The substance of new research has thus been placed on an antiquated armature.

Moreover, these oppositional categories also had the effect of intensifying central debates about continuity and change in family history. For if historians such as Stone and Shorter used the oppositional and developmental categories to emphasise how the family in early modern England was just emerging from its 'traditional' state, revisionist historians used the same categories to emphasise that the family in sixteenth- and seventeenth-century England was in fact already 'modern'.[23] When used by scholars of the revisionist school, as Wrightson explains, these categories had the effect of over-modernising the distant past and playing down the alien character of some aspects of past experience.[24]

Indeed, the most significant effect of the heavy reliance on categories borrowed from the social sciences was that they barred historians from taking seriously terms and categories used by the historical actors themselves. While historical materials have been pounded all too often into anachronistic models, simple historical questions have not been sufficiently pursued: questions such as what concepts of the family did people in the past have? What did the family mean for them? In what terms did

[23] It is worth noting at this point that a new idea, proposed or intimated by scholars, was that England was the first to march along the route to modernity because in some fundamental ways its enduring nuclear family structures have made it essentially 'modern' for a very long time. See, for example, how Wrigley connects the history of the English family to the origins of industrialisation: '[t]he predominance of the small conjugal family household antedates the industrial revolution by many centuries . . . the prior existence of a society composed of small conjugal families – where marriage came late, implied economic independence, involved neolocal residence and was associated with high levels of mobility – was strongly congenial to relatively high real incomes, adaptability and growth': Wrigley, *People, Cities and Wealth*, p. 13. The most extreme hypothesis that both traces the attenuated nature of English kinship to the remote past and links it strongly to modernity is proposed by Macfarlane, who sees the unique characteristics of the English family and kinship system as an important component of what he defines as 'English individualism', the essential precondition of subsequent social, cultural, and economic developments: A. Macfarlane, *The Origins of English Individualism: The Family, Property and Social Transition* (Oxford, 1978), see e.g. statements on pp. 196, 198. See also A. Macfarlane, 'The myth of the peasantry: family, and economy in a northern parish', in Smith (ed.), *Land, Kinship and Life-Cycle*, pp. 333–49. Macfarlane agrees that 'there is no necessary correlation between the predominance of the nuclear family and industrial growth', but he also contends that a special association exists between the nuclear family and modernity: Macfarlane, *The Family Life of Ralph Josselin*, p. 159; Macfarlane, *Individualism*, e.g. pp. 25, 146, 198–201. In a later work Macfarlane emphasises the close tie between 'the Malthusian marriage system' and economic growth: Macfarlane, *Marriage and Love in England, 1300–1840* (Oxford, 1986), e.g. pp. 321–3. See also A. Macfarlane, *The Culture of Capitalism* (Oxford, 1987).

[24] Wrightson, 'The family in early modern England', p. 13.

they understand family relations, household residence, kinship relationships, friendship, and patronage?[25] It is at this point in particular that *Family and Friends in Eighteenth-Century England* seeks to make a distinctive intervention. It takes seriously concepts of the family used by people in the past. It seeks to understand these concepts, analyse them, and reconstruct the social views implicit in them and their uses. It is in this way that this book seeks to investigate anew central issues in the history of the family in eighteenth-century England.

This is an objective that requires us to attend to language. Terms and categories are expressed in words. In order to understand concepts of the family current in the eighteenth century we therefore need to turn our attention to the language in which familial and social terms were coined, expressed, and negotiated. What, for instance, did people in the eighteenth century mean when they spoke or wrote about 'families'? Was it really the nuclear family that they mainly had in mind, or were there perhaps other concepts of the family that were significant for these people and that were also expressed through their words? And when people at that time made references to 'relations' or 'kindred', what sort of groupings did they have in mind? What, indeed, were the relationships that they thought of when they used rudimentary terms such as 'mother', 'son', or 'sister'? Usages such as these, this book emphasises, could be far from straightforward. If we investigate them closely, we can see that they contain complex and historically specific meanings that shed new light on the history of the family and require us to rethink our understanding of many social ties in eighteenth-century England and the early modern period more broadly. Focusing on the eighteenth century, *Family and Friends* cannot present a full answer to the question of continuity and change in family history. But it will, I hope, open new paths for debate and propose a new way forward.

Indeed, the study of historical concepts of the family, I argue, must inevitably branch from relationships of blood and marriage to other social ties. This is not only because relationships of blood and marriage were extremely significant in early modern society and culture, but also because the boundaries between familial and non-familial ties, as we shall see, were different then and now. Such different boundaries were also manifested in linguistic terms, and the study of keywords such as 'family', 'friend', and 'connexion' will enable us to trace them. We will thus be able

---

[25] Archaic usages have been documented and studied by historians to a degree, but their implications have rarely been fully pursued in establishing new frameworks for analysis. Important attempts at re-conceptualisation, however, can be found in Cressy, 'Kinship and kin interaction', esp. pp. 65–9; Cressy, *Coming Over*, ch. 11; O'Hara, 'Ruled by my friends'. See also pp. 19–20, 118–22, 167–72 below, and notes there.

to re-locate historical family forms within rich webs of kinship, friendship, patronage, economic ties, neighbourhood ties, and, not least, political ties. We will be able to understand better how familial and social relationships worked, and how they were understood when they so often failed to work.

This historical analysis of language and social concepts requires a methodology and texts upon which to practise. It is therefore important at this point to explain this book's approach to method and to texts. *Family and Friends* accepts the challenge posed by 'the linguistic turn'. But unlike many other cultural studies, it retains a firm interest in social history, in the realities and experiences of men and women in the past. It also differs from many cultural studies in that it mostly does not focus on the general level of discourse, but rather offers detailed analyses of language usages. If a systematic study of contextualised linguistic usages is valuable in historical studies in general, the study of active usages, I believe, is indispensable for investigating the terms in which complex and dynamic relationships of family and kinship were conducted. My main research method, then, consists of pursuing keywords and phrases in texts, and analysing them as much as possible within full textual contexts and identifiable social contexts. For example, as I traced a keyword such as 'friend' in an eighteenth-century diary, I noted all its occurrences and tried to assess each time who were the 'friends' referred to, by analysing both the immediate context of each utterance and the broader context of the text. When appropriate I also continued to pursue these 'friends' in various archival sources. In order to test the 'representativeness' of my findings I also examined usages of keywords in many personal, legal, prescriptive, and literary sources, as well as historical dictionaries. Occasionally I relied on examples drawn from works by other scholars.[26]

Let us turn, then, to the principal texts examined. The first is the personal diary of an eighteenth-century shopkeeper, Thomas Turner. It consists of 111 notebooks written between 1754 and 1765.[27] The second

---

[26] In some cases I did so for reasons of convenience, and in some cases to draw attention to the fact that concepts that I analyse also feature in the context of other historical discussions. When using broadly surveyed examples I was not always able to exercise the same rigour as I did when analysing some specifically studied texts. But I tried as far as possible to take account of the performative contexts of usages and to trace them within their textual contexts.

[27] The original diary probably included 116 or 117 volumes. Turner's diary and documents relating to it are kept at Yale: Thomas Turner Papers, Manuscripts and Archives, Yale University Library. This work has been based mostly on my reading of the microfilm copy of the diary. See also T. Turner, *The Diary of Thomas Turner, 1754–1765*, ed. D. Vaisey (Oxford, 1985). This excellent edition, which contains a rich selection of extracts from the original diary, also includes very helpful notes and commentaries. I would like to thank David Vaisey again for allowing me to check my reading of Turner's manuscript against his unpublished transcriptions.

and third are conduct treatises, one for male apprentices and the other for maidservants: Samuel Richardson's, *The Apprentice's Vade Mecum: or, Young Man's Pocket-Companion*, and Eliza Haywood's *A Present for a Servant-Maid: or, the Sure Means of Gaining Love and Esteem*.[28] The last three texts are popular novels, Samuel Richardson's *Pamela: or, Virtue Rewarded*, Richardson's *Clarissa: or, The History of a Young Lady*,[29] and Eliza Haywood's *The History of Miss Betsy Thoughtless*.[30] I supplemented these texts with comparable examples drawn from many other sources. For instance, my study of Turner's diary is supplemented by other papers relating to Turner and his circle.[31] Some broad conceptual and chrono-logical arguments presented in this book, however, have been based initially on a wide range of examples drawn from many personal, prescrip-tive, legal, administrative, and literary sources from different historical periods.

It is important to stress that the principal texts were not selected on the grounds that their content was necessarily 'representative'. Indeed, many aspects of their content were clearly unrepresentative. The marriage of a gentleman and his servant-maid provides a plot for *Pamela* precisely because such a marriage was highly unusual. Certain aspects of Thomas Turner's life were also untypical, such as the level of education that he

[28] S. Richardson, *The Apprentice's Vade Mecum* (London, 1734); E. Haywood, *A Present for a Servant-Maid* (London, 1743). Editions quoted here: S. Richardson, *The Apprentice's Vade Mecum* (London, 1734), ed. A. D. McKillop, The Augustan Reprint Society, publication numbers 169–70 (Los Angeles, 1975); E. Haywood *A Present for a Servant-Maid* (Dublin, 1743), facsimile reprint, The Garland series (New York and London, 1985). Richardson's treatise is based on a letter written to his nephew and apprentice, Thomas Verren Richardson. The letter was reprinted at the start of the nineteenth century by the Stationers' Company and presented to youths bound at the hall ever since, see T. C. D. Eaves and B. D. Kimpel, *Samuel Richardson* (Oxford, 1971), pp. 50–4; Richardson, *Vade Mecum*, Introduction, p. 1, and references there to S. Richardson, 'An unpublished letter; from Mr Samuel Richardson to his nephew, Thomas Richardson', *Imperial Review: or, London and Dublin Journal* 2 (Aug. 1804), 609–16.

[29] Examples from *Pamela* were compiled from reprints of the first edition and the last revised edition: S. Richardson, *Pamela* (London, 1740), ed. T. C. D Eaves and B. D. Kimpel (Boston, 1971); S. Richardson, *Pamela* (London, 1801), ed. P. Sabor, Introduc-tion by M. A. Doody (Harmondsworth, 1980). Following quotations refer mostly to the latter. *Clarissa* was first published in London, 1747–8. The edition used here is *Clarissa: or, The History of a Young Lady*, ed. A. Ross (Harmondsworth, 1985).

[30] E. Haywood, *The History of Miss Betsy Thoughtless* (London, 1751). Edition quoted here: E. Haywood, *The History of Miss Betsy Thoughtless* (1751), Introduction by D. Spender (London and New York, 1986).

[31] These include letters of Turner to his children, 1786–90, medical prescriptions collected by Turner, notes listing the landholdings in East Hoathly, etc. See the 'Special Files' and 'Worcester Material', Thomas Turner Papers, Manuscripts and Archives, Yale Univer-sity Library. Other documents relating to Turner's relations, friends, and to Turner himself are kept in ESRO, CKS, and among the Newcastle Papers in the British Library, and are cited below.

acquired by his own efforts and his residence in proximity to the influential Pelham family. One of the main methodological points proposed here is that the general cultural elements of these texts can be found not necessarily in their content, but in their language. Although artificial, this distinction between text-content and word-content is nevertheless important, and I would like to suggest that by focusing on the level of word-content one can gain insight into the meanings of historical terms. Moreover, this insight, as I suggest, can be gained by inferring content from context, rather than by relying largely on isolated examples detached from their broader contexts.

The generic variety of the main sample of texts is also intentional. For the purposes of this book, each genre has different virtues. The personal diary is the least mediated of the genres used here. It is a large and detailed autobiographical record, containing a rich account of everyday life. Diaries are often used by historians of the family, and this diary matches well with other well-studied sources such as Ralph Josselin's diary or the diary of Samuel Pepys. Conduct manuals have also been studied often by historians of early modern England. Their merit is that they strive to conform to – and also display – prescriptive values and norms. The popular novels have the advantage of containing a wide range of characters and social situations, which are particularly valuable for tracing linguistic usages in diverse contexts. Additionally, the literary and prescriptive texts invite us to proceed from the analysis of verbal usages to the study of related constructs; these enable us to bind the history of familial and social concepts yet more closely to the cultural history of eighteenth-century England.

Yet despite their generic differences, I contend, the texts studied here reveal many similar usages, for these personal, prescriptive, and literary texts all shared a similar world of linguistic concepts. We can imagine the authors of our main texts as belonging to the same eighteenth-century 'language community'. The language they shared was a written language; as such it was not accessible to everyone in the eighteenth century. It also coexisted alongside numerous sociolects and regional dialects.[32] But this written language, too, I suggest, had its community of users. Samuel Richardson, Eliza Haywood, and Thomas Turner were all literate people of 'the middling sort'. Richardson, born in Derbyshire, was a joiner's son who became a master printer; only at the age of fifty did he publish his first

---

[32] The important question whether, considering the great linguistic diversity of early modern England, it is possible to speak of a linguistic community there at all is raised by P. J. Corfield, 'Introduction: historians and language', in P. J. Corfield (ed.), *Language, History and Class* (Oxford, 1991), p. 28.

novel.[33] Haywood was probably the daughter of a London hosier and
shopkeeper.[34] She wrote and published extensively, probably to support
herself and her two children.[35] Thomas Turner was the son of a Kentish
yeoman and shopkeeper; he, too, became a shopkeeper.[36] Evidently,
middling people such as these could use the written language well: they
read some similar texts, they even read some of each other's texts, and
those that they wrote reveal many similarities.[37] Furthermore, if we take

[33] See the extensive biographical study by Eaves and Kimpel, *Samuel Richardson*. A more
concise biography can be found in Eaves and Kimpel, 'Introduction', *Pamela*, ed. Eaves
and Kimpel, pp. v–xvi. See also A. D. McKillop, *Samuel Richardson, Printer and Novelist*
(Chapel Hill, 1936).

[34] Little is known of Haywood's background. She is traditionally identified as the daughter
of a London tradesman. Her first biographical account, written not long after her death,
describes her as London born and her father as being 'in the mercantile way': 'Mrs Eliza
Haywood', in D. E. Baker, *Biographia Dramatica, or, Companion to the Play House*
(London, 1764), pp. 215–16. According to her own testimony, her maiden name was
Fowler. Accordingly, Haywood's biographer, Whicher, suggested she was the daughter
of a London hosier and shopkeeper, Robert Fowler. Blouch sees the merit of Whicher's
identification and adds two other possibilities: (1) that Haywood was the daughter of
another London tradesman named Fowler; (2) that she was the sister of Sir Richard
Fowler of Harange Grange, Shropshire, to whom she claimed in one letter to be 'nearly
related' (E. Haywood to an unknown addressee, BL Add. MS 4293, f. 82). On the basis
of Haywood's early biography, writing, and career it seems to me more likely that she was
the daughter of a London tradesman than the sister of a Baronet. It is significant that she
made claims to gentility. As discussed in ch. 4, however, the words 'nearly related' could
designate various relationships. By 19 Feb. 1756 a 'Mrs Haywood' is listed in a Westminster poor-rate book and assessed 'no money'. She probably died shortly afterwards: see
G. F. Whicher, *The Life and Romances of Mrs. Eliza Haywood* (New York, 1915); C.
Blouch, 'Eliza Haywood and the romance of obscurity', *Studies in English Literature* 31
(1991), 535–52, and references there esp. in nn. 3, 15, 58; E. Haywood, *Love in Excess*
(1719–20), ed. D. Oakleaf (Peterborough, Ontario, 1994), pp. 7–35.

[35] She described her marriage as 'unfortunate': BL Add. MS 4293, f. 82. Little is known
about her husband, however, and her children were possibly illegitimate: see Blouch,
'Eliza Haywood and the romance of obscurity'. Haywood's complete list of publications
numbers at least seventy titles. Between 1720 and 1730 only she composed thirty-eight
novels, romances, 'secret histories', and scandal stories. See Whicher, *The Life and
Romances of Mrs. Eliza Haywood*, and esp. pp. 200–1. See also J. Richetti, *Popular Fiction
Before Richardson: Narrative Patterns, 1700–1739* (Oxford, 1969), chs. 4–5; M. Heinneman,
'Eliza Haywood's career in the theatre', *N&Q* n.s. 20 (1973), 9–13; R. Ballaster, 'Eliza
Haywood', in J. Todd (ed.), *Dictionary of British Women Writers* (London, 1989), pp.
322–6; J. Spencer, *The Rise of the Woman Novelist: From Aphra Behn to Jane Austen*
(Oxford, 1986), e.g. pp. 8–9, 61–2, 76; J. Todd, *The Sign of Angellica: Women, Writing and
Fiction, 1660–1800* (London, 1989), pp. 146–60; G. M. Firmager, 'Eliza Haywood: some
further light on her background', *N&Q* n.s. 38 (1991), 181–3; R. Ballaster, *Seductive
Forms: Women's Amatory Fiction from 1684–1740* (Oxford and New York, 1992), esp. pp.
153–95; Haywood, *Love in Excess*, ed. Oakleaf, pp. 7–35 and further references there.

[36] See Turner, *Diary*, ed. Vaisey, esp. pp. xvii–xxxix.

[37] See, for example, critical comments on Haywood's work in Richardson's correspondence: *The Correspondence of Samuel Richardson*, ed. H. L. Barbauld, 6 vols. (London,
1804), vol. IV, pp. 55–6. Richardson also printed Haywood's comedy *A Wife to be Lett* in
1735. On the reading of Richardson's work in Turner's household, see N. Tadmor, 'In
the even my wife read to me: women, reading and household life in the eighteenth
century', in J. Raven, H. Small, and N. Tadmor (eds.), *The Practice and Representation of*

the popularity of our main texts into account, we can postulate that this 'language community', shared by Haywood, Richardson, and Turner, was probably shared by a larger number of people. Richardson's conduct manual, first published in 1734, was advertised until 1744 and reprinted until the end of the century.[38] Eliza Haywood's manual was still advertised thirty years after its original publication in 1743 as 'a well-designed and valuable tract'.[39] The novels, particularly *Pamela* and *Clarissa*, enjoyed remarkable popularity. Between 1747–8 and 1800 *Clarissa* went through nineteen editions and *Pamela*, published in 1740, went through twenty-four.[40] Haywood's novel went through only ten editions from its publication in 1751 until 1800, but in terms of her total number of editions its author ranks as the most popular female novelist in the eighteenth century.[41] A conservative estimate of the 'language community' in which these texts circulated, then, would include at least 180,000 readers from the middle of the eighteenth century to 1800.[42] The readers of these texts, we may suppose, amounted to only a part of the population that would have understood and used the linguistic usages examined in this book.

This 'language community', I would like to emphasise, was not united

Reading in England (Cambridge, 1996). See also Turner, *Diary*, ed.Vaisey, Appendix D, on Turner's reading more broadly. Finally, Haywood's familiarity with at least some of Richardson's work is evident from the fact that she published and possibly also wrote *Anti-Pamela: or, Feigned Innocence Detected* (London, 1741). In addition, some of her acquaintances, such as Richard Savage, and especially Aaron Hill, were also close to Richardson's circle.

[38] Richardson, *Vade Mecum*, Introduction, and reference there.

[39] See reference in Whicher, *The Life and Romances of Mrs. Eliza Haywood*, p. 146, to the *Monthly Review* 46 (April 1772), p. 463. See also Whicher, *The Life and Romances of Mrs. Eliza Haywood*, pp. 145–8. *A Present for a Servant-Maid* was published in 1743 for T. Gardiner and sold for the price of 1s, as advertised in *The Gentleman's Magazine*, June 1743. It was followed by two pirated editions printed in Dublin in 1743 and in 1744. In 1745 it was reprinted in London. The next edition appeared in 1771.

[40] J. Raven, *British Fiction, 1750–1770: A Chronological Check-List of Prose Fiction Printed in Britain and Ireland* (Cranbury, 1987), p. 15.

[41] Raven, *British Fiction*, pp. 14–15. This indeed was also her most popular novel.

[42] To minimise risk, let us estimate all these texts as having an overlapping circle of readers. We can also estimate a readership of five persons for each copy; this is a low but safe estimate which takes account of library and personal borrowing, and the second-hand book-trade, as well as the usual practice of reading aloud.The number of copies in each edition is more difficult to assess. Raven estimates that Haywood's novels were launched in editions of about 1,000 copies, lower than a print-run of 1,500 volumes per edition that he estimates as the most economical to produce (Raven, *British Fiction*, pp. 16, 40, and n. 108). When printing his own successful novels, however, Richardson clearly went above this safe figure. The second edition of *Clarissa*, for example, was issued in 3,000 copies. The first edition of *Sir Charles Grandison* had 4,000 copies. The third edition of *Sir Charles Grandison*, printed only four months later, still had 2,500 copies (see McKillop, *Samuel Richardson*, pp. 154, 215). If we take a rough but safe figure of 1,500 copies, using *Pamela*'s editions as our only index, we reach a readership of 180,000 from *Pamela*'s publication in 1740 until 1800. This can be used as a minimum figure for estimating the extent of the 'language community'.

by any common textual experience. My working proposition is much more basic: namely, that when Haywood, Richardson, or Turner wrote words such as 'family' or 'friend' they generally understood what these words meant. They probably also shared this understanding with at least some of their contemporaries. It is this understanding that I wish to explore and analyse. Another point that should be clarified here concerns the terms used in this book. It is important to acknowledge that many analytical terms used in this book, such as 'the household-family' and 'occupational relationships', are rooted in present-day terminology. I do not simply assume that it is possible to delve into the minds of people long dead and understand their culture 'in its own terms'. The aim of the terminology used here, rather, is to illumine some social and familial concepts in past time while also addressing the analytical concerns of modern scholarship. Finally, it is important to add a note about the conceptual organisation of this book. Different concepts of the family are presented here separately, although in effect there could be swift shifts of focus between them, as well as overlapping and ambiguous usages. The conceptual differentiation employed here, however, is essential for the sake of analysis. Furthermore, as I try to show, it is well supported by many common eighteenth-century usages.

The first three chapters of this book thus analyse concepts of the family, focusing on usages of the keyword 'family', whereas the last three focus on concepts of kinship, friendship, and patronage, tracing the keyword, 'friend'. Between them is a large chapter devoted to the language of kinship. Chapters 1 and 2 thus discuss the concept of the family as a household unit, and chapter 3 examines the family as a concept of lineage and ancestry. Starting from usages of the keyword 'family' to refer to kin, chapter 4 presents a new set of organising principles for understanding the language of kinship used in the seventeenth and eighteenth centuries, whilst also placing those within a historiographical context. Chapters 5, 6, and 7 lead us once more from the broad conceptual and chronological analysis to more specific and closely contextualised studies. Chapter 5 explores dynamic relations between related and non-related 'friends'. Chapter 6 proceeds to investigate 'friendship' ties within the context of eighteenth-century political life. Chapter 7 investigates ideas and representations of 'friendship' in prescriptive and literary texts.

This book, then, aims to offer distinct contributions in three respects. First, it aims to contribute substantively to the history of the family in eighteenth-century England, and indeed, more broadly, the early modern period. The analyses in this book are often highly focused, but their concerns are broad. By attending to the ways in which people in the past expressed and negotiated familial and social relationships, *Family and*

Friends proposes to discuss anew historical concepts of family and household, kinship, friendship, and patronage. *Family and Friends* does not aim to offer a new chronology of familial continuity and change from the early modern period to today: one might indeed wonder whether there was a single chronology that could embrace so many relationships. But I hope that the findings of this book will be used to reflect anew on currently used chronologies and typologies, and indeed on the debates about familial continuity, difference, and change.

Secondly, this book aims to offer a methodological contribution. The systematic analysis of historical linguistic usages offered here is new. Its merit, I contend, extends beyond any etymological analysis based largely on the study of isolated usages. I believe this methodology can be useful in various historical inquiries, for it enables us to understand better what people in the past meant when they used keywords and concepts. In an area such as the history of the family, however, I think this methodology can be particularly useful, because designation and negotiation are especially important in the context of close and dynamic familial relationships; moreover, some of the currently used terms and concepts, drawn from the social sciences, have left such a problematic legacy in the historiography of the family. Rather than importing into history the theoretical concepts of other disciplines (the frequent practice in many inter-disciplinary studies), this book thus proposes a method that will help us to historicise theoretical concepts and terms.

The third distinct contribution this book seeks to offer regards the integration of the history of the family into other areas of historical research. *Family and Friends* explores new links between the history of the family and eighteenth-century social and cultural history. It explores new connections between the history of the family and the history of eighteenth-century politics. It even pursues new ways of linking the history of the family and the historically oriented reading of literary texts.

Thus, in all these ways this book seeks to explore new paths for investigating household, family, kinship, friendship, and patronage in eighteenth-century England.

1   The concept of the household-family

Introduction

In seventeenth- and eighteenth-century England, we are told, the English family was characteristically nuclear. This depiction can be traced from the path-breaking studies of the Cambridge Population Group to the broad interpretative survey of Ralph Houlbrooke; from the aggregate analysis of parish registers to the individual testimony of Ralph Josselin's diary. Since the 1960s and 1970s it has become clear that the extended family household, what William Goode termed 'the classical family of Western nostalgia', was not the predominant household and family form in early modern England. English people in the early modern period did not have very large completed families, and did not live in large and complex households.[1]

But what concepts of the family did people have in seventeenth- and eighteenth-century England? Did they focus exclusively on the nuclear unit as the prototype of household and family relationships, or were other

---

[1] Goode, *World Revolution and Family Patterns*, p. 6. The earliest formulations of this thesis include J. Hajnal, 'European marriage patterns in perspective', in D. E. Glass and D. E. C. Eversley (eds.), *Population in History: Essays in Historical Demography* (London, 1965), pp. 101–43; D. E. C. Eversley, P. Laslett, and E. A. Wrigley, *An Introduction to English Historical Demography from the Sixteenth to the Nineteenth Century* (New York, 1966); Laslett, *The World We Have Lost*; Laslett and Wall (eds.), *Household and Family in Past Time*; Macfarlane, *The Family Life of Ralph Josselin*; R. S. Schofield, 'Age-specific mobility in an eighteenth-century English parish', *Annales de démographie historique* (1970), 261–74; E. A. Wrigley, 'Family limitation in pre-industrial England', *Economic History Review* 19 (1966), 82–109; E. A. Wrigley, *Population and History: From the Traditional to the Modern World* (London, 1969). Other perceptions of the nuclear family have been developed by, for example, L. Stone, 'The rise of the nuclear family in early modern England: the patriarchal stage', in C. E. Rosenberg (ed.), *The Family in History* (Philadelphia, 1975), pp. 13–57; Shorter, *The Making of the Modern Family*. For a broad survey emphasising the nuclear family, see Houlbrooke, *The English Family*. See also, for example, Wrightson, *English Society*, pp. 44–5; J. A. Sharpe, *Early Modern England: A Social History* (London, 1987), p. 60, and a more recent and critical perspective in R. O'Day, *The Family and Family Relationships, 1500–1900: England, France and the United States of America* (London, 1994), pp. 1–28.

concepts of the family significant in their world view? If we attend to the language people used, it seems that the latter was the case. Very often, when English people spoke or wrote about 'families', it was not the nuclear unit that they had in mind. 'Family' in their language could mean a household, including its diverse dependants, such as servants, apprentices, and co-resident relatives. Accordingly, Samuel Johnson defined 'family' as 'those who live in the same house'.[2]

This meaning of the term has been noticed by many scholars: indeed, it is mentioned in the opening pages of several studies of the history of the family.[3] But though they have noted this contemporary usage, historians rarely focus upon it when establishing their own guidelines for analysis. Some historians simply mention the archaic usage while clarifying the terms of their discussion, but then proceed to attend to what they regard as family relationships; and, most importantly, these have been the nuclear family relationships. Others have devised and developed their own detailed categories for defining household and family types measuring exact degrees of complexity and extension. These categories, first proposed by Louis Henry and then developed in the path-breaking introduction to Laslett and Wall's *Household and Family in Past Time*, have become extremely influential in family history.[4] Their main purpose has been to facilitate quantitative research and to enable comparative studies of household and family types across different cultures and historical

---

[2] S. Johnson, *Dictionary of the English Language* (London, 1755), s.v. 'family'.

[3] See Stone, *The Family, Sex and Marriage*, p. 28; Stone, *Road to Divorce*, pp. 45–6; Flandrin, *Families in Former Times*, pp. 3–4; Houlbrooke, *The English Family*, p. 19; B. A. Hanawalt, *The Ties That Bound: Peasant Families in Medieval England* (Oxford, 1986), p. 4. The rich significance of the term 'family' is, however, indicated by Snell, *Annals of the Labouring Poor*, esp. pp. 320–1. See also A. Kussmaul, 'The pattern of work as the eighteenth century began', in R. Floud and D. McCloskey (eds.), *The Economic History of Britain Since 1700*, 3 vols. (2nd edn, Cambridge, 1994), vol. I, p. 2. For 'family' as a historical and cultural keyword, see R. Williams, *Keywords: A Vocabulary of Culture and Society* (London, 1976), pp. 108–11.

[4] Laslett, 'Introduction: the history of the family', in Laslett and Wall (eds.), *Household and Family in Past Time*, pp. 23–89, esp. pp. 23–44, 86–9; L. Henry, *Manuel de démographie historique* (Paris, 1967), ch. 2, esp. pp. 44–6, referred to in Laslett, 'Introduction', p. 33. See also C. A. Hammel and P. Laslett, 'Comparing household structure over time and between cultures', *Comparative Studies in Society and History* 16 (1974), 73–109; Laslett, *Family Life and Illicit Love*, pp. 96–7; P. Laslett, 'Family and household as work and kin groups', in R. Wall, J. Robin, and P. Laslett (eds.), *Family Forms in Historic Europe* (Cambridge, 1983), pp. 513–63. For a criticism of some of the limitations of a conjugal-based system of analysis, and further modifications to it, see L. James and J. Gjerde, 'Comparative household morphology of stem, joint, and nuclear household systems: Norway, China, and the United States', *Continuity and Change* I (1986), 89–111. See also Laslett, 'The character of familial history', pp. 277–81. For criticism on 'the Hammel–Laslett classification scheme', see A. Plakans, 'Interaction between the household and the kin group in the Eastern European past: posing the problem', in Hareven and Plakans (eds.), *Family History at the Crossroads*, pp. 164–6.

periods. Nevertheless, one may ask, how illuminating are these categories if they do not engage in dialogue with the terms used by historical actors? This is a question to which I will return in the course of this chapter.

In contrast with much recent work, this chapter does adopt an archaic concept of the family – the household, including its possible dependants – as its central concept for analysis. This concept, it is argued, should be seen as fundamental in two senses. First, it was fundamental in contemporaries' own understanding of what families and households were. Second, and following from this, this concept also illuminates a wide canvas of social action; for example, when people left households or joined them, as servants, apprentices, wards, or even long-term guests, their actions were very often understood as familial actions. To be sure, there were concepts of 'family' in seventeenth- and eighteenth-century England emanating from relationships of blood and marriage.[5] But, as this chapter aims to show, there was a related yet different, and highly significant, concept of the family emanating from relationships of co-residence and authority.[6]

As explained in the introduction, the archive in which I trace this concept is linguistic. My premiss is that a systematic study of words and expressions – that is, active usages employed in the eighteenth century when referring to families – can yield important information about the ways in which family ties were understood; and the keyword on which this chapter focuses is 'family' itself. I have traced it through a variety of texts and noted each of its occurrences, which I have then analysed within both the immediate context of the utterance and the broader context of the entire text. For example, when I encountered an entry in a diary where the author refers to 'my family at home', I tried to establish the identity of the family members referred to, and then compared the entry with other references to this family and with references to other families in the text. After analysing a large number of examples I was able to see the pattern which I present here.

The next section of this chapter thus presents a basic pattern of the concept of the household-family. The examples demonstrating this pattern are drawn here initially from four mid-eighteenth-century texts, written by authors of 'the middling sort': Samuel Richardson's *Pamela* and *The Apprentice's Vade Mecum*, Eliza Haywood's *The History of Miss Betsy Thoughtless*, and the diary of the eighteenth-century shopkeeper,

---

[5] See especially pp. 41–2 below, and chapters 3, 4, and 5 below.
[6] See N. Tadmor, 'The concept of the household-family in eighteenth-century England', *P&P* 151 (1996), 110–40. Different concepts of the family are also discussed in N. Tadmor, '"Family" and "friend" in *Pamela*: a case study in the history of the family in eighteenth-century England', *Social History* 14 (1989), 289–306. The concept of the household-family and its historiographical implications, however, are not developed in '"Family" and "friend" in *Pamela*'.

Thomas Turner.[7] As explained in the introduction, my premiss is that the language usages found in these texts will give us insight into concepts of the family current among a broader eighteenth-century 'language community'. Later in this chapter and in the next chapter I shall compare these usages with others drawn from a range of personal, literary, documentary and prescriptive sources from the middle of the seventeenth century to the early nineteenth century.

Having presented the concept of the household-family in the first section, I shall continue to examine it in the second section with the aid of a close case-study based on the diary of Thomas Turner. This section will investigate the structure of Turner's household-family, the nature of its internal relationships, and its durability over time. The last section of this chapter will then proceed to re-assess the standard categories for classifying households and families, so important in early modern English history. This section will also include a discussion of comparable manifestations of the concept of the household-family drawn from other sources.

The concept of the household-family

The concept of the household-family is widely current in eighteenth-century texts, and it is also well represented in our sample of texts. The meaning of language usages cannot be precisely quantified and there are endless contextual variations, but it is nevertheless possible to detect this concept in all but a few of the hundreds of references to 'families' in Thomas Turner's diary and in the dozens of similar references in the conduct book and novels under discussion. The following quotations present a set of ordinary but well-defined examples that demonstrate some of its main features.

I dined on the remains of What *my Family* had for dinner . . .

I went and serch'd John Joness but found no one there but *his own family*.

I would be a little justified to *my family*, that you have no reason to complain of hardships from me.

I have had the command of *his family*, and lived with him in all things like a wife, except the name.

In each of these examples a '*family*' is referred to, but who are these families? What is their social organisation? The answers can be found by examining the context of each utterance.

When Thomas Turner wrote the words of the first example,[8] he was a

---

[7] See the discussion of the sources, Introduction, pp. 11–16.
[8] Thomas Turner, Diary, 22 Apr. 1764, Thomas Turner Papers, Yale University Library.

childless widower. Both his parents were also dead, and his relatives were living elsewhere. In other words, it is impossible that on this occasion he was referring to anyone from either his nuclear family or his extended family. Who, then, were the persons whom he designated as '*my family*'? The people who on that day remained and dined at home were Thomas Turner's maidservant and the assistant in his shop. Both were members of Turner's household, but neither was related to him by blood or marriage.

In the second example Thomas Turner, while serving as a parish officer, goes to the house of his neighbour John Jones in search of 'disorderly fellows'.[9] He finds there none but John Jones's 'own family'. Jones, too, was at that time a childless widower.[10] He was also an alehouse keeper, and the persons referred to here as 'his family' were probably the servants who helped him run the public house.

The speaker in the third example is a literary character, Mr B. from Samuel Richardson's novel *Pamela*.[11] Like Thomas Turner and John Jones, Mr B. is a single man. He is also an orphan. However, he is not a widower but a bachelor. The persons he refers to as 'my family' are his numerous household servants, and in these lines he rebukes one of them while justifying himself towards the rest.

The speaker in the fourth example is another literary character, the French mistress in Eliza Haywood's novel *The History of Miss Betsy Thoughtless*. The family that she refers to belongs to her lover, Mr Thomas Thoughtless. This family, too, consists of household servants.[12]

Each of these references can be seen as a statement in which a group of persons is identified as 'a *family*'. This group can then be attributed to a person, as in '*my* family', or '*his own* family'. While defining these groups as 'families', various assumptions are also made about the nature of the family and its relationships. All these families have some characteristics in common. They are household units: they consist of people living under the same roof and under the authority of a householder. The heads of these families are single persons, in each case single men. Finally, there are no kinship relations between the heads of these families and their family members. We can call these families 'single persons' families', or,

---

[9] *Ibid.*, 5 Feb. 1758; see also 2 Apr. 1758.
[10] His wife Grace died in 1756. His only son, also named John, was baptised on 9 Jan. 1749 and buried on 25 Dec. 1750: East Sussex Baptism Index, 1700–1812, kept in the ESRO. John Jones remarried in 1761. I am grateful to Roger Davey, East Sussex County Archivist, for helping me find this information about John Jones's son. See also Turner, *Diary*, ed. Vaisey, pp. 333–4.
[11] Richardson, *Pamela*, ed. Sabor, p. 106.
[12] Haywood, *Betsy Thoughtless*, p. 535. The changing composition of Thomas Thoughtless's family is discussed below, pp. 48–50.

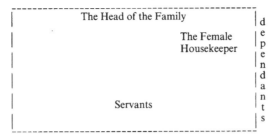

Figure 1   The household-family framework

specifically in these cases, 'single men's families'. In present-day terms these definitions may sound awkward, and probably none of these units would be referred to today as a 'family' except perhaps in a metaphorical sense. Nevertheless, they bear witness to a significant form of social and familial organisation. They present an extreme, though by no means a rare formation of the household-family, and therefore provide us with a key for understanding some of the basic principles of this historical family concept.

The outlines of these household-families can be graphically represented as in figure 1.

Each of these 'single persons' families' has two participating parties, the head of the family and the dependants. The head of each family is male and the dependants are mostly servants. The master's place on the one hand, and the servants' place on the other, mark the boundaries of the household-family. The family also includes a set role for a female housekeeper: she can be a wife, a sister, or any other woman who is invested with the office of housekeeping. This household-family framework is both permeable and flexible. It can expand and contract and include many individuals. One phrase that recurs in the context of such changes is '*to be taken into a family*'. For example, the apprentice-boy in Samuel Richardson's treatise *The Apprentice's Vade Mecum* is said to be 'taken into a Family in so intimate a Relation as that of an Apprentice'.[13] Mr Thomas Thoughtless objects to 'taking [his sister] into his family', although he does take his brother into it.[14] But whether the household-family is densely populated or not populated at all, its basic framework remains essentially unchanged. Many elaborate household units can therefore be understood as variations on this basic household-family form.

[13] Richardson, *Vade Mecum*, p. 45; see also *ibid.*, pp. 3, vi–vii.
[14] Haywood, *Betsy Thoughtless*, p. 303.

The framework of the household-family sketched so far has focused on male householders, but there are also references in the texts to 'families' ascribed to women. Mrs Munden, formerly Betsy Thoughtless, wonders whether the fellow pacing outside her house 'wanted to speak with some one or other of *her family*'.[15] At this point her establishment includes four servants, in addition to Mr Munden. Similarly, Mrs Wellair is eager 'to get home to *her husband and family*'.[16] There are references in the texts to 'single women's families' as well. When Thomas Turner writes about '*all my Mothers Family*' who went to church one Sunday, he is referring to the persons living under the care of Mrs Elizabeth Turner, a widow and a thriving shopkeeper.[17] These verbal expressions acknowledge the position of the mistress of the house and manifest her authority. In these texts, however, the acknowledged authority is usually explicitly male. Most of the references to household-families are made in relation to men, and when households are referred to in a general manner, most often they are defined in relation to their masters, as in '*Mr Piper's Family*',[18] '*Mr B.'s family*',[19] or '*the family of Mr Goodman*'.[20] The framework of the household-family thus manifests concepts of authority and possession, but in many cases patriarchal authority seems to be built into it as well.

The boundaries of these household-families are not those of blood and marriage, they are the boundaries of authority and of household management. But how did this family framework operate? How did people use it at different points in their lives? Let us examine these questions in the diary of Thomas Turner.

---

[15] *Ibid.*, p. 503.   [16] *Ibid.*, p. 335.

[17] 'my Wife and I set out for Framfield . . . My mother, Wife, Brother & *all my Mothers Family* was at Church in the Morn, Except my Sister, & Nephew who together with my Self Staid at home to get dinner', Thomas Turner, Diary, 21 May 1758; 'In the Morn my Wife Self and nephew went over to Framfield . . . my Wife *and my Mother's Whole Family* (except my Sister and my self) at church in the Morn', *ibid.*, 3 Oct. 1756. Turner's participation in preparing the Sunday dinner on this occasion should be noted, but cooking probably did not usually form part of his daily routine.

[18] *Ibid.*, 30 Jan. 1758. Piper's family consisted at this point of his second wife, a baby daughter, a manservant, and a maidservant, and possibly also a younger brother.

[19] Richardson, *Pamela*, ed. Sabor, p. 137. Mr B.'s family consists at this stage of servants only.

[20] See this and 'Mr Goodman's family' in Haywood, *Betsy Thoughtless*, pp. 170, 225, 229. During its most populated phase, Mr Goodman's family included a wife, her daughter by a previous marriage, a female ward, and various servants. See, for example, some similar references to families ascribed to males: 'Please our love to . . . Mr Dent's family . . . Doctor Chaytor, Doctor Rudd and Mr Barnett's families'; 'Mr Nelson's family here desires their compliments to you and their uncle's family', T. S. Willan, *An Eighteenth-Century Shopkeeper: Abraham Dent of Kirkby Stephen* (Manchester, 1970), Appendix IV, pp. 177–8, 191. 'Mr Eyres and Mr Smith's Familys make their best respects to you and sister Witeley', in T. S. Ashton, *An Eighteenth-Century Industrialist: Peter Stubs of Warrington, 1756–1806* (Manchester, 1961; 1st edn 1939), p. 145.

'My family at home': Thomas Turner's diary

In 1750, at the age of twenty-one, Thomas Turner set up business for himself as a mercer in the village of East Hoathly, Sussex. He married Margaret (Peggy) Slater in October 1753. A diary entry from January 1755 laconically records the death of their child: 'This morn about 1 OClock I had the misfortune to loose my little Boy Peter Aged 21 Weeks 3 days p[ai]d for flour and other small things 16*d* at home all day . . .'.[21]

These lines introduce the nuclear unit of Thomas and Peggy Turner and their deceased child. He was, in fact, the only child born to them during the years of their marriage. A present-day reader might think of this unit as 'a family', but this was not the unit that Thomas Turner defined in his diary as his family. There are two types of regular entries that appear throughout most of the diary and present an illuminating angle from which Turner's concept of his own family can be viewed: the near-weekly entries about the household attendance at church, and the near-daily entries about the household consumption of food. Thomas Turner was conscious of his religious duty as the head of his family and he kept a record of the attendance of his household members at church. He also had a very strong sense of his family as an economic unit and of himself as the family administrator and provider: he recorded the consumption of food in his house, and when he dined out he noted what was served at home in his absence. In these entries he refers to family members. Sometimes they are listed explicitly, as, for example, 'my Wife & maid dined on the remains of yesterday['s] diner'.[22] or 'my Self, wife and maid at church in the forenoon'.[23] At other times they are referred to collectively as 'my family': '*my Family at home* Dined on the remains of Yesterdays Dinner', [24] and '*My Family* all at Church in the afternoon'.[25] These references to the 'family' recur in the diary again and again. Many of the records for 1754 are missing and in 1755 the entries take various forms, but from 1756 onwards they conform to a consistent pattern. Turner notes church attendance and food consumption while either noting his household members, or referring to them collectively as 'my family'. But in different instances these references apply to entirely different sets of people. The flexible and permeable framework of the household-family thus surfaces repeatedly in Thomas Turner's words: his 'family' is a household-family, headed by a householder and populated by related and non-related dependants.

No matter who the household-family contained at any particular moment, however, it was normally conceived of by Turner in his diary as

[21] Thomas Turner, Diary, 16 Jan. 1755.   [22] *Ibid.*, 7 Mar. 1756.
[23] *Ibid.*, 2 May 1756.   [24] *Ibid.*, 19 July 1756.   [25] *Ibid.*, 29 July 1759.

an entity separate from his non-resident kin, however nearly related. This can be seen in the following examples:

I dined *with* my mother (*my family* dining on a p[ie]ce pork & Greens).[26]

my Bro[ther] staid at my House . . . and dined *with* my Family . . . [27]

my whole Family at Church . . . *as also* my Brother and Sister . . . [28]

my Family *&* my Mother Slater dined on a roast Shoulder of Lamb . . . [29]

There are many similar examples in the text. In each of them Turner distinguishes between his relations, and the members of his household whom he calls 'my family'. This distinction also holds when referring to relatives who in modern sociological terms form 'the nuclear family of origin' of either Turner or his wife. In the first entry Thomas Turner refers to his visit to his mother's house. Elizabeth Turner, a widow, lived in a neighbouring village. Turner's younger brother, sister, and nephew were at that time living with her.[30] But this group of near kin is listed separately, while the wife and the non-related servant-maid are grouped together as 'my family'. In the next two entries Turner's brother and sister are listed apart from the regular household members. The same principle is evident in the case of the mother-in-law in the fourth entry, referred to as 'my Mother Slater'. But, as we shall see, if any of these relations came to reside in Turner's house, he or she could also be counted among the family at home.[31]

When referring to his relatives by blood or marriage, Turner used several terms. Individual relatives were referred to by kinship terms, names and surnames.[32] When making *general* allusions to kin, however, he tended to use the terms '*friends*' and '*relations*'.[33] Just as 'family' was an inclusive term that could embrace various household members, so could 'friends' and 'relations' refer to various kin: parents, siblings, in-laws, and others. Thus when Turner complained, saying 'living so near *my Friends*

[26] *Ibid.*, 22 Apr. 1756.   [27] *Ibid.*, 11 Oct. 1756.   [28] *Ibid.*, 26 Sept. 1756.
[29] *Ibid.*, 28 Sept. 1756.
[30] Thomas Turner's complex relationship with his mother is examined below in chapter 5, on Turner's 'friends'.
[31] Figure 2 on p. 32 below shows various relations, such as a brother, sister, niece, and mother-in-law, who stayed in the house and were referred to by Turner as among his 'family' who dined at home in his absence.
[32] Such usages are discussed in detail in chapters 4 and 5 below.
[33] On a handful of occasions he used the term 'family' in this respect. It is also important to note that the term 'friend' was used to refer to non-kin, too. Usages of 'family' referring to kin are discussed on pp. 41–2, 103–7. Turner's relations are discussed in ch. 4, and Turner's related and non-related 'friends' are discussed more specifically in chs. 5 and 6.

is I think a very great disadvantage', he was probably referring to his mother and siblings who lived in the neighbouring village.[34]

To summarise, Turner's concept of the family, as expressed in his diary, was first and foremost a concept of household organisation. Two main criteria qualified one to be counted as a member of the household-family: co-residence and submission to the authority of the head of the household. A relationship by blood or marriage did not form a necessary criterion for family inclusion. Turner's non-resident kin were generally conceived of by him as an entity separate from his family at home.

But if an eighteenth-century family such as Thomas Turner's was not simply held together by ties of blood and marriage, what were the relationships that bound its members and turned them into one family? In answering this question, it is possible to identify four facets of household-family relationships. First, when people were 'taken into the family' their arrival was often preceded by an agreement setting the terms for their inclusion. The household-family relationships established in these cases can therefore be called 'contractual'. Different family contracts varied greatly in their formality. The marriage contract was formal, life-long, and (for all but a few) indissoluble. The apprentice's indenture was also formal, but its duration was limited and it could be dissolved. The service contract and the boarding agreement were very often made orally, but they were nevertheless binding.[35] This, for example, is Thomas Turner's record of the agreement that settled the terms of Mary Martin's membership in his household: 'mary martin Came to live with me at 30s a year'.[36] And this is the agreement that preceded the arrival in the family of Thomas's nephew, Philip: 'I agreed to take Philip Turner of my Mother at £5,,0,,0 a year to Board and Cloath him.'[37] The contractual

---

[34] Ibid., 16 Sept. 1757. At various stages Mrs Turner's household also included other kin.

[35] For forms of sealing agreements between servants and masters at hiring fairs and the binding force of such contracts, see Kussmaul, Servants in Husbandry, pp. 31–2, 59. See also the discussion of contractual agreements in C. Muldrew, The Economy of Obligation: The Culture of Credit and Social Relations in Early Modern England (Basingstoke, 1998), ch. 8 and esp. p. 207.

[36] Thomas Turner, Diary, 25 Mar. 1754. This is how this household-family contract was dissolved: 'This day my Wife gave our servant Mary Martin Warning to provide her self with another service at New Lady day next', ibid., 30 Dec. 1757. And, finally: 'this day my Wife Paid Mary Martin our Servant in Cash and goods 40s in full for one Years Wages and she accordingly went away', ibid., 28 Mar. 1758. Records reveal a number of Mary Martins in Thomas Turner's 'catchment area'. One possibility is that she was a widow living in Framfield, Turner's village of origin. This suggestion, which has been kindly communicated to me by David Vaisey, has been made by Patricia Hope.

[37] Thomas Turner, Diary, 15 Feb. 1757. Accordingly, Philip was brought to the house: 'in the afternoon my Brother Moses Brought Over Philip according to our agreem[en]t a [sic] Tuesday last', ibid., 17 Feb. 1757. Following the death of his main guardian and step-grandmother, Philip Turner was placed in the house of a neighbour, the shoemaker Master Hook: 'my brother Came over and brought Philip who is to board at master

household-family relationships were not always so explicit, and they tended to be less explicit in the case of related persons. Some agreements could also be short term, or intentionally flexible and open to change. The important point, however, is that the household-family relationship was formed by agreement: an offer had been made and accepted.[38] Indeed, if we look carefully it would seem that legitimate children were probably the only individuals whose relationship to the household-family was not initially contractual.

The second point is that many household-family contracts involved an exchange of work and material benefits. We can therefore say that these relationships were instrumental. Thomas Turner's concept of his family is best understood in institutional and instrumental rather than sentimental terms: indeed, it is impossible to explain the many changes in his family by searching the diary for evidence of emotional life. This, however, is not to say that emotions were unimportant in the context of the household-family. Early research in the history of the family assumed instrumentality to be in opposition to sentiments and affection, but in the case of Turner's family this contrast does not hold.[39] Turner was not emotionally attached to all the members of his household-family. Different members were attached to him in different measure, and he was also strongly attached to many people outside his household. But various persons became members of Turner's household-family, or derived greater benefit from the household-family relationship, because they had an emotional attachment to its head, as we shall see below. In the case of Thomas Turner's household-family, instrumentality and affection often went hand in hand; indeed, an increase in affection often led to an increase in instrumentality.

A third point follows from the previous two: namely, that many of the household-family relationships were both domestic and occupational. Various household-family members had specific occupational tasks, such as cooking, cleaning, working in the shop, or nursing an invalid. This was

Hooks upon the following terms . . .': *ibid.*, 12 June 1759. Philip, baptised in Framfield on 13 Mar. 1749, was thus nearly eight years old when he came to his uncle's house: ESRO, Baptism Index.

[38] It is worth noting that although familial residence did not necessarily correlate with parish settlement, formal family contracts did have a decisive significance as far as parish settlement was concerned. Lawful marriage, legally bound and fully served apprenticeship, or a year's service carried with them parish settlement. See for example the case of James Marchant, below, n. 46.

[39] Material interests in marriage and parent–child relationships were especially seen as opposed to 'domesticity' and 'romantic love'. See H. Medick and D. W. Sabean, *Interest and Emotion: Essays on the Study of Family and Kinship* (Cambridge, 1984). The importance of combining affection with familial and material interests in the choice of marriage partners is stressed in Ingram, *Church Courts, Sex and Marriage in England*, esp. pp. 134–42.

manifested in double-purpose titles, such as 'servant', 'master', or 'wife' or 'mistress', which indicated one's place in the family as well as one's possible occupational role.[40]

Finally, the contractual, instrumental, or occupational nature of the household-family relationships should not be taken to imply that ties of blood and marriage were of little significance. On the contrary, such ties were extremely effective in Thomas Turner's life, and they were also very useful in gaining access to his household-family. Many of the members of Turner's household-family were recruited from among his kin,[41] but the effectiveness of his kinship networks should not be confused with the structure of his household-family. Similar processes of recruitment enabled Turner to take non-related persons into his family as well. In both cases family ties were linked with patronage, and in both cases they were also heavily dependent on life-course changes, occupational ties, and conditions of domestic hardship brought on by poverty, sickness, or death.[42]

These properties of household-family relationships can be illustrated by examining two particular cases. The first is the case of Hannah Marchant, the second that of Thomas Turner's younger brother, Richard. Both show how contractual, instrumental, and occupational household-family relationships were also entwined with networks of patronage and kinship, in the case of Hannah Marchant extending vertically from the middling household-family to the level of the village poor. Hannah came to the family as a temporary servant, as her service agreement records: 'This Day Hannah Marchant Came to be w[i]th us a little Time to help Clean the House &c.'[43] But her service proved satisfactory and turned into a long-term connection. She lived in the house for a period of at least six years and nine months; indeed, after Peggy Turner's

---

[40] It is interesting to note that the occupational household-family roles were not always gender-specific: shop-assistance, for example, was performed at various times by the master, the mistress, two maidservants, and two journeymen.

[41] See p. 32, figure 2. The close ties among Turner's kin support Cressy's argument for the effectiveness of kinship ties, see Cressy, 'Kinship and kin interaction'. For a discussion of effective kinship ties in a later period, see Anderson, *Family Structure in Nineteenth-Century Lancashire*. See further references and discussions in chapters 4 and 5.

[42] See P. Laslett, 'Family, kinship and collectivity as systems of support in pre-industrial Europe: a consideration of the "nuclear hardship" hypothesis', *Continuity and Change* 3 (1988), 153–75.

[43] Thomas Turner, Diary, 22 Sept. 1758. Hannah Marchant, baptised in Ticehurst, Sussex, on 19 Oct. 1735, was thus twenty-three years old when her service began: ESRO, Baptism Index. It is possible that Turner did not want to engage her on the basis of a yearly contract in order to prevent her from gaining legal settlement in East Hoathly. Hannah came from a poor family. Her brother James, who was also living at the time in East Hoathly, lacked settlement in the parish and at one time was removed from there to his parish of origin, Ticehurst.

death she remained the main long-term family member.[44] During this time Thomas Turner was also associated with many of Hannah's 'friends', that is her relatives by blood and marriage, including her father, aunt, brother, sister-in-law, sister-in-law's sisters and their husbands. He employed them, lent them money, assisted them in various legal matters, gave them away at their weddings, and entertained them at Christmas.[45] But he also benefited from many of these transactions, and when he was obliged to remove Hannah's brother from the village, in his capacity as overseer of the poor, he evidently performed his duty.[46]

In the case of Thomas Turner's younger brother, Richard, the networks of patronage and kinship extended horizontally among fellow tradesmen and across neighbouring towns and villages, and reveal a continual shuffle of household-family members. Richard Turner was taken from his mother's house and shop and placed as an apprentice in the family of one Mr Beard,[47] who had previously been a servant of Thomas Turner. Richard Turner was then hired as a servant by one of Thomas Turner's main suppliers: Thomas made the arrangements for his brother's service and recorded the details of the contract.[48] Subsequently,

[44] Editors of Turner's diary have been impressed by Turner's recurring references to Mary Martin and described her as the 'favourite servant'. The main long-term servant in the household, however, was Hannah Marchant.

[45] James Marchant, Hannah's brother, married Elizabeth Mepham, a frequent visitor and an occasional employee at the Turner household. At their wedding Turner acted as 'what is commonly Call'd Father', giving the bride away. He also gave away Elizabeth's sister Lucy at her wedding: Thomas Turner, Diary, 7 Feb. 1763, 2 Jan. 1764. The Marchants and the Mephams remained in close touch and continued to work for Thomas Turner every now and again. On 14 Aug. 1764 Turner lent money to the widow Marchant. Around the same time he was involved in a complex affair settling the Mepham sisters' inheritance and distributing their share in their father's estate. He handed Lucy's and Elizabeth's shares to their husbands, but held the third sister's share promising to pay it when claimed: ibid., 28–9 Sept., 24–5 Oct. 1764. He was also actively involved in the affair of James Marchant's settlement (see next note). Christmas was celebrated in 1756, 1757, and 1758 with James, Hannah, and the widow Marchant, and in 1759, 1761, 1762, 1763, and 1764 with Elizabeth Mepham and with James and Elizabeth's daughter as well (at Christmas 1764 the widow Marchant was not present).

[46] Ibid., 17 Apr. 1763. James Marchant, a pauper, was apprenticed to his uncle in East Hoathly for the duration of seven years, but the uncle refused to bind him with formal indentures to prevent his future settlement in the parish, and also James left before his term was up. James remained in East Hoathly, but his right to live there remained questionable. After his marriage he was removed to his parish of origin, Ticehurst. The matter was brought before the quarter session at Lewis on 15 July 1763. Throughout the affair Turner both assisted the Marchants and represented his parish interests. A settlement certificate was finally delivered to Turner by Hannah and James's father. It can still be found among the East Hoathly parish records: ibid., 15 July, 11 Oct. 1763; ESRO PAR 378; Turner, Diary, ed. Vaisey, pl. 6.

[47] Thomas Turner, Diary, 1 Jan. 1761.

[48] The contract was signed for the period of two to three years. Thomas Turner's record of it includes such particulars as who should pay for the hire of a horse when Richard Turner and his master went to London or visited a fair: Thomas Turner, Diary, 27 Dec. 1760.

one of Richard Turner's fellow-servants became a member of Thomas Turner's family, and some time later Richard himself joined the family.[49] He worked in his brother's shop, went on errands, and collected debts on his behalf, and also socialised with him in the same circle of friends.[50] When Thomas Turner was courting the woman who was to become his second wife, Richard joined them as a companion.[51] A few days before their marriage he left the house and bargained to hire himself out as a yearly servant.[52] Richard Turner's membership in his elder brother's household-family was therefore both domestic and occupational, and it was clearly a life-course phenomenon. But it also involved long-term ties of affection and of kinship-based patronage, both of which persisted after he had left the household-family. Years later Richard Turner died in his elder brother's house.[53]

Finally, it is important to examine how Thomas Turner's concept of the family accommodated changes over time. This chronological survey is very significant, because it allows us a new and close insight into phases of change and continuity in a middling eighteenth-century household. The changes in Turner's household-family are summarised in figure 2, which lists the persons referred to by Turner as 'my family' together with the dates of their inclusion within the household-family. The starting date is 1756, when Turner's 'family pattern' was already clearly established.

It can be seen that during the years 1756 to 1765 Thomas Turner's household-family underwent many changes. But the concept of the family, which Turner used throughout this period, produced an enduring continuity of structure despite the comings and goings of individuals. As soon as a new person came to live in the house, he or she was subsumed into the household-family and was referred to among the family members who dined at home or went to church; conversely, when a family member left the house, he or she was removed from the list and was no longer included within the family. Philip Turner, for example, is referred to

---

[49] Henry Dodson arrived on 16 Apr. 1764, and Richard Turner on 26 Dec. 1764.
[50] See, for example, Thomas Turner, Diary, 3, 5, 10 Jan., 26 Apr. 1765.
[51] Ibid., 24 Mar. 1765. Another female companion was also present.
[52] Ibid., 16 June 1765.
[53] 'My Brother Richard Turner died Monday the 21st of February 1774 at my House in EastHothly and was buried at Framfield Fryday the 25th 1774 aged 32 Years': 'Notes on Family History', ESRO, SAS/SM 210; see also T. Turner, The Diary of Thomas Turner of East Hoathly (1754–1765), ed. F. M. Turner, with an introduction by J. B. Priestley (London, 1925), p. 111; T. Turner, The Diary of a Georgian Shopkeeper, a selection by R. W. Blencowe and M. A. Lower, with a preface by F. M. Turner, ed. G. H. Jennings (Oxford, 1979), p. 83. (The title 'Notes on Family History', by which the document is known, however, does not appear in the original manuscript.)

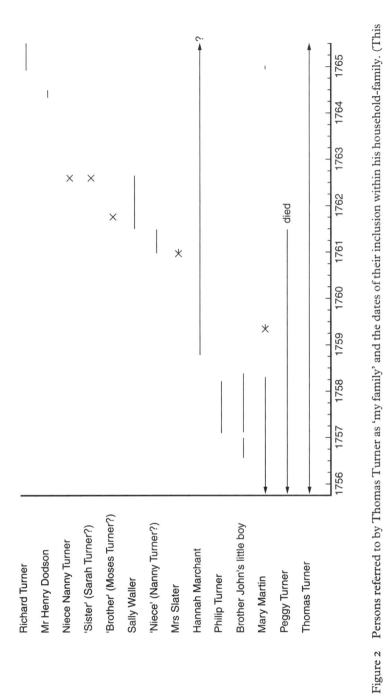

Figure 2   Persons referred to by Thomas Turner as 'my family' and the dates of their inclusion within his household-family. (This figure does not record every occasion when such frequent visitors as Mary Martin and Moses Turner stayed at the house, but only when Thomas Turner referred to them as 'my family'.)

among the family on 21 February 1757, four days after he joined the household. The servant Mary Martin is listed among the family church-goers on 26 March 1758, nearly three months after she had been given notice and only two days before she actually went away. Once she left, she was promptly referred to as 'my former servant' or 'my late servant'.[54] At times, when she returned to the house for a few days' visit or to do some casual work, she was again referred to among 'my Family at home'.[55] Turner's concept of his family, with its basic independence from kinship ties, also accommodated the greatest change that occurred in his life during these years, the death of his wife. With Peggy Turner's death, this family ceased to contain a nuclear unit. But its structural framework continued to exist as a 'single man's family', and years after his wife's death we still find Thomas Turner referring to 'my family at home'.

Turner's concept of the family appears to have required the presence in the household of more than one dependant. When there was only one such person in the household, he hardly ever referred to 'my family', but as soon as a new dependant joined the household he quickly reverted to his record of 'my family at home'.[56] For example, after the middle of August 1762, when Thomas Turner remained at home with only his servant Hannah Marchant, the references to 'my family' were suspended for a period of about nineteen months. But on 16 April 1764 a new dependant arrived at the house, the shop assistant Mr Henry Dodson.[57] Two days later Turner once more referred to 'my Family at home'.[58]

Altogether, the number of persons who were referred to by Turner as members of 'my family' during these years amounts to at least eleven, not counting Thomas Turner himself. But the number of persons who ac-tually lived in the house at one and the same time was normally no more

[54] Such references to this faithful former servant recur again and again years after her departure: see, for example, Thomas Turner, Diary, 2 Apr. 1761, 27 Feb. 1762, 16 Oct. 1764, 18 Feb. 1765.
[55] For example, she arrives at the house on 31 Dec. 1764 and is referred to among the family diners on 4–5 Jan. 1765. On Sunday 6 Jan. she is counted as 'my late serv.' among the churchgoers, and on the same evening she goes away.
[56] A notable exception is Turner's entry on 28 May 1758 in which he refers to his wife and himself as his 'family': 'My Whole Family at Church in the morn (that is my Wife and Self).' It is possible to read this as a self-conscious entry in which Turner acknowledged the recent changes that occurred in his family: the departure of his two nephews and maidservant and his wife's deteriorating health. Turner then suspended his references to 'my family at home' and resumed them only on 27 Sept. 1758, five days after Hannah Marchant had joined the family.
[57] On 16 Apr. 1764 Turner records Dodson's entry into the household-family as well as his occupational role: 'My old acquaintance Mr Henry Dodson Came in the afternoon to stand the shop for me.'
[58] Thomas Turner, Diary, 18 Apr. 1764. References to the 'family' are suspended yet again after Dodson's departure in June, but are resumed six months later when Richard Turner joins the household: ibid., 4 Jan. 1765.

than two or three: for about fifty-eight months in all the household-family included three members, and for about thirty months it included two. Even in its most densely populated phases, the number of household-family members probably did not exceed five. The two noticeable periods of surge in the family population (from February 1757 to March 1758, and from February 1761 to the following June) can be associated with phases in the life-course. The former was a phase of relative strength, when the young and childless couple were in a position to assist some needy relations, while in contrast the latter phase was characterised by sickness and death, and both Peggy and Thomas Turner themselves needed help. In terms of its size, however, the Turner household appears very ordinary throughout these diverse transformations – no different from many other households numbering between two and five members, which according to Laslett constituted more than three-fifths of English households at Thomas Turner's time, and in which more than two-fifths of the population lived.[59]

Nor can the changes that occurred in the population of the Turner household – frequent and radical as they were – be regarded as unusual, or as the result of extraordinary circumstances. Some similar changes were no doubt experienced by a large part of the contemporary population. The fluctuating composition of Turner's household-family should be seen in the light of some basic contemporary social and demographic conditions, all of which could lead to changing and complex living arrangements. At a time in which about one marriage in three was broken by the death of a partner before the end of the wife's fecund period there could be a significant fluidity in household composition.[60] Illness and widowhood could bring about new domestic arrangements, re-marriage could lead to the creation of complex families with half-relations and step-relations, and orphanhood could necessitate various forms of boarding and fostering.[61] Schooling, too, often involved some boarding, and

[59] P. Laslett, *The World We Have Lost – Further Explored* (Cambridge, 1983), p. 95. These figures are based on a sample of one hundred English settlements between 1754 and 1821.
[60] D. Levine, *Reproducing Families: A Political Economy of English Population History* (Cambridge, 1987), p. 79. 'It was only in the early 1770s that half of any marriage cohort could have celebrated a silver wedding', says Anderson: 'What is new about the modern family?', p. 76. For mortality and life expectancy, see Wrigley and Schofield, *The Population History of England*, e.g. pp. 228–36, 248–53, 412–17, 452–3; for marriage, see *ibid.*, e.g. pp. 189–91, 257–65, 421–30.
[61] This, for instance, may have been the lot of at least some of the 16 per cent of late eighteenth-century children who were motherless by the age of eleven, the 20 per cent who were fatherless, and the 4 per cent who were total orphans by the age of fifteen. By the time they reached their first marriage, 45 per cent were motherless and 49 per cent fatherless. The figures for the late twentieth century are radically different: 2 per cent motherless by the age of eleven and 3 per cent fatherless, and 16 per cent motherless or fatherless by their first marriage. See Laslett, 'Family, kinship and collectivity', 153–75,

children were also sent away to the houses of relations and friends for periods that could last between a few weeks and a few years.[62] The institution of life-cycle service was also very significant. By the time they reached their mid-teens, as many as two-thirds of young men and women left home for formative periods of 'life-cycle service', during which they lived for years as servants and apprentices in other households before setting up on their own.[63] The institution of service was indeed so prevalent that between a quarter and third of all households contained servants.[64] The majority of English people in the eighteenth century thus no doubt married and established new family households for themselves;[65] but the majority probably also lived at some stage in their lives in households to whose members they were not related. Finally, we should remember that there were also at that time strong social, cultural, and religious norms that promoted notions of household governance. Considering all this, it is not surprising that people in the eighteenth century used a flexible and inclusive term for designating the domestic group, while not necessarily conflating it with kinship ties.

Categorical definitions and further usages

This case-study of Thomas Turner's family, drawing as it does on contemporary records made over several years, has revealed phases of change and continuity in an eighteenth-century household which neither household reconstitution studies, depending on disparate and sometimes

---

and esp. p. 163; P. Laslett, 'La parenté en chiffres', *Annales: Economies, Sociétés, Civilizations* 43 (1988), 5–24, esp. p. 13. I would like to thank Peter Laslett for suggesting these references to me. See also Anderson, 'What is new about the modern family?', p. 76. On complex living arrangements due to familial hardship see Chaytor, 'Household and kinship in Ryton'.

[62] Ben-Amos, *Adolescence and Youth*, pp. 39–68, 165–7.

[63] Kussmaul estimates that between 1574 and 1821 servants constituted around 60 per cent of the population aged fifteen to twenty-four: Kussmaul, *Servants in Husbandry*, p. 3. Macfarlane notes that the vast majority of children left home at an early age or worked for people other than their parents, *Marriage and Love in England*, p. 86; for modifications, see *ibid.*, p. 87. On life-cycle service see also Schofield, 'Age-specific mobility'; Laslett, *Family Life and Illicit Love*; R. Wall, 'Leaving home and the process of household formation in pre-industrial England', *Continuity and Change* 2 (1987), pp. 77–101; Ben-Amos, *Adolescence and Youth*.

[64] 'at any moment a quarter or a third of the households of a community would contain servants', Laslett, *The World We Have Lost – Further Explored*, p. 15; see also pp. 3–4, 64–5, 293 n. 6. See also P. Laslett, 'Mean household size in England since the sixteenth century', in Laslett and Wall (eds.), *Household and Family in Past Time*, p. 152.

[65] There was indeed a strong social norm of 'neo-local residence', according to which married couples were expected to set up on their own, rather than join a parental home, for example. As this analysis suggests, however, this did not necessarily imply that such households remained 'nuclear'.

unrelated records, nor census data limited to a single day, can in any way capture. The concept of the household-family has emerged in this case-study as a structured framework within which many familial and social changes were both experienced and understood. The salience of this concept enables us to return to the question posed at the beginning of this chapter: how illuminating are the standard categories of classification, and the concept of nuclearity itself – so influential in the history of the English family – if they do not engage with the terms used by historical actors?

If we try to map the changes in Turner's family according to the classical categories postulated (for example) by Laslett and Wall, the results are bewildering. During a relatively short period of around ten years Thomas Turner's family passed through numerous phases. It started as a simple family household without offspring, became a simple family household with offspring, and was reduced once more to a simple family household without offspring. It proceeded through at least four different phases of downward or upward extension. It then became a single man's family (in classical terms, 'a solitary type "a"'), though this phase was punctuated by brief periods of lateral and downward extension. It then evolved to a phase of 'no family type "a"', before finally reverting once more to a simple family household. Some of these phases lasted no more than several weeks. The longest period of stability lasted twenty-eight months.[66]

But do these categories assist us in understanding the principles underlying the organisational structure and the dynamics of this family? Do they, moreover, have any bearing on Thomas Turner's own concepts? This entirely external system of classification contributes little to our understanding of Turner's family; indeed, it obscures our ability to perceive its organisation and the many changes that took place within it. No doubt this external classificatory system has important uses: without it, it would be extremely difficult to conduct comparative studies across cultures and periods. But it would be a mistake to accept the external system as if it were a historical structure. A better way forward, as this book argues, is to complement it with a methodical analysis of the terms

---

[66] Laslett, *The World We Have Lost – Further Explored*, esp. pp. 93–4, stresses that the family population could change enormously during the life-cycle, but he argues that in the English simple family system such a cycle 'occurred only once of course in every individual case'. In view of Thomas Turner's case, this conception of the life-cycle seems far too schematic. Laslett also argues that the family composition could change temporarily and rapidly, but he stresses that 'most alterations in the family itself changed its size rather than its kinship composition'. As this chapter argues, a different approach to the concept of 'family composition' can affect this conclusion.

in which a historical culture defined itself.[67] Of course, it is important to emphasise once more that the concepts proposed here, such as 'the household-family' and 'contractual relationships' are (like those they seek to complement) also based on a present-day terminology. We cannot simply delve into the minds of eighteenth-century people and understand their concepts 'in their own terms'. Rather, the terminology used here intends to illuminate concepts of the family used in the past, while also addressing questions raised by present-day historians.

The main difference between Thomas Turner's concept of the household-family and the standard categories of classification is that the latter rest on the concept of the nuclear family, and particularly the conjugal unit. Thus, for example, households that include relatives beyond the nuclear core are defined as 'extended', whereas households that include no nuclear core are defined as 'solitaries'. Household and family types are then further classified according to the exact relationships of blood and marriage between the members. In this way, a household consisting of co-resident siblings (for example) falls into the category of 'no family'. In contrast to these definitions, the phenomena of 'the single man's family' or 'the single woman's family' show that in the eighteenth century families could exist quite apart from notions of conjugality. Moreover, families could consist of various types of extension, consanguinity or solitariness – and indeed could evolve very rapidly through these types – without fundamentally changing their social definition as families or their householders' status as heads of families.

The concept of the household-family also enables us to question the usefulness of the term 'extended family'.[68] If nuclear households could absorb and shed extended family members such as siblings, nephews, and nieces without apparently changing their contemporary definition as families, then perhaps the structural boundaries between the 'nuclear family' and the 'extended family' were less clear than is commonly assumed.[69] Indeed, the distinction appears still less relevant when we take

---

[67] In a survey of the history of the family, Tamara Hareven noted that 'ideally, historians should juxtapose the actors' categories and definitions of kin with externally defined notions', while believing that the limitations of traditional historical sources make such a project extremely difficult. This study, I hope, shows that such work is both possible and fruitful. See Hareven, 'The history of the family and the complexity of social change', p. 110.

[68] See also ch. 4, below. See also Goody's broad and effective critique: Goody, 'The evolution of the family'.

[69] See Chaytor, 'Household and kinship in Ryton', esp. pp. 29, 38. See also the questioning of the category of the 'extended family' and 'the myth of the extended family' in Goody, 'The evolution of the family', esp. pp. 119 and 124; see also Segalen, *Historical Anthropology of the Family*, p. 14.

into account that, as we have seen, households could also absorb and shed non-related members, with the use of some similar procedures and often for similar reasons.

These issues are brought sharply into focus if we consider the place of servants. The servants' presence in the household, and their subordinate role, are greatly emphasised by Laslett and Wall. At the same time, however, the servants are not seen as having a modifying effect on the final or permanent structure of the household. Each of the classical categories can appear in one of two ways, with or without servants – thus minimising the impact of the servants on the household structure.[70] Laslett also argues that, because of their great mobility, servants must not be regarded as permanent members of the household.[71] But, as this study has shown, the category of 'permanence' is often problematic. There were both servants and relatives who came into Thomas Turner's family and then left after relatively short periods of time, just as there were both servants and relatives who stayed in the household-family for extended periods.

Finally, we reach the place of other possible co-residents in the household, such as lodgers, boarders, and other sojourners. If we look at the classical categories, these persons are listed under the heading of 'the houseful'.[72] This residual category, however, can also prove problematic. As this study emphasises, the boundaries between kin, servants, boarders, and guests can be difficult to define, and those people who might be treated as 'residual' can also be members of the household.[73] Philip Turner, for instance, was both a relative, a boarder, and probably also a child-servant, whereas Henry Dodson, a journeyman and an 'old acquaintance', fulfilled many of the same roles as Thomas Turner's brother Richard.

Thus, with the use of the standard categories of classification the simple, nuclear family household – with or without servants – emerges as

---

[70] As Laslett explains, 'because servants always modify the membership of households, we allot all domestic groups to one of two classes, those with and those without servants'. He then adds '[n]evertheless servants can hardly be said to affect the final structure of the household', Laslett, 'Introduction', in Laslett and Wall (eds.), *Household and Family in Past Time*, p. 29.

[71] Examining the turnover in the population of servants in Clayworth and Cogenhoe, Laslett says: 'These close details make it plain that servants must not be regarded as permanent members of the households where they worked, even if some of them stayed so long that they became the family retainers of literature and sentiment': Laslett, *Family Life and Illicit Love*, p. 72.

[72] Laslett, 'Introduction', in Laslett and Wall (eds.), *Household and Family in Past Time*, esp. pp. 34–9.

[73] This difficulty is also emphasised by Laslett, who, however, continues to postulate a clear difference between a 'familial' connection with the household and an 'economic' one: *ibid.*, pp. 35–9.

the leading residential pattern in early modern England: but an initial focus on the nuclear family, and the marginalisation of servants, apprentices, boarders, and other co-residents, itself dictates this conclusion. Historians using this system of classification sometimes complain that concepts of 'house' and 'family' are used in the records in confusing ways, making it difficult for the modern investigator to sift the nuclear family members from other related and non-related persons.[74] The analysis of Thomas Turner's concept of the household-family shows that it is not a confusion that the sources display: the reason why early modern people did not identify households by their conjugal core is not because their concepts were confused, but because their concepts were different.

Indeed, Thomas Turner was not the only one to have used this concept of the household-family. More than one hundred years before Thomas Turner wrote his diary, another diarist, Ralph Josselin, referred to the marriage of his servant in the following words: 'our former Mayde Lydia Weston having dwelt with mee I year and almost 3 quarters marryed into our Towne, *the first that marryed out of my family*'.[75] Note also Josselin's account of Lydia's contractual position in his household-family, the duration of her household-family membership, and her present position as a 'former servant'. Lydia, like the faithful Mary Martin, continued to render help: 'Lydia my former servant nursd my litle daughter . . . ', wrote Josselin, recording the child-care arrangements made when he and his wife went away for a few days.[76] In 1660 Samuel Pepys invoked in his diary the same household-family framework: 'I lived in Axe=Yard, having my wife, and servant Jane, and no more in *family* than us three.'[77] In the following year he noted with satisfaction: 'I am now almost settled – *my family* being, myself, my wife, Jane, Will Ewre, and Wayneman, my

---

[74] 'There is ample evidence . . . to suggest that the confusion between "houses" and "families" persisted into the eighteenth century': R. Wall, 'Mean household size in England from the printed sources', in Laslett and Wall (eds.), *Household and Family in Past Time*, p. 166. Past writers, such as Gregory King and Richard Price, are thus criticised for their failure 'to make the appropriate distinction between the houseful and the household', *ibid.*, pp. 161, 173. See also Laslett, 'Introduction', in *ibid.*, pp. 25–8.

[75] R. Josselin, *The Diary of Ralph Josselin, 1616–1683*, ed. A. Macfarlane, Records of Social and Economic History, n.s., 3 (Oxford, 1991), 8 Aug. 1644, p. 15. A contemporary dictionary gives a definition that supports this view: 'Family' is described as 'An Household consisting of persons of diuers sexes, ages, stature, strength &c. Also kindred', T. Wilson, *Christian Dictionary* (London, 1612).

[76] Josselin, *Diary*, 31 Aug. 1646, p. 68.

[77] S. Pepys, *The Diary of Samuel Pepys*, ed. R. Latham and W. Matthews, 11 vols. (London 1970–83), vol. I, p. 1 (1659/60). See also, for example, 6 Dec. 1660, *ibid.*, p. 311: 'After much free discourse with my Lord, who tells me his mind as to his *enlarging his family* and desiring me to look him out a mayster of the horse, and other servants.' For an illuminating analysis of Pepys's household, see Earle, *The Making of the English Middle Class*, ch. 8.

girl's brother.'[78] More than a century later, we find the same concept used by John Arbuthnot. Speaking of a farm of 800 acres, he says: 'If the tract is in the hands of one man, *his family* will consist of himself, a wife, three children, twelve servants . . . Thus the farmer's family – 17.'[79]

This concept of the household-family was also so obvious in the eyes of Gregory King that, when assessing the share of different estates and occupations in the national income, he took into account not only nuclear families but also all household dependants and servants. His table was appropriately entitled 'A scheme of the income and expense of the several *families* of England'.[80] In the case of the temporal peers, for example, he counted 160 families, with a yearly income of £2,800 each, and with *forty* members per family. He then divided the income per head, reaching an average of £70 a year for each of the members in the families of peers. John Locke, too, was well aware of this concept of the household-family. Notwithstanding his fierce attack on the idea of patriarchal sovereignty (as expressed in Filmer's *Patriarcha*), Locke's use of the concept in his *Second Treatise of Government* shows that he shared the contemporary notion of the household-family as a unit of co-residence and authority.[81] Indeed, as a member of Lord Shaftesbury's household, Locke was himself counted as a part of his patron's 'family': in a letter of 7 March 1704/5 Shaftesbury mentions an account he wrote 'of Mr Locke from the time of his coming into our family'.[82]

Eighteenth-century documents are full of similar usages. If we turn to the volumes of Samuel Richardson's personal correspondence, we can trace further the currency of the concept of the household-family among our eighteenth-century 'language community'. For example, Aaron Hill, poet, dramatist, and failed entrepreneur, described one of the members of his family: 'We have a lively little boy *in the family* . . . but, alas, for him,

---

[78] Pepys, *Diary*, vol. II, p. 1 (1660/1). Elsewhere he also calls them 'my people'. For example, 'at dinner was very angry at *my people* eating a fine pudding . . . without my wife's leave', *ibid.*, 27 Jan. 1761, vol. II, p. 24, and see also, for example, p. 67.

[79] J. Arbuthnot, *An Inquiry into the Connection between the Present Price of Provisions and the Size of Farms* (London, 1773), p. 26, quoted in Snell, *Annals of the Labouring Poor*, p. 321. Compare the following: '[t]he *family* consisted of the master, and mistress, her mother, three or four prentices, (my lovely Miss Macpherson, being one) a fore-woman, and maid', J. Carter, *The Scotch Parents: or, The Remarkable Case of John Ramble, Written by Himself (in the Month of February, 1773)* (London, 1773), p. 10. I am grateful to Stephen Bending for this reference.

[80] *Seventeenth-Century Economic Documents*, ed. J. Thirsk and J. P. Cooper (Oxford, 1972), pp. 780–1. See also Wall, 'Mean household size in England', pp. 159–66.

[81] J. Locke, *Two Treatises of Government*, ed. M. Goldie (London, 1993), treatise II, pp. 77, 85–6. I am grateful to Mark Goldie for this reference and for directing my attention to Locke's correspondence.

[82] *Original Letters of John Locke, Algernon Sidney and Lord Shaftesbury*, ed. T. Forster (2nd edn, London 1847; repr. Bristol, 1990), p. 161.

poor child, quite unfriended and born to no prospect. He is the son of an honest, poor soldier . . .'[83] The high-born Mrs Delany conveyed to Mr Richardson her sister's thanks for having got a new governess '*into her family*'.[84] '*Mine is an increasing family*', wrote poor Laetitia Pilkington, as she noted the addition of an illegitimate grandchild to the tally of her wretched dependants.[85] Mrs Scudamore commented on the size of the family to which she arrived as a young bride, '*a large family*, to the number of twenty-three'. But she expressed her pleasant surprise at finding 'so many conveniences in the kitchen, parlour and hall, considering it was till now only occupied by a bachelor'.[86] Furthermore, the concept of the household-family was so prevalent in the eighteenth century that it could be used in an institutional context. The large group of paupers who removed from the Old Duke's Palace Workhouse in Norwich to a new workhouse, for example, is described in a report from 1805 as 'a family of near 600'.[87] The transformations of the concept of the household-family in the nineteenth century remain to be explored. It is significant, however, that in 1863 the office of the Registrar General still produced the following instruction for the census:

The family in its complete form consists of a householder with his wife and his children; and in the higher classes with his servants. Other relatives and visitors sometimes form a part of the family; and so do lodgers at a common table who pay for their subsistence and lodging.[88]

These additional examples show clearly that the concept of the household-family was well known and widely used in the eighteenth century. Before concluding, however, two more points have to be made. First, it is important to stress again that there were other concepts of the family that existed alongside, or in conjunction with, the concept of the household-family. Most notably, there was a concept of the family as a lineage,

[83] *The Correspondence of Samuel Richardson*, vol. I, p. 56.   [84] *Ibid.*, vol. IV, pp. 40–1.
[85] *Ibid.*, vol. II, p. 144.   [86] *Ibid.*, vol. III, pp. 324–5.
[87] A letter by John Gurney in the *Gentleman's Magazine*, Dec. 1805, in reply to a letter by James Nield, *Gentleman's Magazine* Oct. 1805, reproduced in *The Poor Law in Norfolk, 1700–1850: A Collection of Source Material*, ed. S. J. Crowley and A. Reid (Norwich, 1983), p. 57. So a house of correction could be discussed in 'familial' terms: 'I know not why an house of correction may not be conducted with so much regularity as any other house where *the family* is equally numerous', John Howard in *The State of Prisons in England and Wales, with Preliminary Observations, and an Account of some Foreign Prisons* (Warrington, 1777), p. 40, quoted in M. Ignatieff, *A Just Measure of Pain: The Penitentiary in the Industrial Revolution, 1750–1850* (New York, 1978), p. 190.
[88] Quoted in Davidoff, Doolittle, Fink, and Holden, *The Family Story*, p. 161. This study suggests that what the family has meant – in terms of constructions of kinship and friendship, home and household, and the understanding of widely prevalent arrangements of service and lodging – was more complex and less straightforward than previously assumed: e.g *ibid.*, pp. 77–83, 86, 101, 158–82. See also Reay, 'Kinship and neighbourhood in nineteenth-century rural England'.

studied in chapter 3, and a concept of the family as a circle of kin, discussed at the start of chapter 4. For instance, Thomas Turner, as we shall see, used the concept of the lineage in his diary mainly in relation to the Crown, the nobility, historical events, and his near neighbours, the Pelham family.[89] Later in life he also constructed a sense of his own lineage. Furthermore, there was also a concept of the family as a circle of kin from which, significantly, the servants were excluded. For example, when Turner described a festive dinner that he and his wife had in company with '*Mr Pipers Family*',[90] or a tea party with 'Bett Fuller & their Own Family',[91] he most probably excluded the servants of both the Piper and the Fuller households. This was perhaps the nearest that he came in his diary to expressing an idea of the family as an exclusive and co-resident nuclear unit. And, of course, many usages could have overlapping connotations. For example, when Turner worried that his trade 'will hardly answ[e]r the Expences of *a family* w[hi]ch might in all probability be the Consequence of Marriage',[92] he was combining both notions of kinship and household-family dependency.

Secondly, we must take into account that the family could be perceived differently from different points of view. It may well have been the case that a household-family such as Turner's included other – and possibly dissenting – voices that were not represented in the householder's chant about 'my family at home'.[93] Take, for the sake of comparison, the case of the Lancashire governess Miss Weeton. Writing in 1812, she was evidently still acquainted with the concept of the household-family. When she wished to describe the household of one Mr Armitage, for example, she resorted to a pattern of description that we can now well recognise: 'The old gentleman's *family* consists of himself, his wife, and one daughter, a little younger than myself; two women servants, and a boy in livery.'[94] She was even able to see herself as a member of a household-family: when her master's daughter died, for example, she described 'the grief it has occasioned throughout the *family*', no doubt counting herself among the

---

[89] Note, however, that I use the term 'lineage' not in the specialised anthropological sense, but to refer to general notions of ancestry, pedigree, and lineal descent.

[90] Thomas Turner, Diary, 30 Jan. 1758.   [91] *Ibid.*, 9 Oct. 1763.

[92] *Ibid.*, 4 Feb. 1763.

[93] The novels, with their diverse characters and social situations, and complex narratives contain many fascinating examples of overlapping and ambiguous concepts of the family. In this sense, they might be said to present a richer and therefore possibly more faithful historical record of complex family concepts, compared to the relatively unified perspective of the personal diary.

[94] E. Weeton, *Miss Weeton's Journal of a Governess*, ed. E. Hall, 2 vols. (Oxford, 1936–8; reprinted with a revised epilogue, Oxford, 1969), vol. II, p. 71, 22 Dec. 1812. See also 'Edward Smith, his wife, and little boy (about 8 years old), compose the whole of the family, besides myself', vol. I, p. 140. See also also p. 191.

affected.[95] But although Miss Weeton knew the concept of the house-hold-family and invoked it as a social and cultural construct, she did not necessarily approve of it or of her place within it. At times she felt comfortable in her 'situation', as she described it, but at times she resented deeply her servile position and the authority of the people in whose households she lived.[96] Writing to her brother one day, she ex-claimed 'Oh!, my brother, my heart longed to be with thee.' She hoped in vain that he would find her 'a residence, a habitation' near him.[97]

Other chapters of this book will continue to explore additional overlap-ping and conflicting notions of family and kinship. As I have tried to show here, however, the concept of the household-family was a central one: central in its social significance and its historiographical implications. This concept was extremely significant for both describing and under-standing the domestic life of a middling eighteenth-century family such as Thomas Turner's. It was also important for understanding the experi-ence and social actions of many individuals around him. The interpreta-tion presented here differs from – but also complements – an existing body of knowledge derived from quantitative archival research and the categories of historical sociology. It has been the argument of this chapter that through a rigorous examination of the language of texts we can develop a better understanding of the eighteenth-century household: one which takes greater account of the notions and practices of the historical actors themselves.

[95] Indeed, when she took her position in Mr Pedder's household she regarded herself as 'wonderfully fortunate getting into such a family', Weeton, *Journal of a Governess*, vol. I, pp. 219, 241. This 'family' consists of Mr Pedder, his wife, his daughter by a previous marriage, two men servants, and three maids, in addition to Miss Weeton, who is hired as a governess, housekeeper, and companion to the lady of the house.

[96] She deeply resented her master's tyrannical manner towards both his wife and herself: see, for example, Weeton, *Journal of a Governess*, vol. I, pp. 268, 278–9, 316–17. See also her sentiments: 'I would not be understood to argue that woman is superior to man; I should blush to advance so weak an opinion. I would only affirm that they are *equal*, and ought to be treated as such in every respect': *ibid.*, p. 312 (italics in the original). Similarly, while living in the Chorley family, she resented the fact that the mistress of this 'kind family' saw herself as 'answerable to her conduct', and thus asked to inspect the content of her letters: *ibid.*, pp. 106, 111, 132–3. Another time she wrote: 'They give me food and lodging, but they pay themselves again in the spleen they vent on me', *ibid.*, p. 129.

[97] *Ibid.*, p. 281, undated – beginning of Aug. 1810.

2 The concept of the household-family in novels and conduct treatises

Introduction

It is clear that Thomas Turner used the concept of the household-family not only because it made sense to him personally, but because it made sense in the context of the world in which he lived. Furthermore, the comparative examples discussed at the end of chapter 1 show that this concept was known and understood throughout the eighteenth century. Nevertheless, any research based primarily on a single source is bound to raise the question of 'representativeness'. Additional test-cases must be explored. It is important, moreover, to go beyond individual examples and study test-cases with systematic care. This is the aim of the present chapter. This chapter will present a detailed analysis of the concept of the household-family in four mid-eighteenth-century texts: two novels and two conduct treatises. The two novels are Richardson's *Pamela: or, Virtue Rewarded* and Haywood's *The History of Miss Betsy Thoughtless*. The conduct books are *The Apprentice's Vade Mecum: or, Young Man's Pocket-Companion*, a conduct treatise for apprentices by Samuel Richardson, and *A Present for a Servant-Maid*, a conduct treatise for servant-maids, by Eliza Haywood.

These texts offer us additional verbal usages and they also take us from the realm of the personal diary to a much more public arena. Conduct books and novels were well-known genres in the eighteenth century. These specific texts were also written by popular authors and were widely circulated. The two conduct treatises remained in print until the end of the century, while *Pamela* and *The History of Betsy Thoughtless* rank among the most popular literary texts of their time. A conservative estimate suggests that an audience of at least 180,000 managed to read these texts in the middle and latter decades of the eighteenth century. The readership of these texts thus embraced a considerable body of individuals.[1]

---

[1] For details regarding these texts and their circulation, see above, Introduction, pp. 11–16, and esp. n. 42.

The circulation of these texts and the popularity of their authors are important for consolidating this book's claims. As explained in the introduction, the premiss of this book is that verbal usages can give us insight into contemporary social and cultural concepts. Thus, we saw that Thomas Turner's usages of a word such as 'family' give us insight into contemporary concepts of the family, and also help us to explore an array of related concepts and phenomena. But it is important to go beyond the personal diary and trace the ways in which words were used in more publicly circulated texts. The four texts analysed in this chapter link Turner's personal diary to a broader 'language community'. Thomas Turner, Eliza Haywood, and Samuel Richardson, it is argued, were participants in a single cultural milieu: Turner read Richardson's work, Richardson read Haywood's, Haywood was familiar with Richardson's. There were also other texts that they all shared as a part of their cultural vocabulary. As this chapter aims to show, they also shared similar concepts of the family. On the basis of this contextualised evidence, we may presume that these concepts were also shared by a broader readership.

Beyond extending the range of samples and providing evidence of a broader 'language community', the texts analysed in this chapter will also allow us to examine more closely how the concept of the household-family featured in eighteenth-century representations of social life. It will enable us to investigate how historical concepts of the family were used as materials in literary production, from the configuration of characters to the construction of plots. The analysis of the conduct books will allow us to explore the concept of the household-family further, but also examine more specifically how servants and apprentices were conceived of in relation to it. Advice literature is studied often by historians of the family, but the investigation of conduct literature for servants and apprentices is less usual in this context. As servants and apprentices could be members of household-families, however, it is important to look more closely at literature dedicated to them. Finally, we shall be able to explore how even specific narrative formulae relating to the concept of the household-family can be traced fruitfully across our generic boundaries. Historians are aware of the role of narrative formulae in the construction of legal and testimonial narratives.[2] This chapter will thus investigate the ways in which a formulaic notion of the household order and time could be manifested in some similar ways in our principal texts.

[2] See N. Z. Davis, *Fiction in the Archives: Pardon Tales and their Tellers in Sixteenth-Century France* (Cambridge, 1988); L. Jardine, *Reading Shakespeare Historically* (London and New York, 1996), e.g. pp. 19–34; Gowing, *Domestic Dangers*, esp. pp. 52ff; M. Gaskill, 'Reporting murder: fiction in the archives in early modern England', *Social History* 23 (1998), 1–30.

The analysis of the novels thus occupies the first section of this chapter. The second section deals with the conduct books. The third section traces notions of household order and time from the conduct treatises and the novel to Thomas Turner's diary.

The concept of the household-family in two novels

The concept of the household-family is clearly evident in our two mid-eighteenth-century popular novels. Moreover, characters, roles, and narrative developments are constructed in these novels within the parameters of the concept of the household-family. Many households are referred to as 'families' both in *Pamela* and in *The History of Miss Betsy Thoughtless*: the family of Mr Goodman, the family of Mr Thoughtless, the family of Mr Munden, the family of Miss Towers, the family of Mr Peters, and others.[3] Many of these families contain kin and non-kin who live together under the authority of masters and mistresses. For example, Mr Munden's family in *The History of Miss Betsy Thoughtless* consists of Mr and Mrs Munden and their male and female servants. When Mr Munden wants to economise and dismiss his wife's footman, he announces his decision in the following words: 'I think *my family too much encumbered*; you have two maids . . . I have a man . . .'.[4] He then proceeds to suggest the footman's dismissal. Relationships within these literary families are also similar to those observed so far. For instance, when Pamela describes her arrival at the B. household, she explains how she has been 'taken into the family', thus suggesting the servant's contractual and instrumental affiliation to her family of service: 'I was a young creature who had been *taken into Mr B.'s family* to wait upon his mother.'[5]

Characteristic features of the household-family are also displayed in these novels in relation to families headed by single householders. In fact,

---

[3] See, for example, Mr Goodman's family, Haywood, *Betsy Thoughtless*, pp. 11, 15, 225, 229, 239; Mr Thoughtless's family, *ibid.*, pp. 303, 534–5; Mr Munden's family, *ibid.*, pp. 469, 472, 489. See Miss Towers's family, Richardson, *Pamela*, ed. Sabor, pp. 82–3; Mr Peters's family, *ibid.*, pp. 383, 389; see also, for example, Sir Simon Darnford's family, *ibid.*, pp. 201, 226, 383, 389; Mr Carlton's family, *ibid.*, p. 401. See further examples relating to Mr B.'s family in *ibid.*, pp. 59, 82, 97, 98, 104, 105, 106, etc. See also Tadmor, '"Family" and "friend" in *Pamela*'; N. Tadmor, 'Concepts of the family in five eighteenth-century texts', unpublished PhD dissertation (Cambridge, 1992), chs. 6–8; Tadmor, 'The concept of the household-family in eighteenth-century England', 137–9.

[4] *Betsy Thoughtless*, p. 469.

[5] *Pamela*, ed. Sabor, p. 137. See Tadmor, '"Family" and "friend" in *Pamela*'. Interestingly, in the first lines of the abridged version of *Pamela*, edited by Richardson, or possibly by Oliver Goldsmith, this household is referred to as Mrs B.'s family, and Pamela is said to have been taken into 'her Family'. See S. Richardson, *The Paths of Virtue Delineated: or, the History in Miniature of the Celebrated Pamela, Clarissa Harlowe, and Sir Charles Grandison, Familiarized and Adapted to the Capacities of Youths* (London, 1756).

three of the most important families in *The History of Miss Betsy Thoughtless* have single masters during significant parts of the plot: the family of Mr Thomas Thoughtless, the family of Sir Bazil, and the family of Mr Goodman. In *Pamela*, too, the main household is headed by a single man, Mr B. His is a large household with many servants. When Pamela's father arrives looking for his daughter, he asks: 'what *family* the 'squire had down here?' The reply presents the following list: 'A housekeeper, two maids, and, at present, two coachmen, and two grooms, a footman, and a helper.'[6] The changes that occur in the population of these households are also understood within the concept of the household-family. When Mrs Munden escapes from her husband's house, leaving him with only his man and a servant-maid, the text reads: '*his family* was now reduced to two, her own man and maid having followed her'.[7] When Mr Goodman, wishing to divorce his wife, is preparing to live as a single man he announces the appointment of a new female housekeeper: 'I have a kinswoman, who I expect will . . . take care of the affairs of *my family* henceforward.'[8] The size of these households and the specialised roles of their servants are meant to signify wealth and prestige. But from a structural point of view, these literary and genteel households reveal the familiar outlines of the house-hold-family. They are household units. They are headed by masters and mistresses, and they include related and non-related dependants.

Female characters in the novels are also constructed as mistresses of families and female housekeepers. Thomas Turner described his wife Peggy as 'a Prudent & good OEconomist in *her Family*'.[9] In a similar way, *Pamela* presents women in the neighbourhood of Mr B.'s house accord-ing to their 'character in their families', namely their behaviour within their households and their management of the household affairs. Thus, for example, one Mrs Brook is described as having 'no bad character in her family', whereas Mrs Arthur is said to be 'pretty passionate in her family on small occasions'.[10] And of course, the heroines of both novels are also presented as mistresses of 'families'. Pamela looks forward with pleasure to her management of Mr B.'s family,[11] whereas Betsy, once a frivolous young lady, redeems herself by becoming a virtuous wife and a model housekeeper.

The concept of the household-family is so deeply embedded within these novels that many episodes should be understood with this concept

---

[6] *Pamela*, ed. Sabor, pp. 325–6.   [7] *Betsy Thoughtless*, p. 556.   [8] *Ibid.*, p. 239.
[9] Thomas Turner, Diary, 23 June 1761.   [10] *Pamela*, ed. Sabor, pp. 82–3.
[11] For instance, Mr B. lays down 'rules for the family order' for her, similar to those practised in the house in his mother's time. At another time Pamela looks forward to being 'settled' and applying herself 'to the duties of the family'. After the hubbub of her marriage, she hopes to 'subside into a family calm', to make herself 'a little useful to the household of my Mr B.', *Pamela*, ed. Sabor, pp. 393, 490, 515.

in mind. See, for example, how the familiar characteristics of the house-hold-family emerge in two episodes in *The History of Miss Betsy Thought-less*: first, the way in which the Frenchwoman Mademoiselle de Roquelair joins the household of her lover, Thomas Thoughtless, and, secondly, the way in which Betsy Thoughtless later joins the same household. When Mr Thoughtless plans to return to England from his 'grand tour', the family guardian hires him a house and provides it with 'all such furniture as he thought would be necessary for a *single gentleman*'.[12] Thus Mr Thoughtless, a single man, becomes the master of a family, and he decides to take into it his beautiful French mistress. In doing so he nominates her as his female housekeeper. Characteristically, this position is arranged contractually. In this case, the exchange takes the form of a 'promise': 'he [Mr Thoughtless] had *promised* her the sole command of his house and servants, and that she should appear as his wife in all respects except the name'.[13] The mistress later describes the same posi-tion, referring to it in familial terms: 'I have had the command of *his family* and lived with him in all things like a wife, except the name.'[14] Clearly, it is naive of Thomas Thoughtless to entrust his household affairs to the management of a kept mistress. Secretly, and 'without raising any suspi-cion in the *family*', she receives in the house another lover, a mercer who calls on her under the pretence of bringing patterns of silk.[15] Thomas Thoughtless discovers the treachery with the aid of his 'family', namely his household servants, and the mistress escapes from the house by the skin of her teeth.[16] The flexible framework of the household-family, however, soon permits the affiliation to the family of another female housekeeper. This time it is Thomas's sister Betsy, who has just run away from her mean and adulterous husband. The agreement settling her affiliation to her elder brother's household-family takes the form of an open invitation: '[he] *invited* her . . . to remain in his house as long as she should think fit'.[17] Her appointment to the role of the female housekeeper is also announced with the aid of a similar formula: 'He desired her to take upon her the sole command and management of *his house and family*.'[18]

This turnover in the population of Thomas Thoughtless's family sug-gests that, just as it was possible to trace the changes that took place in Thomas Turner's family over time, so too it is possible to trace the chronological changes in a literary family. As we saw, Thomas Thought-less's family starts on its way as a 'single man's family'. The addition of the French mistress turns it into a mock-conjugal unit. But while the mistress is in charge of the family, there are two other individuals who want to join it: Thomas's younger brother Francis, and his sister

[12] *Betsy Thoughtless*, p. 224.   [13] *Ibid.*, p. 247.   [14] *Ibid.*, p. 535.
[15] *Ibid.*, p. 540.   [16] *Ibid.*, pp. 540–1.   [17] *Ibid.*, pp. 556–7.   [18] *Ibid.*

Betsy.[19] Both are minors, and after their guardian's death they pass into Thomas's care. But despite the close ties of blood, guardianship, and affection, it is significant that the young brother and sister are not seen as having an automatic place in their elder brother's family. When they are taken into it, and eventually they both are, it is because it is his wish and the circumstances are right for it, not because it is their right and his unquestionable duty. As long as the French mistress is in the house, decency prevents Thomas Thoughtless from taking his sister into his family.[20] In addition to the moral objection there is a structural obstacle, for Betsy might lay claim to the role of the female housekeeper, currently held by the mistress. Thus Betsy goes to board with another family in town. The reasons for her exclusion from the family are hinted while describing how Francis joins it: 'Those objections which had hindered Mr Thomas Thoughtless from *taking her [Miss Betsy] into his family*, had not the same weight in relation to Mr Francis, whose sex set him above meddling with those domestick concerns.'[21] However, sometime later Mr Francis goes away. Soon afterwards Betsy, now Mrs Munden, is invited to join the family.[22] But Betsy's stay in the family also does not last long. Soon she retires to the country. The next woman who enters Mr Thoughtless's family to take the role of the senior female housekeeper is his lawful wife.[23]

Comparing these changes in Thomas Thoughtless's family to the chronological changes in Thomas Turner's family, we can see that there are obvious dissimilarities in the composition of the two families due to the socio-economic status of their householders. Whereas Thomas Turner's family includes members such as a shop assistant, Thomas Thoughtless's family includes a French mistress. But beyond these differences, the range of members who are incorporated in both families amounts to a rather similar repertoire of servants, siblings, wards, boarders, and wives. In both the Turner and the Thoughtless families there are also contractual agreements settling the affiliation of members to the family. In both cases there are instrumental ties as well: for example, both

---

[19] It is, of course, not accidental that it is the elder brother who is the head of a household-family. See N. Tadmor, 'Dimensions of inequality among siblings in eighteenth-century novels: the cases of *Clarissa* and *The History of Miss Betsy Thoughtless*', *Continuity and Change* 7 (1992), 303–33.   [20] See *Betsy Thoughtless*, p. 211.   [21] *Ibid.*, p. 303.

[22] As seen above, this takes place in the context of the breakdown of her marriage. Betsy's affiliation to the family is yet another instance of kinship-based patronage. As in the diary of Thomas Turner and in the conduct treatises, such effective kinship ties are referred to in terms of '*friendship*', see below chs. 4 and 5, and especially ch. 7.

[23] *Betsy Thoughtless*, p. 588. As in the case of Turner's second marriage, this new phase in which the family grows to accommodate a conjugal unit is reported only briefly. Both texts – the literary and the personal – break soon after the climactic news of the master's nuptials.

Thomas Turner and Thomas Thoughtless manage many financial affairs for their siblings. In both cases familial relationships are often also affective and sociable, and in both cases they are entwined with many long-term ties of 'friendship' and kinship-based patronage. Finally, in both cases phases of household-family affiliation are often temporary.

Although the concept of the household-family appears in these novels in similar manifestations to those we found in Turner's diary, the broad social canvas of these novels also contains some familial forms that cannot be detected in the more limited scene of East Hoathly. For example, there are some detailed episodes in these novels in which institutions such as a boarding-house or a boarding-school are referred to as 'families'.[24] When Miss Betsy and her friend Flora arrive for a visit in Oxford they lodge at a boarding-house headed by a landlady. This establishment and its staff are described as a 'family'. Thus, for example, when the two young ladies decide that they do not wish to dine at home, a footman is sent 'to acquaint *the family* the ladies would not dine at home'.[25] Unlike other householders, such as Thomas Turner and his mother, the mistress of this household has a partly servile position in relation to her paying guests, all the more so as they are clearly her social superiors. But it is significant that even such a landlady retains the position of moral authority, typical of the mistress and householder. It is her duty to maintain the good order and reputation of her establishment, and when Miss Betsy and Miss Flora are involved in a scandal, she remonstrates with them.[26] Another establishment, a boarding-school, is also referred to in *The History of Miss Betsy Thoughtless* as a 'family'. The head of this 'family' is a 'governess' who is a gentlewoman and a widow. As the text shows, this family includes, besides the governess, a tutoress, a nurse, possibly other servants, and some young ladies. In view of what we know about contemporary boarding-schools, this setting is not unlikely, for boarding-schools were often located in private houses and numbered about ten or a dozen girls.[27] One

[24] See also the references in chapter 1 to the dwellers of a workhouse as a 'family', p. 41, and n. 87.   [25] *Betsy Thoughtless*, pp. 45, 47.
[26] 'They dreaded to expose themselves to fresh insults, if they stirred out of doors; and at home they were persecuted with the unwearied remonstrances of their grave landlady', *ibid.*, p. 57.
[27] On the growth of boarding-schools for girls, see J. Lawson and H. Silver, *A Social History of Education in England* (London, 1974), p. 208: 'A typical boarding school for girls' from the later seventeenth century 'might be kept by a widowed or maiden gentlewoman, who boarded in her ample house ten or twelve girls of mixed ages'. See also R. O'Day, *Education and Society, 1500–1800: The Social Foundations of Education in Early Modern England* (London, 1982), pp. 186–90; S. Skedd, 'Women teachers and the expansion of girls' schooling in England, c. 1760–1820', in Barker and Chalus (eds.), *Gender in Eighteenth-Century England*, pp. 101–25, and many references there. Similar institutions were also found at a later period by committees for reforming women's education. See J. C. Pedersen, 'The reform of women's secondary and higher education: institutional

of these pupils is Miss Forward. She is a gentleman's daughter, her mother is dead, and her father has remarried. Sadly for her, she falls under the influence of a French tutoress with an 'amorous disposition'. The illicit love affair, on which Miss Flora embarks with the aid of this tutoress, serves as the context for a number of references to the 'family' of the boarding-school. When Miss Forward goes to meet her lover, for example, it is said that 'The tutoress knew well enough how to excuse our staying out so much longer than usual; and neither the governess, nor *any one in the family*, except ourselves, knew any thing of what had passed.'[28]

The concept of the household-family is thus articulated throughout in the language of these texts. Furthermore, this concept furnishes our novels with social structures and a gallery of roles and relationships. The social framework of the household-family provides a literary and conceptual framework for *Pamela* and *The History of Miss Betsy Thoughtless*. The social landscape of these novels is punctuated with household-families, just as the social landscape of Turner's East Hoathly. Characters make their ways through families and change their familial roles and affiliations. While the cast of characters moves around, household-families expand and contract. The plot of *The History of Miss Betsy Thoughtless* consists of a picaresque ramble through many household-families. Miss Betsy, the heroine, is removed from her father's house and is placed in a boarding-school. She is then placed in the family of Mr Goodman.[29] She continues to board elsewhere, until she becomes the mistress of the family of Mr Munden. She is then taken into her elder brother's family,[30] goes to reside with yet another family, and finally becomes the mistress of the family of her second husband. The flexible framework of the household-family makes it possible to relocate this character across the literary scene, whilst attaching her to various households and assigning to her a range of familial roles as befits her sex, age, kinship ties, and financial and marital status.

In contrast, the plot of *Pamela* is located within a single household-family. Pamela enters the family as a twelve-year-old waiting-maid,[31] and

---

change and social values in mid and late Victorian England', *History of Education Quarterly* 19 (1979), 69.

[28] *Betsy Thoughtless*, pp. 78–9. See also, for example, a letter dated 1805 written by the school-mistress Martha Cochan at Wigan to her pupils' parents: 'I am happy to add the young ladies are well and in good spirits, and they have been very good girls during their residence in *my family*', in Ashton, *An Eighteenth-Century Industrialist*, p. 145.

[29] '[Lady Trusty] resolved . . . to take all the opportunities that fell in her way, of giving Miss Betsy such instructions as she thought necessary for her behaviour in general, and especially towards *the family in which it was her lot to be placed*', *Betsy Thoughtless*, p. 11.

[30] *Ibid.*, pp. 556–7. There she is also given 'sole command' of the 'family'.

[31] At the start of the novel she is fifteen years old. We are told that she has been taken into the family at the age of twelve.

she remains in the family after her mistress's death.[32] The next set of events, which centres around Mr B.'s assaults on Pamela, also explores the tension between her attempts to move out of his family and her confinement within it. Pamela is given warning and even begs her master to leave, but she stays nonetheless. Plans for her departure from the B. household do not materialise. Even her longed-for exodus from the family turns out to be yet another re-location within Mr B.'s domain: she leaves his Bedfordshire house only to find herself carried to his Lincolnshire house. In terms of the household-family framework, she enters a state of limbo. No longer a servant, she declines Mr B.'s proposals to take charge of his house as a kept mistress, but her way out of the family is blocked.[33] Finally Mr B. allows her to go. His voluntary release is then reciprocated by her voluntary compliance. On her way to her father's house, Pamela turns back. Shooting vertically through the household-family framework, she takes the position of Mr B.'s lawful wife.

The concept of the household-family is therefore very important in Richardson's construction of this tightly controlled story. But it is interesting to note that this concept also created problems that both Richardson and his critics tried to negotiate. After all, Pamela is a contractually bound servant, not an abject slave, and in real life, as Richardson and his readers well knew, servants were usually much more free to come and go. How, then, is it possible to explain why Pamela does not break her contract with the family sooner, or more effectively? And having finally left Mr B.'s family, why does she return to it so soon? In Fielding's *Shamela*, for example, her desire to remain near Mr B. forms a part of a calculating scheme to trap him into marriage.[34] Revisions of *Pamela* also reveal that Richardson tried to make these points more credible, whilst also emphasising his heroine's virtue. In the last edition, for example, Pamela's half-hearted and abortive attempt to escape receives a better justification.[35] Her reason to return to Mr B.'s house is also amended. In the first edition she is motivated by passion, but by the

---

[32] At this point she is given a new task: to take care of her master's linen. She is relieved that she does not have to find a new place, for, as she says to her parents, 'it was not *every family* that could have found a place that your poor Pamela was fit for', *Pamela*, ed. Sabor, p. 43. However, later Mr B. doubts Pamela's usefulness, and asks the housekeeper 'do you think her of any use in the *family*?', *ibid.*, p. 59.

[33] This is a contractual proposal in which Mr B. offers Pamela a financial settlement, promises that she will be 'Mistress of my Person and Fortune', that all his servants will be hers, and that she will 'appear with Reputation, as if you was my Wife'. He also promises that he will extend his favour 'to any other of [her] Relations', and hopes she will comply on such terms 'as will make [herself], and all [her] Friends, happy': *Pamela*, ed. Eaves and Kimpel, pp. 164–7.

[34] H. Fielding, *An Apology for the Life of Mrs Shamela Andrews* (1741), ed. J. Hawley (Harmondsworth, 1999), pp. 3–43.

[35] See *Pamela*, ed. Sabor, p. 188, and n. 137.

last edition is moved by a sense of obligation and fear for Mr B.'s life.[36]

The stories that these novels tell are in many ways unlikely. Poor servant-maids did not usually marry their rich masters and bad husbands such as Mr Munden did not normally perish so quickly to make way for faithful lovers. But although these stories are exceptional, the building blocks from which they are constructed contain an array of historical materials. The concept of the household-family belongs to this category of historical building blocks. It evokes a past world of great demographic and geographic mobility. It reveals a social and economic order, and closely related hierarchies of age and gender. This world order reverberates in the language of texts, despite differences in authors and boundaries of genres.

The concept of the household-family in two conduct treatises

the Family being gone abroad

raise any Disturbance in *the Family*

the Family are in Bed

In all well-governed *Families*[37]

the Rules of an orderly *Family*

Family-Engagements

[to be] taken into *a Family*[38]

These are some typical references to the 'family' from *A Present for a Servant-Maid* (first set) and *The Apprentice's Vade Mecum* (second set). These references are general, almost opaque, and at a first glance they seem unilluminating: they reveal very little about the possible composition of the 'families' referred to, their size, or the possible relationships between their members and their householders. Clearly, such general references are appropriate for the genre of the conduct book, for they suit its strategy to present universal directions that can apply to all sorts of familial circumstances.

On closer examination, however, it seems that even these general and

---

[36] '. . . he has got too great Hold in my Heart', she says; eleven lines later she expresses her decision to obey him, not least in order to make herself and others happy by means of 'a generous Confidence': *Pamela*, ed. Eaves and Kimpel, pp. 217–18. In the last edition, she declares 'my *heart is free*' (italics in the original), and enters upon an exposition about obligation and duty, and her fear that Mr B. should die: *Pamela*, ed. Sabor, pp. 288, 290, and nn. 218, 219. See also T. C. D. Eaves and B. D. Kimpel, 'Richardson's revisions of Pamela', *Studies in Bibliography* 20 (1967), 61–88.

[37] Haywood, *Servant-Maid*, pp. 19, 34, 38, 39.   [38] Richardson, *Vade Mecum*, pp. ix, 8, 45.

apparently unilluminating references manifest what are by now familiar characteristics of the concept of the household-family. The general nature of these references actually corresponds well with the flexible and inclusive nature of the household-family. The idea of the family as an organisational framework is suggested by the fact that the 'family' is seen here as having boundaries: there are those who are in it, those who are outside it and do not partake in its activities, and those who are 'taken into' it. The use of the singular noun 'family' together with the plural verb 'are' – 'the Family are in Bed' – also suggests that the family is perceived as a collective unit. In addition, three of the above references emphasise notions of order, and thus bring to mind related notions of authority. Finally, the references to 'the family' as going abroad, or as lying in bed also convey the close association between the family and the home that serves as its base.

The characteristic outlines of the household-family emerge yet more clearly if we examine the possible family members envisaged in these treatises. Chief among them is the master, who is often also associated with broader notions of authority and order. The 'family' members are grouped collectively in relation to him, as in the expression 'Master and his Family', or 'Master or his Family'.[39] In these texts, as in Turner's diary, the master's marital status is not always structurally significant. Sometimes he is imagined as a married man, or at least as having a female partner; however, the possibility of a single man's household-family is also suggested when Haywood warns the servant-maid to beware of the master's temptations if 'a single Man'.[40] Characteristically, however, the role of the female housekeeper is also emphasised in these treatises. For instance, the apprentice in Richardson's treatise is instructed to be dutiful to his mistress,

[39] Ibid., pp. 45–6. Similarly, the opening lines of this treatise propose two parties – the master and his dependants referred to collectively as a 'family' – as Richardson addresses 'all Masters of Families'. Male authority in the family is assumed by Haywood as she describes, for example, the maid's correct behaviour to the master and 'your Master's son': Servant-Maid, pp. 37–9, 45–50. Other males mentioned in this context are servants, apprentices, and boarders and lodgers.

[40] Servant-Maid, pp. 45–7. This is followed by a similar warning against a married master (pp. 47–8). Always pragmatic, Haywood explains that the single master is likely to try to seduce the maid but is unlikely to marry her. Yielding to a married master is even more pointless, for the maid will not only damage herself and her future prospects but will turn her mistress against her. Interestingly, Haywood does not mention the possibility of a single woman's family. As we know, there were many women at the time who were independent householders and also employed servants. The absence of an explicit reference to them therefore does not reflect a historical reality. One possible reason for this absence is that despite the currency of female-headed households, the idea of the male-headed household served as an influential cultural stereotype which Haywood naturally used. Another reason might be that Haywood did not focus on single mistresses of families because they did not present an obvious threat to the servant-maid's sexual virtue. Female householders are also discussed in Earle, The Making of the English Middle Class, esp. pp. 166–74.

too.[41] In Haywood's treatise it is indeed the mistress who is mentioned most often as the person directly in charge of the servant-maid.[42]

The main family members proposed and discussed in these treatises are thus the master, the mistress, the apprentice, and the servant-maid. The characteristic features of the household-family framework also come to mind if we try to gauge the possible number of these family members. This is clearly open to endless variations. The possibility of there being more than one apprentice in the family is noted when Richardson instructs the apprentice to behave with condescension, if the fellow-servant is his junior, or with complaisance if he is his senior.[43] Richardson also mentions the possibility of there being 'divers Journeymen' employed in the master's business and other 'Fellow-Servants'.[44] Similarly, in Haywood's treatise there are references to families with a single servant-maid, as well as to families with diverse servants of both sexes. Significantly, the latter are still referred to as *'People of the same Family'*.[45]

Beyond these figures, the treatises propose other possible family members. Both treatises mention the possibility that there may be children in the family. For example, at one point Haywood explains to the maid that '[i]f you happen to live in a *Family* where the Mistress either suckles, or brings an Infant up by Hand at home, Part of the Duty of a Nurse will fall to your Share'.[46] Richardson's treatise, too, mentions children and possibly other relations as the apprentice is told to behave obligingly not only to the master but 'to all his, to his Children and Friends'.[47] Other members of the household referred to by Haywood are 'Gentlemen Lodgers' and 'Boarders'. The maid is warned to guard herself against their temptations and to watch their behaviour.[48] If they violate the family timetable by keeping late hours, for example, she is advised to report them to the master or mistress. They, then, should try and curb these transgressing lodgers and boarders and make them conform to the conduct of *'well governed Families'*.[49]

---

[41] *Vade Mecum*, p. 19.
[42] See, for example, the introductory words to *Servant-Maid*: 'A due Observance of the Rules contained in this little Treatise, cannot fail of making every *Mistress of a Family* perfectly contented, and every *Servant-Maid* both happy and beloved' (italics in the original). This treatise does not propose an explicit sexual division of the household labour, but several references indicate that there is a female part of the household, referred to on one occasion as the *'common Affairs of the Family'*, that includes tasks such as child-minding, sewing, cooking, and cleaning. When the servant-maid is 'taken into the Family', she thus joins this female labour force and comes under the direction of the mistress: for instance, *Servant-Maid*, p. 41.   [43] *Vade Mecum*, p. 28.
[44] *Ibid.*, pp. 28–9.
[45] *Servant-Maid*, p. 35. This instruction appears in the context of a special section entitled 'Behaviour to fellow-servants'.   [46] *Ibid.*, p. 16.   [47] *Vade Mecum*, p. 19.
[48] *Servant-Maid*, pp. 49–50.
[49] *Ibid.*, p. 39. In the same context, an older male child – 'your Master's son' – is also mentioned as a potential hazard. Further discussion on the position of lodgers and boarders in the 'family' appears in the next section.

Lastly, while the presence in the house of masters, mistresses, servants, apprentices, lodgers, and boarders is understood in familial terms, members of the servant's family of origin are described as 'parents', 'friends', and 'relations'.[50] These usages convey the importance of these close relationships, but they also highlight the structured position of the servants within their family of service. Similar references were noticed in the context of Turner's family. Thus, the young apprentice in *The Apprentice's Vade Mecum* is told to seek the advice of his 'friends' in any important affair, and to conduct himself in a way that will not shame them or spoil their investment in his upbringing.[51] The maid in Haywood's treatise is advised to visit her 'friends' around holiday and fair times, or on some Sundays if no other time is possible.[52]

References to the family current in these treatises thus require us once more to think of the family in structural terms. The family conceived of in these treatises bears the characteristic features of the household-family: here, too, the family is presented as a household framework with various co-resident members. Notions of household management and order are strongly emphasised. But when it comes to the status of the family members, their possible number, or their possible relationships to the master and mistress, there are very many permutations. At times the family is referred to as containing a nuclear unit with a spouse and children, at another time we are presented with a 'single man's family'. Boarders and lodgers are also envisaged as family members, while servants and apprentices are counted throughout as members of the family, and relationships with them are discussed in detail. In other words, here, too, the idea of the family as a household framework supersedes many specific and restricting notions of family composition.

If we now turn to the ways in which apprentices and servant-maids are 'taken into' a family, we find once more some familiar features. The chronological survey of Turner's family has shown the great number of related and non-related individuals who became members of the family for various periods of time, and by means of various agreements. The affiliation of these members of the family was instrumental, but often also sentimental. This was often also related to certain phases in the life-cycle. The conduct treatises, though clearly more abstract and theoretical,

50 See, however, the rare but significant references to the 'family' conveying notions of ancestry and lineage, as discussed in ch. 3.
51 *Vade Mecum*, pp. vii, 24, 37, 38. On p. vii the apprentice's previous carers are referred to as 'Parents, or such as had the Care of their Education'. This possibly reflects the contemporary demographic regime in which a significant number of youths lost one or both parents and therefore had to be cared for by others, see above, pp. 34–5.
52 She is warned, however, not to engage her mind with worldly matters on those days 'which ought to be devoted to Heaven alone'. If that happens whilst visiting her 'friends', she is advised to 'visit them less often, th[ough] not totally neglect them', *Servant-Maid*, p. 40.

present a similar procedure and similar relationships.

The actual affiliation of apprentices to their masters' families is referred to in Richardson's treatise in very strong terms, and with the aid of a potent image: '*the Families into which they are transplanted for a Series of Years* the most important and most critical of their whole Lives'.[53] Another expression used in the treatise is to be 'taken into' a family. The apprentice is said to be '*taken into a Family in so intimate a Relation, as that of an Apprentice*'.[54] Once he is taken in, the apprentice is seen as a part of the family. Thus, for example, Richardson discusses the 'inviolable Regard which Servants *taken into a Man's Family, and who are become a Part of it*' ought to have to the reputation and profit of their masters.[55] Indeed, the new phase in the boy's life, his apprenticeship, is seen as a rite of passage, a transplantation from boyhood to manhood: 'remember that you are now taken from the company of giddy Boys, to that of serious men; that you are *transplanted* from Play to Business'.[56]

Such phrases manifest in powerful terms the apprentice's affiliation to his new family of service. The fact that this affiliation is contractual is also plainly evident. Richardson not only discusses one by one the articles of the apprentice's indenture, the contract that binds him to his master and settles his position in the family, but even refers to this contract by the biblical word 'Covenant' thus emphasising both its contractual nature and its solemnity.[57] It is important to note, however, that while describing the indenture in exalted terms Richardson is familiar enough with the contemporary reality to suggest the possibility of this contract's violation, and even untimely termination.[58] Alongside the ideal figure of the good

---

[53] *Vade Mecum*, pp. vi–vii. See also 'the Rules of the Family into which you are transplanted', *ibid.*, p. 33. See also p. xii.   [54] *Ibid.*, p. 45.   [55] *Ibid.*, p. 3.
[56] *Ibid.*, p. 23.   [57] *Ibid.*, p. vii.
[58] According to Earle, for example, the drop-out rate among London apprentices was around 50 per cent, although he suggests that figures normally quoted on the decline of London apprenticeship from 1600 are misleading due to the uncharted growth in suburban apprenticeship, where most of the industrial and artisanal work was done by 1700. Within the city apprenticeship was still the commonest way to become a full member of a Livery Company and acquire the freedom of the city, a status which gave both important rights and social prestige. The great majority of those who became rich in London (like Samuel Richardson) started their career with apprenticeship: P. Earle, *A City Full of People: Men and Women in London, 1650–1750* (London, 1994), esp. pp. 61–3; Earle, *The Making of the English Middle Class*, pp. 85ff, and references there. See also at this point Brooks's argument concerning the growing differentiation in patterns of apprenticeship by the middle of the eighteenth century and its eventual decline, but also its survival in the eighteenth century and the importance of apprenticeship as a feature of identity and the focus of some of the most characteristic social and cultural values of the middling sort: C. Brooks, 'Apprenticeship, social mobility and the middling sort, 1550–1800', in J. Barry and C. Brooks (eds.), *The Middling Sort of People: Culture, Society and Politics in England, 1550–1800* (Basingstoke, 1994), pp. 52–83. On the decline of apprenticeship, see also: Snell, *Annals of the Labouring Poor*, pp. 228–69, and references there; J. G. Rule, *The Vital Century: England's Developing Economy, 1714–1815* (London and New York, 1992), pp. 24–5, and references there; Earle, *The Making of the English Middle Class*,

apprentice, the treatise presents the shadowy figure of the disorderly, idle, dishonest, and impudent lad, who thinks himself above 'being confin'd to the necessary Rules of an orderly *Family*'.[59] At this point conformity to the family order is seen not only as a key to future success, but also as a means of minimising the risks of future difficulties and failure.[60]

While emphasising the contractual bond between the apprentice and his master, it is interesting that Richardson does not discuss the possibility that they might be otherwise related. Though this was not a commonplace phenomenon, youths in eighteenth-century England could be apprenticed to relations.[61] One might have thought that a detailed treatise such as Richardson's would say something on this score. Furthermore, one might expect this treatise to contain some advice about how related masters and apprentices should conduct themselves if only because of the fact that this particular treatise was elaborated by Richardson on the basis of instructions to his own nephew and apprentice, Thomas Verren Richardson. In his sequel to *Pamela* Richardson expresses strong views against binding relations as apprentices ('better to have *any body* than relations'), but later, after the death of Thomas Verren, he proceeded to take yet another nephew, William Richardson, as

esp. pp. 85–6; and Earle, *A City Full of People*, p. 63 and references there. See also Griffiths, *Youth and Authority*; Ben-Amos, *Adolescence and Youth*.

[59] *Vade Mecum*, p. 52.

[60] Richardson suggests that the relations of such a lad would do well to spare the honest tradesman and themselves much mortification, disappointment, time, and money, and instead of binding him as an apprentice, send him to sea. One can recall at this point the image of Hogarth's idle apprentice, who makes his way first from his master's workshop to sea, and finally to the gallows. For the fear of downward mobility among middling autobiographers, see M. Mascuch, 'Social mobility and middling self-identity: the ethos of British autobiographers, 1600–1750', *Social History* 20 (1995), 45–61. For risk in business more broadly, see J. Hoppit, *Risk and Failure in English Business, 1700–1800* (Cambridge, 1987). For the fear of ruination, see J. Raven, *Judging New Wealth: Popular Publishing and Responses to Commerce in England, 1750–1800* (Oxford, 1992), pp. 183–200.

[61] Houlbrooke's study of apprentices enrolled in Tudor and early Stuart Norwich shows that only 4 per cent of the apprentices bore the same surnames as their masters: Houlbrooke, *The English Family*, p. 46. Other studies suggest some possibly closer links between service and kinship. Rappaport shows that 15 per cent of the 266 entrants and 460 masters in his London sample engaged at least one apprentice during their lives with the same surname as themselves: S. Rappaport, *Worlds Within Worlds: Structures of Life in Sixteenth-Century London* (Cambridge, 1989), p. 80. Earle notes the infrequency of recurring surnames among masters and apprentices, but also points out the existence of close social networks and possible kinship ties between masters and apprentices: Earle, *The Making of the English Middle Class*, p. 90. Brodsky Elliot suggests that although only 1 per cent of London apprentices in her sample bore the same surnames as their masters up to a tenth may have been bound to London resident kin, if one also takes account of maternal kin: V. Brodsky Elliot, 'Mobility and marriage in pre-industrial England', unpublished PhD dissertation (Cambridge, 1979), pp. 209–10; see also *ibid.*, p. 213. Ben-Amos estimates that in provincial towns such as Bristol, Norwich, and Southampton the rates of servants related to their masters may have also been relatively high: Ben-Amos, *Adolescence and Youth*, p. 167, and n. 65.

his apprentice and potential successor.[62] Indeed apprenticeship could even be used in early modern England as a means of adoption, in the absence of an adoption procedure.[63] In the light of all these circumstances, the absence of instructions to related masters and apprentices in Richardson's treatise seems to emphasise all the more the importance of their contractual bond which stems from the 'Covenant' of the indenture.

The occupational aspect of the apprentice's relationship with his master is self-evident. The apprentice is contracted to the master to learn his trade and business. The word 'master' thus serves here in a double meaning, for the master of the family is also the master of his trade. The instrumental nature of this relationship is also obvious. During his term the boy is to serve the master faithfully, but it is by the effect of the master's 'Cares, and his Example' that he is 'to be built up to Business', and to 'have a Foundation laid' for his own prosperity.[64] Richardson's treatise is thoroughly imbued with notions of dutiful work, considerations of future success, and awareness of possible failure. The relationships between the master and his apprentice, however, are never seen as simply instrumental and calculating. This relationship is also described in terms of 'love'. The apprentice is told to show '*Love* and *Submission*' to his master, so as not to 'imbitter his Pleasures, and make his Time of Service to a Master he does not love, appear *tedious* and *irksome*'.[65] He is also advised to 'study his Master's Temper' and show towards him 'Sweetness of Disposition'.[66] The language of these instructions seems to suggest a similarity between the master–apprentice relationship and the relationship between husband and wife, for wives, too, were expected to study their husbands' temper and show them sweetness of disposition, love and submission. It seems that just as the marriage contract created a binding family relationship between the husband and wife, so did the 'Covenant'

---

[62] Samuel Richardson had great hopes that William would continue his business. He took him in 1748, and in May 1759 William was still working for his uncle. But by the end of that year he preferred to marry and set up business on his own. Richardson was disappointed and blotted out the original bequest intended for William in his will, leaving him only three guineas: see Eaves and Kimpel, *Samuel Richardson*, pp. 51, 500–3, and references to *Pamela* there.

[63] See G. Mayhew, 'Life cycle and the family unity in early modern Rye', *Continuity and Change* 6 (1991), 222. On service and adoption, see also Macfarlane, *Individualism*, p. 150; on adoption more broadly see Goody, *The Development of the Family and Marriage*, e.g. pp. 42, 74, 99–101, 195ff, 204. According to Blackstone, parents could dispose of the custody of a child, born or unborn, to particular guardians. The Poor Law Act of 1889 empowered Poor Law guardians to assume parental rights over deserted children. Adoption, however, was only introduced in England in 1926: W. Blackstone, *Commentaries on the Laws of England*, 4 vols. (Oxford, 1770), vol. I, p. 461; A. Bainham, *Children – The Modern Law* (2nd edn, Bristol, 1998); S. M. Cretney and J. M. Masson, *Principles of Family Law* (6th edn, London, 1997), p. 873. I am grateful to Jonathan Herring for these reference on modern family law.   [64] *Vade Mecum*, p. 25.

[65] *Ibid.*, p. 46. Italics in the original.   [66] *Ibid.*, p. 47.

of the indenture create a family relationship between the apprentice and his master. In both cases this family relationship entailed submission to the authority of the male householder, in both cases it required duty, and in both cases it was expressed in terms of 'love'. This notion of love, however, is probably best understood not as spontaneous and emotive (such a relationship was often described in the eighteenth century with terms such as 'affection' or 'tender affection'), but as a highly committed, formal, and even ritualised form of sentiment.

In Eliza Haywood's treatise, too, a servant who enters service is said to 'be *taken into the family*'.[67] Once she is taken into the family, the servant-maid is also bound by familial ties to other persons in her newly acquired family. In the section entitled '*Quarrels with Fellow-Servants*', for example, the maid is advised to behave towards her fellow-servants in a temperate and pleasant manner, for 'there is nothing so engaging as a mild affable Behaviour, especially to *People of the same Family*'.[68] Another phrase that recurs in *A Present for a Servant-Maid* in the context of the maid's family of service is 'the *Family where you live*'.[69] Following this logic, a previous place of service is called '*the Family you lived in before*'.[70] It is thus also clear that the servant-maid can experience 'serial affiliation' to different families in succession.[71] This is implicit in the concluding lines in which Haywood explains that by following her instructions the servant will gain 'the Blessing of God, and the Love and Esteem of the *Families* in which you live'.[72] Although the servant-maid is clearly imagined as being attached to her family of service, her affiliation is described in looser terms than that of the apprentice. Nor is this relationship solemnised by as binding and long-term a contract as the apprentice's indenture. Nonetheless, a phrase recurring in the context of the household service in this treatise – 'the family where you live' – can suggest the demanding nature of this service, as it refers to it in terms of 'life'. Such a service, as we know, could often be arduous and leave the servant very little time and space for a life of her own.

As in *The Apprentice's Vade Mecum*, the occupational nature of the servant-maid's affiliation to the family is also self-evident. In this case, too, the relationship is also seen to be instrumental in both the short term and the long term. Faithful service is the key not only to a good and happy period of employment, but also to many future benefits. This also leads to

---

[67] *Servant-Maid*, p. 50.
[68] *Ibid.*, p. 35. Italics in the title in the original. The 'People of the same Family' are then specified as '*those we converse or have any Business with*', thus suggesting the contractual and instrumental nature of the servant-maid's position in the family.
[69] *Ibid.*, p. 13, see also pp. 7, 16.   [70] *Ibid.*, p. 12.
[71] However, the benefits of a loyal and long-term service to a single family are emphasised, as described below, and see also *ibid.*, pp. 7, 50.   [72] *Ibid.*, p. 74.

the sentimental aspect of this relationship. Without a formal contract such as the apprentice's indenture, the cultivation of the maid's affiliation to the family depends greatly on her own behaviour and choice. If the relationship is successful, its loose contractual ties can be strengthened, it can become more committed and its instrumental benefits can also increase. In this case the mistress gains 'an old and tried servant' on whom she can depend,[73] while the maid gains a loyal patroness on whom she can rely for many important matters. The success of this relationship is also manifested in the way in which it is described in terms of kinship, for the old and loyal servant is looked upon 'as a *Relation*'. The advantages of a long and happy term of family affiliation are spelled out by Haywood:

I shall only add a few Words to remind you of the Advantages of living a great while in *a Family*. Those of you who go young to Service, and continue in one Place eight or ten Years, will be then of a fit Age to marry, and besides being entitled to the Advice of your Mistress, will be certain of her Assistance in any Business you shall take up; your Children, if you have any, partake her Favour, perhaps some of them *be taken into the Family*, and both you and yours receive a Succession of good Offices. If your Husbands behave well to you, they will be encouraged for your Sakes; and if ill, you may depend on Protection from them. An old and tried Servant is looked upon *as a Relation*, is treated with little less Respect, and perhaps a more hearty Welcome.[74]

This leads to the final point: in both treatises service is perceived as a life-course experience. In the above quotation it is presented as a period of 'eight or ten years', after which the servant is 'of a fit Age to marry'.[75] Other instructions to the servant-maid reveal the same view. For instance, she is advised to make the most of her service not only so that it will be more pleasant, but also to advance her prospects for the next stage: marriage and housekeeping. Thus she is told to prove herself '*a good Housewife*' by showing industry and frugality, 'two very amiable Parts of *a Woman's Character*'.[76] This, according to Haywood, will guarantee the servant-maid her mistress's favour, 'the Esteem of Mankind', and will also increase her chances of getting 'a good Husband'. It is implicit in the treatise that the servant-maid's future position is likely to be more modest than her mistress's. But this is yet another reason why the servant-maid

---

[73] *Ibid.*, p. 50.

[74] *Ibid.*, p. 50. See also the warning against too frequent changes of 'family', p. 7.

[75] *Ibid.*, p. 50. Hill mentions that in 1851 66 per cent of female servants were under twenty-four, *Women, Work and Sexual Politics*, p. 132. See also I. K. Ben-Amos, 'Women apprentices in the trades and crafts of early modern Bristol', *Continuity and Change* 6 (1991), esp. pp. 243–5. The effects of service on women's age at marriage are also seen in V. Brodsky Elliot's study of native and migrant women in London, 'Single women in the London marriage market: age, status and mobility, 1598–1619', in Outhwaite (ed.), *Marriage and Society*, pp. 81–100.

[76] *Servant-Maid*, p. 41.

should polish her housewifery skills as a sound investment for the future. 'Consider, my dear Girls', says Haywood sagaciously, 'that you have no Portions, and endeavour to supply the Deficiencies of Fortune by Mind. You cannot expect to marry in such a Manner as neither of you shall have Occasion to work, and none but a Fool will take a Wife whose Bread must be earned solely by his Labour.'[77]

In *The Apprentice's Vade Mecum*, too, service is depicted as a life-course experience. The apprentice lives as a servant so that he himself will one day be able to become master. Throughout this treatise, too, good conduct in service is presented as the key to future prosperity.[78] Thus, Richardson warns the apprentice to avoid the vice of extravagance, which will be very harmful for him as a tradesman and will also deprive him of 'the Means of being *just*, not on only to *your Family, when you come to have one*, but to the rest of the World'.[79] In accordance with the articles of the apprentice's indenture, he is also warned not to disrupt the orderly course of his life by marrying before his time is up. He who marries too young 'may come to have a *Family of Children* while he himself is but a Boy, and while he is deprived of all *honest Means* of maintaining them'.[80] Unlike the servant-maid in Haywood's treatise, who is seen as socially inferior to her mistress both in the present and the future, the apprentice and his master are perceived as possible future equals, even future competitors. This, too, forms a part of the apprentice's ideal life-cycle, and the treatise contains advice about how he should conduct himself so as not to hurt his master while setting up his independent business.

The analysis of these two treatises reveals yet again some basic and shared notions concerning the concept of the household-family. In these treatises, as in Turner's diary, the family is seen as a flexible framework that can include kin and non-kin: masters, mistresses, servants, lodgers, and boarders can all conceivably share familial quarters with children and other relations. The characteristic pattern of familial authority is also present. The household-family relationships, investigated in the context

---

[77] *Ibid.*, p.41.
[78] See, at this point, Thomas Turner's similar advice to his own son Philip, a servant at Brighton, 'do be always careful to perform to the very utmost of your Power that is to be a good Servant, as it is not only a duty you owe your Employers but your own Interest will likewise result from it, for a prudent Sober, industrious Servant is a Character valuable and will always recommend itself to the esteem of worthy & sensible people'. He then adds: 'be careful of what connections you form for in such Public Place of Resort as Brighton Vice lurks at every Corner to ensnare and ruin the unwary youth who is entrapped in her ways, therefore my Dᵣ Child let Virtue and Prudence direct your steps . . . in the due discharge of all the duties of your Station . . .': Thomas Turner to Philip Turner, 24 July 1789, 'Special Files', Thomas Turner Papers, Manuscripts and Archives, Yale University Library.
[79] *Vade Mecum*, p. 41. Italics for 'just' in the original.
[80] *Ibid.*, p. 4. Italics for 'honest Means' in the original.

of Turner's diary, are also evident here. In these treatises, too, the family relationships are both domestic and occupational, contractual and instrumental, but also sentimental.

The analysis of these treatises also reveals some shared notions concerning the possible social roles of the household-family more broadly. The household-family emerges in these texts, as it does in Turner's diary, as a central social institution and an agent of socialisation. This is emphasised in the ways in which it is presented as an almost cyclical concept, linked to notions of the life-cycle. Servant-maids and apprentices are to join the family, study domestic and occupational roles, and subject themselves to the family order. They should strive to endear themselves to their masters, mistresses, and to other family members. Successful integration within the family is portrayed alongside the shadow of possible disruption. If the service period is successful, however, it should also come to an end. In due course the servants should leave the family and hopefully form a family of their own. In these latter stages they are also seen to carry with them the family pattern and perpetuate it within a future generation.

The family timetable

The concept of the household-family can also be detected in our texts in some specific formulae and narrative patterns. We have already seen that this concept furnishes our texts with some central social structures, literary materials, and a gallery of possible roles and relationships, but our texts even include specific formulae and narrative patterns which relate directly to the concept of the household-family. If we look at concepts of time and timekeeping, for example, we can see recurring formulaic usages and narrative constructs that reveal notions of a household-family timetable. Before turning to these, however, it is important to examine more broadly how notions of time and the household-family timetable are manifested in our texts.

The economy of the family time is discussed most explicitly in the two conduct treatises. In the context of the household service, time is a commodity, for when servant-maids and apprentices are 'taken into the family', their time is engaged for the household-family service. Thus the servant in *A Present for a Servant-Maid* is told that as long as she is in 'the Condition of a Servant', her 'Time belongs to those who pay [her] for it'.[81] Similarly, when the apprentice is 'transplanted' into his master's

---

[81] *Servant-Maid*, p. 13. See also the reference to servants 'having given their Time and Labour to their Master by Agreement', in W. Fleetwood, *The Relative Duties of Parents and Children, Husbands and Wives, Masters and Servants* (London, 1705), Garland Publishing (New York and London, 1985), p. 366.

family, his time becomes the master's property: '[y]ou must remember, that you have no Portion of Time during the Term of your Apprenticeship, that you can call your own', states this treatise.[82] Subjection to the family timetable, therefore, is perceived as part and parcel of the servants' place in the household-family. In a special section, entitled '*Hours for Business, etc. to be determined by the Rules of the Family*', Richardson explains to the apprentice in the most explicit terms that his 'bounden Duty' as an apprentice is inseparable from his duty to observe the family timetable.

As to the Time of your going to Rest and Rising in the Morning, the Hours of Working and Business, Holidays or Spare time, and the like, *you are wholly to be govern'd by the Rules of the Family into which you are transplanted*: And remember that an exact Conformity to such Rules, for the Ease and Quiet of your Master, is your bounden Duty, and will be your future Benefit.[83]

Furthermore, both treatises emphasise the moral significance of maintaining the family timetable. Our treatises instruct servants in detail not to misspend that time that does not belong to them. Both Haywood and Richardson go as far as defining the servant's waste of his or her employment time as an act of '*Robbery*', performed by the servant against the master and mistress.[84] Various moral injunctions, such as instructions to avoid idle gossiping, gambling, or haunting taverns and play-houses, are also justified on the grounds of their effect on the economy of time. For example, Richardson warns the apprentice not to keep 'ill Hours' with idle companions and loose women, for this will prevent him from resting well during the night, and then working well during the day.[85] The connection between the household-family timetable and its moral order is so clear in these treatises that the violation of the family timetable is presented as a sign of social disorder and misrule more broadly. Haywood's description of the unruly apprentice reveals the exact counterpart of Richardson's warning to the apprentice, described above. The servant-maid is instructed to beware of the young apprentices of the family who keep late hours and 'come home in Liquor': 'for as no laudable Business, nor innocent Recreation, could make him transgress in this Manner', explains Haywood. The servant-maid is thus advised to report the unruly apprentice to her master, so that steps can be taken to keep him '*within the Bounds of Duty and Regularity*'.[86] Other figures who are also mentioned as

[82] *Vade Mecum*, p. 25. In addition to allowing the master to benefit from the full worth of the apprentice's service time, the subjection of time is meant to teach the apprentice a good lesson, 'for to a *Handicrafts-Man*', says Richardson, 'Time is the same thing as Money', *ibid.*, p. 26 (italics in the original), and see similar expressions in pp. 6, 8. Quoting the words of the indenture, Richardson reminds the apprentice that he is not to '*absent himself from his Master's Service Day nor Night unlawfully*', *ibid.*, p. 19 (italics in the original).   [83] *ibid.*, p. 33.   [84] *Ibid.*, pp. 8–9, *Servant-Maid*, p. 13.
[85] *Vade Mecum*, p. 8.   [86] *Servant-Maid*, pp. 38–9.

possible transgressors of the family timetable and its moral order are gentlemen boarders and lodgers. If they, too, come home late at night, when the rest of the family is asleep, and then also take advantage of the late hour to 'proceed to Rudeness' and make indecent proposals to the servant-maid, she is advised strongly to report the matter to the mistress and refuse any bribe, or any attempt to silence her.[87] The order of the family timetable is thus linked here very closely to the family's moral and sexual order, and the maid is urged not to keep silent if order is at stake.

If we turn to a novel such as *Pamela*, we find there, too, awareness of the orderly family timetable. Just as the master and mistress in the conduct manuals set '*the Rules of an orderly Family*',[88] so does Mr B. lay down for his wife the '*rules for the family order*'. These rules stipulate regular hours for rising and going to bed, and regular mealtimes.[89] Bedtime is to be at eleven, rising at six.[90] Breakfast is to be served at nine, dinner at three, and supper at nine. The aim of these family rules is to preserve order, regularity, and good health, thus linking the family timetable, in this case, too, to broader benefits: 'For man is as frail a piece of machinery, and, by irregularity, is as subject to be disordered as a clock', says Mr B.[91] The social significance of the family timetable is further emphasised when Mr B. calls these rules 'old fashioned', but declares that he is proud of maintaining them nonetheless. He also expects his guests to abide by them and he hopes to propagate them in the neighbourhood. Mr B.'s '*rules for the family order*' in the first edition of *Pamela*, however, are even more old-fashioned, for there dinner is to be fixed for two, and supper for eight.[92] It seems that one can clearly detect here the voice of the prudent City tradesman, Samuel Richardson, behind the words of the reformed gentleman, Mr B.

Awareness of a regular family timetable is also evident in the diary of Thomas Turner. In this case, too, the family timetable also has broader significance in terms of a social and moral order. But in order to examine Turner's notions of his family timetable, we should first place them within the broader context of his methods for accounting for the passage of time. Turner was greatly aware of the passage of time and he used in his diary three methods for accounting for it. The first was according to clock-time. Turner's account specifies whole hours, half hours, and ten-minute intervals past the hour. He did not normally register time by single minutes or seconds, but his frequent use of the qualifier 'about' while recording time suggests that he was aware of small units of measurement, and that he knew that he was measuring time by near proximity only. See,

[87] *Ibid.*, p. 50.   [88] *Vade Mecum*, p. 52.   [89] *Pamela*, ed. Sabor, p. 393.
[90] This applies to the summer months, although the considerate husband suggests that Pamela might want to lie half-an-hour longer.   [91] *Ibid.*, p. 394.
[92] *Ibid.*, p. 394, and p. 534 n. 284, and see the editor's reference there.

for example, the following entries: 'About 10m[inutes] p[ast] 10 my Bro[ther] Came Over'; 'we arrived about 20m [past] 12'; 'This day ab^t 30mp1 We had a very remarkable shower of Rain.'[93] Turner's second method of measuring time was according to the passage of the day. Noon was the central point that split the day into morn and forenoon, followed by the afternoon, even, and night. The third method, which was related to it, was measuring time according to the orderly routine of the household-family. Here the main milestones were the family meals: breakfast, dinner, and supper.[94] The temporal value of the household-family routine is thus evident in the diary in numerous entries such as '*after breakfast* I set out',[95] or '*After dinner* my Brother Came Over.'[96] This orderly operation of the household-family timetable is of course also evident in its continuation in the master's absence, as recorded in numerous references to the 'family' who dined at home while Turner himself was away.[97]

An orderly family timetable, in which the day is devoted to honest work and the night to sound sleep, is also perceived by Turner as a mark of virtuous, wholesome, and industrious living. Not unlike Mr B., he drew up 'Rules of proper Regimen' for a simple and wholesome life, including a moderate and healthy diet, a limited consumption of rich food and heady drinks, and a regular and early bedtime as far as possible.[98] Turner wrote these rules after attending church and meditating religious thoughts, thus emphasising further the link between irregularity and 'wickednesses and Irreligion'.[99] It was possibly due to this regimen that he started recording in his diary the food consumption and church attendance of his household-family. Indeed, when this beneficial order was disrupted after some late-night revels and heavy drinking, Turner complained in terms that show his disapproval and fear of disorder. Like Mr B. in *Pamela*, he is afraid that his body and mind are 'disorder'd' by the irregularity. As in *The Apprentice's Vade Mecum*, he is concerned that this disorderly conduct is inconsistent with 'the Duty of a Tradesman' to pursue his business 'with Vigour, Industry and pleasure'.[100]

In his famous article on 'Time, work-discipline, and industrial capitalism', E. P. Thompson has suggested that concepts of time and work have undergone a developmental process, from the irregular, flexible, and task-oriented notions of time, typical of pre-industrial societies, to the

---

[93] Thomas Turner, Diary, 21 June, 12 July, 19 July 1758. The letters 'mp' stand for 'minutes past'.
[94] Festive meals which took place in the evening and the night were also called 'dinner'. Tea-drinking was sometimes also mentioned, especially if guests happened to call at the house.   [95] Thomas Turner, Diary, 5 Sept. 1762.   [96] *Ibid.*, 18 Sept. 1762.
[97] See also the following reference indicating the temporal value of meals: 'After dinnertime (for I need not Say after diner on acct I eat none)', *ibid.*, 29 Jan. 1756.
[98] *Ibid.*, 6 Feb. 1756.   [99] See *ibid.*, 8 and 29 Feb. 1756.   [100] *Ibid.*, 1 Feb. 1760.

regular time division of industrialised societies.[101] In industrialised societies, Thompson argues, work-time is purchased from the worker, and is strictly regulated by the employer. A separation between work-time and leisure time thus comes into being in industrialised societies, as well as growing alienation between the worker, the process of production, and the product. Although Thompson recognises the existence of capitalist labour relations in the early modern family economy, he invests those with a spirit of joint and communal enterprise. But if we turn to our findings so far, we can see that they do not quite fit this description. In fact, the picture seems rather mixed. The family timetable and work, discussed so far, can be described as 'task-oriented' in the sense that they allow little separation between 'life' and 'work'. Yet they are also invested with strong notions of regularity and order, and they also stem from various contractual relationships. On the whole, the notions of family time and work identified here seem to bear a closer resemblance to the idea of the worker as a 'hand', than to any notions of spontaneous cooperation. Admittedly, the eighteenth century is presented in Thompson's thesis as a transitional period, and it might be that this is why our time-work system appears so mixed. But then it is also worth noting that the regular notions of time and work, identified here, are located not in the mill or the factory but in the family home. Ideas about lingering time and spontaneous living, often romantically construed, are thus not necessarily appropriate in the context of the eighteenth-century household-family.

Indeed, notions of the family timetable are so ingrained in our texts that they are manifested in some formulaic usages, which are also employed significantly in broader narrative contexts. Note, for example, the formulaic references to the household-family timetable in the following entries. In the first group of examples the orderly family timetable is used to designate nighttime, in the second it designates daytime.

at night, at an hour when . . . *all the family would be in bed*[102]

all the family were gone to their repose[103]

I got out of the house when *all the rest of the family were asleep*[104]

---

[101] E. P. Thompson, 'Time, work-discipline, and industrial capitalism', *P&P* 38 (1967), 56–97. See also the broader interpretation in D. S. Landes, *Revolution in Time: Clocks and the Making of the Modern World* (Cambridge, Mass., 1983). See Hunt, *The Middling Sort*, pp. 53–6. See also the reference in *ibid.*, p. 56 n. 37 to the *Spectator* 15 (1710–11) (Oxford, 1965), vol. I, pp. 66–8. Hunt argues that for the middling sort in the eighteenth century promptness was closely associated with ideas of moral rectitude. In this respect, she also argues that the careful observance of time had preceded the introduction of clock time. My analysis develops similar ideas.   [102] *Betsy Thoughtless*, p. 80.
[103] *Ibid.*, p. 81.   [104] *Ibid.*, p. 534.

On her coming home, she found *the family not yet gone to bed*, though it was then near one o'clock[105]

[I] got into my chamber *before any of the family were stirring*[106]

he rose that morning . . . *before the greatest part of the family had quitted their beds*[107]

soon after daylight . . . *before the family was up.*[108]

the family was soon raised[109]

Such usages suggest the household-family routine; they may well indicate a domestic routine evolving initially around a central source of heat and light. Note also the recurring combination of the singular noun, 'family', and plural verbs, as in 'the family *were* stirring', 'the family *were* gone to their repose'. Such usages convey a notion of the family as a collective body. This is also suggested in the repeated references to the whole family: '*all* the family', '*any* of the family', '*any one* of the family'.[110]

It is due to the conventional depiction of the household-family time-table and its social and moral resonances that formulae such as these can be used in our texts in evocative ways. Let us examine closely some particular episodes. The first example shows how formulaic references to the household-family timetable convey ominous signs in the context of one episode in *The History of Miss Betsy Thoughtless*. The second reveals how they are used more positively in the context of two other episodes in *The History of Miss Betsy Thoughtless* and *Pamela*. Finally, we shall see how Turner used a similar formula while constructing a narrative in his diary.

Formulaic references to the household-family timetable are employed as ominous signs in the context of the sad story of Miss Forward. Miss Forward makes her first appearance in *The History of Miss Betsy Thought-less* as a young gentlewoman in boarding-school. We have already noted above how this boarding-school is referred to as a 'family': as we saw, this 'family' includes a governess, a nurse, a tutoress, pupils, and possibly various others.[111] Miss Forward violates the order of this family in a way that leads to her utter ruin, and her transgression is both moral and

[105] *Ibid.*, p. 173.   [106] *Ibid.*, p. 85.   [107] *Ibid.*, p. 569.
[108] *Pamela*, ed. Sabor, p. 126.   [109] *Ibid.*, p. 126.
[110] See also J. Austen, *Northanger Abbey* (1818), ed. J. Davie (Oxford, 1971), p. 150: '[t]o be kept up for hours, after *the family were in bed*, by stupid pamphlets, was not very likely. There must be some deeper cause: something was to be done which could be done only while the household slept.' See also 'Catherine found herself to be hurried away by Miss Tilney in such a manner as convinced her that the strictest punctuality to *the family hours* would be expected at Northanger', *ibid.*, p. 128. Similarly, Miss Weeton, whilst staying at the family of one Mrs Chorley in Liverpool in 1808 complains about 'the early rising of the family here' which makes her feel 'fidgety', Weeton, *Journal of a Governess*, vol. I, p. 105.   [111] *Betsy Thoughtless*, pp. 77–8.

temporal. Her downfall starts as she comes under the bad influence of a French tutoress, who helps her to conduct a fatal liaison with a libertine named Mr Wildly. The tutoress is very resourceful in making secret assignations – for herself and her pupil – without the knowledge of '*the family*'. Ultimately, Miss Forward commits a grave act of temporal and moral transgression: she meets her lover at night, in a dark and secluded garden, while the rest of 'the family' are asleep. Such a meeting, Miss Forward explains, 'could not be done by day without a discovery'. 'I therefore fixed the rendezvous at night, at an hour when I was positive *all the family would be in bed.*'[112] In this context, the reference to the family timetable strikes an ominous note. A young woman who wanders alone at night in a dark garden, while the rest of the family is asleep is clearly up to no good. This notion is intensified as Miss Forward continues her story, while repeating the formulaic reference to 'the family': 'Night came on – *all the family were gone to their repose* – and I, unseen, unheard, and unsuspected, quitted my chamber.'[113] This repeated reference to the sleeping 'family', as well as the reiterated confirmation that Miss Forward has committed the deed unnoticed – 'unseen, unheard, and unsuspected' – all serve to strengthen the impression that her story is ill-fated. Sadly for Miss Forward, she does indeed manage to go and return unseen. Even old Nurse Winter, the lightest sleeper of all the 'family', who usually gets up at the slightest suspicion of an unusual noise, does not rise.[114] Finally, the formula is evoked ominously yet again as Miss Forward concludes her account of these events: 'I then went back with the same precaution . . . locked all the doors softly, and got into my chamber *before any of the family were stirring.*'[115]

Miss Forward's departure from the family timetable is a fatal mistake indeed. She becomes pregnant, her lover forsakes her, and her relations reject her. Her baby, born in shameful conditions, soon dies. Miss Forward then makes her way alone in London, sinking deeper and deeper into degradation. The eighteenth-century reader was no doubt familiar with this narrative pattern of 'the harlot's progress': literary heroines such as Fanny Hill, Roxana, Moll Flanders, Clarissa, and many others are presented with similar career choices. The formulaic references to the family timetable, however, anticipate this sad turn of events, for the temporal transgression can be associated so clearly with notions of moral and social transgression.

In another case in *Pamela* the formula of the family timetable is used in a less blatant way, although here, too, it is employed evocatively. See the wording of the following episode.

---

[112] *Ibid.*, p. 80.   [113] *Ibid.*, p. 81.   [114] *Ibid.*, p. 84.   [115] *Ibid.*, p. 85.

travelling all night, [Goodman Andrews] found himself soon after daylight at Mr
B.'s gate, *before the family was up*: and there he sat down to rest himself, till he
should see somebody stirring.
    The grooms were the first he saw, coming out to water their horses; . . . 'is the
'squire at home, or is he not?' 'Yes, but he is not stirring', said the groom . . . *The
family was soon raised*, with the report of Pamela's father coming to enquire after
his daughter.[116]

In this episode, as in Miss Forward's sad story, time is indicated in
relation to the movements of the household-family, and is also expressed
in similar words: '*before the family*', and '*after the family*'. Indeed in this
case, too, the temporal formula has ominous connotations: Goodman
Andrews sets out on his journey as he believes his daughter's virtue is in
danger. But in this case, the formula also suggests positive irregularity, for
it reveals the father's readiness to act on behalf of his daughter and
confirms his extraordinary virtue and love.
    In another episode in *The History of Miss Betsy Thoughtless* we find a yet
more positive use of the same formula. This time, we are told that Mr
Trueworth has risen early in the morning '*before the greatest part of the
family had quitted their beds*'.[117] Like Miss Forward, he proceeds to walk in
a secluded garden. But in this case the conventional signs indicate a
positive message. Mr Trueworth's stroll takes place not under the cover
of the night, but at the break of a new day. His actions are innocent and
open, and his intentions are honourable. Fortuitously, Betsy, who in her
days in London has always '*kept late hours*', is now also charmed by the
freshness and solitude of the early morning hour and the 'soft sincerity of
a country life'.[118] She, too, proceeds to the same garden, and it is in this
setting that the two reveal their true love.
    When Thomas Turner came to construct in his diary his own narrative
of the story of Lucy Mott, he resorted to these formulaic elements. To aid
the analysis, let me reproduce Turner's narrative:

This day a Mellancholy affair broke out in this Neighbourhood /Viz/ Lucy Mott
serv[t] to Mr Jer. French, last Night absconded her self from her service (*privately
and quite unknown to any one in the Family*) and from many Corroborating
Circumstances there is great probability to think she hath committed that rash
action of Suicide She went off in her worst apparel, and left behind her all her
money and had taking more than Common Care in laying up all her Cloths and
collecting it together in such a manner that it might be the more Easy to find by
her relations. there is also the greatest reason imaginable to think she was pregnant for by some reasons given by her Mrs it seems plain and on the 18th Ult. she
wanted of my Wife 2 Oz jallap but upon her saying we had not such a quantity in

---

[116] *Pamela* ed. Sabor, p. 126. See also E. Haywood, *The Fortunate Foundlings* (3rd edn,
    London, 1748), p. 28: 'and so sat waiting till she heard some of the family were
    stirring'.   [117] *Betsy Thoughtless*, p. 569.   [118] *Ibid.*, p. 568.

the house and telling her she must be either mistaken in the name or Quantity for that must be Enough for 20 People to take she seem'd greatly confus'd and pretended it was not to take ... so that I should rather think her intentions might be then rather to destroy the Foetus than her self.[119]

The basic fact, namely, the disappearance of Lucy Mott during the night, is extended here by Turner to form a grave narrative. However, this grave narrative is constructed with the use of conventional formulae and signs. First, Lucy's actual disappearance is referred to as the disorderly departure of a servant from her place of service. After mentioning her name and her employer's name, Turner pronounces that she has '*absconded her self from her service*', thus indicating her breach of her contractual obligations. The suspicion is then presented that this abrupt and mysterious departure signifies yet a greater departure, a departure from life. Furthermore, the unruly manner of Lucy's departure is suspected to signify 'the rash action of Suicide'.[120] Conventionally, the fact that these sad deeds have occurred in the dead of night adds to the sense of danger and mystery, for nighttime is when young women such as Lucy Mott and Miss Forward should be safe indoors. Like Miss Forward, however, Lucy Mott wanders away. Like her, she also goes '*privately*', and '*and quite unknown to any one in the Family*'. The narrative of Lucy's transgression is thus presented as a transgression against the order of the household-family.

Furthermore, as in the case of Miss Forward, these acts of temporal and familial transgression are linked to acts of female transgression. '[T]here is also the greatest reason imaginable to think she was pregnant', says Thomas Turner. He then brings further evidence to suggest that Lucy Mott tried to buy a large quantity of a purgative drug, with the aim of inducing abortion.[121] Her disappearance and supposed suicide are thus tied to her supposed illicit pregnancy and desperate state. Other details reinforce this grim impression. Like Pamela, who expresses her departure from Mr B.'s household-family in a symbolic divestment and transformation of dress, so does Lucy Mott prepare to leave this world in her worst apparel, thus, supposedly, showing consideration to her 'relations', who are to inherit her best clothes and small savings.[122]

Clearly, Thomas Turner constructed this narrative with caution and

[119] Thomas Turner, Diary, 8 Mar. 1760.
[120] The archaic use '*hath* committed' recalls the language of biblical moral injunctions.
[121] See Turner, *Diary*, ed. Vaisey, p. 203.
[122] See also Pamela's desperate attempt to run away, leading to a temptation to take her own life, *Pamela*, ed. Sabor, pp. 209–17. This event, too, includes an account of clothes and money. Pamela takes 'one shift, besides what I had on, and two handkerchiefs, and two caps, which my pocket held . . . and all my stock of money, which was but five or six shillings, to set out for I knew not whither'. However, she is driven to this distress because 'she preferred her honesty to her life', *ibid.*, pp. 209, 212.

care. He hinged his suspicion on an array of carefully produced signs, which he referred to as '*Corroborating Circumstances*'. Beyond the quasi-legal signs, however, there are other, cultural, and formulaic signs. These are the signs of familial misrule, and of female transgression, abandonment, and ruin. The story of Lucy Mott thus presents an interesting case of the construction of a narrative in which the formulaic patterns, used by a single individual in his diary, resemble greatly those narrative patterns used in contemporary literary texts. However the similarity between the story of Lucy Mott and our literary examples is even more striking, for, as it happened, Turner's construction of the signs was untrue. Lucy Mott did not commit suicide. On 1 June 1760 the banns for her marriage were called in a local parish church.[123]

Conclusion

Evidently, Thomas Turner was not the only one to have used the concept of the household-family. This concept was current in a wide range of other sources from the mid-seventeenth to the early nineteenth centuries. Moreover, the detailed analysis has shown that this concept was employed in many significant ways by members of an eighteenth-century 'language community'. Samuel Richardson and Eliza Haywood invoked this concept in their texts. They made similar verbal usages, invested them with similar verbal and social meaning, and used this concept more broadly in the construction of their texts. Characters, roles, relationships, and even entire episodes and narratives were envisaged and written down with the concept of the household-family in mind. Finally, as the last section of this chapter has shown, Haywood, Richardson, and Turner also used some specific and similar formulae, based on the concept of the household-family. The concept of the household-family, with the notions of order implicit in it, was thus significant in constructing notions of time, linked to notions of a sexual and moral order. The tensions between day and night, right and wrong, obedience and misrule, success and failure were all constructed with the aid of the concept of the household-family.

The concept of the household-family thus reverberates in our principal texts, and indeed in many others, regardless of differences in authors and boundaries of genres. It not only formed a part of the cultural vocabulary of our 'language community', and was extremely important in its members' understanding of social experience but also attests to the social and cultural world in which they lived.

[123] Thomas Turner, Diary, 18 May, 1 June 1760.

3   The concept of the lineage-family

Introduction

However important the concept of the household-family was in eighteenth-century society and culture, there were also other concepts of the family that existed at the same time. The main subject of this chapter is the concept of the lineage-family.[1] This concept of the family was both very significant and probably the one furthest removed from the concept of the household-family. The first section of this chapter examines the manifestations of the concept of the lineage-family in the diary of Thomas Turner. The second section offers a closer examination of Turner's references to the lineage-family with which he had the closest contact, the Pelham family. This chapter will also enable us to see how a middling eighteenth-century man such as Turner related to notions of lineage and ancestry, and the role such notions played in his cultural perceptions and social interaction.

Having established the main characteristics of the concept of the lineage-family, and having explored its usages in Turner's diary, we shall proceed to investigate its manifestations in our other texts. The third section will focus on the two conduct treatises, *The Apprentice's Vade Mecum* and *A Present for a Servant-Maid*, and the fourth section on *Pamela* and *The History of Miss Betsy Thoughtless*. These sections will allow us to ascertain the broad currency of the concept of the lineage-family within an eighteenth-century 'language community', and also to show how this concept was used as a building-block in the construction of eighteenth-century texts. These sections will also discuss some differences between our principal sources and examine the concept of the lineage-family as a point around which contested ideas are manifested.

---

[1] The term 'lineage' is used here not in the anthropological sense but as referring more broadly to notions of ancestry, pedigree, and lineal descent.

Thomas Turner's concept of the lineage-family

On Friday 21 January 1757 Thomas Turner leafed through Benjamin Martin's *General Magazine of Arts and Sciences* and found there a reference to his place of birth, Groombridge near the Sussex–Kent border. He noted the exact location of Groombridge in relation to the nearest town, Tunbridge Wells, and he noted the parish to which Groombridge belonged. He also noted the name of the family who once held its ancient seat in the place, '*the Noble Family of Cobham*'.[2] What sort of family did Turner refer to here? Even on the basis of this limited context it is possible to say that this usage suggests a notion of progeny, especially male progeny: it implies that there were men under the name of Cobham who married and produced Cobham offspring, who then continued further the Cobham line. It also suggests a sense of both plurality and collectivity, for in the course of the years there must have been many individuals belonging to the family of Cobham. In this context, the family name appears as an important emblem, marking familial unity and continuity. Finally, it is also possible to see that Turner identified this family while locating it socially and ascribing to it a sense of social importance. He knew that this was a noble family. He may well have been able to tell us more about the Cobhams and their deeds, and he may well have expected others to know about them too.

This reference to the family of Cobham conveys a concept of the family which is different from the concept of the household-family, used so often by Turner in his daily accounts. Whereas membership in Turner's household-family could be gained and lost contractually, membership in a lineage such as the Cobhams' was essentially transmitted by birth and blood.[3] Whereas Turner's household-family was an organisational unit that underwent many changes, the Cobham family persisted over time. We suggest calling the concept of the family conveyed here the concept of the lineage-family.

There are, however, significant similarities as well as differences between the two family concepts. In relation to both concepts, property is important. Just as Turner's concept of the household-family was associated with notions of property ownership and management, so is a lineage-family such as the Cobham family mentioned in relation to its ancient seat.[4] But whereas ordinary household-families are defined by

---

[2] Thomas Turner, Diary, 21 Jan. 1757.
[3] However, a lineage-family such as the Cobhams may have permitted some degree of contractual inclusion for it was possible to be co-opted into a lineage by taking on a family name. This was done to continue the name in the absence of a male heir: L. Stone and J. C. F. Stone, *An Open Elite? England 1540–1880* (Oxford, 1984), p. 47.
[4] It is then mentioned that this property passed out of the Cobham line and 'descended to

Turner according to individual householders, such as 'Mr French's family' or 'my mother's', the body in possession of this family seat is presented as the lineage-family collectively: 'anciently the Seat of the Noble Family of Cobham'.[5] Another point of similarity concerns the importance of marriage, for it was an important bond within the household-family and it was also important for maintaining a lineage-family such as the Cobhams'. Lastly, both concepts of the family enjoy a similar degree of opacity and, hence, flexibility. When Turner described his own domestic group as a 'family', his usage gave little indication as to who the family members might have been at any particular moment. Similarly, a reference to a lineage-family such as the Cobham family provides no information about the actual antiquity of the lineage, the manner of its descent, or its current state. All that this usage allows us to deduce is that there had been some generational continuity associated with the name Cobham and with its ancient property.

How important was this concept of the lineage-family for Thomas Turner? Historians of early modern England have often tried to gauge the exposure of ordinary people to matters of 'high' politics, religion, and culture.[6] Turner's references to familial lineages allow us to investigate further the conjunctions between 'high' and 'low' social and cultural spheres in the world of a middling eighteenth-century man.

First and foremost, national rule was linked in Turner's eyes to notions

---

the Clintons and Wallers', *ibid.*

[5] Tensions between lineage possession and personal possession were also evident in the institution of strict settlement, which probably became increasingly popular among the landed elite at that time. Generally, strict settlement reinforced primogeniture, while at the same time restricting the heir's freedom to sell or mortgage the estate and ensuring provisions for other family members. For the debate on the relationship between strict settlement, primogeniture, and family care, see L. Bonfield, 'Strict settlement and the family – a differing view', *Economic History Review* 41 (1988), 461–6, and E. Spring, 'The strict settlement: its role in family history', *ibid.*, 454–60, and references there. See also L. Stone, 'Spring back', *Albion* 17 (1985), 167–80. Other relevant works are H. J. Habakkuk, 'Marriage settlements in the eighteenth century', *Transactions of the Royal Historical Society* 32 (1950), 15–30; J. P. Cooper, 'Patterns of inheritance and settlement by great landowners from the fifteenth to the eighteenth centuries', in J. Goody, J. Thirsk, and E. P. Thompson (eds.), *Family and Inheritance* (Cambridge, 1976), pp. 192–327; Trumbach, *The Rise of the Egalitarian Family*; C. Clay, 'Property settlements, financial provisions for the family, and sale of land by the great landowners, 1660–1790', *Journal of British Studies* 21 (1981), 18–38; L. Bonfield, *Marriage Settlements, 1601–1740: The Adoption of the Strict Settlement* (Cambridge, 1983); B. English and J. Saville, *Strict Settlement: A Guide for Historians* (Hull, 1983); Stone and Stone, *An Open Elite?*; S. Staves, *Married Women's Separate Property in England, 1660–1833* (Cambridge, Mass., 1990).

[6] In the context of eighteenth-century historiography, the works of Edward Thompson have given additional impetus to the exploration of the relations between 'patricians' and 'plebs' (a question that will also concern us later). See also P. King, 'Edward Thompson's contribution to eighteenth-century studies: the patrician–plebeian model re-examined', *Social History* 21 (1996), 215–28.

of lineage and family. The nation's rule was seen by Turner as invested not only in the monarch, but in the royal family. At the most mundane level, this was manifested in the fact that when he consumed alcoholic drinks, Turner used to make one toast to the health of the king, and one to '*the Royal Family*'.[7] Indeed, Turner knew well the royal genealogy and he even taught it to one of his close companions, the shoemaker Thomas Davy.[8] He also noted in his diary important events in the royal family, such as the death of George II and the birth of George Augustus Frederick, later George IV.[9] Significantly, he referred to these events using both deferential and familial terms. Thus, George II was named by him not only as 'his most August Majesty', but also as '*King and Parent* of this our most happy Isle'. Further personalisation and familiarisation of the royal family was possibly evident in the fact that Turner named three of his own sons by the loyal Hanoverian name, 'Frederick'.[10] During the eighteenth century the celebration of majesty played an increasingly important role in the forging of national sentiments.[11] Throughout the first half of the century it also played an obviously important role in buttressing the Hanoverian claims to the throne. 'Believe me, Gentlemen,' said the Chairman, Henry Fielding, in his address to the Grand Jury at the opening of the Quarter Sessions at Westminster in June 1749, 'there is but one Method to maintain the Liberties of this Country, and that is, to maintain the Crown on the Heads of that *Family* which now happily enjoys it.'[12] It seems, then, that Turner shared this royalist and

[7] The fact that, when describing his daily regimen, Turner lists these as the first and second of the total of four glasses that he allowed himself a day suggests that this may have been a usual habit: Thomas Turner, Diary, 8 Feb. 1756. See the mention of such a toast on 30 June 1758.
[8] He drew for him part of the genealogical table of the royal family, *ibid.*, 18 July 1757.
[9] *Ibid.*, 26 Oct. 1760, 12 Aug. 1762, and the birth of the future Duke of York, 26 June 1764.
[10] Two of them died in infancy. Frederick Turner, born 7 Dec. 1771, died 7 Nov. 1774; Frederick Turner, born 3 May 1775, died 13 June 1775. The third Frederick Turner was born on 17 Dec. 1776. See also Turner, *Diary*, ed. Vaisey, pp. 324–5.
[11] See L. Colley, *Britons: Forging the Nation, 1707–1837* (New Haven and London, 1992), esp. pp. 195–236. In the second half of the eighteenth century, Colley argues, the celebration of majesty also became increasingly personalised around the figures of the monarch and the royal family.
[12] 'A charge delivered to the grand jury at the sessions of the peace held for the City and Liberty of Westminster &c. on Thursday the 29 of June, 1749, by Henry Fielding, Esq; Chairman of the said sessions . . .', *Charges to the Grand Jury, 1689–1803*, ed. G. Lamoine, Camden Fourth Series, vol. 43 (London, 1992), p. 335. See, for example, how in an earlier sermon to the Grand Jury of the county of Gloucester in 1723, Sir Richard Cocks described the flight of King James and the landing of King William, leading to the just and reasonable '*Pacta Conventa*' between 'Great Britain' and 'the *Hanoverian Family*', providing that this family continues to maintain Protestant rule, *ibid.*, esp. pp. 175–80.

pro-Hanoverian public discourse, all the more so as he lived in the midst of a strong Whig constituency, as we shall see later.[13]

Beyond this, Turner's understanding of his country's geography was also marked according to the realms of household-families. Moreover, his notions of historical time and significant historical events were closely linked to the names and deeds of great families and great men.[14] See, for example, Turner's description below of the town of Battle. On Tuesday 11 October 1757 he returned from a market day at the town. He was evidently impressed by the pleasantly situated town, its considerable market, and its school. He then continued to place the town on a broader map of national history and great heroic events, mentioning the local great family and its property as important signposts.

I think Battle to be a pleasant situated Town, and there seems to be a Consider-able Market for Stock &c. on the 2nd Tuesday in every Month the Abbey which belongs to *the family of the Websters* (and which was built just after the Conquest, in memory of the Battle fought near that place between the Conquerer & Harold the then King of England & in which the latter, his 2 Brothers, most of the English Nobility & 97,974 common Men was slain) is the remains of a fine Gothic Structure there is also . . . in the Town a free School . . .[15]

Indeed, if we return to Turner's description of his own birth place, Groombridge, mentioned at the start of this section, we can find that there, too, notions of national geography and historical time are linked to the concept of the lineage-family. After locating Groombridge geographi-cally and identifying it by its parish, and after linking it to 'the Noble family of Cobham', Turner continues to place it on a map of national and

---

[13] See ch. 6, below.

[14] At this point it is worth noting that one of the books that he owned – and to which he returned at various times during the years of the diary – was Collins's *The Peerage of England*. See also Turner, *Diary*, ed. Vaisey, p. 348. Another diarist, Samuel Pepys, also had a similar view of the great lineage-families in the realm. See, for example, his report on Fuller's forthcoming book on '*all the families of England*'. These were, of course, all the great families that mattered, as the full title of Thomas Fuller's book indicates: *History of the Worthies of England* (1662). As the editors note, to Pepys's disappointment, the book contained nothing about his own family: Pepys, *Diary*, 22 Jan. 1661, vol. II, p. 21 and n. 1.

[15] Thomas Turner, *Diary*, 11 Oct. 1757. In this case notions of plurality and collectivity are further emphasised by the plural usage, 'the family of the Websters'. Notions of social status are evident not only in the way in which Turner singles out the Webster family, but also in his description of the historical events, for the men slain in the ancient battle are listed in order of rank. This example also demonstrates how opaque such usages can be as to the actual details concerning the lineage-family. In this case, both the family's title and its ownership of the abbey were rather recent. Sir Thomas Webster, son of Sir Geoffrey Webster, Kt, was created a baronet in 1705. In 1721 he purchased the Battle abbey estates from the Montague family: see J. F. Huxford, *Arms of Sussex Families* (Southampton, 1982), pp. 203–4.

historical importance, providing additional information about great families, great men, and great events.

Groombridge about 3 Miles from Tunbridge Wells in the Parish of Speldhurst, anciently the Seat of *the Noble Family of Cobham* had a Market on Thursday, a Chapel of ease to belong: in to Speldhurst, and since decended to the Clintons and Wallers that renowned Soldier, who in the Reign of Henry the 5th took Charles Duke of Orleans, General of the French Army, Prisoner at the Battle of Agincourt and held him in honourable Custody at Groombridge which a manuscript in the Heralds Office mentions to be 25 Years in the time of which his recess he newly erected the House at Groombridge on the old foundation and was a benefactor to the Repair of Speldhurst Church.[16]

Thus, it would seem that the concept of the lineage-family was not only significant in Turner's understanding of his nation's rule and of national geography and history, but it also assisted him in making broader sense of his own origins. The above entry is one of the rare occasions in which Turner referred in writing to his own past, and the concept of the lineage-family seems to have provided him in this case with a meaningful frame of reference to which he appended his origins. Interestingly, he did not mention Groombridge in this case in terms of personal experience: he did not indicate whether his parents had lived there for long, how long he had lived there, whether he still had any memories of the place or any current connections to it. Rather, he located Groombridge within a broader frame of reference marked by important families, personalities, and historical events. This frame of reference existed comfortably alongside his concept of his own household-family, to which he subsequently referred: '*my Family* to day dined on the remains of Saturdays dinner & I when I came home dined on some Sausages fry'd'.[17]

It is possible to see at this stage that Turner's references to familial lineages were made in a language strongly shaped by public discourse. When writing about lineage-families, he used many formulaic phrases and standard generic expressions. Some of these expressions were taken from the realm of oral conventions and public ritual, some from the world of print. Turner's toasts to the royal family, for example, were patently formulaic. References to events such as the death of the King and the birth of an heir to the throne were reported in solemn formulaic terms.[18] Other references, such as the above reference to '*the Noble Family of Cobham*' and 'the Clintons and the Wallers', were informed by a publication in a contemporary magazine.[19] Even Turner's description of the town of Battle, written after he attended a market in the town, was coined in a style similar to that of contemporary travel literature. Daniel Defoe's

---

[16] Thomas Turner, Diary, 21 Jan. 1757.   [17] *Ibid.*, 24 Jan. 1757.
[18] *Ibid.*, 26 Oct. 1760, 12 Aug. 1762.   [19] *Ibid.*, 21 Jan. 1757.

description of Battle in *A Tour Through the Whole Island of Great Britain*, for instance (which Turner actually read at a later date), contains some similar elements.[20]

But did this concept of the lineage-family have any personal significance for Thomas Turner? Did it have any bearing on the ways in which such a middling eighteenth-century man saw his own family? It seems that for many years the concept of the lineage-family had very little personal importance for Turner. Throughout his diary he did not refer to himself as having 'family' in the lineage sense of the word. Nor did he refer to his relations by blood and marriage as having familial lineages. The nearest he came to expressing such a notion was when he described his future second wife Mary [Molly] Hicks saying 'she comes of Reputable Parents'.[21] But even then he seems to have stressed her immediate parentage as a proof of her good upbringing and possible future fortune, rather than evoking any notions of long-term familial heritage. Similarly, none of Turner's ordinary neighbours – the Fullers, the Durrants, the Davys, the Wellers, etc. – were referred to by him in his diary as having 'families' in the lineage sense of the word. This was not for want of opportunities: one can imagine numerous contexts in which such comments could have been made, such as remarks about the character and reputation of particular neighbours, about marriages and baptisms, or the descriptions of funerals in the neighbourhood in which Turner served as an undertaker and a supplier of gloves, bands, rings, etc. Nonetheless, such references were not made.

Turner's silence about his neighbours' lineage-families is all the more striking in view of the fact that probably a good number of them could claim descent from local 'dynastic families',[22] and perhaps even some links to arms-bearing families. The fact that the 'better sort' in Turner's locality, such as Mr Porter, Mr Coates, or Mr Calverley, came from arms-bearing families is not surprising.[23] However, many among Turner's

---

[20] D. Defoe, *A Tour Through the Whole Island of Great Britain*, 4 vols. (London, 1724–6), ed. P. Rogers (Harmondsworth, 1986), pp. 140–1. This edition recounts 'that memorable fight with Harold, then King of England; in which the fate of this nation was determined'. The 'Sixth Edition with Very Great Additions, Improvements, and Corrections: Which Bring it Down to the End of the Year 1761' (London, 1762), vol. 1, p. 183, also contains a description of 'some remains of the Abbey', which are said to form a part of the house of its present owner, named here as Lord Viscount Montacute. This edition also notes the Sunday and Holyday fairs of this 'handsome Town'. Thomas Turner recorded reading a part of 'a Tour through England' on 24 Nov. 1764, but it is impossible to know which edition he read.   [21] Thomas Turner, Diary, 14 Apr. 1765.

[22] See A. Mitson, 'The significance of kinship networks in the seventeenth century: south-west Nottinghamshire', in Phythian-Adams (ed.), *Societies, Cultures and Kinship*, pp. 24–76.

[23] The Porters of Sussex were probably a younger branch of the Porters of Markham in Nottingham. Mr Coates's title, 'Esq.', and his descent from a York family are inscribed in

neighbours bore names that indicate their descent from well-known local families and conceivably even their links to local arms-bearing families with branches among the county squirearchy and higher ranks of professions and trades.[24] Indeed, had Turner had greater personal regard for familial lineages, he could have boasted more about the substantial yeoman's family, connected with its parish for several generations, from which his future wife descended.[25] He could have tried to trace links with the Sussex arms-bearing family of the same name.[26] Indeed, he could have said something about his own presumed descent from the old Sussex county family of Turners of Tablehurst, in East Grinstead.[27]

At this point, however, it is important to emphasise that at different points in his life Turner clearly invoked different concepts of the family. During the years of the diary, he is notably silent about his own lineage-family and the lineage-families of his neighbours. But there are two additional documents that indicate that his attitude was subject to change. At some point Turner attached to the safeguarded diary volumes a carefully painted coat of arms of the Turners of Tablehurst.[28] Although

a mural in East Hoathly church, in which Mary, the wife of Mr Porter, is also mentioned as 'only daughter and heiress of Christopher Coates Esq.'. Mr Calverley was a descendant of the Calverleys of The Broad in Hellingly: see Huxford, *Arms of Sussex Families*, pp. 192–3, 340; R. W. Blencowe and M. A. Lower, 'Extracts from the diary of a Sussex tradesman, a hundred years ago', *SAC* 11 (London, 1859), 196.

[24] The list of Sussex families bearing coats of arms contains various surnames that also recur in Turner's diary: Burges, Davy, Ellis, French, Fuller, Jenner, Durrant – to mention only a few. For example, the name 'Durrant' was well known in Turner's area. The arms-bearing Durrant family also had branches in Waldron, Lewes, and Framfield – all in Turner's near locality. William Durrant of Framfield, the neighbouring village where Turner's mother lived, was listed in the last heraldic visitation of Sussex in 1662–8. Robert Durrant, gt, of Framfield was still listed among the Sussex electors in 1774. In 1701 a Samuel Durrant of Waldron bequeathed land to his son in Turner's own village, East Hoathly. More than half a century later a Joseph Durrant of East Hoathly still had dealings with land held in the past by one Samuel Durrant. This was probably Joseph Durrant the blacksmith, one of Thomas Turner's nearest neighbours, who was also a freeholder, a fellow parish officer, and a participant in festive dinners held by the principal inhabitants of East Hoathly. In addition, Turner was also in touch with members of the Durrant family in Waldron. Samuel Durrant of Lewes, a wealthy merchant and landowner was one of his suppliers and bankers. See Huxford, *Arms of Sussex Families*, p. 157; *The Poll for the Knights of the Shire to Represent the County of Sussex, Taken at Chichester in 1774 . . .* (Lewes, 1775), pp. 74, 92. See also Robert Durrant's mural in Framfield church and F. Lambarde, 'Coats of arms in Sussex churches', part v, *SAC* 71 (1930), 135. See Turner, *Diary*, ed. Vaisey, p. 330, and exchanges of land among the Durrants in Laughton Manor: ESRO, Laughton Manor Court Books, A2327 1/4/4, ff. 67–8, 480–1; A2327 1/4/5, f. 7. See other references to the Durrant family, e.g. *SNQ* 2 (1928–9), 22–4, 202–4; *SAC* 4 (1851), p. 303.

[25] Blencowe and Lower, 'Extracts from the diary of a Sussex tradesman', 219; Thomas Turner, Diary, 31 July 1765.

[26] The Hickes family of Rotherbridge, see Huxford, *Arms of Sussex Families*, p. 342.

[27] Blencowe and Lower, 'Extracts from the diary of a Sussex tradesman', 183; Huxford, *Arms of Sussex Families*, p. 308.

[28] Blencowe and Lower, 'Extracts from the diary of a Sussex tradesman', 183; Turner, *Diary*, ed. Turner, p. xxvi.

he did not add any verbal statements, his action manifested a claim for gentle descent. Years after he stopped writing his diary, moreover, Turner wrote another document in which he constructed a sense of patrilineal descent, and possibly also a sense of a professional dynasty.[29] He was now older, and he had behind him a rich familial experience.[30] Around these years he was most probably taking steps towards educating his sons and preparing them to take their place as members in a dynasty of Turner tradesmen. It may well have been significant that by this time his economic state had also improved to the degree that he was able to invest in property, thus securing the foundations for the family's upward mobility.[31] It was from this vantage point that he referred to his family's past. He put on paper the names of Turners, dead and living, including his father, both his father's wives and their children, followed by the names of his own wives and children. He added some more biographical details about births, deaths and burials, places of residence, etc., as well as details of occupational training and pursuits, starting from his father's possession of the Framfield shop.[32] Occasionally he added more personal

[29] ESRO, SAS/SM 210, reprinted in Turner, *Diary*, ed. Turner, pp. 105–12; Turner, *Diary of a Georgian Shopkeeper*, pp. 79–84.

[30] The youngest Turner could have been when he wrote that document was forty-eight, when his last son mentioned in the document was baptised (on 10 Jan. 1777). Of course, the document may have been written at any point afterwards.

[31] He managed to purchase his shop in 1766. The main public house in the village, *The King's Head*, previously the *The Maypole*, was purchased in 1772. By the time of his death, Turner was comfortably settled: his estate was assessed as not amounting to £2,000. His pride in his trade is also reflected by the fact that he was described on his gravestone as 'draper'. Indeed, at least two of his sons also became tradesmen, and one of them became one of the most successful mercers in the county with annual commercial returns reaching for a series of years £50,000 and even £70,000. See Turner's will, ESRO, W/A 66 ff. 728–30; Turner, *Diary*, ed. Vaisey, pp. xii n. 1, 293 n. 8, 327; Blencowe and Lower, 'Extracts from the diary of a Sussex tradesman', 183; L. F. Salzman, 'Philip Turner', *SNQ* 16 (1963), 37. Turner's ambition for his son Philip is also evident in a later letter, in which he approves of his behaviour and says 'an unremitted assiduity to business on your Part is best for you, and may in time open a road to your advancement in life (which God grant it may) for with a descreet and Prudent behaviour I hope you need not fear it': Thomas Turner to Philip Turner, 27 July 1790, 'Special Files', Thomas Turner Papers, Manuscripts and Archives, Yale University Library.

[32] John Turner, a Kentish yeoman and shopkeeper, was admitted to the Framfield property on 10 July 1735: ESRO, Framfield Manor Court Book, ADA 117, ff. 24–5; see also Renouncement of claims by William Constable, 9 Dec. 1735, CKS, Streatfield MSS U 908 T158. The people who surrendered the Framfield property to him were John and Avis Constable, who bore the same surname as John Turner's first wife and were most probably related. In the early 1730s John Turner evidently also became known by the name 'Fann', as mentioned in the court records and in his will. This may possibly indicate that either he or one of his predecessors was illegitimate or informally adopted. Research done by Roger Davey, Sussex County Archivist, and myself has uncovered many hitherto unknown details about Thomas Turner's ancestry, but so far no conclusive evidence concerning the birth of John Turner has been found. I am very grateful to Christopher Whittick and especially to Roger Davey for help in exploring the links among the Turner, Constable, and Fann families, as well as the history of the Framfield property.

notes.[33] But on the whole the entries were not extensive. One is also struck by the limited amount of detail about Turner's maternal family and the families of origin of his first and second wives. Clearly, the emphasis in this document is on the Turner line. This document proposed a lineage with Thomas Turner and his father as founding fathers, and it was meant to transmit a sense of this lineage to Thomas Turner's own progeny.

Thus, the concept of the lineage-family was significant for the ways in which Thomas Turner envisaged his world and his place within it. Just as his nation and its history were linked in his eyes to notions of lineage and family, so did he eventually construct a sense of his own history in terms of lineal descent.[34]

The Pelham family

While Thomas Turner was largely silent about notions of lineage and ancestry regarding himself and his ordinary neighbours, there was one neighbour to whom he clearly ascribed such notions. This was the Duke of Newcastle, whose estate at Halland bordered on Turner's village, East Hoathly. His, indeed, was the lineage-family with which Turner had the closest contact. Turner's references to the Duke of Newcastle and his family, the Pelham family, show that the concept of the lineage-family was not only important in Turner's understanding of his world and his place within it, but was also an active force in shaping social relations in Turner's locality.

Thomas Pelham-Holles, First Duke of Newcastle, was one of the most important political figures of his time and probably the single most influential magnate in Sussex. Every summer he used to come to his seat at Halland House, where he was visited by a large number of distinguished guests. Other members of the Pelham family also arrived in the neighbourhood, either to visit Halland or on their way to be buried in the nearby family vault at Laughton.[35] Turner was interested in events that took place at Halland and he was conscious of the Whig political interest in his locality.[36] As a shopkeeper, he was aware all the more of the

---

[33] In the cases of his own children, he added the names of their 'sponsors' and godparents. In the cases of his father and first wife he added personal eulogies, expressed, not surprisingly, in solemn and formulaic terms. The eulogy for Peggy Turner in this document is extremely similar to the recurring eulogies about her in the diary.

[34] It appears that Turner succeeded in this mission. The manuscript was bequeathed from father to son in the course of four generations until it reached the hands of Florence Maris Turner, who published it in 1925.

[35] See Vaisey's witty remark about Henry Pelham who 'appears only as a corpse on his way to the family vault at Laughton', Turner, *Diary*, ed. Vaisey, p. xviii.

[36] See below, ch. 6, and esp. pp. 221–32.

business opportunities that Halland offered to himself and his village shop.

The thriving historiography of the eighteenth-century 'middling sort', among whose ranks Thomas Turner numbered, often has little bearing on the equally thriving historiography of the eighteenth-century aristocracy. Studies of the rising eighteenth-century middle classes also tend to focus on the urban settings.[37] The case of Thomas Turner offers us a good opportunity for observing the ways in which a rural, provincial, and middling eighteenth-century man perceived the near presence of one of the most influential lineage-families of his time.

Turner clearly recognised the Pelham family as a lineage-family and he was able to recognise a good number of its current members as well. On the morning of Friday, 9 July 1756, for example, he went together with one of his neighbours to watch the funeral of the Duke of Newcastle's sister, which was to proceed from Halland House to the neighbouring parish of Laughton. His reference in this context to 'their *Family* Vault at Laughton' shows his recognition of the Pelham lineage-family; the separate burial place also symbolises the social separation and elevation of this lineage, its collective unity and its persistence over time.[38] Turner's exact reference to the deceased lady, 'The Hon. Lady Frances, dowager of Castlecomer', also reveals his knowledge of members of the Pelham family. He was even able to add that she was sixty-nine when she died.[39] Other members of the Pelham family whom Turner identified on this occasion include 'the Hon: Col: Pelham, T. Pelham Esq, John Pelham Esq, and Hen: Pelham Esq', who were among the pall-bearers. He was also able to identify the mourning coach of 'Mr Pelham & Col: Pelham'.

[37] See, for example, the urban settings explored in Earle, *The Making of the English Middle Class*; J. Smail, *The Origins of Middle-Class Culture: Halifax, Yorkshire 1660–1780* (Ithaca, 1994); S. D'Cruze, 'The middling sort in eighteenth-century Colchester: independence, social relations and the community broker', in Barry and Brooks (eds.), *The Middling Sort of People*, pp. 181–207; J. Barry, 'Bourgeois collectivism? Urban association and middling sort', in Barry and Brooks (eds.), *The Middling Sort of People*, pp. 84–112, and further references there.

[38] See C. Gittings, *Death, Burial, and the Individual in Early Modern England* (London, 1984), esp. chs. 8–10. For the importance of aristocratic funerals (including the funeral of the Duke of Newcastle in 1768) see J. V. Beckett, *The Aristocracy in England, 1660–1914* (Oxford, 1986), pp. 344–5. For an earlier period, see M. James, 'Two Tudor funerals', in M. James, *Society, Politics and Culture: Studies in Early Modern England* (Cambridge, 1986), pp. 176–87. On rituals of death and burial in Tudor and Stuart England, see Cressy, *Birth, Marriage and Death*, chs. 17–20. See also the fusion of familial and lineage sentiments in the construction of private burial chapels for the French nobility in N. Z. Davis, 'Ghost, kin and progeny', *Daedalus* 106 (1977), esp. pp. 92–3.

[39] It is interesting that whereas ordinary wives are mentioned so often by Turner as appended to their husbands, he expresses no qualms about the fact that the honourable dowager has returned in death to her original family vault, accompanied mainly by her own kin.

But although this occasion clearly reveals Turner's recognition of the Pelham family and his anticipation of its display of grandeur (later he actually expressed his disappointment that the funeral was not attended by as many people as one might have expected), it is also significant that he watched this grand family from a distance.[40] If he had any personal exchanges with members of the Pelham family, let alone with the Duke of Newcastle himself, he did not report it in his diary.

Just as the concept of the lineage-family was linked in Turner's eyes to notions of property, and especially to the family house, so was his view of the Pelham family shaped by the near presence of their seat at Halland.[41] Indeed many of Turner's diary references to the Duke were made in relation to the Duke's visits to Halland. When the Duke came to Halland Turner was invariably busy, supplying many goods from his shop to the big house. On such occasions he also commented on the Duke's guests, purchases, and the evils of luxury and intemperance.[42] However, the role of Halland House in shaping Turner's view of the Pelham family was emphasised all the more by the fact that the house continued to exercise the Pelham influence even in the Duke's absence. Halland continued to serve as a significant local centre of production and consumption even when the Duke was away. As subsequent examples will show, patronage and charitable donations also continued to be dispensed from Halland in the Pelham name regardless of whether the Duke himself was present. Lastly, the Duke's influence was constantly felt locally through the actions of his agents at Halland. Until 1764, Halland's steward and gardener was Mr Christopher Coates, one of the most powerful men in Turner's parish, who was also connected by marriage to the rich and influential local rector, Mr Porter.

In a famous description Harold Perkin presented the hegemonic influence of the big house in the life of an eighteenth-century rural community.[43] His argument was criticised severely by E. P. Thompson, who proposed a host of other social preoccupations in the life of an eighteenth-century parish.[44] As this case-study suggests, although Halland House did

---

[40] As Beckett observes, it was usual to involve local people in affairs of the big house and what happened within the family was the concern of everyone, whether it was birth, marriage, or death: Beckett, *The Aristocracy in England*, p. 344.
[41] See also the discussion of Turner's political life, ch. 6.
[42] See, for example, Thomas Turner, Diary, 8–9 Aug. 1755, 6–7 Aug. 1757, 8 Aug. 1759, 24 July 1763.
[43] H. Perkin, *Origins of Modern English Society, 1780–1880* (London, 1969), p. 42. See also and compare Beckett, *The Aristocracy in England*, pp. 341–62.
[44] E. P. Thompson, 'The patricians and the plebs', in E. P. Thompson, *Customs in Common* (London, 1991), pp. 20–2. See also Laslett's famous description of the human-size and small-scale nature of pre-industrial English society, dominated by the one group that could be defined as a class, the aristocracy and the gentry: Laslett, *The World We Have*

not serve as the centre of Turner's locality, its influence was felt strongly by Turner. The influence of the Pelham family was felt through it, both directly, and in a mediated manner through the local power-axis that extended from the big house to the level of the parish.[45]

Just as the concept of the lineage-family was linked in Turner's eyes to a public and historical scene, so the Pelham family helped to bring national and international events nearer to Turner. But in this respect, too, it was not only the Pelhams, but their estate at Halland that served as an important channel through which 'high' events were experienced by Turner. This was the case all the more because such events, as suggested above, could also take place in Halland in the Duke's absence. Thus, for example, Halland was the place to which middling people from the neighbourhood went to celebrate victories during the Seven Years War, such as the victory over the French fleet at the battle of Quiberon Bay, celebrated at Halland on 8 December 1759, and a bonfire, supper, and drinks on 7 October 1760 commemorating the fall of Montreal and the taking of Canada.[46] On such occasions Turner also drank to the health and success of 'his Majesty and the Royall Family', followed by a long list of other loyal toasts, among them toasts to the Duke of Newcastle and other members of the Pelham family who were not present at the occasion.[47] The Duke's arrival at Halland was a cause for yet greater celebrations. At the opening of summer assize sessions, before the Lewes races, public days were held. Before a general election, Halland opened its gates to the entire county constituency.[48]

Another important context, in relation to which Turner made references to the Pelham lineage-family, was the distribution of charitable donations. Such acts of charity, performed on behalf of the Pelhams by their stewards, were part of the long-standing ties of philanthropy that connected the local aristocracy and the parish. Turner wrote his accounts of these donations in his diary mostly while acting as overseer of the poor for his parish. Early modern historians trace the gradual weakening of aristocratic charity. While some eighteenth-century historians see the gradual weakening of artistocratic paternalism as a major shift in class relations, others stress the enduring force of aristocratic patriarchalism

---

Lost – Further Explored, esp. ch. 2. See Thompson's response in 'Patricians and plebs', pp. 19, 22–3.
[45] These relationships are investigated further in ch. 6, below.
[46] Thomas Turner, Diary, 8 Dec. 1759, 7 Oct. 1760. See also Turner, *Diary*, ed. Vaisey, p. 194 and n. 25, p. 212 and n. 25.
[47] Thomas Turner, Diary, 30 June 1758. See also Turner, *Diary*, ed. Vaisey, p. 156 and note there.
[48] See Thomas Turner, Diary, 7 Aug. 1757, 5 Aug., 1759, 24 July 1763. For the gathering before the general election of 1761, see *ibid.*, 5 Apr. 1761, and ch. 6.

and indeed the deference of ordinary people.[49] Turner's accounts of the
Pelham charity allow us to investigate these issues through a particular
case-study. They lead us to examine the possible process of change within
a context of contested customary and legal practices.[50]

From the linguistic point of view, these references contain what by now
can be classed as characteristic features of the concept of the lineage-
family. Typically, Turner invokes a collective notion of the Pelham
lineage-family together with its long-term time-span, as he mentions '*the
ancest[rs] of the Pelham family*' and their customary charity dating '*from Time
immemorial*', and promised '*forever*'.[51] Typically, these usages are imprecise: the lineage is mentioned generally, agency is ascribed to it collectively, and the long time-span is patently inexact. Turner's language in
writing about the familial charity is also characteristically formulaic. This
time, the repeated patterns suggest ritualised formulae derived from the
realm of oral tradition and custom. Lastly, the Pelham seat, Halland
House, is also mentioned in this context as an important location. The
mediating role of the Duke's agent is specified as well. The following
entries demonstrate how all these characteristic elements are manifested
in recurring entries in Turner's diary.

About 10 m[inutes] p[ast] 3 we arose to perform our task /Viz/ *Some of the
Ancestors of the Pelham Family have order'd that on this day (for Ever)* there should
be given to Every Poor Man or Woman that shall come to dem[d] it 4*d* and every
child 2*d* and also to Each a draught of Beer and a Very good Piece of Bread.[52]

[49] See, for example, F. Heal, *Hospitality in Early Modern England* (Oxford, 1990), esp. chs.
     2–4 and pp. 190–1; Perkin, *Origins of Modern English Society*, esp. pp. 51, 184–8. Com-
     pare, for example, Clark, *English Society*, pp. 42–3; see also the family as a patriarchal
     framework, *ibid.*, pp. 80–7. See also Beckett, *The Aristocracy in England*, pp. 350–9, on
     aristocratic charity.
[50] On the significance of such notions in eighteenth-century social conflicts and on chang-
     ing customary practices more broadly see, for example, Thompson, *Customs in Common*,
     esp. p. 6; R. W. Malcolmson, *Life and Labour in England, 1700–1780* (London, 1981), ch.
     4; B. Bushaway, *By Rite: Custom, Ceremony and Community in Eighteenth-Century Eng-
     land, 1700–1800* (London, 1982); P. King, 'Customary rights and women's earning: the
     importance of gleaning to the rural labouring poor, 1750–1850', *Economic History Review*
     44 (1991), 461–76; P. King, 'Gleaners, farmers and the failure of legal sanctions in
     England, 1750–1850', *P&P* 125 (1989), 116–50; J. Neeson, *Commoners: Common Rights,
     Enclosure and Social Change in England, 1700–1820* (Cambridge, 1993); S. Hindle, 'Persua-
     sion and protest in the Caddington Common enclosure', *P&P* 158 (1998), 37–78. On
     contested notions of written and oral tradition see especially A. Fox, 'Custom, memory
     and the authority of writing', in P. Griffiths, A. Fox, and S. Hindle (eds.), *The Experience
     of Authority in Early Modern England* (Basingstoke, 1997), pp. 89–116.
[51] 'Time immemorial' is specified by Turner at one time as being 'upwards of hundred
     years', Thomas Turner, Diary, 30 Sept. 1764. On the concept of 'time immemorial' see
     Thompson, *Customs in Common*, p. 4. In defining this concept, Thompson uses also R.
     Burn, *The Justice of the Peace and the Parish Officer*, 4 vols. (14th edn, London, 1780) vol. I,
     p. 408. This book was known to Turner and it was read by him in Feb. 1758.
[52] Thomas Turner, Diary, 21 Dec. 1759.

In the Even went down to Halland where I supp'd & staid all night in Order to assist Mr Coates in distributing of a gift left by *some of the ancesters of the Pelham family for Ever* to be giving yearly on St. Tho[mas] Day to Every man and Woman 4*d* Each.[53]

My Bro. Came Over in the Even in Order to stand in my Shop to Morrow during my absence I having Promis'd Mr Coates to assist him in the morn in distributing *a Gift Left by Some of the Pelham Family for Ever* and annually giving upon St Thomas's day that is 4*d* Each to Every man and Woman & 2*d* to Every Child Come from where they Will and a P^{ce} of Bread and draught of Ale to Each.[54]

My Brother Came over in the Even in Order to stand the Shop for me whilst I assist Mr Coates to Morrow in distributing *a Gift left by Some of the ancestors of the Pelham Family* to be distributed Yearly on St. Thomas's day.[55]

Alongside this long-lasting philanthropic tradition, Turner mentions in his diary another Pelham charity. This charitable donation consisted of a more frequent distribution of similar basic goods: a bushel of wheat made into bread every Sunday, and a quantity of beer every Thursday and Sunday. Typically, the agents bearing the expense of this considerable gift were specified as 'his Present Grace the Duke of New Castle and his ancestors': in other words, the Duke is seen here as the present embodiment of his long line of lineage-family. This charitable donation was also said to have continued '*without any alteration*' and '*for Time immemorial*'. As in the case of the previous gift, the distribution of this charity was performed on fixed days, and from the significant and fixed location, Halland House. The recipients were also fixed: eight poor from the parish of East Hoathly, and twelve from the parish of Laughton. Over the years, moreover, individual recipients and their parishes got used to seeing this charity as their 'right'. This led, as Turner explains, to an unequal distribution of goods, 'some having a Claim as suppos'd to double the Quantity another had'.[56]

Paradoxically, the same notions of imprecise familial agency and a long-term temporal span, which characterised Turner's references to the lineage-family and to this charity more specifically, and which were seen as the source of this charity's sanction, also helped in bringing about its end. The collective notions of agency and the long-term temporal span served to cast a veil over the fact that it was actually unknown who had initiated this particular donation, and when. This was discovered when Mr Coates, the old steward and gardener at Halland retired from his post, and a new steward was appointed in his place. Turner described the new steward, Mr Baley, as 'fam'd for OEconomy and frugality (tho I should

[53] *Ibid.*, 20 Dec. 1761.   [54] *Ibid.*, 20 Dec. 1762.   [55] *Ibid.*, 20 Dec. 1763.
[56] *Ibid.*, 30 Sept. 1764.

rather think it deserv'd the name of niggardlyness & done to Gain Self applause)'.[57] Indeed, Baley had plans for improving Halland's economy, and one of his reforms consisted of putting an end to the old and expensive charity.[58] He thus gave the parish notice of its imminent end. This drove the parish to action in an attempt to defend what it regarded as its 'right'. It was indeed a right worth fighting for, as the annual value of this charitable donation amounted to fifty pounds' worth of poor relief. But it soon became clear – as happened in so many disputes over customary rights in the course of the early modern period – that the parish had no deed in writing to uphold its right.[59] It now appeared to have been only a 'Prescriptive Right', and Turner doubted whether, 'Considering the Greatness of the Person We have to deal with', such a 'Prescriptive Right' could be contested successfully in a court of law. But this charity was too valuable to let go. Thus, the parish decided to send Turner to search the wills of 'the ancest'[s] of the Pelham Family' for a written proof to validate the claim.[60] The search proved unsuccessful. Presumably the custom ended. But although the parish lost its case, its stand, as communicated by Turner, was expressed in a firm language of 'rights'. It was also seen to be grounded in a respected legal tradition, despite the fact that the balance between the oral and customary components of this tradition was in this case contested. Going back to the terms of the historiographical debate, we can see that a middling eighteenth-century plebeian such as Turner, and others of a similar status in his community, were determined to fight their case. They were also equipped with the means to do so (for they had access to legal knowledge and professional legal advice), if only they could find the right evidence. Notions of patriarchal patronage, which were undoubtedly part of Turner's world view – and which were also part of his concept of the lineage-family and his view of the Pelham family and their great house – should thus not be mistaken for a servile attitude on behalf of either Turner or his parish.

Thus, in the context of Turner's locality the concept of the lineage-family was linked to active and influential forces in social relations. Clearly, a provincial and middling man such as Turner had knowledge of the main lineage-family in his locality, the Pelham family, and he was also fascinated

[57] *Ibid.*, 30 Sept. 1764. Interestingly, Turner accuses here the steward and his niggardliness, while the Pelhams themselves remain free of blame. It may be that Turner and the parish could square their deference for the Pelhams with their desire to defend ancient rights by blaming the niggardly Baley for what happened. I am grateful to Adam Fox for this insight.
[58] Vaisey makes the very plausible suggestion that Baley's policy was connected to his discovery of Coates's mismanagement and possible corruption. See Turner, *Diary*, ed. Vaisey, pp. 174, 329; A. Baley's Letter Book, 1763–73, ESRO, SAS Ha 310.
[59] See Fox, 'Custom, memory and the authority of writing', and references there.
[60] Thomas Turner, Diary, 30 Sept. 1764. See also Turner, *Diary*, ed. Vaisey, p. 306, and n. 30.

by their grandeur. But his engagement with the Pelham family was often mediated, and the mediating factors were themselves important players in the local scene. Turner's references to the Pelham family were thus infused with meanings derived from both elite influence and local power. But although he was faced with such power, Turner's attitude towards the Pelham family and their agents was never merely subordinate. Undoubtedly deferential, it was also active, instrumental, and critical.

The concept of the lineage-family in two conduct treatises

Neither *A Present for a Servant-Maid* nor *The Apprentice's Vade Mecum* reveals many references to the concept of the lineage-family. This is hardly surprising: treatises aimed at women and working lads are not the context in which one would naturally expect to find references to lineage-families. The absence of such references is especially clear in the case of Haywood's treatise. Although she mentions some large and affluent households, these are referred to as active household frameworks, not as the present carriers of notions of long-term familial continuity.[61] Indeed, the 'high' national and historical scope in which Turner made many of his references to lineage-families is almost entirely absent from this treatise.

Likewise, 'families' in *The Apprentice's Vade Mecum* appear almost entirely as household frameworks in which masters and apprentices live and work. These 'families' are also set in the context of the busy world of urban merchants and tradesmen. The one or two instances in which there are references in this treatise to the concept of the lineage-family, however, are both telling and significant. Having identified the characteristic features of the concept of the lineage-family in the context of Turner's diary, we can better appreciate Richardson's usage of this concept and his argumentation. See the following lines at the opening of the treatise.

TRADE is of so much Honour and Importance to this Kingdom, that many of our *best Families*, who are the greatest Ornaments to their Country, both among the Nobility and the Gentry, owe originally their Rise and Fortunes, their Splendour and Dignity, to it: And as the Bodies of our Nobility and Gentlemen receive constant Augmentations from this Source it is therefore of the highest Importance to cultivate the Minds of this most useful and most numerous Part of the Commonwealth.[62]

From the linguistic point of view, we can see that the concept of the lineage-family is used here with its characteristic features, as identified

---

[61] For instance, at one place Haywood refers to the household of 'an Alderman in the city', with whom she claims to be 'well acquainted'. Another time she speaks of the house of a 'Person of Condition' where there are many men servants: see Haywood, *Servant-Maid*, pp. 17, 36, and also pp. 31, 32.   [62] Richardson, *Vade Mecum*, pp. xi–xii.

above in our analysis of Turner's usages. Richardson proposes in these lines the concept of the lineage-family in its broadest national scope, speaking of the '*best Families*' in the country. Notions of nationhood are further emphasised by naming them '*our* best Families'. A historical perspective is evident here, for the 'best Families' are mentioned with a temporal scope dating from their original rise. Typically, however, this original rise is not measured according to any precise time-scale. Use of publicly circulating idioms, including clichés and formulaic phrases can also be detected here: 'best Families', 'Ornament to their Country', 'Rise and Fortunes', 'Splendour and Dignity', etc. Indeed, Richardson's words quoted here bear great resemblance to other well-known expressions of similar sentiments, such as Steele's *The Englishman* (1713) or Defoe's *A Plan of English Commerce* (1727) and *The Complete English Gentleman* (1729).[63]

Richardson thus uses here the concept of the lineage-family with its typical characteristics. But rather than plain acceptance, let alone identification, his words convey a sense of distance. Clearly, Richardson's main aim here is not to exalt the great families of the realm but to glorify trade and inculcate pride in their profession in the hearts of young future tradesmen. That Richardson chooses to convey this message by invoking the concept of the lineage-family, however, is significant. At the time Richardson wrote this treatise, the public images of tradesmen and trade were a complex and contested matter. While English society developed 'a broad commercial consensus' and the importance of trade was widely appreciated, eighteenth-century moralists also denounced the malignant consequences of luxury, associated, among other things, with trade.[64] A

---

[63] See N. McKendrick, '"Gentleman and players" revisited: the gentlemanly ideal, the business ideal and the professional ideal in English literary culture', in N. McKendrick and R. B. Outhwaite (eds.), *Business Life and Public Policy: Essays in Honour of D. C. Coleman* (Cambridge, 1986), pp. 110–11; Raven, *Judging New Wealth*, e.g. pp. 1–2, 84, 89–90, 91.

[64] 'The intermingling of the supposedly distinct worlds of finance, trade and agriculture did much to promote the sense of a broad commercial consensus in the age of Walpole and Pelham.' By the end of the eighteenth century, Langford says, 'it seemed difficult to appreciate the bitterness which had once marked relations between landed and moneyed men': P. Langford, *Public Life and the Propertied Englishman, 1689–1798: The Ford Lectures Delivered in the University of Oxford* (Oxford, 1991), pp. 308, 310. According to Massie, 19 per cent of all families in 1760 were engaged in trade and distribution: quoted in Hoppit, *Risk and Failure in English Business*, p. 4. Earle, for example, also describes how gentlemen's sons permeated the London business world in the seventeenth and early eighteenth centuries. These men were not seen as defiled by trade, rather, they raised the social status of trade: Earle, *The Making of the English Middle Class*, esp. pp. 7–13, 86–9, 94, 108–9. Brooks argues that in the seventeenth and eighteenth centuries an increasingly large proportion of apprentices came from the gentry and the lesser gentry, thus creating a cultural contact point between the middling sort and the gentry in terms of cultural values. He also discusses continuing notions of tension between gentility and trade:

revival in elite education, the expanding civil service, enhanced military and colonial enterprises, and the rising professions also offered new opportunities for the sons of the gentry.[65] By the second half of the eighteenth century, a decline in the public image of tradesmen was evident in contemporary literary works: indeed, the eighteenth-century businessman continued to be judged not just by his own merits, but according to a gentlemanly ideal.[66] Richardson's glorification of trade in the above lines, coined in terms of the lineage-family, thus reflects some of the contemporary complexity surrounding the status of trade and the public image of the tradesman. Richardson emphasises the debt owed to trade by the great families of the realm, both for enabling their original rise and for supporting their current splendour. But in doing so, he judges trade not by its own merits, but by its contribution to the nation's uppermost ranks.

But all is not lost. Although in these opening lines tradesmen are marked by their distance from – and services to – the great families of the realm, tradesmen can strive to develop gentleman-like behaviour, and thus join the ranks of the socially honourable. This, Richardson explains, is within the apprentice's reach, if he only follows the guidelines for a determined but generous conduct, as Richardson suggests:

This Conduct will ingage you many Friends, who, as they will grow up with you into Life and Business, may be of very great Service to you. You will also hereby gain the Name of a *generous* and *Gentleman-like* Man, Epithets in no sort incompatible with Trade and Business, and wipe away those little Aspersions which the low and sordid Selfishness of some narrow Minds have put into the Mouths of Gentlemen, and others, who are not Tradesmen, against Men of Business; or at

Brooks, 'Apprenticeship, social mobility', esp. pp. 78, 78–81. See also Colley, *Britons*, ch. 2. For luxury, see J. Sekora, *Luxury: The Concept in Western Thought, Eden to Smollett* (Baltimore and London, 1977). See also J. G. A. Pocock, *Virtue, Commerce and History: Essays on Political Thought, Chiefly in the Eighteenth Century* (London, 1985); I. Hont and M. Ignatieff, *Wealth and Virtue: The Shaping of Political Economy in the Scottish Enlightenment* (Cambridge, 1983); Raven, *Judging New Wealth*, esp. e.g. pp. 12, 82, 99, 157–82; C. J. Berry, *The Idea of Luxury: A Conceptual and Historical Investigation* (Cambridge, 1994), pp. 126–76.

[65] See, for example, J. Cannon, *Aristocratic Century: The Peerage in Eighteenth-Century England* (Cambridge, 1984), p. 42; G. Holmes, *Augustan England: Professions, State and Society, 1680–1750* (London, 1982); P. J. Corfield, *Power and the Professions in Britain* (London and New York, 1995); G. Holmes and D. Szechi, *The Age of Oligarchy: Pre-Industrial England, 1722–1783* (London and New York, 1993), pp. 147–58, and references there; J. Rosenheim, *The Emergence of a Ruling Order: English Landed Society, 1650–1750* (London and New York, 1998), e.g. pp. 39–42, 166–7, 82, 228–30, and references there.

[66] For the changing representations of trade and tradesmen and their declining image, see Raven, *Judging New Wealth*. As Raven shows, however, the characterisation of the English overseas trader remained unblemished throughout the period. For discussions of merchants and gentility, see esp. *ibid.*, pp. 83–111, 256–8. See also McKendrick, '"Gentlemen and players" revisited', p. 117.

least your Conduct will make you, on all Occasions, a laudable Exception to the general Rule. And it must be not a little agreeable to you, that you shall be placed, by your beneficent Disposition, in such a Point of Light, that you shall not only *reflect Honour to your Name and Family*, but also be an Ornament your Profession, and a Credit to Trade in general.[67]

The last reference to the apprentice's '*Name and Family*' can be read in more than one way. It can be interpreted as a reference to the apprentice's future household and family (as in another usage in this treatise '*your Family, when you come to have one*'[68]), or as referring to the apprentice's family of descent, or perhaps both. In one way, then, these lines, like the previous example, convey the importance of the gentlemanly ideal for judging the tradesman's success. With the aid of commendable conduct, the successful tradesman can extract himself from the crowd of ordinary tradesmen and place himself among the ranks of those whose family and name are associated with aristocratically oriented notions of honour. But while emphasising the importance of the gentlemanly ideal, these lines also convey a sense of professional ambition and pride, probably not unlike those sentiments that inspired Thomas Turner in constructing his own lineage of a trading family.

Thus, despite their almost insignificant number of occurrences, references to the lineage-family still constitute a conceptual background that informs Richardson's treatise. If the first reference to the 'best Families' conveys a broad national scope, a historical scope, and a hierarchical view of the social order, the second reference to the apprentice's family provides a frame of reference for evaluating notions of social success, stratification, and status mobility.

The concept of lineage-family in two novels

The plot, the characterisation, the social setting, and the themes of eighteenth-century novels such as *Pamela* and *The History of Miss Betsy Thoughtless* give scope to many references to lineage-families. Let us first see how the concept of the lineage-family is manifested in the language of these novels. We shall then proceed to examine its significance in establishing the social profile of characters, and in the construction of plots.

Having established the typical characteristics of the concept of the lineage-family, we can briefly examine their manifestation in the follow-

[67] *Vade Mecum*, p. 40. The words 'generous' and 'Gentleman-like' appear in italics in the original. Compare the usefulness of deportment, genteel behaviour, etc., as means of 'procuring . . . many Friends and Acquaintances, who will promote and serve' a man, S. Philpot, *Essay on the Advantage of a Polite Education Joined with a Learned One* (London, 1747), pp. 52–3. I am grateful to Stephen Bending for this reference.
[68] *Vade Mecum*, p. 41.

ing lines from *Pamela*. The speaker here is Lady Davers, sister of the novel's hero, Mr B., and she is reprimanding her brother for his love for his maidservant, Pamela.

> Consider, brother, that ours is no upstart *family*. It is as ancient as the best in the kingdom: and, for several hundreds of years, it has never been known, that the heirs of it have disgraced themselves by unequal matches: and you know you have been sought to by some of the first *families* in the nation, for your alliance.[69]

The concept of the lineage-family is manifested here with its typical long-term yet inexact temporal scope, and its fullest national scope: the family in question is said to be 'ancient', as the best in the 'kingdom'. Other 'first families' are mentioned subsequently in the context of 'the nation'.[70] Characteristic notions of honour are emphasised, as well as a hierarchical social view. Although these lines do not include a specific reference to the family estate, the importance of property is implicit here in the degrading reference to 'upstart families', in the reference to the family 'heirs', and in the reference to the family's previous splendid alliances. *The History of Miss Betsy Thoughtless* also gives us a view of similar typical features. For example, the 'family' of Mr Trueworth, one of the novel's main characters is described as 'ancient', and, indeed, 'by the mother's side, honourable'.[71] A further description of the mother's side as 'the honourable and well-known Oldcastles, in Kent' places that family within a national-geographical setting and suggests connections to landed property, notions of honour, and the importance of the family name. The family name itself, 'Oldcastle', brings to mind further notions of heraldry and antiquity, often associated with the lineage-family.[72]

Various qualifiers, which appear alongside usages of 'family', further emphasise the importance of lineage and ancestry in these novels. *The History of Miss Betsy Thoughtless*, for example, contains references to a 'reputable family', a 'very worthy family',[73] as well as a 'very ancient and honourable family' and a 'noble family'.[74] Another qualifier in this novel is 'good family',[75] marking considerable wealth, a genteel way of life,

---

[69] Richardson, *Pamela*, ed. Sabor, p. 293.

[70] In contrast, upstart families are also described in Lady Davers's following words as families 'of yesterday', and those further down the social scale are described as 'dirt': 'If you were descended from a *family* of yesterday, from one who is but a remove or two from the dirt you seem so fond of, that would be another thing': *Pamela*, ed. Sabor, p. 293.

[71] Haywood, *Betsy Thoughtless*, p. 64.

[72] *Ibid.*, p. 98. On his paternal side he is 'descended from the ancient Britons'. This evokes further a national and historical scope and notions of pride and fame. In this context, however, it might also suggest that on his father's side Trueworth is seen as having more newly accumulated wealth.

[73] *Ibid.*, pp. 307, 549. See also *Pamela*, ed. Sabor, pp. 127, 370, and 'a family of great repute', p. 124.   [74] *Betsy Thoughtless*, pp. 354, 52. See also *Pamela*, ed. Sabor, pp. 418–19.

[75] *Betsy Thoughtless*, pp. 3, 27–8, 327, 383. See also *Pamela*, ed. Sabor, pp. 45, 108.

but not necessarily ancient ancestry. Yet another usage stressing the importance of the concept of the lineage-family is the shorthand phrase '*of family*', meaning that the individual concerned is well descended. For example, at the start of the novel, Pamela writes about one of the ladies of the neighbourhood's gentry, describing her as being '*of family*'.[76] Another lady is described in the same context as 'well descended, though not of quality', and another is said to be a countess, 'not only noble by marriage, but by birth'.[77]

Such usages are important for establishing the social profile of characters. They declare their social position, and place them in relation to other characters. For example, Betsy Thoughtless is said to be 'of a good family'.[78] She later defines it as 'a family of some consideration in the world'.[79] Other references indicate that she is the daughter of a man titled 'gentleman', with close connections to county gentry as well as to the higher echelons of London trade.[80] Mr Trueworth, with his 'ancient' and 'honourable family' is thus placed above Miss Betsy's 'good family', although the two are clearly within marriageable bounds.[81]

We have already seen that references to lineage-families can be shaped by public discourse, including, not least, the use of formulaic phrases and clichés. When it comes to the social positioning of characters, formulaic phrases evoking the concept of the lineage-family play an important role. See, for example, the following phrases from *The History of Miss Betsy Thoughtless:*

Miss Betsy's family, fortune, and character[82]

A gentleman of family, fortune, and character[83]

a woman of fortune, family, and reputation[84]

Miss Betsy's family, circumstances, and manner of life[85]

---

[76] *Pamela*, ed. Sabor, p. 85. Mr B. also uses this shorthand phrase when he criticises '*proud fools of family*'. See also *Pamela*, ed. Sabor, p. 295, '*pride of family*'. See also, for example, the following lines from the *Guardian*: 'There is nothing more easie than to discover a Man whose Heart is full of his *Family*. Weak minds that have imbibed a strong Tincture of the Nursery, younger Brothers that have been brought up to nothing, Superannuated Retainers to a great House, have generally their Thoughts taken up with little else', the *Guardian* (London, 1714), no. 137, p. 291.

[77] *Pamela*, ed. Sabor, p. 83. Indeed, the word 'birth' often has similar usages to 'family', indicating notions of ancestry and lineage. A similarly used set-phrase is 'birth and fortune'. For example, it is said that when young ladies '*of birth and fortune*' marry they like 'to chuse their own servants', *ibid.*, p. 105. Mr B. also speaks of his 'pride *of birth and fortune*', *ibid.*, p. 116.   [78] *Betsy Thoughtless*, pp. 3, 27.   [79] *Ibid.*, p. 211.

[80] One of Betsy's guardians, described as her late father's friend and neighbour, is an old knight who retired to the country some twenty years past. Her other guardian is a still active London tradesman, but in the course of the novel he also contemplates retirement to the country.

[81] See *Betsy Thoughtless*, pp. 354–5: 'she considered, too, that his estate was much beyond what her fortune could expect, and even his family was superior to hers'.

[82] *Ibid.*, p. 73.   [83] *Ibid.*, p. 97.   [84] *Ibid.*, p. 201.   [85] *Ibid.*

a woman of fortune, family, and an unblemished character[86]

a young lady of family and character[87]

a woman of any family and character[88]

The recurring components here – words such as 'family', 'fortune', and 'character' – fuse together and turn these into rhythmic and emblematic phrases. These, then, are waved as a sort of a social passport, announcing that a character has the right social qualifications and can gain access to social circles. Such phrases are especially useful for the purposes of social introduction. For example, when Betsy's brother wishes to introduce a suitor to his sister, he presents him to the family guardian as a 'gentleman of family, fortune, and character', and asks the guardian to promote the match.[89] Another gentleman, whose son is interested in Betsy, hastens to acquaint himself with her 'family, fortune, and character'.[90] In addition to serving as formulae of introduction, such references to 'family' are also used for announcing yet again the social position of already known characters. In *The History of Miss Betsy Thoughtless*, such announcements recur especially when the social compatibility of characters is considered for the purposes of courtship and marriage.

The force of such usages of 'family' is evident all the more in view of the fact that the emblematic phrases in which they appear are often opaque. Beyond providing a general stamp of approval, these phrases often reveal very little about either the family, or the fortune, or the personal merits of the characters concerned. Opacity is further emphasised when such phrases appear in the text with few additional details to support them. For instance, although Mr Trueworth is presented above by the virtues of his 'family, fortune, and character', very little is said in the text about his family background and only one of his relations makes a brief appearance in the novel. Another gentleman 'of family' and 'estate', Mr Munden, appears in the novel with hardly any additional details at all. The details, however, are not important. More important is the general impression that these are men who enjoy a prestigious social position, due to their ancestry and financial circumstances. That much is conveyed by the emblematic formula.

Indeed, because of their opacity, the emblematic references to 'family' can also be used to create special effects. For instance, when Trueworth declares to one of his friends that Betsy is 'a woman of fortune, family, and reputation',[91] the formula is employed to demand respectful conduct towards Betsy. When Miss Flora writes a letter, introducing herself as a

---

[86] *Ibid.*, p. 275.   [87] *Ibid.*, p. 346.   [88] *Ibid.*, p. 377.
[89] *Ibid.*, p. 97. The announcement is made in the context of a letter to the family guardian, informing him about the suitor and asking his help in promoting the match.
[90] *Ibid.*, p. 73.   [91] *Ibid.*, p. 201.

woman of 'fortune, family, and an unblemished character', the formulaic phrase is manipulated in a number of ways. In addition to providing Flora with words of introduction, this phrase allows her to hide behind the conventional usage and thus avert unwanted elaboration. To the reader, this usage also creates irony, for the reader knows well that if Miss Flora has pretences to 'family', she certainly lacks both fortune and feminine virtue.

Decades after the publication of *The History of Miss Betsy Thoughtless*, Jane Austen could still harp on similar formulaic usages, remarking on the 'fortune and birth' of Elinor Dashwood,[92] or on Mrs Churchill's 'pretence of family or blood'.[93] She could give the formula an ironic twist in a phrase such as 'her fortune was large, and our family estate much encumbered'.[94] An arrogant character such as Lady Catherine de Bourgh is given an entire speech that consists of a tirade of formulae, as she advertises the splendours of her daughter's match with Darcy, due to their respective families and fortunes, while damning Elizabeth Bennet as 'a young woman without family, connections, or fortune'.[95] In this case, the pompous speech is clearly meant to present Lady Catherine in a negative light. However, similar formulaic usages could also be employed in the eighteenth century in many other areas of life that are not always represented in romantic novels. For instance, in 1761 the Dean of Lincoln used the same formula of introduction as he wrote to the Duke of Newcastle, recommending to his favour and patronage a young gentleman from Suffolk 'of a good family and fortune'.[96] As possible candidates were considered to stand for the Pelham interest in Lewes in the 1763 election, the name of William Wyndham was suggested with the aid of a similar formula as 'a Gentleman of Family & Fortune of a most Unexceptionable Character'.[97] Eventually, another candidate received the Duke's blessing. He was introduced to the borough's electorate as 'a man of Family & great Fortune, greatly allied and greatly supported'.[98]

[92] J. Austen, *Sense and Sensibility* (1811), ed. T. Tanner (Harmondsworth, 1969), p. 365.
[93] J. Austen, *Emma* (1816), ed. J. Kinsley (Oxford, 1992), p. 280. See also, for example, the description of the Woodhouses, settled for several generations at Hartfield, as 'the younger branch of a very ancient family', compared to the Eltons who 'were nobody' *ibid.*, p. 123.   [94] *Ibid.*, p. 215.
[95] J. Austen, *Pride and Prejudice* (1813), ed. J. Kinsley (Oxford, 1989), p. 316.
[96] I. Green, Dean of Lincoln, to the Duke of Newcastle, 29 Jan. 1761, Newcastle Papers, BL Add. MS 32,918, f. 126.
[97] 'Persons thought of for Lewes', 29 Jan. 1763, Newcastle Papers, BL Add. MS 32,946, f. 244.
[98] Mr Hurdis to Mr Michelle, 13 Feb. 1763, *ibid.*, f. 396, introducing Mr Plumer. In this case, too, the conventional formula was also useful for averting unwanted elaboration, for this was a superimposed candidate, brought from afar. See also, for example, how the supporters of Sir John Trevelyan introduced him in an election contest as 'an Englishman of an antient and most respectable family, possessed of a large permanent estate'. Charles

The concept of the lineage-family has, then, a crucial role in establishing the social profile of characters – real and fictional – and positioning them in relation to other characters. Related to this is the role of the concept of the lineage-family in the social dynamics of the plot. Let us first examine the case of *The History of Miss Betsy Thoughtless*, and then turn to the more complex case of *Pamela*.

In *The History of Miss Betsy Thoughtless*, the concept of the lineage-family is invoked at some significant moments in the plot, setting the social situation and even anticipating further developments. For instance, as seen above, the initial positioning of Betsy and Mr Trueworth in terms of their 'families' is essential for the dynamics of the plot. It not only places the hero and heroine within a social landscape, but also sets a chain of expectations, for marriage to a gentleman of 'ancient family and estate' such as Mr Trueworth is an advantageous prospect to a young lady of 'good family' such as Betsy. Thus, as this courtship proceeds, other characters also reflect on the merit of this alliance, while considering Betsy and Trueworth's 'families'. But unfortunately, the thoughtless Betsy risks her reputation to the degree that she not only loses Trueworth, but is also pushed to the point that she has to marry any available suitor with the basic qualifications, namely, '*any man that was of a good family and had an estate*'.[99] That man happens to be Mr Munden. At this stage, considerations of Trueworth's 'family, estate, person, and accomplishment' serve to highlight Betsy's loss, and anticipate her future unhappiness. Note the formulaic presentation of the social profile of this lost lover.

[S]he now wondered at herself for having been so blind to the merits of Mr Trueworth's *family*, estate, person, and accomplishments; and accused herself, with the utmost severity, for having rejected what, she could not but confess, would have been highly for her interest, honour, and happiness, to have accepted.[100]

Additionally, in *The History of Miss Betsy Thoughtless* the concept of the lineage-family also appears in the context of encounter and contest. In the following case, for example, we see a comic encounter, which raises nonetheless some serious and contested issues. When a London alderman (aptly named Alderman Saving) discovers that his son has been corresponding with Betsy, he immediately interferes to break up their

Jenkins, Secretary to the Treasury, submitted to Grenville a letter in which John Henniker, a big London merchant was introduced as '[a] friend of mine, a merchant and a man of fortune and character, and a friend to Government – is desirous to represent Fowey', quoted in L. B. Namier, *The Structure of Politics at the Accession of George III* (London, 1957; 1st edn 1929), pp. 98, 320.
[99] *Betsy Thoughtless*, p. 383.   [100] *Ibid.*, p. 441.

relationship. Betsy's guardian, offended by this treatment of his ward, protests that she is 'of a *good family*'.[101] At this point the alderman rebuffs him with the following words: 'A good family! – Very pleasant, i'faith. Will a good family go to market? Will it buy a joint of mutton at the butcher's, or a pretty gown at the mercer's?'[102] This encounter between the City merchant and the retired West End tradesman highlights the urban milieu in which *The History of Miss Betsy Thoughtless* is set, with active and recently retired tradesmen, alongside members of the landed gentry and even members of the nobility. In this mixed setting, there were indeed different and contesting ways of evaluating social prestige, including the importance of 'family'. But while the merchant's view is obviously presented in this scene as vulgar (in line with a more general negative depiction of tradesmen, as discussed above), it is significant that similar points of criticism about the uselessness of overly genteel wives were voiced by many early eighteenth-century moral critics.[103] The novel's ambiguous attitude to notions of gentility and rank is further evident in the fact that elsewhere in the text life at the fashionable West End, 'the other End of Town', is also criticised for its associations with immoral conduct. Eventually, the alderman's view is probably largely vindicated in the novel, for poor Betsy first has to redeem herself by becoming a useful wife.

If in *The History of Miss Betsy Thoughtless* considerations of lineage-family appear at key moments in the plot and provide materials for an occasional contest, in the case of *Pamela* they underlie the plot of the entire novel. In a nutshell, the basic premiss of *Pamela* is that Mr B., 'a man *of family*, and ample fortunes', 'not destitute of pride', eventually decides to marry his mother's waiting-maid.[104] Needless to say, this waiting-maid has no splendid lineage-family behind her. A pending question during a significant part of the novel is therefore how the compatibility of Mr B. and Pamela can be justified. Mr B.'s ancestry and fortune are to be weighed against Pamela's virtue, faith, prudence, modesty, as well as her great beauty and other accomplishments.

An added complication, however, is that in the course of *Pamela* the concept of the lineage-family is also contested. Despite her general deferential conduct and attention to etiquette, Pamela proves her exemplary virtue not least by showing little regard for notions of lineage and ancestry. For example, after describing the neighbourhood's gentry in a letter

---

[101] *Ibid.*, p. 27.   [102] *Ibid.*, p. 28.
[103] See Tadmor, 'In the even my wife read to me', and references there to Defoe, Addison, etc. See also Mr B.'s speech against useless and spoiled ladies of birth and fortune, 'well read in nothing, perhaps, but Romances', *Pamela*, ed. Sabor, p. 463.
[104] *Ibid.*, p. 297.

to her parents, she criticises explicitly the idea that *'family and birth'* should be taken as a source of pride and prestige. 'But don't you wonder to find *me* scribble so much about *family* and *birth*?' she asks her parents. She then assures them that even if she had reason to boast of her own 'family', she would little value herself upon it, for 'VIRTUE *is the only nobility*.'[105] After Pamela ascends the social ladder and becomes betrothed to Mr B., she still questions the justification of *'pride of family'*. Invoking the temporal scope of the concept of the lineage-family, for instance, she wonders whether poor families, who have not kept records of their ancestry for hundreds of years, might not be as 'deeply rooted' as the great families of the gentry and the nobility.[106]

Contested notions of lineage and ancestry are also evident in the fact that when other characters in the novel slight Pamela for her lack of 'family', they actually place themselves in a negative light. Thus, for example, the neighbour Sir Simon Darnford dismisses Pamela's appeal for protection in his house, saying: 'Why, what is all this, my dear, but that our neighbour has a mind to his mother's waiting-maid! . . . He hurts no *family* by this.'[107] But in doing so he only highlights his own sinfulness and poor judgement. In another episode Mr B.'s proud sister reproaches Pamela for *'setting up for a family'*. She even anticipates that as Mrs B. Pamela will 'occasion a search at the Herald's Office', in an attempt to append a lineage to her 'wretched obscurity'.[108] From the point of view of the verbal usage, we can see that the sister invokes here the concept of the lineage-family in its typical historical and national scope. The effect of her tirade, however, is not to glorify notions of lineage and ancestry but to expose her own proud and violent temper, and thus to cast doubt on any claims to honourable birth that are not also backed by honourable conduct.

Thus, although Pamela proves her virtue by her lack of regard to notions of lineage and ancestry, eventually she receives her reward by being integrated into the illustrious B. family as Mr B.'s wife, and the mother of the future heir. Indeed, it is her lack of a lineage-family that allows her to become totally integrated into the B. family. On the two occasions that Betsy marries, her husbands are expected to mix with the Thoughtless network of relations and 'friends'. When trouble arises, members of this network intervene to mediate between the husband and wife. It is precisely this sort of intervention that Mr B. seeks to avoid by

---

[105] *Ibid.*, p. 83. Italics in the original. The passage is absent from the first edition.

[106] *Ibid.*, pp. 294–5. She further raises the possibility that in the course of the years some of these great families will be reduced to 'the dung-hills', while others, presently denounced as 'upstart families', will revel in their estates.

[107] *Ibid.*, p. 172. The italics in *'family'* appear in the later edition, and are absent from the first, *Pamela*, ed. Eaves and Kimpel, p. 122.   [108] *Pamela*, ed. Sabor, p. 419.

marrying a grateful servant, not a woman 'of family'. When Mr B. justifies his marriage to a woman of low birth, he explains that whereas a woman who marries beneath her demeans herself, a man who marries his social inferior only raises her to his own ranks, for a wife always joins her husband's line. He mentions as an example 'the royal family of Stuart', which allied itself into the comparatively 'low family of Hyde'.[109] Furthermore, he states that his marrying a malleable young woman with no claims to '*birth and fortune*' increases his chances for matrimonial happiness.[110] His depiction of marital discord at the upper rungs of the social ladder, in those cases where both husband and wife have been spoiled by the advantages of their high rank, brings to mind Hogarth's 'Marriage A-la-Mode', and indeed also the fate of Betsy Thoughtless in her first marriage to Mr Munden.

Thus, in both *Pamela* and *The History of Miss Betsy Thoughtless* the concept of the lineage-family plays an important role in the social configuration of characters, in placing them in relation to other characters, and in the dynamics of the plot. The use of formulaic phrases, which can also be traced beyond the literary context further emphasises the social impact of statements about 'family'. As we saw, however, the concept of the lineage-family could also be contested. In the case of *Pamela*, opposition mounted in the name of virtue was particularly forceful. But, whether contested or endorsed, it is possible to say by now that the concept of the lineage-family was clearly a part of the social and cultural vocabulary of people in eighteenth-century England. When people in the eighteenth century referred to themselves, or to other people, as being 'of family', they not only understood what they were talking about, but they could also understand the significance of their words within a broader and shared world of social and cultural concepts.

Conclusion

From the quantitative standpoint, references to the concept of the lineage-family were not always significant. The novels provided us with a rich source, but if the diary of Thomas Turner still contained a reasonable sample of relevant usages, Richardson's treatise had only one or two and Haywood's had none. However despite the occasional paucity of usages, mostly context-dependent, it is clear that the concept of the lineage-family provided eighteenth-century writers with a very significant frame of reference. A middling and provincial eighteenth-century man such as Turner did not use this concept in his daily life to describe either his own

---

[109] *Ibid.*, p. 441.   [110] *Ibid.*, pp. 463-4.

family, or notions of lineage and ancestry among his near neighbours and friends. Nonetheless, the concept of the lineage-family was significant in his understanding of his country, its geography, its history, and its national rule. It also informed his perceptions of the local aristocratic family, the Pelham family, and its nearby country seat. Finally, at crucial points in his life, Turner also envisaged his own origins and progeny in terms of lineage and ancestry.

Tracing references to the concept of the lineage-family from Turner's diary to other texts, we detected many similarities. Characteristic features – such as a long-term but imprecise temporal scope, a broad social and national scope, general notions of honour, and the importance of property and the family name – were all traced through different texts. Comparative examples drawn from personal and literary sources beyond our principal texts highlighted further the broad currency of this concept. Furthermore, it became clear that in many cases references to the concept of the lineage-family were shaped by public discourse and coined in formulaic usages, thus highlighting their currency within our eighteenth-century 'language community'. In the context of the novels, this concept also served as a fundamental building block in the construction of characters and plots.

Throughout this chapter, however, we also saw that the concept of the lineage-family was invoked while contesting the value or the power of lineage and ancestry. Thomas Turner, for example, referred to the Pelham family as a lineage-family while criticising its conduct and contesting its parochial policy. The urban setting of *The Apprentice's Vade Mecum* brought to light well-known tensions between notions of lineage and ancestry, and trade. In a novel such as *Pamela*, the concept of the lineage-family was placed in opposition to notions of virtue. From the methodological point of view, such contested usages raise once more an important point.[111] The fact that the word 'family' was used so conventionally to refer to notions of ancestry and lineage does not necessarily imply that these notions were always embraced. Indeed, people could clearly speak about such notions in ways that tested them, contested them, or, indeed, negated them. The important point is that whether affirmed or negated, notions of lineage and ancestry were still conveyed with the aid of conventional language usages, which attest to the general currency of the concept of the lineage-family in eighteenth-century society and culture.

Thus, we can see that for many people in eighteenth-century England the concept of the lineage-family was very significant. It formed a part of a

[111] See also above, ch. 1, pp. 42–3.

general frame of reference, with strong national overtones. But it also seems that on many occasions the concept of the lineage-family was related to notions of social distance. People used this concept not simply to describe situations, or express agreement, but also to voice criticism and engage in conflict.

4   The language of kinship

The kinship-family

Having reached this point we are faced with the question of kinship. If people in seventeenth- and eighteenth-century England could understand relations with non-kin in familial terms, and if within families kin and non-kin could be contractually bound, yet if at the same time notions of lineage were also valued – how in view of all this did people perceive relations with kin? And how can their language help us to probe further concepts of family and kinship current in seventeenth- and eighteenth-century England?

Starting from our main keyword so far, we can see that the word 'family' was also used in the eighteenth century to refer to circles of kin both within and beyond households. To present-day English speakers, this concept of the kinship-family seems obvious. This is the main usage of the word today, and English speakers have no difficulty in identifying it when it also appears in texts from the past. For instance, when present-day readers find in an eighteenth-century novel, such as *The History of Miss Betsy Thoughtless*, that Betsy thanks another character for his goodness to her and 'all our family', they can easily understand that this single and childless heroine is referring to her near kin, members of her nuclear family of origin.[1] Similarly, when we read in Thomas Turner's diary that he refused to draft a will for one of his neighbours, Mr Piper, for fear that because of his inadequate legal knowledge he might 'bring Trouble into the *family*', we can guess that he was referring to Piper's wife and children, for whom Piper intended to provide under the rule of primogeniture, as well as to Piper's brother, who may have still resented the fact that the old and childless Mr Piper had decided, less than a year after his wife's death, to marry his young household servant.[2] The historically oriented and

---

[1] Haywood, *Betsy Thoughtless*, p. 248. On this occasion, when Betsy thanks her guardian, Mr Goodman, she is in fact living in his house as a member of his 'family'. But if her familial position in her guardian's house is a matter that requires some historical explanation, we have no difficulty in identifying Betsy's near kin as her 'family'.
[2] See Thomas Turner, Diary, 20 Apr. 1761, and William Piper's will, ESRO, Lewes

often counter-intuitive understanding, which we employed in order to understand the concept of the household-family, is not necessary for understanding usages such as these.

When we examine other eighteenth-century sources we can find many similar usages. As their meanings seem obvious, a small number of examples can demonstrate the point. When one Anne Cooper complained before a local Justice of the Peace that her husband had deserted her, 'leaving her & her *family* to perish', we can readily understand that she was referring to herself and '3 small Children', whom she had indeed mentioned to the JP.[3] 'I shall now live solely for *my family*', declares Marianne Dashwood in Jane Austen's *Sense and Sensibility*, published in 1811. Her following words explain the meaning of 'family' in this case, for Marianne asserts that her mother and two sisters 'must henceforth be all the world to me'.[4] In a similar manner the Mayor and Alderman of Nottingham wrote a letter to Lady Howe desiring her 'to chuse *one of her family*' to stand as a candidate in an election campaign: the family member that she chose was her son.[5] James Oakes, of Bury St Edmunds used the word 'family' to refer to a broader group of relations by blood and marriage. On one occasion, for example, he described '*The whole Family*' who dined together. This family circle probably included a sister and brother-in-law, father-in-law, and two of his wife's uncles and their children who came for a family visit.[6]

People in the eighteenth century were also able to use the word 'family' to single out circles of kin within households, thus drawing boundaries

Archdeaconry Wills Register W/A6o ff. 352–5. Turner noted in his diary that he agreed to undertake the role of guardian and trustee of Piper's children, together with the village rector Mr Porter, for Mr Piper on his death bed 'could not prevail on anyone else'. William's brother is not mentioned in this context. In William Piper's will, however, his 'loving Brother' John Piper is named as executor and administrator together with Thomas Turner and the Rev. Thomas Porter. The three were to manage Piper's estate in trust, and provide the widow with her annuity of twelve pounds. They were to make special arrangements in case the estate proved inadequate for this provision. Later they were to dispose of the property, transferring the bulk of the estate to William's elder son. William's widow, Mary, was promised only meagre provision for her old age.

3 R. Paley (ed.), *Justice in Eighteenth-Century Hackney: The Justicing Notebook of Henry Norris and the Hackney Petty Session Book* (London, 1991), case 191, p. 25. See also case 582, and reference there, p. 100; case 602, p. 103; a warrant signed to apprehend Solomon Price for leaving 'his family charge to the parish'.

4 Austen, *Sense and Sensibility*, p. 338. Similarly, when Mr Collins, one of Austen's characters in *Pride and Prejudice*, goes to visit Mr and Mrs Bennet and their daughters, he is described as being received 'with great politeness by *the whole family*': Mr and Mrs Bennet and their daughters. In an earlier exchange, Mr Bennet announces his arrival to his wife saying 'I have a reason to expect an addition to our *family party*.' See Austen, *Pride and Prejudice*, pp. 53, 57.

5 Quoted in Namier, *The Structure of Politics*, p. 94.

6 J. Oakes, *The Oakes Diaries: Business, Politics and the Family in Bury St. Edmunds, 1778–1827*, ed. J. Fiske, 2 vols. (Woodbridge, 1990–1), vol. I, 6 Aug. 1781, p. 219.

between related members of 'families' and other household dependants. We have noted this usage in the first chapter in the context of the analysis of Thomas Turner's diary, and we can find it in many other sources. If we return to James Oakes's diary, for example, we can see that he also referred to servants as 'family' members.[7] Like Turner, he also made references to his 'Family at home' which included a changing composition of family members, and which continued after his wife's death, when he remained a single male householder.[8] But while such references to the 'family' may have included related and non-related persons, they may have also been aimed in particular at circles of co-resident kin. For example, when Oakes noted in his diary 'Family at home alone', he may have been referring in particular to the presence of co-resident kin in the house with no additional company.[9] Similarly, when he described how one Miss Moyle dined and drank tea with 'my Family', or how he went together with his 'Family' to 'Tea & Supper', he was probably referring not to his complete household, including its servants, but to circles of kin, those whom we would probably also identify as the 'family' within the household.[10]

The correspondence between some eighteenth-century and present-day references to the kinship-family may lead us to think that the kinship concept of the family was largely the same then as now. This conclusion would be justified if it were not for two additional complications. First, usages could shade into each other and even apparently obvious usages could be less transparent than they appear at first sight. Take, for example, the examination of the wheelwright John Simmons of Holt in 1817, which records that he was 'born in the parish of Briston of lawful

[7] For instance, when he noted supplying four bottles of beer to his 'family' during Christmas, he was clearly referring to the household servants: *ibid.*, vol. I, 25 Dec. 1796, p. 340. See also 'hav[in]g 3 Servt more in [the] Family': *ibid.*, vol. I, 22 Sept. 1787, p. 248. 'All the Family black silk Gloves' was probably a reference to the gloves received by his servants at his wife's funeral: *ibid.*, vol. II, 2 Dec. 1802, p. 33. In a similar manner, he also spoke broadly about other 'families' as units of household management. For instance, during a grain shortage, Oakes noted the measures for reducing the grain consumption in his town, namely, that 'every Family should abate 1/3 of their usual Consumption': *ibid.*, vol. I, 14 Dec. 1795, p. 319. See also the editor's comment that 'when James Oakes referred to his family, the term included his servants': *ibid.*, vol. I, p. 167.
[8] There are many such references in the diary. See, for example, 5, 19, 25, Sept., 5–6 Oct. 1798: *ibid.*, vol. I, pp. 368–9, or the following references to the 'family' after the death of Oakes's wife's, which also included kin such as a sister, nieces, and nephew: *ibid.*, vol. II, 12, 18 Mar. 1803, p. 37; 6 July 1803, p. 41; 22 July 1803, p. 42; 21, 25 Nov. 1803, p. 49.
[9] See, for example, *ibid.*, vol. I, 25 July 1793, p. 228; 16 Mar. 1797, p. 344; 5 May 1797, p. 347.
[10] See, for example, *ibid.*, vol. I, 1 Apr. 1790, p. 263; 15 June 1787, p. 248; see also, e.g., 23 Nov. 1795, p. 318; 19 Oct. 1798, p. 369. Note, however, that references such as these can be inconclusive, as it may be that some 'family' groups referred to in the diary on such occasions included some servants, or a governess accompanying children.

parents . . . *with whom he resided as part of their family* until he was nearly 14 years old, when he was bound apprentice by a regular indenture'.[11] If this usage contains a recognition of Simmons's 'family' as a kinship group, it also contains a recognition of it as a household unit, and an implicit understanding that it was possible to live in other 'families'. In a similar way, Turner's record that when he visited 'his mother's' he was 'received very coldly' not only by her but by *'all the Family'* can be read as a reference to his near kin who lived in the house.[12] But at the same time, one might take account of the fact that Mrs Turner's 'family' was a complex domestic and occupational unit, consisting of various relations, step-relations, and non-related residents which also changed over time. Turner's other references to this 'family', as we saw, are shot through with significant notions of household possession and management. This particular usage, then, might also be more complex than it first appears. The same applies to references that invoke both the concept of the kinship-family and notions of lineage. We can imagine that when Sir John Rushton, MP, wrote to the Duke of Newcastle: 'my whole ambition centres in the hopes of a peerage for *my family'*, he was referring both to himself and to his kin, who would have enjoyed the promotion, as well as to his lineage and all it stood for, that he wished to ennoble.[13] This usage, therefore, may have also been richer than it first appears.

The second reason why references to the kinship-family may be more complex than they initially seem is that, alongside the apparently transparent usages, our texts include many references to kin that are not at all self-evident and that clearly require a historical explanation. Such, for example, are the usages of kinship terms current in the eighteenth-century such as 'relations', 'connexions', or even 'friends'. Terms such as 'kinsman' and 'cousin' also had significant usages that tell us much about perceptions of kinship in eighteenth-century society and culture. Indeed, as we shall see, even apparently self-evident terms such as 'brother', 'son', or 'mother' had a range of historical meanings, as well as conventional usages that require observation and elucidation.

It is time, then, to turn to the study of historical usages of the language of kinship. In order to prepare the ground, however, let us first place the language of kinship within the broader context of scholarly debates on the

---

[11] J. Hales, *'On The Parish': Recorded Lives of the Poor of Holt and District, 1780–1835*, ed. S. Yaxley (Dereham, 1994), p. 29. See also the examination of the cordwainer Richard Fuller from 1795, declaring that 'he was born of lawful parents' and 'resided as part of their family until he was about 11 years of age', when he entered service for the first time: *ibid.*, pp. 25–6.

[12] Thomas Turner, Diary, 22 Feb. 1756. Indeed, in the same context Turner continues to complain about his 'friends'.

[13] Quoted in Namier, *The Structure of Politics*, p. 13.

history of kinship in the early modern period. The subsequent sections will then proceed to offer a new model for understanding the language of kinship in seventeenth- and eighteenth-century England.

The historiography and the language of kinship

Until about the 1960s, there seems to have been a broad understanding about the general trajectory of English kinship: as the modern nuclear family arose, extended kinship ties became less significant. This narrative can probably be traced back to a set of developmental assumptions current in nineteenth- and early twentieth-century social thought.[14] By the 1960s it had been further buttressed by accounts drawn from the modern social sciences that emphasised the close fit between the nuclear family and conditions of modernity.[15] Since the 1960s and 1970s,

[14] See Wrightson's discussion of this 'old master narrative' in 'The family in early modern England', esp. pp. 2–10. See also Anderson, 'What is new about the modern family?', esp. pp. 67–73; Hareven, *Family Time and Industrial Time*, pp. 1–3; Hareven, 'The history of the family and the complexity of social change', esp. pp. 95–6. The details vary greatly, as do the interpretative emphases of different thinkers. The history of the Western family, however, has been set by influential thinkers within the broad context of developmental changes from tribes and clans to the nuclear family, from status to contract, from feudalism to capitalism, or from *Gemeinschaft* to *Gesellschaft*: see, for example, H. S. Maine, *Ancient Law: Its Connection with the Early History of Society and Its Relation to Modern Ideas* (London, 1905; 1st edn 1861); F. Engels, *The Origin of the Family, Private Property and the State*, Introduction by M. Barrett (Harmondsworth, 1985; 1st edn 1884); F. Toennies, *Fundamental Concepts of Sociology (Gemeinschaft und Gesellschaft)*, trans. and supplemented C. P. Loomis, *American Sociology Series* (1904; 1st edn 1887); E. Durkheim, 'Review on Ferdinand Toennies, *Gemeinschaft und Gesellschaft*', in E. Durkheim, *On Institutional Analysis*, trans. and ed. M. Traugott (Chicago and London, 1978), pp. 115–22 (originally published in *Revue philosophique* 27 (1889), 416–22), and Durkheim, 'The conjugal family', in *ibid.* (originally published in *Revue philosophique* 90 (1920), 1–14), and esp. pp. 229, 238–9.
[15] See, for example, Parsons, 'The kinship system of the contemporary United States'; Parsons, 'The social structure of the family'; Parsons and Bales, *Family, Socialization and Interaction Process*; Goode, *World Revolution and Family Patterns*, esp. chs. 1 and 2; Ogburn, 'Social change and the family', pp. 58–63; Goode, 'The role of the family and industrialization', pp. 64–70, and see also and compare Winch and Blumberg, 'Social complexity and familial organization', pp. 70–92, and references there. See also Hareven, 'The history of the family and the complexity of social change'; Wrightson, 'The family in early modern England', esp. pp. 2–3. It is important to note that the nuclear family has also been studied as a universal human grouping either as the sole prevailing form of the family or as the basic unit from which more complex familial forms are compounded, and that the necessary correlation between it and industrial growth has been questioned: e.g. Murdock, *Social Structure*, esp. p. 2; Greenfield, 'Industrialization and the family in sociological theory'. Macfarlane, for example, agrees that 'there is no necessary correlation between the predominance of the nuclear family and industrial growth'. He also explains that in 'peasant societies' the joint residential unit is often more of an ideal than an actuality. But he also argues that a special association exists between the nuclear family and modernity: a kinship system that highlights the individual and the nuclear family is 'particularly well adapted to an industrial and individualistic system' and indeed

however, this narrative has been challenged by new research. Some structural features were identified that seemed to indicate that the English kinship system in the early modern period was by and large flexible and loose, often limited in its extent and shallow in its genealogical depth, and highly focused on the nuclear family. Contrary to the myth of the extended family of old, it now appeared that only a minority of households in studied localities contained extended family households, populated with various kin.[16] Nor did this appear to be a sedentary 'traditional society': population turnover could be surprisingly high and geographical mobility could reduce the density of kin within single parishes.[17] Labour was thus hired usually from ser-

facilitated England's precocious economic and social development in the eighteenth and nineteenth centuries: Macfarlane, *The Family Life of Ralph Josselin*, p. 159, and n. 4; Macfarlane, 'The myth of the peasantry', pp. 344–5, and see also n. 38; Macfarlane, *Individualism*, and specifically pp. 146, 201.

[16] See P. Laslett and J. Harrison, 'Clayworth and Cogenhoe', in H. E. Bell and R. L. Ollard (eds.), *Historical Essays, 1600–1750, Presented to David Ogg* (London, 1963), pp. 157–84; Laslett, *The World We Have Lost*; P. Laslett, 'Size and structure of the household in England over three centuries', *Population Studies* 23 (1969), 199–223; Laslett and Wall (eds.), *Household and Family in Past Time*, esp. 'Introduction', and pp. 125–58. For variations as a result of industrialisation, see Anderson, *Family Structure in Nineteenth Century Lancashire*; Nair, *Highley*, pp. 113–14, 201–5, 255. For regional and temporal variations, see R. Wall, 'Regional and temporal variations in English household structure from 1650', in J. Hobcraft and P. Rees (eds.), *Regional Aspects of British Population Growth* (London, 1979), pp. 89–113, esp. p. 103; P. Laslett, 'Characteristics of the Western family considered over time', *Journal of Family History* 2 (1977), 89–115, reprinted in Laslett, *Family Life and Illicit Love*, esp. table 1.2, pp. 22–3; Laslett, 'Mean household size in England', esp. p. 154. Compare different evidence from wills: M. Spufford, *Contrasting Communities: English Villagers in the Sixteenth and Seventeenth Centuries* (Cambridge, 1974), pp. 114–15.

[17] Young men and women left their village to work as servants and apprentices or to marry, families of labourers came and went in search of work, and even thriving farmers could move in quest of new opportunities: see Laslett and Harrison, 'Clayworth and Cogenhoe'. See also P. Clark, 'Migration in England during the late seventeenth and early eighteenth centuries', *P&P* 83 (1979), 57–90; Kussmaul, *Servants in Husbandry*; D. Souden, 'Movers and stayers in family reconstitution populations', *Local Population Studies* 33 (1984), 11–28; R. M. Smith, 'Some issues concerning families and their property', in R. M. Smith (ed.), *Land, Kinship and Life-Cycle* (Cambridge, 1984), esp. pp. 57–8. There were, of course, significant local variations and much depended on the availability of economic opportunities. However the effects of population turnover on kinship density are noted in a number of local studies. In Terling, Essex, in 1671 less than half of the 122 householders were even distantly related to other householders, and most of those related to other householders were related to only a single household in the village. This kinship density was lower than in the village of Gosforth in the 1950s, and much weaker than in a sample of three eighteenth-century French villages. In Whickham in 1666 only 13.6 per cent of households were related to others in the parish. Data from a London suburb between 1620 and 1626 reveal that 18 per cent of households were related to others. In both the parishes of Myddle and Highley in Shropshire, kinship networks were denser and more stable than in Terling, and the population turnover lower. Stability was greatest in Myddle. In Highley, kinship networks were more extended in 1550 to 1620 than in 1620 to 1780, and in the latter period they were similar to Terling's 1671

vants and labourers, who tended to be non-kin.[18] Debt and credit relations certainly existed among kin, but more so among friends and neighbours.[19] Property was usually left to near kin.[20] Even the poor relief system was structured by the Tudor Poor Laws not on the principle of

level. By 1851, however, hardly any heads of households were related to any others, and only 30 per cent were born in the parish. In Limpsfield, Surrey, in 1851, for example, 30 per cent of households were related to others: Wrightson and Levine, *Poverty and Piety*, pp. 82–91; Wrightson, 'Kinship in an English village', pp. 315–23; Levine and Wrightson, *Whickham*, p. 333; Hey, *An English Rural Community*, pp. 203–4, 207–9; Nair, *Highley*, pp. 65–8, 154–5, 253, and see also K. Wrightson, 'Postscript: Terling revisited', in Wrightson and Levine, *Poverty and Piety*, p. 190, and further discussion pp. 189–92; Boulton, *Neighbourhood and Society*, pp. 250–3; E. Lord, 'Communities of common interest: the social landscape of south east Surrey, 1750–1850', in Phythian-Adams (ed.), *Societies, Cultures and Kinship*, pp. 165–7, and further examples there. See also Reay, 'Kinship and neighbourhood in nineteenth-century rural England'.

[18] See, for example, Laslett, 'Clayworth and Cogenhoe'; Laslett, *The World We Have Lost*; Schofield, 'Age-specific mobility'; Wall, 'The age at leaving home'; Kussmaul, *Servants in Husbandry*; Brodsky Elliot, 'Single women in the London marriage market'; Houlbrooke, *The English Family*, pp. 25, 46; Wrightson, *English Society*, pp. 42–4; M. K. McIntosh, 'Servants and the household unit in an Elizabethan English community', *Journal of Family History* 9 (1984), 3–23; P. Clark, 'Migrants in the city: the process of social adaptation in English towns', in P. Clark and D. Souden (eds.), *Migration and Society in Early Modern England* (London, 1987), esp. pp. 271–3; Rappaport, *Worlds Within Worlds*; Ben-Amos, *Adolescence and Youth*, esp. pp. 165–70. The implications of this pattern are conceptualised in Laslett, 'Characteristics of the Western family considered over time', in Laslett, *Family Life and Illicit Love*, pp. 12–49; Macfarlane, *The Family Life of Ralph Josselin*, pp. 205–10; Macfarlane, *Individualism*, pp. 147–50; Macfarlane, *Marriage and Love in England*, e.g. pp. 83–8. See also the discussion above, ch. 1, p. 35, and ch 2, pp. 57–9.

[19] In Highley, for example, between 1550 and 1619, 89 per cent of debt transactions were with non-kin, of which 30 per cent were with neighbours, whereas only 11 per cent were with kin: Nair, *Highley*, p. 69. Macfarlane shows that only one tenth of the property acquired by the seventeenth-century Essex clergyman Ralph Josselin came from kin, and only one tenth of his money transactions were with kin: the rest were with friends and neighbours: Macfarlane, *Family Life of Ralph Josselin*, p. 149. See also B. A. Holderness, 'Credit in English rural society before the nineteenth century, with special reference to the period 1650–1720', *Agricultural History Review* 24 (1976), 97–109; Wrightson and Levine, *Poverty and Piety*, pp. 100–1; Spufford, *Contrasting Communities*, pp. 212–13. Mitson, 'The significance of kinship networks', pp. 62–70. See also Muldrew's comprehensive study of debt and credit relations, *The Economy of Obligation*, and esp. pp. 95–172.

[20] The range of kin recognised in wills was most often narrow. Single or childless people were most likely to seek more distant kin such as nephews and nieces and leave their property to them, and women's wills recognised a wider circle of kin then men's. Primogeniture existed in both law and custom but it was also constantly checked by the desire of parents to provide for all their children. See, for example, Wrightson, 'Kinship in an English village', pp. 323–9, and specifically pp. 323–4; Wrightson and Levine, *Poverty and Piety*, pp. 91–9, and specifically p. 92; R. T. Vann, 'Wills and the family in an English town: Banbury, 1550–1800', *Journal of Family History* 4 (1979), 346–67; C. Howell, 'Peasant inheritance customs in the Midlands, 1280–1700', in Goody, Thirsk, and Thompson (eds.), *Family and Inheritance*, pp. 112–55, esp. p. 141; Howell, *Land, Family and Inheritance in Transition*, pp. 255–7. See similar practices in the medieval period: Smith, 'Some issues concerning families and their property', pp. 56–8. For a discussion of kinship recognition in wills, see also Cressy, 'Kinship and kin interaction', esp. 53–65; Wrightson, 'Postscript', in Wrightson and Levine, *Poverty and Piety*, esp.

kinship support, but on parochial support.[21] Finally, and most significantly for the argument of this book, influential observations were made
about the structure of the English kinship system which were also used to
support the new hypothesis that extended kinship ties in early modern
England were largely circumscribed. Specifically, scholars argued, the
very patterns of kinship terminology and recognition both reflected and
promoted a social structure focused strongly on the nuclear family, with
only a narrow range of largely loose and flexible kinship ties beyond it.[22]

pp. 192–4. For a decline in kinship recognition in wills, see Vann, 'Wills and the family in
an English town', esp. pp. 363–7, and Nair, *Highley*, pp. 67–8, 155–8. For female legatees,
see Erickson, *Women and Property*, esp. pp. 86, 212–16, and references there. The
moderation of primogeniture is also emphasised, e.g. in Spufford, *Contrasting Communities*, pp. 85–7, 104–11, 159–61; Houlbrooke, *The English Family*, pp. 19, 41; L. Pollock,
'Younger sons in Tudor and Stuart England', *History Today* 39 (1989), 23–9. The
significance of primogeniture among the elite is a contested matter, especially in relation
to strict settlement: see also my discussion in Tadmor, 'Dimensions of inequality among
siblings in eighteenth-century English novels', 311–12, and references there.
[21] The Poor Relief Act of 1601 obliged grandparents, parents, and children to support one
another, and consequently there were cases of grandparents being forced to take in
grandchildren, or children being forced to contribute to their parents' maintenance; but
these people were very often not in a position to give much assistance and the obligation to
support them thus fell on the parish. Parish officers, who were wary of increasing the
number of the poor in their parishes, could also prevent people from taking in needy kin. P.
Slack, *Poverty and Policy in Tudor and Stuart England* (London and New York, 1988), esp.
pp. 84–5. See also, for example, P. Laslett, 'The family and the collectivity', *Sociology and
Social Research* 63 (1979), 432–42; Wrightson, *English Society*, pp. 46–7; Goose, 'Household size and structure in early Stuart Cambridge'; R. M. Smith, 'The structured
dependence of the elderly as a recent development: some skeptical historical thoughts',
Ageing and Society 4 (1984), 409–28; Smith, 'Some issues concerning families and their
property', pp. 72–85; T. Wales, 'Poverty, poor relief and the life-cycle: some evidence from
seventeenth-century Norfolk', in Smith (ed.), *Land, Kinship and Life-Cycle*, pp. 351–404;
W. Newman Brown, 'The receipt of poor relief and the family situation: Aldenham
Hertfordshire, 1630–1690', in Smith (ed.), *Land, Kinship and Life-Cycle*, pp. 403–22.
[22] See especially Macfarlane, *Individualism*, esp. pp. 144–7, 196; Wrightson, 'Household
and kinship', 155; Wrightson, *English Society*, pp. 46–8; Houlbrooke, *The English Family*,
pp. 19, 40; Hanawalt, *The Ties That Bound*, pp. 79–80. See also Ralph Josselin's recognition of kin and his relationships with them, Macfarlane, *The Family Life of Ralph Josselin*,
pp. 158–60, and pp. 105–60 more broadly; C. Issa, 'Obligation and choice: aspects of
family and kinship in seventeenth-century County Durham', unpublished PhD dissertation (St Andrews, 1987). Note also Wrightson and Houlbrooke's broader discussions on
paternal descent, the uses of kinship, possible regional and occupational differences, and
the importance of extended kinship ties and notions of lineage and descent among the
elite. However '[d]ynastic sentiments and awareness of one's lineage', as Houlbrooke
explains, 'played little part in the lives of the great majority of the population'. 'There was
no well defined group of kinsmen larger than the elementary family to which most
individuals owed loyalty': Wrightson, 'Household and kinship', 155–7; Wrightson, *English Society*, pp. 44–51; Houlbrooke, *The English Family*, chs. 2–3 and quotations on p. 19.
As Hurwich explains, even those who could boast a lineage also had their own flexible
universe of kin, traced through both the paternal and maternal sides: J. Hurwich,
'Lineage and kin in the sixteenth-century aristocracy: some comparative evidence on
England and Germany', in A. L. Beier, D. Cannadine, and J. M. Rosenheim (eds.), *The
First Modern Society: Essays in English History in Honour of Lawrence Stone* (Cambridge,

The fact that these patterns were then identified from the sixteenth century to the present, and even in the medieval period, has lent further credence to the hypothesis that the English kinship system was also marked by continuity.[23] Admittedly, the study of kinship has attracted less interest than the study of the nuclear family and its relationships. In 1986 Cressy observed that English historians' remarks on kinship are still 'scattered, hesitant and relatively spare'.[24] In subsequent years important studies were produced but there was no major rise in the scholarly interest in the field.[25] At the same time, however, the chronological and conceptual frameworks of the history of early modern kinship were also contested. Not all scholars agreed that the early modern period was typified by an enduring focus on the nuclear family and largely attenuated kinship ties beyond it. Stone's monumental study *The Family, Sex and Marriage in England 1500–1800*, for example, presents the nuclear family not as a socially salient feature in early modern England, but rather charts its ascent at the expense of kinship and neighbourhood ties mainly from 1450 to 1630.[26] Chaytor's

1989), pp. 33–64; see also Goody, *The Development of the Family and Marriage*, pp. 232–9.

[23] For continuity, see Macfarlane, *Individualism*, and esp. e.g. pp. 144–7, and note also the discussion of change, p. 147; Wrightson, *English Society*, p. 46; Houlbrooke, *The English Family*, p. 40; Hanawalt, *The Ties That Bound*, pp. 79–80. Goody discusses changes and argues that standard and local terminologies existed side by side; however, he also argues that as a system or structure capable of being analysed in its own right 'the terminology has remained much the same since the Norman conquest': Goody, *The Development of the Family and Marriage*, pp. 262–78, and quotation on p. 277. On kinship in medieval times, see also Hanawalt, *The Ties That Bound*, esp. pp. 79–83; B. Phillpotts, *Kindred and Clan in the Middle Ages and After. A Study in the Sociology of the Teutonic Races* (Cambridge, 1913), pp. 205–63; L. Lancaster, 'Kinship in Anglo-Saxon society', *British Journal of Sociology* 9 (1958), 236–9; T. M. Charles-Edwards, 'Kinship, status, and the origins of the hide', *P&P* 56 (1972), 3–33. See also and compare the broad study of historical and overlapping usages in Goody, *The Development of the Family and Marriage*. On changes in medieval family and kinship ties, see Z. Razi, 'The myth of the immutable English family', *P&P* 140 (1993), 3–44.

[24] Cressy, 'Kinship and kin interaction', 38–9, and see the references there to similar earlier comments by Wrightson and Stone; see also Cressy, *Coming Over*, p. 274. Cressy's article contains many useful references to studies on kinship up to 1986.

[25] See, for example, Cressy, *Coming Over*; O'Hara, 'Ruled by my friends'; Phythian-Adams (ed.), *Societies, Cultures and Kinship*; Hunt, *The Middling Sort*; Levine and Wrightson, *Whickham*, esp. pp. 329–38; Wrightson, 'Postscript', in Wrightson and Levine, *Poverty and Piety*, pp. 187–97; Rollison, *The Local Origins of Modern Society*, chs. 4–5; Ben-Amos, *Adolescence and Youth*, pp. 165–70; Johnston, 'Family, kin and community'; Reay, 'Kinship and neighbourhood in nineteenth-century rural England'; Cressy, *Birth, Marriage and Death*; Grassby, 'Love, property and kinship'; Davidoff, Doolittle, Fink, and Holden, *The Family Story*, esp. chs. 1–2.

[26] Notions of lineage and 'allegiance by the kin' are said to have declined, as 'this traditional society' eroded due to major social, economic, and cultural changes, thus giving way to the rise of the nuclear family. 'Intensified affective bonding of the nuclear core at the expense of neighbours and kin' is seen as one of the hallmarks of this new family, fully established by 1750. However, the main decline of lineage is dated 1450 to 1630. The

investigation of late sixteenth- and early seventeenth-century households in the Tyneside village of Ryton revealed complex family households, filled with step-children and foster-children and assisted by various relatives. This led her to question 'the distinction between conjugal unit and wider kinship system'.[27] By 1986 Cressy challenged what he now identified as the 'new orthodoxy' concerning the weakness of the extended kinship ties in early modern England. While he agreed with the new emphasis on the primacy of the nuclear family and with the fact that testamentary evidence reveals a narrow range of kin, he also emphasised the importance of qualitative rather than quantitative evidence and highlighted interactions among extended kin.[28] In the following years studies by O'Hara, Mitson, Lord, and Grassby, for example, questioned aspects of the 'new orthodoxy' further.[29]

Some of these disagreements may have stemmed from the particular issues under discussion: while Laslett and Wall focus on the presence of kin within households and Wrightson and Levine examine the role of kinship ties in the social structure of parish communities, others emphasise their significance in broader neighbourhoods, interpersonal relations, business connections, etc.[30] Some of these disagreements may have concerned definitions. Relationships studied at times under the category of 'the nuclear family', as we shall later see, could be debated at other times under the rubric of 'the extended family' or 'kinship' – and vice versa.

period 1550 to 1700 is already marked by 'the restricted nuclear family' and 1640 to 1800 by the 'close domesticated nuclear family': Stone, *The Family, Sex and Marriage*, and specifically e.g. pp. 22, 28–9, 70. See also, for example, the major shifts in the role of parents and 'friends' in the choice of marriage partners from 1660 to 1800: Stone, *Road to Divorce*, p. 10. See also, for example, M. Slater, 'The weightiest business: marriage in an upper gentry family in seventeenth-century England', *P&P* 72 (1976), 25–54; S. H. Mendelson, 'Debate: the weightiest business', *P&P* 85 (1979), 126–35; rejoinder by M. Slater, pp. 136–40; Trumbach, *The Rise of the Egalitarian Family*.

27 Chaytor, 'Household and kinship in Ryton', pp. 25–60, and esp. p. 38; cf. Wrightson, 'Household and kinship', 151–8.

28 Cressy, 'Kinship and kin interaction', and specifically p. 44, and see also his criticism of Stone, *The Family, Sex and Marriage*, p. 40; cf. Wrightson, 'Postscript', in Wrightson and Levine, *Poverty and Piety*, esp. pp. 192–7. Cressy's subsequent major study showed dense and active kinship networks among settlers in seventeenth-century America, and between them and their relations in England: Cressy, *Coming Over*, esp. pp. 263–91.

29 O'Hara, 'Ruled by my friends'; Mitson, 'The significance of kinship networks', esp. p. 35; Lord, 'Communities of common interest', esp. pp. 162–4; Grassby, 'Love, property and kinship', 1. See also Reay, 'Kinship and neighbourhood in nineteenth-century rural England'; Davidoff, Doolittle, Fink, and Holden, *The Family Story*, pp. 31–3, 39, 86.

30 Wrightson's working hypothesis that 'kinship ties beyond those of the nuclear family were of limited significance in the social structure of village communities', Cressy's argument that the English kinship system was 'valuable, versatile and wide-ranging', or Mitson's suggestion that 'dynastic families' permeated regional neighbourhoods are not necessarily conflicting: Wrightson, *English Society*, p. 45; Cressy, 'Kinship and kin interaction', 53; Mitson, 'The significance of kinship networks', e.g. pp. 70–3.

As the dust settles on the old debates, it is possible to see that, while by and large many of the broad structural features delineated by pioneering historians hold, there is also evidence to suggest that kinship ties in seventeenth- and eighteenth-century England may have been richer, more complex, and altogether more significant than sometimes estimated. Take, for example, the question of kinship density at the level of individual parishes. Within single parishes, the absence of kin could indeed leave nuclear family households isolated.[31] But as scholars suggest, the dearth of kin at the level of parish communities may well have played an important role in patterns of short-distance and long-distance migration, so typical of early modern England, thus connecting a parish to its locality, to the capital, or even to overseas migration.[32] There is significant evidence to show that relationships among kin could be kept successfully within a radius of five, ten, or fifteen miles.[33] Networks of kin could even thrive within regional neighbourhoods, forming 'dynastic families'.[34] However kinship ties could evidently also be maintained in migration over longer distances – whether migration to towns,[35] or

[31] See the references above, n. 17. A particular case that also demonstrates this in the course of the life-cycle can be seen in Levine and Wrightson, *Whickham*, p. 337.

[32] Cressy, 'Kinship and kin interaction', 51; Wrightson, 'Postscript', in Wrightson and Levine, *Poverty and Piety*, p. 196, and also the points raised in pp. 194–7.

[33] For example, of all the kin mentioned in wills from Terling between 1550 and 1699, 24 per cent lived more than fifteen miles away from the village, 32 per cent more than ten miles away, and 44 per cent lived less than ten miles away from their kin in Terling: Wrightson, 'Kinship in an English Village', p. 326. Mitson's study of eleven parishes in south-west Nottinghamshire reveals similar short-distance kinship networks: members of these parishes were linked together in extended networks that formed 'dynastic families' and permeated through the neighbourhood: Mitson, 'The significance of kinship networks', pp. 24–76, and see also her reference to similar findings by Everitt and his definition of 'dynastic families', *ibid.*, pp. 25, 71, 73. Mary Carter's study of St Ives shows similar dense networks both within and around the town: M. Carter, 'Town or urban society? St Ives in Huntingdonshire, 1630–1740', in Phythian-Adams (ed.), *Societies, Cultures and Kinship*, pp. 127–30. See also Wrightson, 'Postscript', in Wrightson and Levine, *Poverty and Piety*, esp. pp. 194–7, and references there. Kinship networks are also evident in a larger urban setting. Boulton suggests that '[i]t seems possible . . . that a substantial minority of Boroughside households were involved in locally based kin networks', despite the low presence of kin within parish boundaries: Boulton, *Neighbourhood and Society*, p. 260.

[34] Mitson, 'The significance of kinship networks'. The case of Thomas Turner may also support this view. Although both he and his parents experienced geographical mobility, and were 'movers' in Souden's terms rather than 'stayers', they had links with a regional kinship network stretching over neighbouring towns and villages, and they were also integrated more broadly in the social fabric of the neighbourhood. See also below, chs. 5–6.

[35] 'Local ties may have been less common but more useful to a newcomer, at least initially': Boulton, *Neighbourhood and Society*, p. 259. Migrants to towns and cities thus came to live with their kin and benefited from their support: see e.g. P. Clark, 'The migrant in Kentish towns, 1500–1700', in P. Clark and P. Slack (eds.), *Crisis and Order in English Towns, 1500–1700* (London, 1972), pp. 135–9; Brodsky Elliot, 'Single women in the London

migration overseas,[36] and there were also processes of 'chain migration' in which kin followed in each others' footsteps to new locations.[37] Distance and separation could thus sever kinship ties, but they could also reshape them.[38] Relations living far away were not necessarily 'effectively lost'.[39] News by word of mouth, a letter, or a visit could mean a lot. Ralph Josselin noted with concern the news heard of his relations, many of whom he could not see regularly.[40] Thomas Turner and John Penrose took care to call on their relations when their journeys took them in their direction. If Turner complained about his uncle's hospitality and his cousin's meanness, Penrose felt free to treat himself to a supper at his cousin's house although she happened to be away.[41] 'I be verrie fond of

marriage market', pp. 93–5; Ben-Amos, *Adolescence and Youth*, pp. 166–70. Apprentices also corresponded with their parents and siblings: *ibid.*, p. 161. See also Anderson, *Family Structure in Nineteenth-Century Lancashire*, esp. pp. 152–61; Clark, 'Migrants in the city', pp. 271–3. Kinship ties were also important in channelling immigration from Ireland to Victorian London, or migration to late nineteenth- and early twentieth-century American cities: L. H. Lees, *Exiles of Erin: Irish Migrants in Victorian London* (Manchester, 1979); T. K. Hareven, 'The dynamics of kin in an industrial community', in J. Demos and S. S. Boocock (eds.), *Turning Points: Historical and Sociological Essays on the Family* (Chicago, 1978), pp. 151–82.

[36] Morgan, Cressy, and Thompson show how immigrants to America maintained their connections with relatives in England, and vice versa. In these cases, the claims of cousinage could extend very far and include people who had never met: E. S. Morgan, *The Puritan Family: Religion and Domestic Relations in Seventeenth-Century New England* (rev. edn, New York, 1966), pp. 150–60; Cressy, 'Kinship and kin interaction', 44–9; Cressy, *Coming Over*, pp. 263–91; R. Thompson, *Mobility and Migration: East Anglia Founders of New England, 1629–1640* (Amherst, Mass., 1994), esp. pp. 189–204; Wrightson, 'Postscript', in Wrightson and Levine, *Poverty and Piety*, p. 196, and references there.

[37] For example, of the eight youths who left the village of Shepshed, Leicestershire, to be apprenticed in the Brewer's Company in London, four were related either through marriage or blood, with relations ranging from brother, brother-in-law, and cousin. The remaining four were from the same parish: Brodsky Elliot, 'Mobility and marriage', pp. 209–10. 'Apprenticeship was kept in the family, so to speak', Brodsky Elliot concludes, *ibid.*, p. 213. See also studies by Anderson, Lees, Hareven, above, n. 35.

[38] See also Cressy, *Coming Over*, ch. 11.   [39] Wrightson, *English Society*, p. 45.

[40] See, for example, the following references from Ralph Josselin's diary: news on 'cousin Benton', Josselin, *Diary*, 1 Sept. 1644, p. 18; 6 Nov. 1646, p. 74; news delivered by 'Cosin John Hudson' of 'the welfare of my freinds', *ibid.*, 30 July 1653, p. 307; a letter from 'uncle Josselin' reporting on their welfare, *ibid.*, 30 Aug. 1653, p. 309; sad news of 'Cousin Hurril', *ibid.*, 12 July 1663, p. 499; 24 Jan. 1663/4, p. 504; 30 Jan. 1663, p. 505, etc. See also Cressy, 'Kinship and kin interaction', 42.

[41] 'Supper at Coz: Mason's tho' she is at Tiverton with a sick Uncle of her Husband', *Letters from Bath, 1766–67, by the Rev. John Penrose*, with an Introduction and Notes by B. Mitchell and H. Penrose (Gloucester, 1983), 12 June 1766, p. 160; see also 9 Apr. 1767, p. 163. The exact relationship between these cousins is unknown. Thomas Turner also called on his aunt on his way to or from Tunbridge Wells: e.g. Thomas Turner, *Diary*, 10 July, 14 Aug., 16 Aug. 1756. Turner complained about his uncle Hill's hospitality when he went to visit him, and was served 'a leg of very ordinary ewe mutton', a roasted pig 'with a rind as tough as any Cow Hide', and a sauce 'which looked like what is Vomited up by Sucking Children': *ibid.*, 17 Oct. 1756. From 26 to 29 Apr. 1764 he stayed with his cousin

Cousin Ned, and verrie pleased he can come avisiten us', said the farmer's wife Anne Hughes as she prepared for her cousin's visit.[42] Londoners such as Samuel Pepys and his father were visited by many kin and they even entertained 'cousins' whom they had never met.[43] For Parson Woodforde and his niece Nancy, the week-long visit of Nancy's brother Sam was the culmination of years of separation and longing.[44] Indeed, as Cressy has shown, migration over the Atlantic may have even had the effect of heightening the sense of membership in some extended families.[45]

In a similar way, kinship and service could also be mutually reinforcing, rather than structurally and practically conflicting institutions. Certainly, servants and apprentices were usually non-kin, but this does not mean that kinship was not important, or that kinship ties were weak. As Krausman Ben-Amos explains, when it came to apprenticeship of youths kinship ties were 'simply indispensable'. Kin were mobilised to assist in the selection of masters, to provide lodging to migrant youths they might never have met before, and they even risked themselves in signing bonds. They were entrusted with money, and if trouble arose between the youth and his master, they were called upon to help.[46] Far from severing kinship

Charles Hill. Turner had lent this cousin money and, according to his testimony, had always entertained him generously. He was therefore mortified when his cousin permitted him to pay the expense of his horse, which amounted to 5s. See also below, pp. 189–91.

[42] A. Hughes, *The Diary of a Farmer's Wife, 1796–7* (Harmondsworth, 1980), 8 Mar. 1797, p. 126.

[43] For example, on 4 Oct. 1660 Samuel Pepys was introduced by his cousin Thomas Pepys to two gentlemen whom he had never met before, one of whom was also named Pepys, and the other's aunt was married to Samuel Pepys's great uncle. He accepted both as 'my two new Cosins' and sat drinking with them: see Pepys, *Diary*, vol. 1, pp. 258–9; see also Houlbrooke, *The English Family*, pp. 56–7. London was of course the greatest point of attraction for migration and geographic mobility: E. A. Wrigley, 'A simple model of London's importance in changing English society and economy, 1650–1750', *P&P* 73 (1967), 44–70. Pepys recognised over eighty living relations, for the most part quite distant, as it is often difficult to understand his exact relationships with them. This tailor's son also owed his education and career to his second cousin and patron, the Earl of Sandwich. As Flandrin notes, Pepys's kinship recognition is all the more striking in view of the fact that he lacked affinal kin, as he married the daughter of a French *émigré*: Flandrin, *Families in Former Times*, p. 33.

[44] See, for example, the following reports in Nancy Woodforde's Diary: '[h]ave been expecting Br Sam all this Week'. 'Am much disappointed at not hearing or seeing my Br Sam this week'. 'In great Hopes that Br. Sam would have been here but I have heard nothing of him at which I am much vex'd and almost angry with him'; 'received a Letter from Br. Sam informing me that he should set of in the Mail Coach on Tuesday Evening at 8 o'Clock for Norwich . . . I am quite rejoiced to find that he is coming for have not seen him for Seven Years': N. Woodforde, 'Nancy Woodforde: a diary for the year 1792', in *Woodforde Papers and Diaries*, ed. D. Woodforde (London, 1932), 6, 7, 13 July 1792, 11 Aug. 1792, pp. 64, 68.   [45] Cressy, *Coming Over*, p. 263.

[46] Ben-Amos, *Adolescence and Youth*, pp. 169, 165–70. On apprenticeship and parental affection, see also Rappaport, *Worlds Within Worlds*, pp. 80–1; Brooks, 'Apprenticeship, social mobility', esp. pp. 73–4.

ties, she suggests, the mobility of youth tended to 'awaken kinship ties' and to reinforce the special social and moral obligations associated with them.[47]

Nor is the evidence concerning the relative dearth of extended kin within households as conclusive as it appears at first sight. Laslett's pioneering studies of household composition in one hundred communities between 1574 and 1821 reveal not only a majority of households with no co-resident kin, but also a snapshot of a significant and consistent minority of households with kin, including more than a quarter of gentry households, about a sixth of yeomen households, and about an eighth of the households of craftsmen and tradesmen; even 7.7 per cent of pauper households included kin consistently between 1574 and 1821.[48] This seems to accord well with the permeable concept of the household-family, discussed in the first chapter of this book, which permitted the inclusion of kin within the household in various capacities, for various periods of time, and on a fluctuating basis. As we saw in our chronological survey of Thomas Turner's household-family, any snapshot taken at a single moment would have seriously underestimated the number of kin who, for a period, were members of that household. It may be that some of the co-resident kin recorded by Laslett also formed part of a broader and fluctuating flow of kin who may have been taken into households due to occupational needs, support in case of hardship, the extension of hospitality, or in the processes of mobility and migration.

Beyond all this, there is also much evidence to suggest that kinship ties can be detected in the context of business and occupational ties throughout the seventeenth and eighteenth centuries, from the kinship networks among the humble families of Oxford boatmen from the sixteenth to the nineteenth centuries,[49] to Northampton innkeepers between 1560

---

[47] Ben-Amos, *Adolescence and Youth*, p. 169.

[48] In this large sample 27.6 per cent of gentlemen's households included kin beyond the nuclear family, 17 per cent of yeomen households, 12.3 per cent of the households of craftsmen and tradesmen, 7.9 per cent of labourers' households and 7.7 per cent of paupers' households. On the whole 10.9 to 11.9 per cent of all households in the communities studied by Laslett between 1599 and 1854 included kin: Laslett, 'Mean household size in England', p. 154; Laslett, 'Characteristics of the Western family considered over time', in Laslett, *Family Life and Illicit Love*, pp. 22–3. Note, however, regional and temporal variations: Wall, 'Regional and temporal variations in English household structure from 1650'. In the poor parts of early seventeenth-century Cambridge, for example, as few as 3.1 per cent of households contained resident kin: Goose, 'Household size and structure in early Stuart Cambridge', 376. See also Berkner, 'The use and misuse of census data'.

[49] M. Prior, *Fisher Row: Fishermen, Bargemen and Canal Boatmen in Oxford, 1500–1900* (Oxford, 1982). See also the discussion and references in Cressy, 'Kinship and kin interaction', 44–53.

and 1760,[50] seventeenth-century overseas merchants,[51] and eighteenth-century tradesmen and entrepreneurs.[52] They could play a role in the life of a seventeenth-century Puritan such as Nehemiah Wallington,[53] as well as possibly in the spread of the eighteenth-century Evangelical Revival.[54] Links between kinship and political connections can be detected from the Oxfordshire rising of 1596,[55] to the Sussex gentry in the period of the Civil War,[56] and on to political connections among mid-eighteenth-century politicians.[57] There is also evidence to suggest that kin could be significant in the context of poor relief, even if they did not actually house needy relatives.[58] Finally, in matters of courtship and marriage the 'multilateral consent' of a range of relations and friends was also important.[59]

It is at this point that we should return to the question of language. Ties among kin were expressed in language. Their very relational structure was coined linguistically. Any claim of recognition, any denial of support were also expressed and negotiated in words. But how did the language of kinship work in the seventeenth and eighteenth centuries? How accurate and useful are the current scholarly accounts of its structure, vocabulary, and meanings?

[50] A. Everitt, 'The English urban inn, 1560–1760', in A. Everitt, *Landscape and Community in England* (London, 1985), esp. pp. 193–8. These dynastic innkeepers, however, rarely continued in innkeeping for more than three or four generations, and they comprised only a minority of the inn holders in the town.

[51] Grassby, 'Love, property and kinship'.   [52] Hunt, *The Middling Sort*.

[53] P. S. Seaver, *Wallington's World: A Puritan Artisan in Seventeenth-Century London* (Stanford, 1985), pp. 69–95, esp. pp. 78–85.

[54] Everitt's study of the subscription lists to Philip Doddridge's *Family Expositor* shows extensive ties bound with religious networks, suggesting the role of dynastic connections in the spread of the Evangelical Revival: A. Everitt, 'Springs of sensibility: Philip Doddridge of Northampton and the Evangelical tradition', in Everitt, *Landscape and Community in England*, esp. p. 233.

[55] J. Walter, 'A rising of the people – the Oxfordshire Rising of 1596', *P&P* 107 (1985), 105.

[56] A. Fletcher, *A County Community in Peace and War* (London, 1975), pp. 44–8, 52, also quoted in Wrightson, *English Society*, p. 48, and see other references there.

[57] Namier, *The Structure of Politics*. One does not have to be an avid 'Namierite' to see how dense and useful such connections could be.

[58] For instance, Wales stresses the importance of parish support but also argues that it is important to emphasise the presence or possibility of kin support to poor relatives: T. Wales, 'Poverty, poor relief and the life-cycle', pp. 384–5; see also Newman Brown, 'The receipt of poor relief and the family situation', pp. 406–7. Boulton suggests that local kin in a seventeenth-century London suburb 'could play an integral part in the system of parish poor relief': Boulton, *Neighbourhood and Society*, p. 259. See T. Hitchcock, P. King, and P. Sharpe (eds.), *Chronicling Poverty: The Voices and Strategies of the English Poor, 1640–1840* (Basingstoke, 1997); Ottaway, 'Providing for the elderly in eighteenth-century England', 391–418, and further references there.

[59] See Wrightson, 'The family in early modern England', pp. 16–17, and reference there to Ingram, *Church Courts, Sex and Marriage*, pp. 134–42. See also Shoemaker's discussion of parental consent and the balance of sentiment and material interest in marriage and courtship: Shoemaker, *Gender in English Society*, pp. 93–7.

One point over which there has been relatively little disagreement among scholars is the structure of the English kinship system in the seventeenth and eighteenth centuries, as also manifested in its terminology. Various studies emphasise the focus on 'ego' and the nuclear family, the system's bilateral structure, its flexibility and looseness, its terminological limitation, as well as the 'vagueness' or inconsistency of some usages.[60] An important contribution in this respect has come from the anthropologist Alan Macfarlane, who first examined the early modern English kinship system in a path-breaking study based on the diary of the seventeenth-century clergyman Ralph Josselin, and then continued to theorise it in subsequent studies.[61] It was he who shaped the field of early modern kinship studies at a formative stage whilst introducing to it methods and questions drawn from modern anthropology and sociology. Even if historians remained sceptical about Macfarlane's broad claims, they benefited from the expertise of this professional anthropologist and their understanding of the kinship system in early modern England is indebted to his.[62]

Three characteristic features regarding the historical language of kinship are thus emphasised by scholars. First, scholars recognise that the historical English kinship terminology was uncongenial for promoting a social system based on the extended family. The terminology itself is portrayed as minimalistic, focused on the nuclear family, and offering

[60] For example, Wrightson emphasises the general structural features that promoted the recognition of only limited and impermanent groups of kin, while highlighting the nuclear family: see Wrightson, *English Society*, esp. pp. 46–8. See also Wrightson, 'Household and kinship', 155. Houlbrooke emphasises the absence of a well-defined kinship group beyond the elementary family to which most individuals owed loyalty and highlights the fluctuating body of the effective kin. The absence of rules giving priority to any one group of kindred is seen to match 'the vagueness of the English kinship terminology, which for the most part did not distinguish consanguinal and affinal kin': see Houlbrooke, *The English Family*, pp. 19, 40. Though Cressy fruitfully departs in important respects from previous interpretations of kinship recognition (see also Macfarlane's, discussed below), he also explains that the language of kinship in England was – and still is – loose and limited, compared to other societies, emphasising the fluidity and imprecision of many usages: Cressy, 'Kinship and kin interaction', 65–6; see the focus on ego and the nuclear family, *ibid.*, 67–8.
[61] See Macfarlane, *The Family Life of Ralph Josselin*, and esp. chs. 7–10 and the diagrams on pp. 156–7; Macfarlane, *Individualism*, and see esp. the discussion of the kinship terminology on pp. 145–7. Macfarlane also argues that for centuries the Englishman has been '[s]ymbolized and shaped by his ego-centred kinship system'. The nature of the structure of the kinship terminology thus forms an important part of this argument: *ibid.*, p. 196. See also Macfarlane, 'The myth of the peasantry', pp. 333–49, Macfarlane, *Marriage and Love in England*, and Macfarlane, *The Culture of Capitalism*.
[62] Thus, for example, Wrightson quotes Macfarlane's studies while discussing kinship structure and terminology, and Cressy acknowledges his debt to Macfarlane: Wrightson, 'Household and kinship', 155; Wrightson, *English Society*, pp. 45–7; Cressy, 'Kinship and kin interaction', 68. See also Cressy, *Coming Over*, p. 286.

flexible but limited recognition of extended kinship ties.[63] This is said to have been the case since at least the central Middle Ages. For instance, relationships such as 'son' or 'mother', as Hanawalt explains, could always be described precisely, whereas relationships such as 'fourth cousin once removed' or even 'grandmother', could only be expressed by clumsy compounds.[64] The exact description of the nuclear family relationships is interpreted by scholars as a mark of their abiding importance, while the lack of words for the extended ties is taken as evidence of their insignificance. The nuclear family terms, as Hanawalt asserts, 'were virtually the only ones that were important', whereas 'the lack of words for extended kin indicates that they were not a part of daily parlance because they were not needed'.[65]

Secondly, the kinship terminology is said to be not only minimalistic, but also gradual in terms of its exactness, with exact terms for naming near relationships and more inclusive and unspecific terms for naming the more distant kin. For example, the term 'father' is mentioned by Macfarlane as an exact term for designating a near relationship, whereas 'uncle' and 'cousin' are both more distant and more vague: 'uncle' indeed applies to at least four different relationships, including maternal and paternal uncles and the husbands of maternal and paternal aunts, whereas 'cousin' can have a wider extension and in the early modern period it was used very widely indeed.[66] Thus the naming system, too, is said both to highlight the near relationships and lump together, or obscure, more distant ties, thus suggesting once more that the English kinship system was ill-fitted for a social system in which extended kinship ties were a central organising principle.

Thirdly, English kinship terminology is also seen to be typified by remarkable continuity. To be sure, archaic usages have been documented, such as the broad extension of the term 'cousin', the fact

---

[63] See, for example, Macfarlane, *Individualism*, pp. 144–7; Wrightson, *English Society*, p. 46; Houlbrooke, *The English Family*, pp. 19, 40.

[64] Hanawalt, *The Ties That Bound*, pp. 79–80, and references there. Hanawalt follows Phillpotts in noting the difference between the sparse English system and the elaborate kinship terms and structures current at the same time on the Continent: Phillpotts, *Kindred and Clan*, pp. 242–63. Hanawalt disagrees with Macfarlane on major issues, but her understanding at this point is similar to his.

[65] Hanawalt, *The Ties That Bound*, p. 80. See also Macfarlane, *Individualism*, pp. 144–7.

[66] Macfarlane discusses the way in which the English kinship system combines exact and descriptive terms as well as almost 'classificatory' terms. In contrast, for example, in the traditional Celtic system it is 'not possible to talk vaguely of one's "cousin" or "uncle"', and such relationships have to be specified as 'father's brother's son', or 'mother's brother': Macfarlane, *Individualism*, pp. 146–7. See also Wrightson, *English Society*, p. 46; Houlbrooke, *The English Family*, p. 40. At this point, Cressy differs significantly, for he argues that all the basic relational terms were used without precision or consistency: 'Kinship and kin interaction', 65–6.

that 'nephew' could also be used to mean 'grandson', the usage of 'friend' as a kinship term, or the application of elementary relational terms to affines (for instance, naming a sister-in-law as 'sister').[67] Scholars have also been struck by the vagueness or lack of precision in the historical use of at least some kinship terms.[68] Such semantic distinctions, however, have rarely been formulated in terms of structural difference.[69] On the contrary, various scholars stress the similarities between the kinship system of the early modern period, and the modern system of today. Ralph Houlbrooke, for example, concludes his study of English kinship in the sixteenth and seventeenth centuries by saying that 'it is hard to point to a change which had much affected the essential character of English kinship'.[70] Scholars of medieval history, as we saw, trace the strands of continuity further back.[71] As Macfarlane explains, 'almost exactly the same terminology has been used from at least the thirteenth century onwards'.[72]

Macfarlane depicts this historical kinship system with the aid of 'the onion model', described by the anthropologist Robin Fox.[73] This model presents the system in the form of layers or concentric circles, like an onion's skins, and it elucidates the main characteristics of the English kinship system as discussed so far.[74] At the centre of the model is 'ego', the individual from whose point of view the kinship ties are traced. Around him, in a series of circles, are his kin. The nuclear family (includ-

---

[67] For archaic usages, see, for example, I. Schapera, *Kinship Terminology in Jane Austen's Novels*, Royal Anthropological Institute of Great Britain and Ireland, Occasional Paper no. 33 (London, 1977); Trumbach, *The Rise of the Egalitarian Family*, Appendix A; Wrightson, *English Society*, p. 46; Houlbrooke, *The English Family*, pp. 19, 40; Goody, *The Development of the Family and Marriage*, pp. 271–2; Macfarlane, *The Family Life of Ralph Josselin*, p. 138; Macfarlane, *Marriage and Love in England*, p. 289; Josselin, *Diary*, pp. 2, 11, 18, 21; S. Wolfram, *In-Laws and Outlaws: Kinship and Marriage in England* (London and Sydney, 1987), e.g. pp. 65, 71; Cressy, 'Kinship and kin interaction', 65–7; Cressy, *Coming Over*, pp. 269–70; O'Hara, 'Ruled by my friends'.

[68] Wrightson, for example, notes that the nuclear family terms were clear enough but the terminology for designating the extended kin was 'singularly unspecific'. Houlbrooke comments on the wide and vague usage of the term 'cousin'. Cressy notes the looseness of the English kinship terminology and that the basic relational terms were used 'without precision or consistency': Wrightson, *English Society*, p. 46; Houlbrooke, *The English Family*, p. 40; Cressy, 'Kinship and kin interaction', 65–7. A valuable critique of the assumed vagueness and flexibility of the kinship terminology can be found in O'Hara, 'Ruled by my friends', esp. pp. 10–11.

[69] See above the Introduction, pp. 9–10.

[70] Houlbrooke, *The English Family*, p. 58.

[71] Hanawalt, *The Ties That Bound*, pp. 79–80, and references there especially to works by Phillpotts, Lancaster, and Goody.   [72] Macfarlane, *Individualism*, p. 147.

[73] R. Fox, *Kinship and Marriage* (Harmondsworth 1984; 1st edn 1967), p. 259; Macfarlane, *Individualism*, pp. 146–7. See also and compare the depiction of receding circles of 'intimate', 'effective', 'non-effective', and 'unfamiliar' kin in Macfarlane, *The Family Life of Ralph Josselin*, p. 157, and see chs. 7–10 more broadly.

[74] I shall use the image of circles and rings following Macfarlane, *Individualism*, p. 146.

ing father, mother, son, daughter) occupies the first circle;[75] grand-relatives, parents and children, occupy the next layer. Aunts, uncles, nephews and nieces occupy the third circle, and beyond them are the cousins. The historical change in this kinship system – or indeed the lack of change – is also understood by Macfarlane with the aid of this model. In the earlier system the second and third rings were merged, as the terms 'nephew' and 'niece' were also used in the sense of 'grandson' and 'granddaughter'. This, however, is the only terminological change that Macfarlane mentions in this context, and it is not seen as a very significant one. As he explains, 'in basic structure the system of terminology had not changed'.[76] Lastly, the gradation of the onion rings also bears a close relation to the exactness of the kinship terminology.[77] The inner circle of the isolated nuclear family is marked by exact terms such as 'father' and 'son' while the terms 'grandfather' and 'grandson' in the second circle are also descriptive. The more distant kin, however, such as 'uncles' and 'cousins', are designated by more inclusive and unspecific terms, as discussed above. The well-focused nucleus thus fades into fuzzy margins, with some points of gradation along the way.

It is easy to see how this understanding of the kinship system could well fit and influence the hypothesis on the centrality of the nuclear family in early modern England and the relative weakness of extended kinship ties. In 1986 Cressy offered a more dynamic model. He allowed for great flexibility and accommodated important archaic usages, while attaching less importance to distinctions between 'effective' and 'non-effective' kin, and near and peripheral kin.[78] He used the model to argue that the kinship system in the early modern period was not shallow or narrow, but variable and wide ranging. However, Cressy dwells little on conventions of usage or questions of historical difference.[79] He takes issue with Macfarlane's assessment of the instrumental value of kinship in early modern England. At the same time, however, Cressy remains close to the structure of kinship that Macfarlane proposed.[80]

[75] See also ego's brother and sister, Fox, *Kinship and Marriage*, pp. 258–9.
[76] Macfarlane, *Individualism*, p. 147. [77] *Ibid.*, pp. 146–7.
[78] Cressy, 'Kinship and kin interaction', 65–9. See also Cressy, *Coming Over*, pp. 286–91.
[79] He argues that the language of kinship in England 'was (and is) limited and loose', and that the relational terms were used 'without precision or consistency': Cressy, 'Kinship and kin interaction', 65–6.
[80] He still highlights the isolated nuclear family (defined narrowly as including ego's spouse and offspring), while also suggesting a concentric model of the kinship system with ego and the nuclear family at the centre, surrounded by 'radiating spheres of extended kin'. He highlights the voluntary nature of kinship recognition: at the centre of the system was 'ego', the individual, who, 'like the sun in Copernican cosmography', was 'free to illumine or eclipse all the rest': *ibid.*, pp. 67–8. Nevertheless, Cressy's criticism of Macfarlane presents an important advance, and one which I found useful and stimulating.

In so far as current scholarly accounts of the early modern kinship system imply that kinship terms were used in similar ways in the past and now, and that they related to each other in similar ways in the past and now, they are, I would like to suggest, misleading. My claim in this chapter is not that terms and their relations were different in every respect, but that in significant respects they were so. Nor is it enough to say that kinship terms in the seventeenth and eighteenth centuries were simply 'unspecific' and 'loose', or usages 'imprecise': it is possible to find a logic within the looseness, and moreover both looseness and imprecision could serve various social purposes. The aim of this chapter, therefore, is to conceptualise practices of the seventeenth- and eighteenth-century language of kinship, pointing out some organising principles, while also elaborating on the ways in which this kinship terminology was different from the terminology used today. These organising principles, I contend, reveal the richness of the historical language of kinship and suggest its great social, cultural, and moral significance. But these organising principles do not agree well with some categorical definitions of 'the nuclear family' and 'the extended family', nor do they conform to the 'onion model'. Indeed, one of the arguments of this chapter is that an 'onion model' is unhelpful for understanding the ways in which people in early modern England named their kin.

Let us proceed, then, to the organising principles of the historical language of kinship. The first set of organising principles is 'recognition and opacity'. The second is 'incorporation and differentiation'. The third principle is 'plurality'. The fourth and last principle, 'diffusion', will indicate some ways in which the language of kinship could shade into the language of friendship, patronage, and community and associational life,[81] an issue that will be examined in greater detail in the last three chapters of this book.

Recognition and opacity

When we examine usages of kinship terms in English texts from the seventeenth and eighteenth centuries, we can see that there were a number of terms that not only did not highlight the nuclear family and separate it from other kinship ties but often served to blur the nuclear family boundaries and submerge them in broader relationships. These were the term 'relation', various derivations of 'kin', the term 'friend', and, particularly in the eighteenth century, the term 'connexion'. All these were normally used as terms of reference: in other words, they were

---

[81] Wrightson describes how 'kinship shaded into friendship': Wrightson, *English Society*, p. 50. I found this expression helpful.

used for talking about kin, rather than directly at them. They were also used commonly in relation to individuals: 'Mr Smith's relations', 'her friends', or 'his kindred'. All these terms, I would like to argue, were employed in some similar ways. They were used to designate individual kin or clusters of kin, but gave little indication as to the identity of these kin or their degree of relationship. Accordingly, these terms served to recognise kin, while at the same time concealing the distinctions between different kinship degrees.

When Samuel Woodforde left his home for Cambridge in June 1687, his mother wrote in her diary the following lines: 'may he do virtuously, and bring a great deal of honour to the name of God, and comfort to himself and *his Relations*'.[82] Surely the mother was counting herself among the 'relations' whom she hoped would draw comfort from her son. Other 'relations' in this case could include Samuel's father, siblings, step-siblings, and diverse others. One hundred years later, Nancy Woodforde was critical about her 'relations': she thanked her uncle heartily for providing her with some money, but complained that 'I never have a farthing from *any other of my Relations* notwithstanding I have a Mother and Brother who have plenty of money.'[83] In other words, she was proposing a group of her 'relations' which included an uncle, a parent, a sibling, as well as unknown 'others'. In Ralph Josselin's case, the category of 'relations' could include a sibling and her son. After Josselin recorded his complaint of his sister and 'cosin', who owed him money and still dared to ask for a new and bigger loan, he concluded saying: 'it greiveth me that *relations* are so unworthy not to bee trusted'.[84] In the case of Sarah Harrold, too, the category of 'relations' probably included near kin. In December 1712 her husband Edmund wrote in his diary: 'my wife lay a-dying from 11 this day . . . she died in my arms, on pillows. *Relations most by.*' A mother, a sister, and the children who 'wept sore' at the funeral were probably among the 'relations' who witnessed this deathbed scene.[85] It is therefore clear from these examples that the term 'relations' could include very near kin, members of the nuclear family. This use of the term

---

[82] M. Woodforde 'Mary Woodforde's Book, 1684–1690', in *Woodforde Papers and Diaries*, ed. D. Woodforde (London, 1932), p. 16.
[83] Woodforde, 'Diary', 9 Jan. 1792, pp. 38–9.
[84] Josselin, *Diary*, 7 Nov. 1657, p. 409. For doubts about trust, see Muldrew, *The Economy of Obligation*, ch. 7.
[85] E. Harrold, 'Diary of a Manchester wig maker', *Remains Historical and Literary Connected with the Palatine Counties of Lancaster and Chester*, The Chetham Society, vol. 68 (Manchester, 1866), p. 190. The sister was given her Bible, the mother her white gloves. The servant, who may have also been present at this death-bed scene was given her worst clothes. Sarah Harrold had at least one infant daughter who died in April 1713. Another daughter, Anna, was probably her step-daughter by Edmund Harrold's previous marriage: shortly afterwards she was removed to her grandparents' house.

may have depended on life-course changes, or even on the circumstances of the conversation. People were more likely to refer to members of their nuclear family as their 'relations' if they were not living with them in the same household, or if they were mentioning them to a third party (another person, or even the pages of a diary). Nonetheless, as these examples show, the term 'relation' could be used to refer to the nearest kin.

A 'relation', however, could also be established by marriage. When John Thomlinson noted in his diary that one Mr Parkes 'had hopes of having me for a *relation*', he was referring to Mr Parkes's hopes that he would marry his daughter.[86] The 'relations' could also consist of sets of maternal or paternal kin. For instance, William Stout described in one of his autobiographical entries a child 'who was brought up by *some of his mother's relations*'.[87] In another entry he described a man who left his estate to his half-brother 'without any respect to *his father's brother or relations*'.[88] In both these cases the 'relations' could include a variety of maternal and paternal kin such as grandparents, uncles and aunts, and diverse others.[89] Lastly, 'relation' could be used for recognising a distant relationship of an unknown degree. This, for example, was the case of one Mr Wallace, who appeared one day in the house of the Gawthern family, as Mrs Gawthern records: 'a Mr Wallace we found in the house who said he was a *relation*; Mr G[awthern] gave him five guineas and he went away that evening'.[90]

Countless similar usages appear in contemporary literary texts, but, because these texts have enclosed sets of characters, it is often easier to establish the identity of the 'relations' referred to. Let us examine, for example, some of the many usages of 'relation' in Richardson's *Clarissa*. '*All my relations* are met', says Clarissa.[91] These relations, as clearly evident from the textual description, include Clarissa's own parents, siblings, uncles, and aunt who watch over Clarissa and negotiate her

---

[86] J. Thomlinson, 'The diary of the Rev. John Thomlinson', in *Six North Country Diaries*, *The Publications of the Surtees Society*, vol. 118 (Durham, 1910), 6 July 1718, p. 128.

[87] W. Stout, *The Autobiography of William Stout of Lancaster, 1665–1752*, ed. D. Marshall (Manchester, 1967), entry for 1703, p. 144.

[88] *Ibid.*, entry for 1701, pp. 134–5. Note, however, that the boundaries of recognition could shift and the brother, who presumably had greater expectations from this inheritance, is mentioned here separately from the other 'relations'.

[89] In a similar way, 'relations' could designate the kin of a husband or wife: a wife who had no children of her own was described by Stout as being 'always bountiful to *her own relations*': *ibid.*, entry for 1738, p. 223.

[90] A. Gawthern, *The Diary of Abigail Gawthern of Nottingham, 1751–1810*, ed. A. Hanstock, Thornton Society of Nottinghamshire, Record Series, vol. 33 (Nottingham, 1980), 14 Sept. 1790, p. 52.

[91] Richardson, *Clarissa*, p. 117. See also 'my assembled relations have taken an *unanimous* resolution . . . against me', p. 217. Italics in the original.

match. Clarissa clearly sees her relations' faults, but she still rebukes Miss Howe for speaking lightly of them: 'I am very angry with you for your reflections of *my relations*, particularly on my father and on the memory of my grandfather.'[92] At the same time, Clarissa is also pleased to have the good opinion of Mr Lovelace's 'relations', whom she lists as follows: 'two excellent aunts, and an uncle, from whom he has such large expectation'.[93]

Sometimes the term 'relation' is also modified by adjectives such as 'near' and 'distant'. But here, too, the boundaries can shift: some cousins can be defined as 'distant', whereas others can be defined as 'near' because in other ways they are closer to the individual concerned. Miss Howe describes her cousin's grandmother as a 'distant relation' of her own mother, while referring to her own future husband as a relation nearer than a papa.[94] Cousin Morden, a distant kinsman whose exact relationship is unspecified, is nevertheless very close to the Harlowe family: he is presented as 'nearly related'.[95] James Harlowe describes himself cynically to Clarissa as '*but* your brother (a very slight degree of relation with you)'.[96] Mr Lovelace awaits his wedding day, when he will make himself happy and also show his duty to his 'nearest relation': in his case, it is his uncle; his other near relations are two aunts by half-blood, and their daughters.[97]

We can see from these examples that the term 'relation' was used as a flexible category to designate kin both within and beyond the nuclear family. The 'relations' in the above examples include parents, siblings, aunts and uncles, cousins, half-relations, in-laws, and possibly various others. The emphasis in these cases, however, is not on the actual degree of the relationship, but on its recognition. At the least, these utterances

[92] *Ibid.*, p. 134.
[93] *Ibid.*, p. 183. These relations wish Mr Lovelace would marry Clarissa: '*all your relations* have it that you do honourably by her'. They even urge him to accept her relations as his: 'you must look at them all as *your relations*; and forgive and forget'. At the same time, Miss Howe hopes that Clarissa will 'meet with the approbation of *[her]* relations' (*ibid.*, pp. 604, 664, 1017). See also Thomlinson's reference to Mrs Hall who was kind to her husband's relations 'as to her own relations', Thomlinson, 'Diary', 4 Oct. 1718, p. 141.
[94] 'I think verily I could like him better for a papa, than for a nearer relation': Richardson, *Clarissa*, p. 207. Her marriage to her suitor is described as 'my prospect in relation to him'.   [95] *Ibid.*, p. 37.
[96] *Ibid.*, p. 223. Italics in the original. Clarissa replies: 'I should endeavour to assert my character, in order to be thought less an *alien*, and *nearer of kin to you both*', referring to her brother and sister. Italics in the original.
[97] *Ibid.*, p. 638. For similar usages, see, for example, the autobiography of William Stout. John Booth, whom Stout takes as an apprentice, is described as '*a remote relation*'. William Stout presents his own nephew as his '*near relation*'. Others, who have claims on an inheritance are described as *near relations*, whereas a man who inherited from his 'cousin' is described as '*his next relation*', see Stout, *Autobiography*, entry for 1711, p. 164; entry for 1731, p. 209; entry for 1723, p. 189; entry for 1716, p. 174.

convey an acknowledgement that an individual has kin. At times, this acknowledgement is also accompanied by an expectation that the relationship might be reciprocal and effective. Such an expectation is implicit even in the many examples where the expectation clearly had not been fulfilled. Nancy Woodforde is plainly disappointed in some of her 'relations', but her sense of disappointment is evidence of her hopes that they should be caring and supportive. Ralph Josselin, too, is disappointed in his unworthy 'relations', but his disappointment reveals their ability to make claims – and his need to justify himself in rejecting them. Beyond these general notions, however, the term 'relations' is remarkably opaque. Except for broad designations such as 'near' or 'distant', it provides no information as to the actual type of relationship. Nor does it provide any information about the number of the 'relations', or the commitments that their relationships entail. One thing, however, we can undoubtedly ascertain: these usages of 'relation' do not emanate from the fixed point of the nuclear family and do not present it as a unit separate from other kinship ties.

Indeed, if we examine these historical usages of 'relation', it would seem that one of their main advantages is that they provided opacity and served to conceal differences. The term 'relation' was very useful in social situations precisely because it enabled speakers to make general allusions to kin without getting into detail, or without revealing very much. This could be desirable for various reasons, whether because the details were little known, or because they were not important in the context in which the utterance was made, or because they were already known and taken for granted, or because for some reason the speaker wished to conceal them. In the case of poor Mr Wallace who arrived one day in his relations' house asking for help, the exact details of the relationship were probably little known. The diarist's reference to him as 'a Mr Wallace we found in the house who said he was a relation' shows that she did not know him, nor did she continue to dwell on the exact degree of his relationship. But the umbrella-term 'relation' was evidently useful enough in this case to demand recognition and to enable Mr Wallace to make a financial claim on his distant kin. In the case of the man who left his estate to his half-brother 'without any respect to his father's brother or relations',[98] the exact details were unimportant: William Stout's main point in making this utterance was to describe a case of wrongful inheritance, rather than to list all the possible kin who did not benefit from this man's estate. In the same way, when Stout referred to the child who 'was brought up by some of his mother's relations',[99] his main point was not to describe exact living

---

[98] Stout, *Autobiography*, entry for 1701, pp. 134–5.   [99] *Ibid.*, entry for 1703, p. 144.

arrangements, but to place the child in the context of a broader story about his mother's imprudence and the family's downfall. This type of opaque usage was useful in many contexts. John Cholwich of Backwaton, Devon, gave his testimony in a settlement examination identifying himself as the deponent's 'relation'.[100] His exact relationship was not specified and was indeed irrelevant in this context. The important detail was that he was a kinsman of the person in whose favour he testified, and that much was conveyed by the unspecific term 'relation'. In contrast, when Clarissa describes the meeting of 'all her relations' the term 'relations' serves as a convenient shorthand to designate a group of kin whose identity is well known to her, to her friend whom she addresses, and to the reader. Similarly, when Edmund Harrold mentions in his diary the presence of 'relations' by his wife's death bed, the general term fits his usual abbreviated style, and no doubt he was familiar with all the persons concerned.

In the case of John Thomlinson, however, the opacity of the term 'relation' served a double strategic purpose. The young Reverend John Thomlinson was looking relentlessly for a living and a wife, and in both negotiations discretion was very important. On 27 March 1722, for example, Thomlinson wrote: 'had proposals from the lady of London for a match with *a relation*, whose name she concealed, some suggested her daughter'.[101] This anonymous reference to a 'relation' highlights the importance of discretion, especially at the early stages of the marriage negotiations when the terms of the proposal were not agreed and gossip could be very detrimental. In this case, however, anonymity was even more important, because Thomlinson was juggling a number of proposals at the same time and these words were in fact addressed to one of his prospective brides, whose father, Thomlinson hoped, would be propelled to action by the news.[102]

In all these usages, then, the term 'relation' conveys the idea that an individual has kin, rather than any specific information about the structure of the kinship relationship. The opacity of the term 'relation' thus served to highlight kinship as a social relationship while glossing over its specific structures. When people spoke about their 'relations', or about the 'relations' of other people, they constructed unspecific but effective notions that individuals have webs of kinship ties: that they are not alone in the world and are attached to others who might give comfort, aid, or trouble. And so, although specific kinship ties were often blurred or diffused, the idea that kinship is important was nonetheless conveyed.

---

[100] The testimony was taken on 2 Mar. 1790: quoted in J. S. Taylor, *Poverty, Migration and Settlement in the Industrial Revolution* (Palo Alto, 1989), p. 96.
[101] Thomlinson, 'Diary', 27 Mar. 1722, p. 167.   [102] *Ibid.*

Derivations of 'kin' could have a similar resonance. When 'kinsman' or 'kinswoman' were used in the singular, the implication seems to have been that these are not relations of the first or second degree, although the exact nature of the relationship was not articulated: the 'kinsman' could be a nephew, a first cousin, a more distant blood-relation, or a relation in law. When used in the plural, 'kindred' designated clusters of kin, including near and distant kin. For example, just as Ralph Josselin denounced one needy sister and her son as unworthy '*relations*', so was he pleased to include another sister among his '*kindred*' whom he could assist (though evidently at a lesser cost to himself):

My sister Dorothy and her houseband with mee, wee gave them such old things as wee any wayes could spare, I paid her 20ˢ. for her legacy. and I lent her 20ˢ. more, the lord be blessed that enables mee to be a freind to *any of my kindred*, it is better to give than receive.[103]

On another occasion we find William Stout using the term 'kindred' more broadly, although he, too, could clearly also use it to designate near kin. When Stout realised that he wished to become a Quaker he feared that he would incur the displeasure of his relations, including 'my mother, brother, sister and *other of my kindred*'.[104] But in the following year he was satisfied that his '*kindred* and acquaintance' accepted his choice, presumably including in this reference his near kin. The use of 'kindred' to apply to a relation beyond the nuclear core is also evident in *Clarissa* when a loan by one character to the nephew of his wife by her half-sister is described as a small favour '*from kindred to kindred*'.[105] In another significant reference Stout explains why he does not claim kindred with one of his neighbours, John Bryer, thus giving us further insight into the possible extension of 'kindred':

John Bryer sone of Edmund Bryer of Kellet by his first wife, whose second wife was Agnes Barker and sister to my father's first wife Grace Barker; but neither of them having any child, we did *not claim any kindred to each other*.[106]

The possible recognition of kindred is traced here through the first marriage of Stout's father and the second marriage of John Bryer's father to a pair of sisters. As neither of these marriages was sealed with the birth of a child, no kindred is claimed between Stout and his neighbour. However, the implication is that had there been a child who would have united the families in both blood ties and financial considerations, kindred would have been claimed. Indeed, the exact relation between

---

[103] Josselin, *Diary*, 20 Oct. 1647, p. 106.
[104] Stout, *Autobiography*, entry for 1686, p. 84; entry for 1687, p. 85.
[105] Richardson, *Clarissa*, p. 212. Mr Hervey is the husband of the half-sister of James Harlowe's mother.   [106] Stout, *Autobiography*, entry for 1687, p. 88.

'kindred' could be so distant or intricate that it was unknown. See, for example, the words of one witness in a testamentary case heard in County Durham, that 'he was both kin to the plaintiff and defendant, but within what degree he knoweth not'.[107] In all these cases, then, the term 'kindred' appears as a general and flexible term that could extend both near and far. In the usages of 'kindred', too, it was the sense of an existing and recognised kinship tie that was conveyed, rather than a certain structured kinship relationship. Consequently, the same opacity that characterised usages of 'relations' also characterised usages of the derivations of 'kin'. When William Stout mentioned in 1722 'Houghton and *his kinsman Stanley*' who did not succeed in the election for the knights of the shire, for example, he was not interested in the exact relationship between Sir Henry Houghton and Sir Edward Stanley, but in their coalition and joint campaign.[108] The identity of the Newgate 'kinswoman' in *Moll Flanders* remains unknown: the important detail is that the speaker had a relation in Newgate whom she visited.[109] In *The History of Miss Betsy Thoughtless* the opaque term 'kinsman' is even used as a literary device to create irony. 'Fortune threw in my way *a kinsman of my mother's* . . . [who] compassionated for my calamitous condition', says Miss Forward obliquely, as she tries to explain the appearance of a hitherto unknown man who takes upon himself to provide for her.[110] As the narrator hints, however, 'it was not by a *kinsman* she was maintained'.[111]

Inclusiveness and opacity were also among the main characteristics of the term 'friend'.[112] We have examined above one case in which Ralph Josselin referred to his sister and her son using the term 'relations' and another in which he referred to a sister and her husband as his 'kindred'. In the following examples he comments on the same sibling relationships using the term 'friends'. When his sister Anna goes away, having received helpful gifts especially from himself and his family, Josselin says: 'my sister Ann departed from us, loaded with *her freinds bounty. esp. ours*'.[113] When he arranges a loan between his sisters Mary and Anna, also paying at the same time a sum of money to Anna's husband on account of his future legacy, he concludes with satisfaction: 'I am glad I am in the condicon to bee helpfull to *my freinds*.'[114] But the term 'friend' could also

[107] Issa, 'Obligation and choice', p. 113.   [108] Stout, *Autobiography*, entry for 1722, p. 186.
[109] D. Defoe, *Moll Flanders* (1722), ed. J. Mitchell (Harmondsworth, 1978), p. 101.
[110] Haywood, *Betsy Thoughtless*, p. 175. See also, for example, Haywood's description in *The Female Spectator* of a wedding that took place after the match was made '*by the kindred on both sides*': E. Haywood, *The Female Spectator* (London, 1745), vol. I, p. 30.
[111] Haywood, *Betsy Thoughtless*, p. 197.
[112] For further discussion of 'friendship', see below, ch. 5.
[113] Josselin, *Diary*, 29 July 1673, p. 570.   [114] *Ibid.*, 9 Oct. 1647, p. 105.

be used more inclusively. Josselin also referred to his wife's relations as 'friends', and he named his cousin and her husband as 'friends'.[115] As in the case of similar terms, however, he also used the term 'friends' to make general references to his whole group of effective kin. For instance, he describes how in his youth, when he needed assistance and support, *'frends* were not so kinde as I expected'.[116] Thus, in all these cases the term 'friends' was used by Josselin as a flexible and inclusive category that could apply to diverse kin. Indeed, this category was applied particularly to those kin who were expected to be effective, but at the same time it did not reveal in any way the identity of these kin, their number, or their exact relationships. About a century later, we still find Thomas Turner making similar usages. Turner complained about the tumults that his marriage caused among his *'friends'*, primarily his mother and brothers. Similarly, Clarissa, though rejected by all her *'friends'*, namely her parents, siblings, uncles, and aunt, still hopes for a reconciliation with them.[117] Frederick James testified in his settlement examination that he needed money to return to his *'friends at Kenton'*, Devon, namely, his relations.[118] The 'friend' who came to the help of the destitute Mrs Maddocks in 1812 was her uncle.[119]

'Friend' could also be modified by adjectives such as 'next' and 'near'. In legal terms, a *'next friend'* had a similar meaning to a *'next of kin'*, or a *'next relation'*.[120] For example, Blackstone explains in his *Commentaries on the Laws of England* that if a person dies intestate, the court is instructed to assign as the executor *'the next and most lawful friend'*, who is interpreted to be 'the *next of blood* that is under no legal disabilities'.[121] A person could also be described as a *'near friend'*, similar to a 'near relation'. For example, a relation writing on a woman's behalf in a courtship matter is presented in a letter as her *'nearest friend'*.[122] It was also possible to say

---

[115] See e.g. *ibid.*, 23 July 1651, p. 252; 'my uncle N. Josselins daughter and her housband came to us, a mercy to bee in a capacity to welcome *our freinds': ibid.*, 21 May 1664, p. 508.

[116] But he also relates how, when he became very ill, his *'freinds'* feared for him: *ibid.*, entries for 1636, 1639, pp. 5, 7.

[117] See, for example, Richardson, *Clarissa*, pp. 456–7, 513, 690.

[118] Taylor, *Poverty*, pp. 47–8. These 'friends' included his grandmother.

[119] 'Her friends were so displeased at her marrying a protestant that, until her husband's death, they would never notice her; then, being in indigent circumstances, a wealthy uncle again became a friend': Weeton, *Journal of a Governess*, vol. II, 15 June to 15 July 1812, p. 37. See also the case of Mrs Dodson's 'friends' who disapproved of her marriage: *ibid.*, p. 21. On another occasion Miss Weeton agrees to remain in Mr Pedder's service encouraged by the fact that this was the wish of her master's 'friends'. These were probably Mr Pedder's relations in Preston, and particularly his father, who had disapproved of Mr Pedder's marriage to his servant but wanted her to at least have a genteel teacher and companion such as Miss Weeton: *ibid.*, vol. I, 14 Mar., 1810, p. 242.

[120] Stout, *Autobiography*, entry for 1711, p. 174. In this case, the next relation is a cousin.

[121] Blackstone, *Commentaries on the Laws of England*, vol. II, p. 496. Italics in the original.

[122] This is a model letter in a letter-writing manual, *The Complete Letter Writer: or, Polite*

that a person is '*come of good friends*', that is, that she comes from good stock.[123] Sometimes it was necessary to differentiate those friends by blood and marriage from other friends, who were not kin.[124] This could be done by naming the related friends as '*natural friends*'. For example, Madan's *Thoughts on Executive Justice*, published in 1785, explains that if a person is convicted, '*his natural friends* might be brought in to aid him'. These are later described as a brother and a sister.[125] In a similar way, when Clarissa makes her will, she assures that '*all my natural friends* are considered'.[126]

Finally, we reach the term 'connexion'.[127] This term became increasingly current in the course of the eighteenth century, particularly in polite speech. It was used mostly in the plural form – 'connexions' or 'connections'. This term could also refer to clusters of kin both within and beyond the nuclear family, and it was also remarkably opaque, designating kin while giving no specific information as to their degree, sex, or number.[128] '[P]ray, Sir, are you acquainted with any of *my connections*?', asks one of the characters in Sheridan's *The School for Scandal*, thus making a general reference to his kin. In the following words he proceeds to specify one of them, his 'dev'lishly rich uncle', from whom he has 'the greatest expectations'.[129] In Jane Austen's *Pride and Prejudice*, 'connexions' refers collectively to the nuclear family of origin and maternal uncles, as it is said that Darcy, the novel's hero, prevents himself from falling in love with Elizabeth Bennet because of 'the inferiority of her *connections*': her vulgar mother and sisters, her eccentric father, and her maternal uncles, who are still actively employed in trade and in the legal profession, are the first among these undesirable kin.[130] Like other terms

English Secretary (London, 1767), Letter xv, p. 110: 'From a Relation of the Lady, in Answer to the above'. The previous letter is 'From a young Tradesman to a Lady he had seen in Public', *ibid.*, pp. 109–10.

[123] S. Richardson, *Familiar Letters on Important Occasions*, ed. B. W. Down (London, 1928), p. 40.   [124] See also the study of 'friendship' below, chs. 5–7.

[125] M. Madan, *Thoughts on Executive Justice, with Respect to our Criminal Laws Particularly on the Circuits* (London, 1785), pp. 98–9, quoted in J. A. Sharpe, *Crime in Early Modern England, 1550–1750* (London, 1992), p. 174.   [126] Richardson, *Clarissa*, p. 1413.

[127] Also spelled 'connection'. This spelling originated around 1725–50, but it was only recognised by lexicographers in Webster's dictionary of 1818, as explained in *OED*, s.v. 'connexion', 'connection'. The following discussion includes both forms of spelling.

[128] Like 'friend', 'connexions' could also designate non-kin. See also below, pp. 161–2, 167–71, 198–211.

[129] R. B. Sheridan, *The School for Scandal*, III: iii (1777), in *Four English Comedies* ed. J. M. Morell (Harmondsworth, 1959), pp. 364–5, also quoted in *OED*, s.v. 'connexion'.

[130] See Austen, *Pride and Prejudice*, p. 45. At another time, the term is used to refer only to the two uncles. It is suggested that, with all her fine qualities, Elizabeth's sister Jane should have been 'well settled', but with 'such a father and mother, and such *low connections*', she is denounced as having 'no chance of it'. These 'connections' are then specified as her uncle the attorney in Meryton, and another uncle 'who lives somewhere near Cheapside': *ibid.*, p. 31.

examined so far, 'connexions' could also be used for step-relations and half-relations, and it could be modified by adjectives such as 'distant' or 'near'. For example, in *Sense and Sensibility*, Mrs Dashwood's step-son and his wife are described as Mrs Dashwood's '*nearer connections*', compared to her more distant cousin who eventually comes to her aid.[131]

Unspecific but suggestive references such as these could be particularly useful in the context of courtship and marriage, as the merits of a match were considered and discussed. For instance, when a gentleman of the Tyrell family of Bury St Edmunds married a young lady of the Ray family of Haughly, they were wished 'much Joy on the Late happy *Connection*' of their respective families.[132] On another occasion the diarist James Oakes anticipated '*A Connection*' between two young people: he was, in other words, anticipating their forthcoming match.[133] References to such 'connections' could even be made in a verbal form. For instance, Jane Austen says of one of her characters that she has '*connected herself* unexceptionally', by giving her family 'neither men, nor names, nor places that could raise a blush'.[134] Unspecific yet suggestive references to 'connexion' were also effective in eighteenth-century political life.[135] For instance, Lord Gage agreed that George Townshend should receive an army regiment as his 'claim to favour' was supported not least by the strength of his 'connections': he was probably referring to Townshend's powerful uncle, the Duke of Newcastle, who was then First Lord of the Treasury.[136] At a later date, however, Sir John Molesworth, an MP from Cornwall, supported a motion for disabling revenue officers from voting in Parliamentary elections in order to reduce the influence of the Administration over '*family connexions*' and the landed interest.[137]

'Relation', 'kindred', 'friends', and 'connexions' were thus all used to recognise a variety of kin, including the nuclear family members. Not only was the nuclear family not isolated by these usages, but they actually served to submerge the nuclear family in broader kinship relationships. This kinship terminology was not marked by the precision assumed in the 'onion model', nor was it marked by careful gradation. Rather than recognition and definition, it offered recognition and opacity. But it was indeed the qualities of inclusiveness and unspecific recognition that made this terminology so useful for so many speakers in the seventeenth and eighteenth centuries, and in so many social situations.

---

[131] Austen, *Sense and Sensibility*, p. 57.   [132] Oakes, *Diaries*, vol. II, 13 June 1801, p. 9.
[133] *Ibid.*, vol. II, 26 Sept. 1819, p. 241. One of them was 'Grandson Henry', the other was one Miss Porteous.   [134] Austen, *Emma*, p. 323   [135] See also ch. 6 below.
[136] Lord Gage to the Duke of Newcastle, 29 Aug. 1758, quoted in Namier, *The Structure of Politics*, p. 27. In eighteenth-century historiography, the study of such 'connections' is indeed famously associated with Namier and his legacy: see further discussion in ch. 6 below.
[137] This motion was proposed in 1770: see Namier, *The Structure of Politics*, p. 64.

Incorporation and differentiation

The second set of organising principles which should be pointed out is incorporation and differentiation. Incorporation is the first to be addressed. When a man and a woman married, their marriage brought about not only the alliance of two kinship groups, but also their incorporation.[138] Incorporation was articulated in some distinct naming conventions. The first convention was that kin incorporated into their kinship group the spouses of their kin. These spouses were incorporated in the same degree as their marriage partners. Parents, therefore, could recognise the spouses of their offspring as 'sons' and 'daughters', and siblings could recognise their siblings' spouses as 'brothers' and 'sisters'. The wives of uncles were obviously recognised as 'aunts', and the husbands of aunts as 'uncles'. Even the spouses of cousins could be recognised as 'cousins'.[139] We can see the ways in which these conventions were used by Ralph Josselin. On 30 August 1670, for example, he wrote in his diary: 'My daughter Jane married to Jonathan Woodthorp':[140] the next time Mr Woodthorp was mentioned he was referred to as 'son'.[141] The husband of Ralph Josselin's other daughter, Elizabeth, was also named 'son'.[142] Following the same principle, the husbands of Ralph Josselin's sisters were

[138] Houlbrooke explains that 'each individual who married belonged to at least two nuclear families', and could later gain 'a new secondary attachment to his or her spouse's family, in which he or she would be accepted as "son" or "daughter"'. Cressy explains that 'affinal kin acquired through marriage were embraced in the network almost as readily as consanguinal kin'. He notes many naming practices also discussed here, and explores such relationships within dense and active networks: see Houlbrooke, *The English Family*, pp. 19, 39; Cressy, *Coming Over*, pp. 27, 269–70, 274–86; Cressy, 'Kinship and kin interaction', esp. 66–8. Macfarlane describes the unity of husband and wife for purposes of tracing descent, quoting Pollock and Maitland: Macfarlane, *Marriage and Love in England*, p. 289. The anthropologist Sybil Wolfram also explains that when a man and a woman married they were regarded 'as one', and also took on each other's relationships. She examines various practices of naming similar to those studied here, and also uses among her sources eighteenth- and nineteenth-century novels. However, she emphasises the way in which such relationships were manifested in the use of the in-law and step- terminology (which also highlights the difference between consanguinal and affinal relations), while the present study suggests more inclusive and diversified historical usages. My analysis is thus similar to some of Wolfram's arguments, but it also suggests that the recognition of relations by marriage has probably undergone greater historical changes than Wolfram observes: Wolfram, *In-Laws and Outlaws*, esp. pp. 16–19, 64–6.

[139] Trumbach explains that such usages gave a consanguinal status to affines, see Trumbach, *The Rise of the Egalitarian Family*, Appendix A. Certainly this is one way of defining this process of incorporation. Another way is by seeing kinship terms as initially open to the potential inclusion of both consanguinal and affinal ties, due to the unity of husband and wife. See also Wolfram, *In-Laws and Outlaws*, esp. pp. 16–19, 64–6.

[140] Josselin, *Diary*, 30 Aug. 1670, p. 555.

[141] *Ibid.*, 18 Dec. 1670, p. 557. On this occasion Ralph Josselin noted the death of his son-in-law's mother, in the same manner that he recorded the death of various other family members.

[142] See e.g. *ibid.*, 3 Apr. 1681, p. 631; 12 Feb. 1681/2, p. 636; 8 May 1683, p. 643.

recognised as 'brothers'. For instance, 'my brother Jo: Humphry came to bee with mee a while' was Josselin's reference to his sister Dorothy's husband.[143] The same principle applied to uncles and cousins: Ralph Josselin's 'Uncle Hudson' was the husband of his paternal aunt Anne, and his 'cousin Benton' was probably a cousin's wife.[144]

Similar examples of kinship recognition can be found in numerous eighteenth-century texts. When John Penrose of Cornwall sent his blessing in 1766 to 'Son and Daughter Coode', he was referring to his daughter and her husband.[145] James Oakes of Bury St Edmunds used the same form of naming at the end of the eighteenth century and the beginning of the nineteenth, as he referred to his two 'daughters', his sons' wives: 'Daughter Eliz Oakes safely delivered' was a reference to the wife of his son James.[146] Indeed, James Oakes continued the incorporation of kin in the lineal line to the next generation. His 'Grandaughter and Grandson' who departed on a journey to Leamington on 21 July 1825 were in fact a grandson and his wife.[147] The spouses of siblings were named in the same manner. When Mary Hardy wrote in her diary 'Brother & Sister & I went to Norwich', she was referring not to her two blood siblings, but to her brother and his wife.[148] 'Brother Bridge' was the husband of one of James Oakes's sisters, whereas 'brother Baker' was the husband of another.[149] Mr Foley was incorporated into Mrs Ann Granville's kinship group as 'Your new Cousin': he was lately married to her cousin, The Honourable Grace Granville.[150]

The second naming convention emphasising the principle of incorporation was that each spouse could also take on his or her spouse's kin and express their relationship to them by naming; in other words, the naming convention discussed above was reciprocal. Husbands and wives thus

[143] *Ibid.*, 19 Dec. 1652, p. 291. Similarly, the person referred to by Josselin as 'Brother Hodson' was the husband of his sister Anne: *ibid.*, entry for 1636, p. 4, and see note there: 'Thomas Hodson, R J's brother-in-law.'
[144] *Ibid.*, 14, 15 Oct. 1646, p. 72. The female 'cousin Benton' who miscarried was probably the wife of Josselin's cousin Jeremy Benton, the son of his paternal aunt Mary by her second marriage: *ibid.*, 1 Sept. 1644, p. 18.
[145] *Letters from Bath*, 25 Apr. 1766, p. 57.
[146] Oakes, *Diaries*, vol. II, 20 July 1811, p. 144. See also references to the same 'daughter': *ibid.*, vol. I, 23 Apr. 1795, p. 311; 23 Mar. 1797, p. 345; *ibid.*, vol. II, 23 Oct. 1806, p. 85. For reference to his son Orbell's wife as 'daughter', see *ibid.*, vol. I, 6 July 1800, p. 390; *ibid.*, vol. II, 25 Mar. 1802, p. 18; 18 Mar. 1803, p. 37; 24 Oct. 1806, p. 85.
[147] Oakes, *Diaries*, vol. II, p. 301. 'Grand Daughter Mrs Henry Oakes', whose birthday James Oakes noted, was also a grandson's wife: 23 June 1825, *ibid.*
[148] M. Hardy, *Mary Hardy's Diary*, with an introduction by B. Cozens-Hardy, Norfolk Record Society, vol. 37, (Norwich, 1968), 25 May 1775, pp. 15–16.
[149] See Oakes, *Diaries*, vol. I, 25 Feb. 1782, p. 224; 27 Mar., 28 May 1787, p. 247; 15 Dec. 1791, p. 276.
[150] Mrs Pendarves to Mrs Ann Granville, in *The Autobiography and Correspondence of Mary Granville, Mrs Delany*, ed. Lady Llanover, 3 vols. (London, 1862), vol. I, pp. 80–1.

routinely recognised each others' parents as 'father' and 'mother'. They recognised not only their siblings' spouses as 'brothers' and 'sisters', as seen above, but also their spouses' siblings. Recognition could extend further to include more distant kin. When Ralph Josselin wrote in a diary entry for 1642: 'My wife now growing bigge and ill *my mother* came from Olny to us',[151] he was referring not to his own mother but to his wife's mother, Mrs Anne Constable. When he wrote '*my father* came home with us', he was referring to his wife's father.[152] Similarly, when Thomas Turner wrote in his diary in 1757 'we Lay at *my Father's* all night', he was referring to his stay at the house of his wife's father.[153] Mary Hardy described her visit to her husband's mother in Lancashire using the same form of recognition: 'went to *mother's* were we were joyfully recd'.[154] The sibling terminology was used in a similar manner. The person referred to by Josselin as '*my brother Jeremy*' was in fact his wife's brother; '*sister Betty*' was probably this brother's wife.[155] The man addressed by Thomas Yorke as 'Dear Brother' was his wife's brother.[156] However, John Penrose's 'Brother Bennet' was the husband of his wife's sister.[157] More distant kin could be incorporated in a similar way. The man referred to by Ralph Josselin as 'my uncle Shepheard' was the husband of Mrs Josselin's maternal aunt.[158] The man whom James Oakes described as 'Our Uncle Mr Richard Adamson' was his wife's uncle.[159]

Taking together these first and second conventions of incorporation, it seems that the only familial roles which were not open to incorporation (not at least without incurring charges of bigamy) were 'husband' and 'wife'. However 'serial monogamy', in the form of widowhood followed by remarriage, could lead to intensive kinship incorporation.[160] The persons referred to by Edmund Harrold as 'father Bancroft', 'mother Bancroft', and 'brother Joseph' were probably the father, mother, and

[151] Josselin, *Diary*, entry for 1642, p. 12.
[152] *Ibid.*, entry for 1641, p. 11. See the editor's note there: 'Here, as often father is used for father-in-law.' See also, for example, 'my mother Stone' and 'my mother Marchant', T. Marchant, 'The Marchant diary', ed. E. Turner, *SAC* 25 (Lewes, 1873), 170, entries for 14 Nov. 1714, 1 Jan. 1715.   [153] Thomas Turner, Diary, 24 Jan. 1757.
[154] Hardy, *Diary*, 4 Oct. 1787, p. 63.
[155] Josselin, *Diary*, 4 Sept. 1644, p. 19; 19 May 1651, p. 246. The same entry also includes a reference to 'Jeremy and wife'.
[156] *The Correspondence of Sir James Clavering*, ed. H. T. Dickinson, The Surtees Society, (Gateshead, 1967), pp. 135, 137, *passim*.
[157] *Letters from Bath*, 12 June 1766, p. 161.
[158] Josselin, *Diary*, 26 Sept. 1644, p. 22. The aunt was referred to as 'my aunt'.
[159] Oakes, *Diaries*, vol. I, 12 Feb. 1800, p. 386.
[160] 'Second and subsequent marriages complicated the picture and increased the possibilities of interaction among kin . . . relationships associated with one marriage did not cease to claim kinship after the death of the linking spouse': Cressy, *Coming Over*, p. 270.

brother of his first wife.[161] Evidently the recognition of kinship did not
cease with this wife's death, as these individuals continued to be named
'father', 'mother', and 'brother' long afterwards. So were they named
even after the death of Edmund Harrold's second wife.[162] Nor did a third
marriage put an end to the kinship recognition. Indeed, it was the same
Mr Bancroft, the first wife's father, who gave away the bride at Edmund
Harrold's third marriage, and after the marriage he continued to be
referred to as 'father Bancroft'.[163]

The third naming convention was that step-relations and half-relations
who were also joined by marriage could also be incorporated into their
new kinship groups. Their incorporation, too, was expressed by naming.
Ralph Josselin referred to his father's second wife by calling her 'my
mother'.[164] When Abigail Anna Frost reported in her diary that she spent
a few days 'with my father and mother', she was probably referring to her
father and his newly wedded wife.[165] The young man referred to by Mary
Woodforde as 'son Heighes' was her step-son, her husband's son by a
previous marriage. Her step-daughter, too, was named by her as a daughter: 'my daughter Alice';[166] when Alice married, her husband was incorporated as 'son' into the step-mother's kinship group and named 'Son
Dalgress'.[167] The sibling terminology could also be extended in a similar
way. The woman referred to as 'my sister Rebekah', who came to visit
Ralph Josselin in September 1671, was probably his half-sister, his father's
daughter by his second wife.[168] Similarly, Thomas Turner recognised his
half-brothers as 'brothers': the diary entry 'we drank Tea at my Brothers'
refers to Thomas Turner's eldest half-brother, John.[169] The entry 'my
Brother Will. Came to see us' refers to the other half-brother, William.[170]

[161] Harrold, 'A Manchester wig maker', 25, 31 Dec. 1712, p. 191; 20 Jan. 1712–13, p. 192;
25–6 Apr. 1713, p. 194. The brother is also named 'brother Bancroft'.
[162] At this stage Anna, Harrold's daughter by his first marriage was removed to 'father
Bancroft's' house: *ibid.*, 19 June 1713, p. 197, 7 July 1713, p. 198.
[163] *Ibid.*, 20 Mar. 1713–14, p. 204. For the marriage of Edmund Harrold and Ann Horrocks,
see *ibid.*, 22 Aug. 1713, p. 200: 'Dr. John Harper married me and my 3rd wife Ann, and
Mr Bancroft was father. This makes 2 wives given by Joseph Bancroft.' It seems that at
this point the third wife was incorporated into the kinship group that included her
husband's first wife's kin. The marriage took place at eight o'clock in the morning and
immediately afterwards the bridegroom went to work and did not return until nine in the
evening. During this time the bride was entertained at Mr Bancroft's: he is then named
pointedly as 'her Mr. and father Bancroft', as if to mark the new and extended kinship
incorporation. The couple also dined at 'father Bancroft's' on the day after the wedding,
ibid., 23 Aug. 1713, p. 200.   [164] Josselin, *Diary*, entry for 1636, p. 6.
[165] Gawthern, *Diary*, entry for 1771, p. 27.
[166] M. Woodforde, 'Book', 21 July 1685, p. 13; 3 June 1686, p. 14; Sept. 1687, p. 16; 20 Sept.
1688, p. 19; 26 July 1689, p. 22.   [167] *Ibid.*, 5 June 1690, p. 25.
[168] Josselin, *Diary*, 10 Sept. 1671, p. 560.
[169] Thomas Turner, Diary, 14 Aug., 10, 28 July 1756, etc.
[170] *Ibid.*, 26 Dec. 1755, 14 May, 5 June 1756, etc.

These conventions of incorporation also appear in literary texts. They are current, for example, in Jane Austen's novels, where they have been traced in detail by the anthropologist I. Schapera.[171] 'Mother' is used not only for a mother by blood and marriage, but also for a husband's mother, and a father's wife. 'Daughter' is used for a son's wife, and 'son' for a daughter's husband. The term 'sister' is commonly used to indicate a brother's wife, a husband's sister, a wife's sister, and a sister by half-blood. Similarly, 'brother' is used for a sister's husband, a wife's brother, a husband of a wife's sister, and a brother by half-blood. 'Nephew' is extended in Jane Austen's works to the son of the husband's sister, and the son of the wife's sister. 'Niece' is extended to the wife of the brother's son, the sister of the son's wife, the daughter of the husband's sister, and the daughter of the wife's sister. 'Uncle' extends to include the husband of the mother's sister, the brother of the wife's mother, and the husband of the sister of the wife's mother. Similarly, the term 'aunt' extends to include the wife of the father's brother, the wife of the mother's brother, the sister of the wife's mother, and the wife of the brother of the wife's mother.[172]

People in the seventeenth and eighteenth centuries were thus able to incorporate into their kinship group their kin's spouses, their spouses' kin, as well as their half- and step-relations. Incorporation seems to have been particularly powerful in the case of near kin. Members of nuclear families, united by marriage, were likely to recognise one another as 'father' and 'mother', 'son' and 'daughter', 'brother' and 'sister'. But, as we saw, the principle of incorporation could extend further to include uncles, aunts, and cousins. The only familial roles in which simultaneous incorporation was legally barred were 'husband' and 'wife'. These incorporated terms were commonly articulated in the language of reference and address: readers of seventeenth- and eighteenth-century texts are no doubt familiar with many other such usages.

The obvious result of these naming practices was that kinship groups were considerably enlarged. Parental and filial relationships could double during the life-course. Sibling groups, too, could double or even triple in size, thus multiplying even more the possible relationships between their members. Any re-marriages could further increase the number of relationships recognised. Ralph Josselin, for example, had by his mid-twenties three women to whom he referred as 'my mother' and two men whom he called 'my father'. Only one of the sons that he begat lived long enough to marry, but in the course of his life Josselin acquired four more men whom he could name as 'sons'. Josselin also had three sisters whom

<hr/>

[171] See Schapera, *Kinship Terminology in Jane Austen's Novels*. I found this study particularly inspiring.   [172] *Ibid.*, pp. 6–7.

he called 'my sisters by my father and mother'.[173] He did well to use this biblical sounding qualification, because by that time he had three more females whom he recognised as 'sisters' and four more males whom he called 'brothers'. The total number of relations by blood and marriage who were recognised by Ralph Josselin in his diary with the use of the nuclear family terms amounts to about thirty.[174] James Oakes, living more than a century later, used the same system of kinship recognition. He gained through his wife an additional set of parents and siblings. He begat three daughters and acquired two more, added one son to his own two, and gained three brothers through his sisters. James Oakes, Like Ralph Josselin, expressed all these relationships – given and acquired – using the nuclear family terminology.

These naming conventions reflect what Macfarlane describes at one point as 'the broad category of the nuclear family'.[175] This category could include one's nuclear family of origin, nuclear family of procreation, married offspring, married siblings, half-relations, step-relations, and even grandparents, and it could yet be further supported by effective ties with members of the spouse's nuclear family, as well as relations such as uncles.[176] This category is broader than the nuclear family of 'the onion model', and much broader than the nuclear-family household as defined in the classical categories used in household composition studies, in which the addition of a single relative beyond the narrowly defined core turns the household into an 'extended family household'.[177]

[173] Josselin, *Diary*, 13 Oct. 1661, p. 483.
[174] Those include all of Ralph Josselin's sisters and children, near affinal kin, as well as 'sister Betty' who can be identified as the wife of 'brother Jeremy', and the husbands of Ralph Josselin's daughters. Those include 'sons' Woodthorpe and Smith, and the likely reference to Josselin's two newly acquired 'sons' in London among 'my six sons and daughters'; see also 'all the children well at London': *ibid.*, 1, 7 July 1683, p. 644. Based on these identifications, there were thirty-two people recognised by Josselin in his diary as near kin, including six 'daughters', eight 'sons', five 'brothers', eight 'sisters', three 'mothers', and two 'fathers'. See also and compare Macfarlane, *The Family Life of Ralph Josselin*, pp. 141–3, 157–8, and see Cressy, 'Kinship and kin interaction', 42.
[175] Macfarlane, *The Family Life of Ralph Josselin*, p. 126.
[176] When Macfarlane argues that 'apart from the nuclear family there was no effective kin group in Josselin's world' it is probably this 'broad category of the nuclear family' that he has in mind. The close relationships he analyses include, among others, Josselin's relationships with the nuclear family of daughter Jane Woodthorpe, the nuclear family of daughter Elizabeth Smith, and the intimate relationship between Ralph Josselin and his three sisters, all of whom eventually married. The continuing warm relationships among Josselin's children is also noted. So are the relationships between Josselin and some members of his wife's nuclear family, while they and one of his uncles are also listed as 'effective': Macfarlane, *The Family Life of Ralph Josselin*, pp. 126, 149, 157, and the discussions in chs. 7–8, 10.
[177] See Laslett and Wall (eds.), *Household and Family in Past Time*, p. 31. A narrow definition of the nuclear family is also presented in Cressy's model, in which the nuclear family is identified with the residential unit of procreation, while parents, parents-in-law, married

The naming practices studied here thus lead us to reflect once more on the categorical definitions used in the history of the family such as the 'nuclear family', 'extended kinship', or the 'extended family'.[178] If the conventions of incorporation analysed here served to highlight kinship ties particularly among the near kin, they also served to stretch and blur the boundaries of kinship groups. Each individual was able to incorporate new members into his or her kinship group and announce their incorporation by naming: the strangers of yesterday could be adopted in the same degree as the nearest kin. At any point in the life-course, moreover, it was possible for individuals to recognise their current group of kin, and to name these kin in a way that separated them from non-kin. But in the course of this process the boundaries of 'nuclear families' could be blurred and specific kinship groups could expand almost beyond recognition. In some ways, then, the kinship terminology studied here separated the nuclear family from other kinship ties, as suggested by the 'onion model'. But in other ways this terminology could also facilitate the extension of the nuclear family to the degree that one wonders whether it still merits the title 'nuclear', or whether perhaps it should be called 'extended'.

The analysis of the conventions of incorporation suggests that this family type was neither nuclear nor extended. Conversely, it might be said that it was both. The highly nucleated system of kinship recognition facilitated the incorporation of an extended group of relations by blood and marriage. Six basic terms indicating the elementary family relationships – 'father', 'mother', 'son', 'daughter', 'brother', and 'sister' – were most commonly known and habitually used in both narrow and broader meanings. Sometimes they were used in ways that anthropologists might define as 'descriptive', that is, they were used to point out the *exact* relationship between individuals: when Ralph Josselin wrote 'my sonne John sadly ill', the term 'son' was used descriptively, indicating the boy's

---

children and their spouses and offspring, siblings and their spouses and offspring are classified among 'the radiating spheres of extended kin': Cressy, 'Kinship and kin interaction', 67. Houlbrooke's understanding of 'the nuclear family' is broader, as he perceives the 'nuclear family' throughout the life-course. Married individuals belonged to at least two nuclear families, and could later gain a secondary attachment to the spouse's nuclear family, in which they would be accepted as 'sons' or 'daughters'. The category of 'the kinsfolk' thus lies outside this large 'nuclear core': Houlbrooke, *The English Family*, esp. pp. 19, 39. Wrightson's understanding is similar. In Terling, 'kin beyond the nuclear family and the nuclear families of origin of married couples' are said to be of little functional importance, thus leading to the conclusion that '[t]he nuclear family was very important indeed': Wrightson, 'Kinship in an English village', p. 332.

[178] See above, ch. 1, pp. 35–9. On the problematic concept of the 'extended family', see Goody, 'The evolution of the family'.

exact relationship to Ralph Josselin.[179] But at other times, the elementary family terms were used in ways that were more inclusive, lumping together various relationships in an apparently undifferentiated manner. And so we find that mothers, step-mothers, and mothers-in-law could be referred to and addressed in exactly the same way, 'my mother', just as siblings, half-siblings, and siblings-in-law could all be referred to and addressed as 'brother' and 'sister'. It has been noted by Macfarlane that the terms 'uncle' and 'cousin' were used in English 'in an almost "classificatory" way', but it appears that significant inclusion and lack of differentiation could be manifested also in historical usages of the nuclear family terms.[180] Familial extension, then, started at the nuclear core. It was not merely reserved for the peripheral kin.

These extended-nuclear usages were indeed so common in seventeenth- and eighteenth-century England because, contrary to any simplistic anthropological account, the language of kinship was used not only to describe relationships by blood and marriage but also to signify social relationships and moral duties. The filial relationship, the parental relationship, the sibling relationship, the avuncular relationship, and even cousinage – all these were potential bonds, as well as possible descriptions of biological connections. The recognition of these relationships by naming, therefore, was an announcement of status and a possible undertaking of obligations. Solidarity, consideration, duty, and support could be expected, even if not given. Indeed, many usages of the language of kinship should be understood within the context of frustrated expectations. Take, for example, the case of Thomas Turner and his wife's mother. When Turner named his wife's mother 'my mother', it was not because he longed for another mother figure in his life, or because he conflated the roles of the mother and the mother-in-law and believed that both were his 'mothers' in the same way. Nor, indeed, did this usage indicate that Turner loved his wife's mother: he did not. The significance of this extended-nuclear usage was in articulating the notion that the marriage of Thomas Turner and wife also created a new filial and parental relationship: it placed Thomas Turner in a filial position in relation to his wife's mother, and placed her in a parental position in relation to him. Theoretically, at least, their relationship should have been that of solidarity and consideration, duty and support. As it happened, these obligations were not undertaken, or at least they were not undertaken by Mrs Slater,

---

[179] Josselin, *Diary*, 21 Feb. 1663, p. 505.
[180] Macfarlane, *Individualism*, p. 146. Robin Fox explains that in the 'Eskimo' system, also typical of England, the nuclear family terms are not used for anyone outside the nuclear family; however, the present analysis suggests that there were some significant historical changes in this respect: Fox, *Kinship and Marriage*, p. 258.

as Turner firmly believed. But when Turner criticised 'my Mother's Nonsense which she is Very full of' he was still expressing his discontent in familial terms.[181] The kinship recognition, then, was the structured framework within which this troubled relationship was conducted. Its expected bond was the yardstick against which Turner measured his disappointment.[182]

From the point of view of textual meaning, however, the result of these extended-nuclear usages is that it is sometimes difficult for the present-day reader to know the identity of the individual referred to by a kinship term, because it is possible that more than one individual – in more than one kinship degree – was designated by the same term. When Anne Godfrey, 'a single woman aged twelve years and a vagrant', testified in her settlement examination that she has 'neither father nor mother', the relationships are clear enough.[183] But when Thomas Turner refers in his diary to 'my brother', it is sometimes impossible to determine which brother, half-brother, or brother-in-law he had in mind. The extended-nuclear usages highlight the importance of analysing kinship terms within their textual and performative context. They also highlight the import-ance of analysing actual usages of kinship terms, while taking account of their complexity, rather than simply attempting to distil an abstract kinship system.

There were nonetheless some recognised forms of naming that enabled people to draw subtle boundaries within their incorporated kinship group and to differentiate between its members. The most important means of differentiation was by affixing kinship terms to Christian names and surnames. Here, too, it is possible trace familiar conventions. Relatives by blood and marriage were usually named by the appropriate kinship term, by their Christian name, or by a combination of both.[184] In contrast, persons incorporated by marriage into a kinship group could be referred to by affixing the kinship term to either the surname, or to the Christian name and surname. This formed the first convention of differentiation.

[181] Thomas Turner, Diary, 6 June 1758.
[182] On one interesting occasion Thomas Turner was so angry that he decided to suspend the kinship recognition: 'I think Mrs Slater (for I am sure her usage to me was never like that of a Mother) Used me with abundance of reflecting scurrillous language tho what for I know not . . . Mrs Slater might do well to sell oisters at Billings gate, but to live amongst Civilized People she must be an Obstruction to theirs and their own happiness': *ibid.*, 28 July 1757. It remains a question whether this defiance was expressed beyond the pages of Turner's diary. The bad relationship between him and his mother-in-law continued, as did his kinship recognition.
[183] The testimony of Anne Godfrey of Exeter, Devon, was taken at Michaelmas 1784: quoted in Taylor, *Poverty*, p. 42.
[184] With the exception of wives and other married women, as seen below. Another excep-tion is the naming of senior siblings by their surname, as examined in Tadmor, 'Dimensions of inequality among siblings in eighteenth-century novels', esp. 304–11.

For example, when James Oakes referred to his wife's father, he named him by his surname, 'my Father Adamson'.[185] The husband of Ralph Josselin's daughter Elizabeth was named by his surname, 'my son Smith'.[186] The spouses of siblings could be named in the same way. Thomas Westmore, the brother-in-law of Thomas Medcalf of Lancaster, was referred to as 'his brother Westmore'.[187] Ralph Josselin named his sister's husband by both his Christian name and surname, 'my brother John Humfreys'.[188] The same applied to the siblings of spouses. Thomas Turner referred to his wife's brother as 'my bro. Slater', or 'my Bro. Sam. Slater'. His wife's sister was called 'my sister Ann Slater'.[189] Finally, the same method was used for naming the spouses of siblings-in-law. For instance, Ralph Josselin referred to the husband of his wife's sister by his surname, 'brother Worrall'.[190] Thus, the reference by the kinship term and surname, or by the kinship term and both Christian name and surname, enabled people to differentiate subtly those who married into a kinship group, while still incorporating them within it.

The second convention of differentiation concerned married women. The same form of naming that designated those who married into a kinship group was also used for designating women who married out of it. Marriage signalled the crucial life-course change in the naming of women, and acquaintances, neighbours, and relations acknowledged the woman's altered state by appropriate forms of naming. Non-kin attached the married woman's surname to various titles, such as 'Mrs', 'Good-wife', or 'Dame'. Kin could use the appropriate kinship terms, but they, too, often attached them to the surname. This form of naming could apply to nearly all female relatives, including married daughters, married sisters, married aunts, and married cousins. Nicholas Blundell wrote his accounts of his daughter's wedding naming her by her new name, 'Gloves given at my Daughter Coppingers Marriage'.[191] Samuel Richardson was quick to refer to his married daughter by her new name, 'my daughter Ditcher'.[192] James Woodforde's way of referring to his beloved sister changed gradually over the years from 'sister Jenny' or 'sister Jane', to

[185] Oakes, *Diaries*, vol. I, 6 Aug. 1781, p. 219; 22 Apr. 1786, p. 241.
[186] Josselin, *Diary*, 3 Apr. 1681, p. 631; 12 Feb. 1681/2, p. 636; 8 Apr. 1683, p. 643; 8 May 1653, p. 643.   [187] Stout, *Autobiography*, entry for 1712, pp. 166–7, and n. 198.
[188] Josselin, *Diary*, 9 Dec. 1657, p. 412.
[189] See, for example, references to Sam Slater in Thomas Turner, *Diary*, 9, 11, 30 Mar. 1761. See reference to Anne Slater: *ibid.*, 12 Aug. 1757.
[190] Josselin, *Diary*, 2 May 1648, p. 124; 1 July 1668, p. 543; 13 Sept. 1676, p. 593.
[191] See also 'Coffipot given to my Daughter Pippard': N. Blundell, *The Great Diurnal of Nicholas Blundell of Little Crosby, Lancashire*, 3 vols. (1720–8), The Record Society of Lancashire and Cheshire, 110, 112, 114, ed. J. J. Bayley, transcribed and annotated F. Tyrer (Preston, 1968–72), vol. III (1720–8), pp. 259, 261.
[192] *Correspondence of Samuel Richardson*, vol. II, p. 46.

'My Sister Pounsett'.[193] Similarly, Mary Hardy referred to her married sister Philis Goggs as 'Sister Goggs'.[194] Other married female relations could be named in the same way. Ralph Josselin's paternal aunt was named by her married name, 'aunt Miles',[195] as were his uncle's daughters, cousins Blundel and Johnson.[196] Mrs Foley's 'dear cousin Dewes' was a female cousin, addressed by her married name.[197]

In addition to all these there were personal ways of differentiation. As we saw, Mary Woodforde expressed her maternal position in relation to her step-children by naming them 'my daughter Alice' and 'Son Heighes'. But the reader of her diary can clearly sense the greater warmth with which she referred to her own offspring: 'my dear little Willy', 'my eldest son Samuel', 'my poor Robin', and 'my dear Mary'.[198] Differentiation was also evident when she wrote of *'my Son Heighes own Mother's friends'*, that is, in present-day terms, her step-son's relatives on his mother's side.[199] Thomas Turner, too, differentiated at times between his full brothers and half-brothers. His way of drawing the boundary was by referring to the former by their Christian names, and to the latter by both their Christian names and surname. 'My brother Moses' was a full brother, whereas 'my brother John Turner' was a half-brother. Mary Hardy, whose two sisters-in-law were both named by her 'Sister Raven', used other means of differentiation: 'went to see sister Raven at the Hall', 'slept at Sister Raven's at the Malthouse'.[200]

Although these conventions of differentiation enabled speakers to draw some boundaries within their incorporated kinship group, the incorporation of kin could still result in a certain degree of opacity. The same forms of naming could apply to diverse relationships, and to diverse individuals. The naming of female relatives could be particularly opaque.

[193] J. Woodforde, *Woodforde at Oxford, 1759–76*, ed. W. N. Hargreaves-Mawdsley (Oxford, 1969), e.g. 15 Dec. 1761, p. 64; 22 Dec. 1761, p. 66; 30 Oct. 1762, p. 90; 8 Nov. 1762, p. 92; 5 Feb. 1763, p. 109; 9 June 1774 p. 230; 2 Dec. 1775, p. 210; 21 Dec. 1775, p. 315, etc.

[194] See, for example, Hardy, *Diary*, 12 May 1791, p. 79. She was also referred to simply as 'sister'.   [195] Josselin, *Diary*, 7 Apr. 1750, p. 195.

[196] *Ibid.*, 17 July 1658, p. 428; Appendix I; Macfarlane, *The Family Life of Ralph Josselin*, p. 138 and n. 1 there, and p. 215. Ralph Josselin's cousin Grace's married name was Johnson. The married name of one of her sisters was probably Blundel. These two sisters were tied together with a third sister in complex inheritance arrangements. Josselin helped them to settle the affair, but it is possible that on this occasion the reference is to these cousins' husbands.

[197] 24 Aug. 1740: *Autobiography and Correspondence of Mary Granville, Mrs Delany*, vol. II, p. 91.

[198] See, for example, Woodforde, 'Book', 14 Jan. 1687, p. 15; 13 Oct. 1687, p. 16; 12 July 1688, p. 18; 22 Oct. 1688, p. 19; 26 Apr. 1689, p. 21.

[199] *Ibid.*, 26 July 1688, p. 22. The term 'friends' here refers to the first Mrs Woodforde's relations, who arranged the second Mrs Woodforde's marriage settlement.

[200] Hardy, *Diary*, 11 Dec. 1783, p. 50; 2 Aug. 1805, p. 120.

Theoretically, the man named by James Oakes as 'Brother Bridge' could be a sister's husband, or the husband of a wife's sister. He could also be related by various half- or step-relationships. However, the options for identifying 'Sister Bridge' were greater. She, too, could be a wife's sister, or the wife of a wife's brother. She, too, could be related in various half- and step-relationships. But she could also be a full sister by blood and marriage named by her married name, which indeed she was. Thus, once more, the qualities of opacity and inclusion alert us to the importance of analysing kinship terms within their textual or other performative contexts, rather than simply charting them according to an abstract scheme. From the theoretical point of view, these qualities lead us back to the first naming convention discussed above, recognition and opacity. Both the means of incorporation and the means of differentiation enabled people to name their kin in ways that recognised them as such, but that at the same time did not disclose the exact nature of the kinship tie. All that the naming system revealed was that a particular individual was related to another in a parental degree, as 'father' or 'mother', in a fraternal degree, as 'brother', in an avuncular degree, as 'uncle', etc. The exact relationship behind these terms – whether, for example, the 'brother' was a brother by full blood, half-blood, by marriage only, or by both blood and marriage – could be obscured, or could at least remain ambiguous without the aid of additional information.

This potentially broad extension of the language of kinship assisted people in making kinship claims. The claiming of kinship was a speech act with which individuals proposed their relationships with one another and announced it by naming. It was an effective statement of both private and public recognition. When Gertrude Booker contested the will of Richard Adey and also made claims to the estate of Edward Jackson junior, the fact that Richard Adey and Edward Jackson senior were known to call each other 'brother' and were heard to do so in company was brought as significant evidence to substantiate her case.[201] When the Reverend John Thomlinson wished to reclaim the money he spent on patterns of silk for his future sister-in-law, he was quick to address her as 'Dear Sister'.[202] The claiming of kinship was also used in contemporary literary texts as a means of creating social situations. When Moll Flanders remains aban-

[201] All that some witnesses could say was that they were known to be brothers by half-blood. The act of naming served in this case as a testimony and helped Gertrude Booker to receive a share in the estate. The disputed will was made by Richard Adey of Sodbury, Gloucestershire. The case was heard on 6 Oct. 1668: J. Addy, *Death, Money and the Vultures: Inheritance and Avarice, 1660–1750* (London and New York, 1992), pp. 109–12 and esp. p. 112. The fact that Gertrude Booker's daughter named Edward Jackson senior 'uncle' was also mentioned as evidence: *ibid.*, p. 110.
[202] Thomlinson, 'Diary', 22 Dec. 1721, p. 162.

doned and near poverty, her friend instructs her to name her 'cousin' (in addition to presenting Moll as a woman of fortune), in order to lend Moll an appropriate air of respectability. The trick works, and Moll soon gets a proposal of marriage.[203] Indeed, the claiming of kinship through naming appears as a conventional pivotal moment in many literary works. When Charles Bingley in *Pride and Prejudice* becomes engaged to Elizabeth's sister Jane, he claims from Elizabeth 'the good wishes and affection of a sister'; after herself becoming engaged to Darcy, Elizabeth asks Jane: 'shall you like to have such a brother?' And when Catherine Morland's brother in *Northanger Abbey* becomes engaged to Isabella Thorpe, she sheds 'tears of joy' at 'the happiness of having such a sister'.[204]

These extended usages of the language of kinship also had significant and broader cultural and political resonances. There is an important resemblance between the extended language of kinship and the biblical rules of incest, set in Leviticus. Many of the relationships forbidden by the biblical rule are also those incorporated by naming in the seventeenth- and eighteenth-century English usages, including the father's wife, the son's daughter, the daughter's daughter, the father's wife's daughter, the father's sister, the mother's sister, the father's brother, the father's brother's wife, the daughter-in-law, the brother's wife, and the wife's sister.[205] Some interdictions are even set in terms of kinship incorporation: 'The nakedness of thy father's wife's daughter, begotten of thy father, *she is thy sister*, thou shalt not uncover her nakedness . . . Thou shalt not uncover the nakedness of thy father's brother, thou shalt not approach to his wife: *she is thine aunt*.'[206] Thus, the biblical interdictions had close resonance in the popular language of kinship. These interdictions also had a significant resonance in the realms of law and politics. The onset of the Reformation in England was inherently bound with debates about the sinfulness of the king's marriage to his 'sister' in the broad sense of the term, that is, his brother's wife, and the validity of papal dispensation in such a case. The exact extent of the prohibited degrees of marriage, consanguinal and affinal, remained a matter of public concern as Henry VIII's statute was changed by Edward VI, repealed by Mary, and reinstated by Elizabeth I.[207] It continued to be debated throughout the

---

[203] Defoe, *Moll Flanders*, p. 92.
[204] Examples quoted in Schapera, *Kinship Terminology in Jane Austen's Novels*, p. 6.
[205] Leviticus 18: 7–18; 20: 11–12, 17–21. The law also proscribes sexual relationships with any woman and her daughter or granddaughter. See also Wolfram, *In-Laws and Outlaws*, esp. ch. 2, and p. 64.   [206] Leviticus 18: 11, 14.
[207] 32 Hen. VIII c. 38; 2 & 3 Edw. VI c. 23; 1 & 2 Ph. & M. c. 8; 1 Eliz. c. 1. See also Wolfram, *In-Laws and Outlaws*, esp. ch. 2, where debates about incest are examined up to the twentieth century.

following century and became once more a focus of concern in relation to the Stuart succession. The claim that the Duke of Monmouth, not the Duke of York, was the rightful heir to the throne was supported with arguments about natural law, the canon law, and the biblical laws of marriage and incest, as can be seen in various contemporary writings such as William Lawrence's *Marriage by the Moral Law of God Vindicated*, Dryden's *Absalom*, or John Locke's *First Treatise of Government*.[208]

Various scholars emphasise the limited extent of the English kinship terminology, presenting it as evidence of a restricted kinship universe. However, the practices of incorporation, current in the seventeenth and eighteenth century, show that this terminology could in fact be used for considerably enlarging the reservoir of recognised kin. A limited set of terms enabled the incorporation into the kinship group of the spouses of kin, the kin of spouses, as well as step- and half-relations: this was particularly the case with the nuclear family terms. Conventions of differentiation permitted the creation of subtle boundaries within the enlarged kinship group, while still pronouncing its solidarity. The extended usages of the kinship terms and the combined usages of terms, names, and surnames, however, could also lead to the creation of opacity. In some ways, then, the kinship terminology served to differentiate kin from non-kin, to distinguish between different kinship degrees, and to differentiate the nuclear family from other kinship ties, as the 'onion model' implies. But in other ways the same terminology also served as a powerful matrix for incorporating new members into the kinship group, for obscuring the boundaries between different kinship degrees, and for tying the nuclear family in extended-nuclear kinship networks.

Plurality

The third organising principle is plurality. There were three important ways in which plurality could be manifested. First, it was possible to refer to the same relationships with the use of more than one kinship term. Secondly, the same kinship terms could be used for referring to different kinship relationships. Thirdly, the plurality of the language of kinship was further intensified due to the currency of colloquial and local usages. The practical implication of all these plural usages was that kin could be named in various and overlapping ways. From the theoretical point of view, the existence of plurality makes it even more difficult to fit the

---

[208] M. Goldie, 'Contextualizing Dryden's Absalom: William Lawrence, the laws of marriage and the case for King Monmouth', in D. B. Hamilton and R. Streier (eds.), *Religion, Literature and Politics in Post-Reformation England, 1540–1688* (Cambridge, 1996), pp. 208–30.

language of kinship, current in the seventeenth and eighteenth centuries, into the 'onion model'.

Plural usages of the same kinship terms have been traced above in detail in the context of other naming conventions. It has been seen that many terms, including the nuclear family terms, could be used in extended ways to refer not only to full relationships by blood and marriage, but also to half-relationships, step-relationships, and in-law relationships. The significance of these extended usages has been discussed, as well as their incompatibility with the accepted model that stresses the straightforward, nuclearly focused, and well-graded structure of the English kinship system. It is now possible to see that, contrary to the accepted view, even the most elementary kinship terms did not remain unchanged throughout the centuries. To be sure, the basic vocabulary of terms changed only little: we still speak of mothers, daughters, brothers, and uncles, etc. But there were changes in the usages of these terms, and there were subtle but significant changes in their meanings. Many of the inclusive ways of naming kin, achieved by using kinship terms on their own or together with names and surnames, have become obsolete. Mary Woodforde's reference to 'my Son Dalgress', the husband of her husband's daughter, or Thomas Turner's reference to 'my father Slater', his wife's father, now sound archaic. Nor are we likely to extend the term 'sister' to include a brother's wife, a wife's sister, or the wife of a wife's brother – as did Ralph Josselin, Mary Hardy, and many others. Thus, it appears that the historical changes in the usages of elementary kinship terms were bound together with subtle semantic shifts, the direction of these shifts being away from plurality and towards growing restriction.

Plurality was more complex in the case of kinship terms whose meanings have undergone greater changes. The main terms that fell into this category were 'nephew', 'niece', 'cousin', and the 'in-law' terminology. The transformations of these historical terms attest to significant changes in the kinship terminology. They also emphasise yet again how difficult it is to fit this language of kinship into the 'onion model'.

The extended usages of 'nephew' and 'niece', first recorded by Morgan, were both old and widespread. The Latin *nepos*, the Old High German *nefo*, and the Old English *nefa* all carried meanings of 'nephew' as well as 'grandson' and this meaning has been retained in various European languages.[209] This extended meaning has also been retained in

---

[209] Goody, *The Development of the Family and Marriage*, p. 266. Macfarlane follows Morgan in describing the restriction of *nephew* and *niece* to the children of the brother and sister of ego (that is, the person from whose point of view the relationship is reckoned), and 'the substitution of grandson and granddaughter in their place in the lineal line': see above, p. 121. Interestingly, the archaic usages of 'nephew' and 'niece' were not necessarily

English for centuries. See, for example, the description of the illustrious familial train of the biblical Judge Abdon, as phrased by the translators of King James's *Authorized Version*: 'Abdon, the sonne of Hillel a Pirathonite iudged Israel. And he had fourty sonnes and thirtie nephewes that rode on threescore and ten asse-colts' (Judges 12: 13–14).

The latter thirty riders are of course not the sons of Abdon's siblings, but his grandsons. The learned translators probably knew well that this was their relationship, not only because they could read the Hebrew original, which in this case describes the connection as *'benei banim'*, meaning 'sons' sons', but because they also had before them earlier commentaries that referred to this as a lineal relationship.[210] For instance, the commentary on this passage in a 1550 Bible concordance reads: 'Loke more in these wordes. The Sonnes Sonne, the childes child. Posteritie.'[211] The term 'nephew' in the sense of grandchild may have remained current in learned and literary usages due to the similar meaning of the Latin term *nepos*, and due to the currency of 'nephew' in the biblical translations. By the middle of the eighteenth century, however, this usage had become archaic. Already in 1755 Samuel Johnson was able to say that 'nephew' in the sense of 'grandson' was 'Out of use'.[212] However this sense of 'nephew' clearly did not disappear altogether: Dr Johnson still used it in one of his letters in 1777.[213] A dictionary of English dialect continued to

gender-specific: the *OED* mentions that 'nephew' could also apply to a brother or a sister's daughter, whereas the *Century Dictionary* produces an example from Wycliffe's translation of Genesis 31: 43, where 'neece' is not necessarily female: *The Century Dictionary: An Encyclopedic Lexicon of the English Language*, prepared under the superintendence of W. Dwight Whitney, 6 vols. (New York, 1889–91), s.v. 'niece'.

[210] Judges 12: 13–14; 'nephew' is also used by Tyndale: 'And after him Abdon son of Hellel a pharathonite judged Israel. And he had forty sons and thirty nephews, that rode on thirty ass colts': *Tyndale's Old Testament, Being the Pentateuch of 1530, Joshua to 2 Chronicles of 1537 and Jonah*, trans. William Tyndale, in a modern spelling edition and with an introduction by David Daniell (New Haven, 1992), Judges 12: 13–14; see also 'neuis' in *The Coverdale Bible* (1535), Introduction by S. L. Greenslade (Folkestone, 1975).

[211] J. Marbecke, *A Concordance, that Is to Saie, a Work Wherein . . . Ye Maie Redely Find Any Worde Conteyned in the Whole Bible* (London, 1550), s.v. 'nephew'; Wycliffe, in a yet earlier translation used a similar descriptive designation: 'Elel Pharatonyt; the which hadde fourty sones and thretti of hem sones sones, siteinge up upon seventi coltis of assis': *The Holy Bible, Containing the Old and New Testaments with the Apocryphal Book in the Earliest English Versions Made from the Latin Vulgate by John Wycleffe and his Followers*, ed. J. Forshall and Sir F. Madden, 2 vols. (Oxford, 1850), Judges 12:13. Compare also *The Holy Bible: New Revised Standard Version* (London, 1989), which conveys the biblical language in accessible and current terms: '. . . Abdon, the son of Hillel the Pirathonite judged Israel. He had forty sons and thirty grandsons who rode on seventy donkeys.'

[212] Johnson, *Dictionary of the English Language*, s.v. 'nephew'.

[213] 'He is by several descents the nephew of Hugo Grotius . . . Let it not be said in any lettered country a nephew of Grotius asked a charity and was refused': Dr Johnson to Dr Vyse, 9 July 1777, quoted in *The Century Dictionary*, s.v. 'nephew'.

report its usage in the nineteenth century.[214] Niece in the sense of grand-daughter clearly also survived: Mrs Radcliffe, for example, still used it in *The Italian* in 1797.[215]

Macfarlane explains these changing usages of 'nephew' and 'grandson' with the aid of the 'onion model'. In the archaic usages the second and third rings of the onion have been fused, there being no separation between the terminology for grandchildren and nephews and nieces, but in the modern usage the onion rings have separated. This, according to Macfarlane, was a notable change, although it did not amount to a basic change in the kinship structure.[216] But if one goes beyond the level of the structure and examines actual historical usages, the onion model appears too orderly and well-graded to explain both the usages and their process of change. The terms 'nephew'/'niece' and 'grandchild' did not simply replace one another in succession, and at any moment during the six-teenth and even the seventeenth centuries they may have existed side by side.[217] Thus, although in general terms Macfarlane's description of this terminological shift holds, it is important to realise that this was a very slow process and that for a long time plural usages could have existed simultaneously. Ralph Josselin, for example, gave a sermon on 11 Novem-ber 1669 on a text from 1 Timothy 5:4: 'If any widdow have *children or nephews*, let them learne first to shew piety at home, & to requite their parents: for that is good & acceptable before god.'[218] Clearly, he was familiar with the biblical usage of 'nephew' and it seems that he also expected his audience to understand it. But when he wrote in his personal diary about his own children's children, he referred to them as 'grandchil-dren': 'all my children and grandchildren with mee at my sisters at dinner'.[219]

The language of kinship also included other and possibly more wide-spread plural usages, which reflected on the relative position of 'nephew' and 'niece' in the kinship structure, and which therefore confused further the neat gradation of the onion rings. Most importantly, while 'nephew' and 'niece' could be used to designate grandchildren, 'cousin' could be used for designating nephew and niece. In other words, not only was it the case that the second and third rings of the onion could be fused together

---

[214] Recorded in Kent: *English Dialect Dictionary*, ed. J. Wright (New York, 1903), s.v. 'nephew'.

[215] *OED*, s.v. 'niece', and see other examples there. See also *English Dialect Dictionary*, s.v. 'niece'.

[216] See Macfarlane, *Individualism*, pp. 146–7. See also the reference to Morgan there.

[217] Goody notes usages of 'grandson' from the sixteenth century: Goody, *The Development of the Family and Marriage*, p. 266.

[218] The sermon was delivered on 11 Nov. 1669, as quoted from the diary of John Bufton of Coggeshall: Macfarlane, *The Family Life of Ralph Josselin*, p. 223.

[219] Josselin, *Diary*, 27 Jan. 1679, p. 622.

due to the plurality of 'nephew', 'niece', and 'grandchild', but the third and fourth rings of the onion could also be fused due to the plurality of 'nephew', 'niece', and 'cousin'.[220] The term 'cousin', imported from the French after the Norman Conquest, has been used for centuries very widely. At the nearest, it was applied to the sons and daughters of siblings: 'Cousin Harlowe, said my aunt Hervey, allow me to say that my cousin Clary's prudence may be confided in.' Mrs Hervey from *Clarissa* was speaking to her nephew about her niece.[221] Similarly, John Penrose of Cornwall, writing in 1767 referred to his brother's daughter as 'Coz: Fanny'.[222] However 'cousin' could also apply to the sons and daughters of aunts and uncles, as in the present-day sense, and it could be used more broadly in recognition of more distant kin. Sometimes it seems that this term was used simply to indicate that a kinship claim existed,[223] rather than to recognise any specific kinship degree. Such plural usages of 'cousin' are well known: historians have traced them in various sources and studied their significance.[224]

The term 'cousin' was thus broadly used in the seventeenth and eighteenth centuries both to recognise the existence of a broad range of kinship ties, or indeed to claim their recognition, in addition to designating the relationships of sons and daughters of siblings, uncles, and aunts. Examples of these usages can be traced in the diary of the seventeenth-century clergyman, Ralph Josselin, where they were also effective in constructing the diarist's universe of recognised kin. In the following case, for example, the term 'cousin' was probably used by Josselin in its nearest designation, referring to a sibling's son. Tom Hodson, mentioned below, was the son of Ralph Josselin's sister Anna, who stood in his debt.[225]

---

[220] According to *The Century Dictionary*, s.v. 'nephew', the plurality of 'cousin' and 'nephew' was further intensified because not only could 'cousin' apply to 'nephew', but 'nephew' could apply to 'cousin'. An example from Shakespeare is quoted to support this usage; however, I found no others.

[221] Quoted in Goody, *The Development of the Family and Marriage*, p. 271. The identification of 'cousin', 'nephew', and 'niece' exists in other Indo-European languages: *ibid.*, p. 266.

[222] *Letters from Bath*, p. 172, and see also pp. 62, 94.

[223] That is, beyond the lineal line and the first degree of lateral kin. The term 'cousin' did indicate that the person concerned is not a grandparent, parent, sibling, or offspring of the speaker, nor the spouse of any of the above.

[224] See, for example, 'The word "cousin" was far wider and vaguer in its use than it is today. Those so addressed included distant affinal relatives on the one hand, nephews and even grandchildren on the other': Houlbrooke, *The English Family*, p. 40; Trumbach, *The Rise of the Egalitarian Family*, Appendix A; Cressy, 'Kinship and kin interaction', e.g. 44–53, 65–7; Morgan, *The Puritan Family*, pp. 154–60.

[225] Macfarlane identifies this as one of Ralph Josselin's first cousins, probably the youngest son of his aunt Anne, née Josselin, and her husband Daniel Hudson. He argues that this incident 'shows both the obligations felt to exist between cousins, and their irritating nature'. However, Joseph Josselin's will (as Macfarlane also notes) lists Hudson's four sons, but not a son named Tom. The surname 'Hudson' is possibly also different from

Tom Hodson, came to borrow of me 20^{li}. I wondered at *my Cosins* boldnes, who had for his mother and selfe borrowed 5^{li} and never yet paid it.[226]

Josselin also used the term 'cousin' to refer to the sons and daughters of his uncles and aunts.[227] In addition, as observed earlier in this chapter, he used the term 'cousin' to extend the notion of cousinage to a cousin's spouse.[228] But Josselin also used the term 'cousin' more broadly to include first cousins once removed, second cousins, and perhaps even more distant kin. Indeed, he may have even used this term not only to describe existing relationships, but also to make effective claims of cousinage on very distant kin. Such, for example, was his claim on his 'cousin' John Josselin. On 31 August 1647 Ralph Josselin wrote: 'rid to Much Lees to see Mrs Ellin that went from her uncle without his consent and married *my Cosin Josselin*'. The actual relationship between these two Josselins – John and Ralph – is unknown. At the nearest they were second cousins and it could be that they were more distantly related.[229] But they were connected not only by the same surname and notions of a shared ancestry, but by personal goodwill and important common associations. Ralph Josselin was the vicar of Earls Colne and also held land there and in a neighbouring manor. John Josselin was the Steward of both manors and apparently also shared Ralph Josselin's religious views.[230] Mrs Ellin was eminently connected: she was the niece of Mr Richard Harlakenden, the lord of the same manors and the patron of Ralph Josselin's living. In this dense network of commitments and relationships, it was no wonder that the vicar was quick to claim the steward's cousinage and even give his blessing to the eloping couple.[231]

the surname mentioned in this entry: 'Hodson'. There are other usages in the family wills in which siblings' sons are referred to as 'cousins'. Lastly, a previous reference to a five-pound loan to Ann Hodson lends further support to my suggestion that 'cosin' in this case refers to Tom Hodson, the son of Ann, Ralph Josselin's sister: 'gave my sister Anna 10^s and lent her 5^{li}', Josselin, *Diary*, 12 June 1656, p. 370; Macfarlane, *Family Life of Ralph Josselin*, pp. 137–8, 214–15.

[226] Josselin, *Diary*, 7 Nov. 1657, p. 409. See the reference to this loan in the note above.
[227] For example, 'I was helpful to end my cosin Blundels, and Johnsons business and also to enlarge Betties portion', was probably a reference to first cousins, the daughters of a paternal uncle: *ibid.*, 17 July 1658, p. 428; Appendix 1. Betty Josselin and Grace Johnson were two of the daughters of Ralph Josselin senior. 'Cousin Blundel' was probably the married name of either Anne or Dorothy, the two other daughters in this family. See also Macfarlane, *Family Life of Ralph Josselin*, p. 138, and n. 1 there, and n. 196 above.
[228] '. . . *my Cousin Benton* miscarryed' was his reference to the wife of Mr Jeremy Benton, the son of a paternal aunt: Josselin, *Diary*, 1 Sept. 1644, p. 18. The aunt is Mrs Mary Benton, née Josselin. See also Macfarlane, *Family Life of Ralph Josselin*, p. 137.
[229] Josselin, *Diary*, p. 102. See also Macfarlane's comment, there: 'John Josselin . . . is not known, actually, to have been related to RJ.' The possibility that they may have been second cousins is raised in Macfarlane, *The Family Life of Ralph Josselin*, pp. 137–8. For a discussion of this relationship, see *ibid.*, pp. 137–9.
[230] Macfarlane, *The Family Life of Ralph Josselin*, pp. 138–9.
[231] *Ibid.* On 14 Oct. 1647 he also witnessed an agreement between his 'cousin' and his patron upon the payment of Mrs Ellin's portion, and on 6 May 1649 he preached at the

Thus, like so many other usages studied above, these usages of 'cousin' manifest the double principles of recognition and opacity, indicating the existence of a recognised relationship while potentially concealing its exact degree. From the structural point of view, these plural usages of 'cousin' do not match the neat gradation of the 'onion model'; still less do they match it in view of the potential plural usages of 'nephew' and 'niece'. Plurality was further intensified due to the currency of other interchangeable usages. Because of their plurality, 'cousin', 'nephew', and 'niece' were also used alongside other general and opaque terms, such as 'kinsman', 'kinswoman', and 'relation'. Henry Horsfall is first named in relation to John Horsfall as his 'cousin', and then as 'his said kinsman'.[232] Ralph Josselin was first mentioned by his uncle in his will as 'my nephew', then subsequently as 'my cousin'.[233] One character in *The History of Miss Betsy Thoughtless* is referred to successively as Lord ****'s 'female relation', 'relation', 'kinswoman', and 'cousin'.[234] Indeed, in literary works these plural usages are often more pronounced because they form part of the literary fabric. In the context of a single letter in *Clarissa*, Mr Antony Harlowe names his brother's daughter six times as '*niece*' and six times as '*cousin*', while describing himself throughout as 'your uncle'.[235] In the same context he also names her once as 'child', and three times more using the title 'miss' with and without her name and surname. 'Come, come, cousin', 'let me tell you, niece', 'I love you dearly still, miss', and 'marriage is a queer state, child' – are therefore all references made in the same context by the same individual and to the same individual. They serve to convey important shades of meaning, steering the text's emotional register from rebuke and anger to tenderness and intimacy.

Other plural usages also show that, contrary to any rigid system of classification, there was more than one way of naming kin. The previous section of this chapter explains how nuclear family terms were commonly used for referring and addressing relations-in-law, whereas subtle differ-

baptism of his 'cousin's' son. It could be that Ralph Josselin used this connection to extend his network of cousinage even further. Who, for example, was 'cousin Hurril' or 'Hurrell', of whose misfortune he reported in his diary and whom he accompanied to London together with Mr Richard Harlakenden? Could she be connected to the Reverend William Hurrell, a relation by marriage of Ellin, 'cousin Josselin's' wife? This claim of cousinage would bring Ralph Josselin yet closer to his patron, as Anne Hurrell was Mr Richard Harlakenden's first cousin: see Josselin, *Diary*, entries for 12 July 1663, p. 499; 30 Jan. 1663, p. 505; 22–4 Mar. 1663/4, p. 506; Appendix I.

[232] Stout, *Autobiography*, entry for 1699, p. 127.

[233] The will of Ralph Josselin, yeoman, of Cranham Hall, Essex, made 27 Nov. 1656. John Hudson was also mentioned as 'cousin' in his uncle Joseph Josselin's will, the will of Joseph Josselin, yeoman, made 7 Nov. 1642. For both wills, see Macfarlane, *The Family Life of Ralph Josselin*, pp. 214–15.

[234] Haywood, *Betsy Thoughtless*, pp. 506, 507, 510, 516.

[235] Richardson, *Clarissa*, pp. 154–8.

entiations between relations by blood and marriage and relations by
marriage only were introduced with the aid of combined usages of terms,
names, and surnames. This, however, is not to say that the in-law terminology was unknown. Rather, both the extended-nuclear usages and the
in-law terminology were known and practised. The naming of relations
by marriage as relations 'in-law' is very old.[236] There are no English terms
that correspond absolutely to the Hebrew terms *hatan* and *kalah*, but
even the earliest translators of the Hebrew Bible chose to name Ruth as
Naomi's daughter-in-law and David as the son-in-law of King Saul.[237] A
1550 Bible concordance lists 'Sonne', in the sense of *filius* as separate from
'Sonne in Lawo', meaning *gener*.[238] Similarly, the Hebrew terms *hoten* and
hotenet, *ham* and *hamot*, indicating the wife's and husband's father and
mother, have been translated into English with the use of the nearest
equivalents, 'father-in-law' and 'mother-in-law'.[239] The in-law terminology was clearly also used in ordinary speech. Mary Hardy reported in her
diary 'got our breakfast at my sister-in laws',[240] and Joseph Polybank, a
carpenter, testified in his settlement examination that his father 'had
placed him with his brother-in-law . . . with whom he lived two years in
the nature of a servant'.[241] Indeed, the in-law terminology was commonly
used in legal documents, among them wills, to enable an exact recognition of the persons concerned: for example, references to 'brother-in-law'
are current in the wills connected with the Josselin family, recorded by
Macfarlane.[242] However, the in-law terminology was also used together
with other overlapping usages. In the context of three consecutive diary
entries, Thomas Turner refers to the same individual as 'my Sister in Law
Anne Slater', 'my Wifes sister', and simply 'my sister'.[243] In other words,

---

[236] Goody dates the use of the in-law suffix to the Norman Conquest: Goody, *The Development of the Family and Marriage*, p. 269.

[237] The other senses of the Hebrew terms *hatan* and *kalah* are bridegroom and bride. See,
for example, Ruth 1:6, 22 and 1 Samuel 18:17–22 in *Tyndale's Old Testament*. The same
usages are found in Wycliffe's translation of the Vulgate. Interestingly, Naomi addresses
Ruth as 'daughter' in both the Hebrew and English version: 'And Naomi said unto Ruth
her *daughter in law*, it is good, *my daughter*, that thou go out with his maidens.'

[238] Marbecke, *A Concordance*, s.v. 'Sonne'. See also a concordance of 1632, where the Latin
equivalent of the Hebrew usage is also mentioned as *gener*: J. Buxtorf, *Concordantiae
Bibliorum Hebraicae* (Basle, 1632). See also Wilson, *Christian Dictionary*, s.v. 'Sonne',
which also mentions the difference between a 'Legal' and 'Natural Sonne', referring also
to a 'Sonne in law'.

[239] See, for example, *ham* in Genesis 38: 13, 25, *hamot* in Ruth 2: 11, 3: 17, *hoten* in Exod. 18:
1, 2, 5, 12, *hotenet* in Deuteronomy 27:23. The Latin term for these relationships is *socer*,
see Buxtorf, *Concordantiae Bibliorum*.   [240] Hardy, *Diary*, 27 Sept. 1775, p. 17.

[241] The same man is later referred to as 'his uncle'. 23 Nov. 1775, West Alvington, Devon:
quoted in Taylor, *Poverty*, p. 52.

[242] See, for example, 'my loving brother-in-law' in John Josselin's will, proved 20 Mar. 1691;
'my brother-in-law Lawrence Shepherd', in Thomas Constable's will, made 2 June
1643, proved 2 May 1648; 'my brother-in-law Daniel Hudson', in Joseph Josselin's will,
made 7 Nov. 1642, proved 6 Dec. 1645: Macfarlane, *The Family Life of Ralph Josselin*, pp.
213–16.   [243] Thomas Turner, Diary, 4–6 June 1758.

he identifies her by her relationship to himself via his wife, by her name, by her relationship to his wife only, and by her relationship to himself only. Numerous similar examples of plural usages can be found in this and other texts, highlighting again and again the diversity of the language of kinship.

The plurality of the in-law terminology was further complicated by the fact that it was also used to refer to relationships that we would now term step- and half-relationships. When Ralph Josselin wrote 'my father was a widdower, and my corrupt heart feared a mother in law', he was referring not to a wife's mother (which at that time he obviously did not have, being but a boy), but to a father's second wife.[244] Tony Lumpkin in *She Stoops to Conquer* refers to his mother's husband as 'father in law'.[245] Thomas Turner's 'sister in law Elizabeth' was his father's daughter by his first marriage,[246] whereas the second wife of Mr Dashwood's late father, in Jane Austen's *Sense and Sensibility*, is described as Mr Dashwood's 'mother-in-law'.[247] These in-law terms were thus used to refer to various relationships established by law – that is, by marriage – rather than only to siblings' spouses or the near kin of one own's spouse. In other words, the seventeenth- and eighteenth-century terminology made no difference at this point between consanguinity and affinity, like the French terminology today, in which *beau-père* and *belle-mère* mean both parents-in-law and step-parents.[248] To emphasise the extension of plurality, it is important to recognise that at the same time the step- terminology was also in use. William Stout described the case of two children who were taken away 'from their stepmother'.[249] Shadwell's *The Volunteers* contains the following question: 'What is that Father's wife of kin to you?', to which the answer is: 'My true Stepmother'.[250] But, as Samuel Johnson explained in his dictionary, the term step 'is now seldom applied but to the mother', whereas terms such as step-father or step-brother were evidently not acceptable usages.[251]

Finally, the plurality of the language of kinship in seventeenth- and

[244] Josselin, *Diary*, p. 2. Note 1 there says: 'Here as elsewhere, Josselin's terminology differs from modern usages. He is referring to his step-mother.'
[245] O. Goldsmith, *She Stoops to Conquer: Or, The Mistakes of a Night* (1773), in *Eighteenth-Century Plays*, ed. R. Quintana (New York, 1952), I: ii; v: ii, pp. 354, 400.
[246] Thomas Turner, Diary, 20 Apr. 1759.   [247] Austen, *Sense and Sensibility*, p. 40.
[248] See also Segalen, *Historical Anthropology of the Family*, p. 45.
[249] Stout, *Autobiography*, entry for 1694, p. 110.
[250] Shadwell, *The Volunteers*, I: ii, quoted in *OED*, s.v. 'stepmother'. Note also the following quotation there from the 1598 translation of Terence's *Hecyra* II: i which highlights the different usages of the in-law and step-terminology: 'with one consent all stepmothers hate their daughters in law'.
[251] Johnson, *Dictionary of the English Language*, s.v. 'step'. Other usages noted here are stepdaughter and stepson, used by the Saxons.

eighteenth-century England could be intensified even further due to the currency of colloquial or local usages. The term 'daddy', for example, has been known as a diminutive for 'father' since at least the early sixteenth century.[252] 'Grand Dada' and 'grandmamma' were only two of the recorded diminutive forms of the formal terms 'grandfather' and 'grandmother'.[253] An aunt could also be called 'auntie' or 'naunt',[254] and in the north of England a child could be called 'bairn'.[255] The child of an uncle could thus be called 'brother-bairn'.[256] Further research will surely uncover more such usages, and it will be interesting to see whether this lexical richness did also amount to any local or rank-specific structural differences.[257] Furthermore, it is important to emphasise in this context that behind any known lexeme, designating a kinship relationship, there were numerous forms of spelling and endless forms of pronunciation. 'Faater', 'fadder', 'fader', 'fadther', and 'fadthre', for example, are only some of the recorded variations of the formal term 'father'; 'grandfer', 'granfa', 'gaffa', 'granfey', and 'grenver' are some of the recorded variations of the formal term 'grandfather'.[258]

Thus, by the seventeenth and eighteenth centuries, the English language had accumulated a rich and diversified kinship terminology. It contained simultaneously existing usages, stemming back to different etymological roots. Some terms could be relegated to different registers, as happened for a while to the literary 'nephew' and the more common 'grandchild', or as continued to be the case with 'father' and 'daddy'. Others could be differentiated at times according to their uses, such as the relatively exact in-law terminology, compared to the more opaque and informal incorporated kinship terms. But many kinship terms simply existed side by side, and were used alternately. Speakers drew on them in order to invest their words with many meanings and shades of meaning.

---

[252] See reference to 'dadyes and All ther yong babyes' by Skelton, quoted in *OED*, s.v. 'daddy'.

[253] See, for example, references to 'grand-dad', 'grandad', 'grandada', or 'grand-daddy' from the late seventeenth to the early nineteenth centuries, recorded in *OED*, s.v. 'grand-dad', 'gran(d)-daddy'. See also references to usages of 'grand-mamma' from the same period, *ibid.*, s.v. 'grandmamma'.

[254] See references in *OED* and the *English Dialect Dictionary*, s.v. 'auntie', 'aunt'.

[255] *OED*, s.v. 'bairn'.

[256] *English Dialect Dictionary*, s.v. 'brother'. The example quoted is from Scotland.

[257] Structural differences could arise from terminological differences, but also from the preference of particular combinations of terms. It is important to note in this context the meticulous and subtle analysis in Issa's unpublished PhD dissertation that reveals that the language of kinship used in seventeenth-century County Durham was the same as that known at that time in other parts of the country: Issa, 'Obligation and choice'.

[258] These are examples of nineteenth-century usages, recorded in the *English Dialect Dictionary*, s.v. 'father', 'grandfather'. It is reasonable to suggest that in the eighteenth century there was similar, if not greater, diversity.

In addition, there were diverse socially recognised conventions that enabled speakers to ascribe different meanings to the same kinship terms. The meanings of the language of kinship in the seventeenth and eighteenth centuries were therefore highly contextualised: their great plurality cannot possibly be charted with the aid of the simple scheme of the 'onion model'. Nor does this linguistic diversity indicate that kinship terminology remained stable for many centuries. On the contrary, it is clear by now that both kinship terms and conventional usages continued to evolve and change.

If we examine the terminological changes from the point of view of the present, we can see that the meanings of some seventeenth- and eighteenth-century terms underwent subtle shifts, as happened to the elementary kinship terms, which lost some of their broad incorporated usages. Other terms were gradually relegated to one or two of their senses: such was the case of 'nephew', 'niece', and 'cousin'. Some terms, such as the derivations of 'kin', became increasingly more archaic, and the collective kinship terms 'friends' and 'connexions' became obsolete. The combined usages of kinship terms and surnames also became largely outdated, and the use of kinship terms only as forms of address became more restricted. The step- and in-law terminologies, however, were considerably expanded and brought into current use. Taking a 'Whiggish' view, it is possible to say that these changes had the effect of defining more clearly familial roles and relationships, and restricting the number of kin recognised by naming. These changes also had the effect of highlighting the biological kin and isolating the nuclear family, while separating it from other recognised kinship ties, and particularly from affinal ties. Collective terms became outdated, relationships by marriage were more clearly differentiated, and the inclusiveness and opacity of many terms and usages was considerably reduced.

But people in the seventeenth and eighteenth centuries lacked this historical perspective. They did not know that they were taking part in a grand terminological transformation. For them the language of kinship, with its diverse and pluralistic usages, was a living reality. Indeed, the richness of the historical language of kinship attests to its vitality. It reveals the importance of kinship recognition in both the context of specific social exchanges, and in the culture more broadly.

Diffusion

While the language of kinship was used so richly in early modern England to designate kin, it was also used in the context of many other social relationships. It would be impossible to cover in this chapter the full scope of the diffused usages of the language of kinship in early modern England. But it is important nonetheless at least to note the principle that the language of kinship could be used well beyond the designation of any circles of kin. From the structural point of view, such diffusion is significant. If the 'onion model' often proved unhelpful for understanding the lexical variety and structural complexity of the language of kinship in seventeenth- and eighteenth-century England, we will now see that it is also unhelpful for disclosing its broad diffusion through other realms of social discourse.

Indeed, if we examine usages of kinship terms in early modern sources, we can see that there was hardly a single kinship term in the English language that was used for designating kin alone. The nearer the kinship term, the broader were its applications. The term 'father', for example, could be used in seventeenth- and eighteenth-century England not only for designating the male progenitor, the step-father, the adoptive-father, and the father-in-law, but also for designating a remote male ancestor.[259] It could also be used as an appellation for any old man, particularly one 'reverend for age, learning, and piety', as Samuel Johnson explained in his *Dictionary of the English Language*.[260] Additionally, 'father' could also be used broadly for designating he who provides an original example,[261] and he who acts with paternal care and tenderness.[262] A close and senior male friend, for example, could thus also be referred to in paternal terms. 'My dear papa', is how Miss Westcomb addressed her 'second father', Samuel Richardson;[263] Miss Highmore referred to him as 'honoured papa Richardson'.[264] He, in turn, referred to them as 'daughter of my heart' (alongside his 'daughters by nature'),[265] and 'my dear girl'.[266] Ceremonially, the term 'father' was also used to designate any friend or senior male relative who gave away a woman at her wedding. When the brother of Thomas Turner's faithful maidservant was married to another occasional employee at the Turner household, for example, Turner acted as 'what is

---

[259] Wilson, *Christian Dictionary*, s.v. 'father'; *OED*, s.v. 'father'; Johnson, *Dictionary of the English Language*, s.v. 'father'.

[260] Johnson, *Dictionary of the English Language*, s.v. 'father'; see also *OED*, s.v. 'father'.

[261] As in the biblical usage 'Jobal was the *father* of all such as handle the harp and organ', Genesis 4: 21, quoted in Johnson's *Dictionary of the English Language*, s.v. 'father'.

[262] 'I was father to the poor', says Job in the 1611 Authorized Version of biblical text. Job 29: 16, quoted in Johnson, *Dictionary of the English Language*, s.v. 'father'.

[263] *The Correspondence of Samuel Richardson*, vol. III, pp. 320–2, 258, 308.

[264] Miss Highmore to Miss Mulso, *ibid.*, vol. II, p. 258.

[265] *Ibid.*, p. 250.

[266] He also referred to her as 'dear Madam', 'dear Lady', 'Madam', and 'my dear sweet friend', etc., *ibid.*, vol. II, pp. 209, 211, 215. See also E. Donoghue, 'Male–female friendship and English fiction in the mid-eighteenth century', unpublished PhD dissertation (Cambridge, 1996), pp. 101–72.

commonly Call'd Father', and gave the bride away.[267] Notions of father-hood were also significant in perceptions of monarchic government. Though it was the subject of so many political and philosophical contro-versies, the idea of paternal and sacrosanct monarchy did not disappear from eighteenth-century social thought.[268] It could also be expressed at the popular level: when King George II died, for example, Thomas Turner described him in his diary as 'King and Parent of this our most happy Isle'.[269] And when it came to religious life, 'father' had very significant usages indeed. It was used for designating the influential ecclesiastical writers of the first century, and it was also known as 'the title of a popish confessor, particularly a Jesuit', as Samuel Johnson explains. It was used, moreover, as an 'appellation of the first person of the adorable Trinity', and indeed as an appellation of the Creator himself.[270] 'Our Father which art in Heaven, Hallowed be thy name', were the first words of the Lord's Prayer, memorised by every child in early modern England.

Broad usages such as these reveal the immense cultural significance of the language of kinship in seventeenth- and eighteenth-century England. Not only did this 'nuclear-extended' kinship system serve as a powerful matrix for incorporating many non-kin into any kinship groups, it also served as a matrix for diffusing models of kinship in many areas of life. It was the moral significance of the language of kinship that facilitated and promoted its broad diffusion. If we look at the above quoted usages of 'father', we can see that they all draw on a certain moral understanding of the quality of 'fatherhood', which included attributes such as authority, seniority, care, and tenderness. This moral understanding no doubt enabled people to make sense of – and employ – such broad usages of 'father', well beyond the purposes of identifying male progenitors and other senior male kin.

In a similar manner, the term 'mother' could be used broadly to manifest a range of maternal attributes, well beyond the identification of 'mothers' by blood and marriage. An eighteenth-century diarist such as James Woodforde, for example, named as 'mothers' various non-related females who performed quasi-maternal roles such as housekeeping and

[267] Thomas Turner, Diary, 7 Feb. 1763; see also 2 Jan. 1764. See also OED, s.v. 'father'.
[268] See references to various thinkers in Clark, English Society, ch. 3.
[269] Thomas Turner, Diary, 26 Oct. 1760. See also, for example, how a novelist such as Richardson referred to the sacrosanct nature of monarchy in Pamela, and also to the related notion of the God-like and beneficent master-father, while still advertising the notion that the laws of the land stand above the king: Richardson, Pamela, ed. Sabor, pp. 309, 428.
[270] Johnson, Dictionary of the English Language, s.v. 'father', see also ibid.: 'the title of a senator of old Rome'.

the provision of food and drink. 'Mother Charles' was a bed-maker in New College, Oxford,[271] whereas 'Mother Yeoman',[272] 'Mother Redford',[273] 'Mother Armin',[274] and 'Mother Holders' were only some of the innkeepers and victuallers whose establishments the young Woodforde frequented.[275] The near-kinship term 'brother' was also used to indicate not only a variety of siblings by blood and marriage, but also much broader relationships of amity, sympathy, and fellowship. 'I am distressed for thee, my brother Jonathan' were the moving words of David's lamentation after the death of his dear friend.[276] The man recognised by Ralph Josselin as 'brother Clarke' was also not his brother by blood or half-blood (for Josselin had none), nor his brother by marriage, related through step-relations or through Josselin's sisters and his wife; rather, he was a fellow-worshipper and fellow-parishioner, a brother-in-Christ.[277] Indeed, in religious language, as Samuel Johnson explained, the term 'brother' could be used very broadly as a reference to 'man in general'.[278] But at the same time it could also be used for designating fellow-members in exclusive associations. 'Brother Goodenough' who came to visit Woodforde on the morning of 10 June 1775, for example, was the secretary of Woodforde's Masonic Lodge, and he was only one of the 'brothers' with whom Woodforde socialised.[279]

If we turn to more distant terms, we find that they, too, could be used broadly. Some usages of 'aunt' and 'uncle', for example, may well suggest how the language of kinship could shade into domestic, servile, and close community relationships. For instance, the *Gentleman's Magazine* of December 1793 recorded that 'it is common in Cornwall to call all elderly persons Aunt or Uncle, prefixed to their names'.[280] In 1830 S. P. Holbrook noted that in many families 'children are taught to address the older servant as uncle or auntee, and this is sometimes more than a figure of speech'.[281] In America 'aunt' and 'uncle' became current appellations

---

[271] To whom Woodforde also referred to as 'Mrs Charles'.
[272] Woodforde, *At Oxford*, 28 Nov. 1761, p. 61; 15 Jan. 1763, p. 105; 28 Jan. 1763, p. 108. [273] *Ibid.*, 16 Oct. 1766, p. 17; 2 Dec. 1761, p. 61.
[274] *Ibid.*, 1 Jan. 1762, p. 68. [275] *Ibid.*, 12, 13 Nov. 1760, p. 20.
[276] 2 Samuel 1: 26.
[277] On this occasion, 'brother Clarke' absented himself from a religious meeting because of his dissatisfaction 'as to the place of worship'. This may have been Ed Clark, referred to on 1644 as 'my Christian friend': Josselin, *Diary*, 2 May 1652, p. 278, and compare 26 Aug. 1644, p. 17. See also Cressy, who noted that 'Brother' could also be used to designate a 'brother in Christ': Cressy, 'Kinship and kin interaction', 66.
[278] Johnson, *Dictionary of the English Language*, s.v. 'brother'.
[279] Woodforde, *At Oxford*, 10 July 1775, p. 288. For other 'brothers', see 'Brother Stinton', who 'supped &c' on 10 Nov. 1774 (p. 257), or 'Brother Wood of Braze-nose'. In the plural, they are called 'brothers': *ibid.*, 9 Mar. 1775, p. 277; 23 Feb. 1775, p. 274; 1 June 1775, p. 286. [280] Quoted in *OED*, s.v. 'uncle'.
[281] S. P. Holbrook, *Sketches by Traveller*, vol. III, quoted in *OED*, s.v. 'uncle'.

to elderly black slaves, used particularly by their white owners and other white people.[282] It is significant, however, that while such broad usages of kinship terms could indicate a general sense of seniority and regard, they could also designate a negative sense of familiarity. Such a sense may well have been implicit in usages of 'uncle' and 'aunt' to black slaves, and they were also evident in usages of 'aunt' denoting an 'old woman or gossip', or 'a bawd or procuress'.[283] Beyond all this, the terms 'aunt' and 'uncle' could also be employed in specific figurative and symbolic usages. For instance, 'Uncle George' was a form of reference to King George III, whereas 'Uncle Sam' was recorded as a reference to the government of the United States from as early as 1813.[284] If we turn to the term 'cousin', we can see that it, too, could be used not only as an appellation for a broad range of kinsmen, but also as a familiar and friendly term of address among non-kin: 'I assure you, my dirty cousin! thof his skin be so white . . . I am a Christian as well as he, and nobody can say that I am base born', declares Mrs Honour in Fielding's *Tom Jones*, as she reflects on her love for Tom.[285] Among kings and noblemen, the formula 'trusty and well beloved cousin' was a standard form of address, as noted by Blackstone in his *Commentaries on the Laws of England*.[286] The term 'cousin', too, also had specific figurative usages. 'Cousin Betty', for example, was a particular form of appellation used to describe a harmless madwoman and vagrant, such as the 'bedlamite, or rather an impudent vagrant', who used to enter the sitting room of families and 'claim kindred' with women and children, as a book on husbandry from 1750 records.[287]

---

[282] *OED*, s.v. 'aunt', 'uncle'; *English Dialect Dictionary*; *Dictionary of American English on Historical Principles* (Oxford, 1938), s.v. 'uncle' and 'aunt', 'auntie'; J. A. Holm with A. W. Shilling, *Dictionary of Bahamian English* (New York, 1982), lists a historical usage of 'uncle' as a term of affection and respect to an elderly black slave or servant, and another usage of 'uncle' by slaves for their white masters.

[283] *OED*, s.v. 'aunt'.

[284] *Ibid.*, s.v. 'uncle', and references there. Such references continue to be used. *Ibid.*, s.v. 'uncle' brings an example of a male announcer or story teller for children's programmes on BBC, referred to as 'uncle' in the *Wireless Weekly*, 8 Aug. 1920.

[285] H. Fielding, *Tom Jones* (1749), ed. R. P. C. Muter (Harmondsworth, 1979), p. 196. See also *OED*, s.v. 'cousin'. The nineteenth-century *English Dialect Dictionary* records the use of 'cousin' as a term of address among non-kin, including the epithet 'dirty cousin', especially in Cornwall and Devon.

[286] Blackstone, *Commentaries on the Laws of England*, vol. I, p. 386, quoted in *OED*, s.v. 'cousin', 'in all writs, and commissions . . . the king, when he mentions any peer of the degree of an earl, always stiles him "trusty and well beloved cousin": an appellation as antient as the reign of Henry IV; who being either by his wife, his mother or his sisters actually related or allied to every earl in the kingdom artfully . . . acknowledged that connexion in all his letters'.

[287] Marchall, *Rural Economy* (1796), vol. II, p. 314; Ellis, *Modern Husbandry* (1750), v. iii: quoted in the *English Dialect Dictionary*, s.v. 'cousin'. She would first ascertain that there was no one in but women and children.

Once we turn to broad terms such as 'friends' and 'connexion', diffusion is evident very strongly indeed. In its early Teutonic and Old English origins, 'freond' was indeed used to denote kinsman or tribesman. In eighteenth-century England, as we saw, 'friend' was still used as a very important kinship term. But by then it had also evolved to designate a much broader range of relationships, too, which were also typified by notions of amity and sympathy. Such broad usages of the term 'friend' will be investigated in the next chapters of this book in detail, thus taking us from the realm of kinship to personally selected friendship, and even to social and political associations and patronage. In the present context, therefore, let us just note briefly how broadly diffused usages of 'connexion' could be. For example, when Madan described in *Thoughts on Executive Justice* how 'the various *connections* which the convicts have formed in life' might be brought to their aid at the point of trial, in addition to the pleas of 'natural friends', he designated relationships formed by service and patronage in addition to kinship relationships.[288] When Mrs Sheridan described how the young wife of a major in the army dreaded the thought of following her husband to America, for she had 'no *connections* there', the word was used most probably to refer broadly to any effective relationship, not only kinship ties.[289] 'Connexions', related and non-related, were also very significant in eighteenth-century England for seeking employment and gaining preferment. Here, too, kin and non-kin could play active roles. In eighteenth-century religious life, too, ties among 'connexions' were extremely important, stretching once more well beyond any circles of kin. Thus, for example, Wesley referred to his Methodist followers as members of his 'connexion', writing about 'the preachers in connection with me', or 'the travelling preachers in our connexion'. He also stipulated those who 'may be received into full connexion with us'.[290] And when it came to eighteenth-century political life, 'connexions' were crucial. Thus, for example, Chesterfield referred in a letter of 6 April 1774 to 'the Rockingham Connection', which 'stands the fairest for the Ministry'.[291]

Thus, just as we saw that the category of 'family' could extend in the eighteenth century to include relationships among kin and non-kin, so we can now see that relationships among 'friends' and 'connexions' could shade into a wide variety of attachments among related and non-related

[288] Madan, *Thoughts on Executive Justice*, pp. 98–9, quoted in Sharpe, *Crime in Early Modern England*, p. 174.
[289] Mrs Sheridan to Samuel Richardson, 8 Feb. 1757, *The Correspondence of Samuel Richardson*, vol. IV, p. 151.
[290] See references in various writings by Wesley from 1757 onwards, quoted in *OED*, s.v. 'connexion'.
[291] In a letter dated 6 Apr. (1774), quoted in *OED*, s.v. 'connexion'.

individuals. These broad categories of effective recognition, however, were part of a range of extended and highly suggestive usages, that served to diffuse the language of kinship very broadly throughout many types of relationships, and many areas of life.

Conclusion

The four sets of organising principles, uncovered and elaborated in this chapter, provide us with a new model for understanding the language of kinship in seventeenth- and eighteenth-century England, which in some respects complements existing models and in some respects presents an alternative to them. These principles highlight the importance of focusing not just on formal kinship terms, but on active usages. They reveal patterns of continuity, but also changes.

The first organising principle presented here was 'recognition and opacity'. There were some widely current usages that enabled people in seventeenth- and eighteenth-century England to recognise kin while giving very little indication as to their exact degree or number. From the structural point of view, such usages were significant: rather than simply highlighting the nuclear family relationships while distinguishing between different kinship degrees in a receding manner – as the structural principles emphasised by other scholars and especially the 'onion model' lead one to expect – these usages served to conceal the boundaries between different kinship degrees and submerge the nuclear family in broader relationships. Scholars studying the language of kinship in early modern England have noted some 'vague' and 'imprecise' usages, but we can now move further and suggest that it was the unique combination of recognition and opacity that made terms such as 'relation', 'friend', 'connexion' and the various derivations of 'kin' so useful in so many social situations.

The second organising principle was 'incorporation and differentiation'. The extension of kinship terms to relations by marriage in the seventeenth and eighteenth centuries has of course been noted by many scholars but this chapter has formulated and examined some widespread conventions that enabled people in seventeenth- and eighteenth-century England to expand systematically their reservoir of recognised kin. The incorporation of kin could extend far, traced through both affinal and consanguinal ties. However the nuclear family relationships were probably prone to the most intensive incorporation, as the nuclear family terms were used habitually to also designate half-relations, step-relations, and a wide range of relations by marriage. Subtle means of differentiation then served to re-draw the boundaries of kinship groups, while linking individuals to extended webs of kinship ties. The outcome of these practices was that kinship groups, and particularly nuclear families, could be so enlarged over time that we have preferred calling them 'extended-nuclear'. From the structural point of view, then, the conventions of incorporation and differentiation enabled us to question yet again existing models for understanding kinship in early modern England, and especially the 'onion model'. While in some ways kinship terms and usages served to distinguish kin from non-kin, and to differentiate between different kinship degrees while highlighting the nuclear family, as various scholars emphasise, in other ways the same kinship terminology provided its users with a powerful matrix for enlarging and modifying networks of kin, while blurring or concealing the distinctions between kinship degrees. Finally, we saw that incorporation and differentiation were not only important conventions of usage employed in the naming of kin, but also could constitute significant interpersonal gestures: it is through usages such as these that speakers placed themselves in relation to others, declared relationships, proposed moral duties, and set expectations.

The conventions of incorporation and differentiation identified here may thus also suggest that although much depended on particular circumstances and choice, the recognition of kin in the seventeenth and eighteenth centuries may have been a less 'permissive', 'voluntary', 'fluid', or 'individualistic' matter than it is sometimes said to have been. Evidently, the conjugal bond effected the recognition and articulation of kinship in ways that were a matter of conventional usage, not merely individual preference. These practices, as we saw, were also especially significant in articulating the kinship and marital status of females.

The third organising principle, 'plurality', led us to examine various multiple and overlapping usages, current in the language of kinship in seventeenth- and eighteenth-century England. Of course, most of the archaic usages explored here have been recorded by scholars, but we examined them within systematic structural and performative contexts. Diverse kinship relationships, we saw, could be designated by more than one term. Similarly, various terms could be used for designating different kinship relationships. Once we take into account usages stemming from different etymological roots, or relegated to different registers, as well as possible usages and conventions typical of different regions, or different social groupings, the historical language of kinship appears still more complex and rich. The outcome of this diversity was that the language of kinship could be employed in subtle and versatile ways. From the structural point of view, this plurality makes it all the more clear how impossible it is to force the historical language of kinship, used in seventeenth-

and eighteenth-century England into any simple model such as the 'onion model'.

The fourth and last principle, 'diffusion', leads from the realm of kinship ties to other social relationships. Indeed, the language of kinship was so significant in seventeenth- and eighteenth-century England, that, contrary to what any simple model might lead us to expect, there was hardly a single kinship term that was used for designating kin alone. The nuclear-family terms were used particularly richly, drawing on relational, moral, and symbolic attributes that could be employed in many contexts. Broad terms such as 'friend' and 'connexion' could also shade to include both kinship ties, and other effective social relationships, as will be studied in greater detail in the following chapters.

Both lexical variety and conventions of usage thus made the language of kinship in seventeenth- and eighteenth-century England culturally rich, and socially extremely significant. Historians have been impressed by the 'flexibility' and 'looseness' of this language and by the apparent 'imprecision' and 'inconsistency' of its usages. The organising principles uncovered and investigated here have enabled us to see that behind the apparent inconsistency, there was a structural logic. Furthermore, there was also a social and cultural logic. Even ambiguous and opaque usages, far from simply reflecting the alleged 'limitations' of the English language of kinship, could serve to render it effective and versatile, and endow it with a great capacity for social and cultural signification.

These conventions of usage alert us yet again to the importance of categorical definitions in the historiography of kinship and the family. Whether 'the nuclear family' was defined broadly and cumulatively over time, whether it was defined to include four elementary relationships only, or whether it was defined as the nuclear unit of residence and procreation – each of these alternatives could powerfully influence the classification of family and kinship ties. A narrow definition of the nuclear family could make it seem isolated, or the potential kinship universe beyond it large; conversely, a broad definition of the nuclear family could partly overlap with the spheres of the 'extended kin' and make them appear depleted. It seems that the relationships identified at some times under the rubric of 'the extended family' or 'kinship' could in fact overlap significantly with those identified at other times under broader categories of 'the nuclear family'. Either way, these relationships could include the nuclear families of origin, procreation, members of the spouse's nuclear family, married offspring, married siblings, possibly grandparents, and a wide range of possible step- and half-relations. Beyond these, there were also uncles, aunts, and cousins, linked by numerous potential ties of affinity and blood.

The social and cultural significance of kinship relationships, as it emerges from this analysis, is probably also greater than some scholars have allowed. Evidently, as the practices of 'diffusion' indicate, the language of kinship had a significance in early modern society and culture above and beyond the mere recognition of relational degrees. Furthermore, it also reverberated broadly in other ways. Debates surrounding kinship appear, for example, in the contexts of religious and political controversies about incest and royal succession. The language of kinship is employed evocatively in eighteenth-century literary texts. The invocation of 'connexions' and 'friends' was also effective in political manoeuvres, from the private politics of courtship and marriage to the politics of the state. Most importantly, however, the language of kinship was employed habitually in a wide range of interpersonal relationships to claim recognition, propose social bonds, set moral and religious duties, and postulate many expectations. Solidarity, consideration, or support could be expected among kin, even if they were not given. Debates about kinship sometimes focus too much on positive outcomes. As we have seen, in investigating relationships among kin, expectations – and indeed frustrated expectations – might also be very telling. It is in the gap between expectations and outcomes that interpersonal dynamics among kin, and broader social and cultural norms concerning kinship, can sometimes be fruitfully detected.

Finally, this language of kinship and its conventions has alerted us to the question of historical change. The old developmental approach describing the decline of kinship ties and the rise of the nuclear family in early modern England has been shown to be misguided; however, there is also evidence to suggest that the counter-argument in favour of long-term continuity in kinship and family structures needs re-thinking. Far from remaining constant over the centuries, as various scholars argue, it now appears that the English language of kinship has been subject to changes relating to both the terminology itself, and – not less important – conventions of usage. The exact trajectory of these changes from the seventeenth and eighteenth centuries to today still remains to be explored. The changes may well have happened over a long period of time, and in overlapping and complex ways.[292] It is also important to note that while our understanding of the language of kinship in seventeenth- and eighteenth-century England has been based on careful research, the

[292] See, for example, Wilmott's study on kinship and social legislation, which shows different forms of kinship recognition used in different modern laws. Thus, for instance, he argues that 'the official liability of kinship has shrunk, but the official recognition of kinship has expanded' in matters such as income tax and recognition of dependence: P. Wilmott, 'Kinship and social legislation', *British Journal of Sociology* 9 (1958), 126–42.

comparison with present-day usages is more intuitive. Nevertheless, if we take two rough points of comparison – then and now – we can see that the language of kinship used in seventeenth- and eighteenth-century England was broader in terms of its extension, broader than today's in terms of its categorical understanding of roles and relationships, and richer in terms of its actively used vocabulary.

However, people in the seventeenth and eighteenth centuries, as we have noted, lacked this 'Whiggish' perspective. For them the language of kinship was not a part of historical process of terminological change, but a framework of recognition to be employed and drawn upon in living realities. In view of the conventions of usage studied here, it would seem that one does not need to look as far as extended networks of cousinage to see that the language of kinship in seventeenth- and eighteenth-century England could well promote the construction of complex and dense webs of kin, endow them with great social and cultural significance, and also project them on to other social relationships such as friendship, neighbourhood ties, occupational ties, associational ties, and patronage. The 'nuclear family' itself, as we saw, had a remarkable capacity for internal extension. 'Effective kinship' could still be charted beyond the enlarged nuclear core. The 'extended-nuclear' ties could also be maintained over time, thus stretching the generational span of kinship networks. These networks could be still further infused by remarriages, and shade into other relationships. Taking this view, it would seem that 'the isolated nuclear family' of early modern England may have been less structurally isolated than it has sometimes appeared. If the rich ties examined here were spread across limited geographical areas – as often happened as a result of short-distance migration – or even if they were spread across greater distances, they could still amount to significant groupings of individuals, who could provide one another with material or mental support, assist one another with advice or useful connections, irritate one another with gossip and envy, shame one another with disreputable conduct, or inflict on one another trouble and grief.

5 Friends

Introduction

In the eighteenth century, the term 'friend' had a plurality of meanings that spanned kinship ties, sentimental relationships, economic ties, occupational connections, intellectual and spiritual attachments, sociable networks, and political alliances. In this chapter, we shall investigate a spectrum of relationships designated in the eighteenth century as 'friendship'.

Today the word 'friend' is not applied ordinarily to designate familial relationships,[1] but in the seventeenth and eighteenth centuries usages of 'friend' to designate kin were extremely common. At the same time, however, 'friend' was used to refer to a wide range of non-related supporters, such as patrons, guardians, employers, and other allies. In addition, 'friend' was used to describe well-wishers, companions, members of social circles, or select friends – as it does today. Ralph Josselin, for example, used the word 'friend' to refer to a wide range of kin, from his sisters, brothers-in-law, uncles, and cousins, to his wife's relations. About a century and a half later, Miss Weeton still described the travails of women who married without the consent of their 'friends', namely, their relations.[2] In contrast, Samuel Pepys used the word 'friend' to designate a non-related patron, as he rushed to the death-bed of one Mr Pierce to

---

[1] See, for example, the definition of 'friend' in a recent dictionary as 'a person with whom one enjoys mutual affection and regard (usu. exclusive of sexual or family bonds)': *The Concise Oxford Dictionary* (9th edn, London, New York, Sydney, and Toronto, 1997), p. 541. Many modern researchers also understand friendship as a voluntary relationship beyond the realm of family relationships. See, for example, *The International Encyclopedia of the Social Sciences*, vol. VI, s.v. 'Friend', esp. p. 12. See also, for example, G. D. Suttles, 'Friendship as a social institution', in G. J. McCall, M. M. McCall, N. K. Denzin, G. D. Suttles, and S. B. Kurth, *Social Relationships* (Chicago, 1970), esp. pp. 95–8; J. P. Wiseman, 'Friendship: bonds that bind in a voluntary relationship', *Journal of Social and Personal Relationships* 3 (1986), 191–211; V. J. Derlega and B. A. Winstead (eds.), *Friendship and Social Interaction*, Springer Series in Social Psychology (New York, 1986), e.g. pp. 2–3, 236–8, 250–1; R. G. Adams and R. Bliesznzer (eds.), *Older Adult Friendship: Structure and Process* (Newbury Park and London, 1989); R. Bliesznzer and R. G. Adams, *Adult Friendship* (Newbury Park and London, 1992).
[2] Weeton, *Journal of a Governess*, vol. I, 15 July 1812, pp. 21, 37.

promise him that he would '*be a friend*' to his wife and family.[3] The rector Benjamin Rogers also named his non-related patron, who had found him employment, as '*the best friend I ever had*'.[4] The economic dimension of 'friendship' was also evident when Richardson advised the apprentice in his conduct treatise not to cause his master the loss of 'a good Customer, and Friend'.[5] In addition, however, usages of 'friend' were widely current in eighteenth-century political life. For instance, James Oakes of Bury St Edmunds noted how, on the occasion of elections in town, 'the *Friends* of ea[ch] party' agreed that 'there should be a union of interests between them'.[6] Other contemporary documents contain numerous similar references to 'The King's Friends', 'my Whig friends', or 'friends of the Government'.[7] 'Friendship' ties were also important in the context of religious and spiritual life. The Manchester wig maker Edmund Harrold, for example, referred to the members of his religious reading circle as 'friends'. The Quakers defined themselves as the 'Society of Friends'. Indeed, 'friendship' ties were significant in eighteenth-century associational life more broadly, as attested by the societies that bore the word 'friend' in their title, such as the 'friendly societies', aimed at providing mutual insurance and assistance,[8] the 'Society for the Friends of the People', aimed at obtaining a parliamentary reform,[9] or the societies for

---

[3] Pepys, *Diary*, vol. II, p. 150.

[4] B. Rogers, *The Diary of Benjamin Rogers (1727–52)*, ed. C. D. Linnell, Publications of the Bedfordshire Historical Record Society, vol. 30 (Streatley, 1950), p. 1, entry for 7 Oct. 1727. See also entry for 5 May 1732, *ibid.*, p. 37: 'I was turn'd out to the Wide World without a penny to help my self. Indeed it pleased Mr Aspinal to make me Usher of the Free school (for which I owe him immortal thanks).'

[5] Richardson, *Vade Mecum*, p. 6.

[6] 'It appeared the unanimous wish of their *Friends* there should be a union of Interests between Them.' Specifically, the head of one party said that 'If *the Friends of ea[ch] Party* thought proper to canvass jointly, it must be as they please. He could not have any Objection to his *Friends* giving their second Voices to Sr John': Oakes, *Diaries*, entry for 19 Mar. 1790, vol. I, p. 263.

[7] Namier, *The Structure of Politics*, pp. 8, 114, 279, to mention only few of many such references. See also, for example, the use of the word 'friend' in the following publications relating to politics: J. Withers, *The Whigs Vindicated: The Objections that are Commonly Brought against Them Answered, and the Present Ministry Prov'd to be the Best Friends of the Church, the Monarch, the Lasting Peace, and Real Welfare of England* (London, 1715); W. Romains, *Friends of the Established Church* (London, 1757); R. Sharp, *A Letter to the Public Meeting of the Friends to the Repeal of the Test and Corporation Acts* (London, 1790); S. Heywood, *High Church Politics, Being a Seasonable Appeal to the Friends of the British Constitution against the Practices & Principles of High Churchmen* (London, 1792).

[8] See, for example, *A Letter to a Gentleman in the Country, Giving an Account of the Two Insurance Offices, the Fire-Office and Friendly-Society* (London, 1684); *The Friendly Society, or, a Proposal of a New Way or Method for Securing Houses from any Considerable Loss by Fire, by Way of Subscription and Mutual Contribution* (London, 1684); *Rules, Orders & Regulations of a Friendly Society, Called the British Assurance Society* (London, 1795).

[9] *Friends of the People, Freemasons Tavern, 30 May 1795, At a General Meeting of the Society of the Friends of the People, Associated for the Purpose of Obtaining a Parliamentary Reform, Held this Day* (London, 1795).

the help of unsettled paupers named 'Strangers' Friends'.[10] At the same time, however, usages of 'friend' to designate sentimental and freely chosen friendships clearly also existed. In 1612, for example, Thomas Wilson described 'friend' in his *Christian Dictionary* as 'one whom wee do entirely love above others and use more familiarly & privately than wee doe others, as David did Ionathan'.[11] He was referring, in other words, to a sentimental friendship, freely chosen between two individuals. 'This correspondence is, indeed, the cement of friendship: it is friendship avowed under hand and seal', wrote Richardson emphatically, more than a century later, to one of his select friends.[12]

Such usages of 'friend', as well as the importance of 'friendship' have been recognised by many scholars. Macfarlane, for example, notes the use of 'friend' as 'equivalent to kin', as well as its usage to designate non-related employers, guarantors, guardians, and distant relatives. His study of the seventeenth-century clergyman Ralph Josselin also emphasises the importance of personally selected friends, and he highlights the importance of friendship in marriage.[13] Wrightson observes the ways in which friendship shaded into kinship on the one hand and into neighbourly relations on the other, and Wrightson and Levine emphasise the importance of friendship in the context of local communities.[14] Slater notes many usages of 'friends' referring to kin and discusses the importance of 'friendship' among members of the Verney family.[15] Laslett also discusses the usage of 'friends' for kinsfolk and other intimates, while also noting the roles of kin in trading connections, migration, etc.[16] Rushton, Ingram, and Stone, for example, highlight the role of 'friends', including kin, in marriage negotiations, separation, and divorce.[17] O'Hara

---

[10] J. Myers Gardiner, *History of the Leeds Benevolent or Strangers' Friends Society, 1789–1889* (Leeds, 1890).   [11] Wilson, *Christian Dictionary*.

[12] *Correspondence of Samuel Richardson*, vol. III, pp. 245; see also vol. II, p. 431.

[13] See Josselin, *Diary*, p. 18, n. 1; Macfarlane, *The Family Life of Ralph Josselin*, e.g. pp. 149–51; Macfarlane, *Marriage and Love in England*, pp. 145–7, 286; cf. Macfarlane, *The Family Life of Ralph Josselin*, pp. 143, 150; see also Macfarlane, *Marriage and Love in England*, chs. 8, 9. See also Issa, 'Obligation and choice', e.g. pp. 173–6, 452; Tadmor, '"Family" and "friend" in *Pamela*'.

[14] See Wrightson, *English Society*, esp. pp. 50, 55; Wrightson and Levine, *Poverty and Piety*, ch. 4; Levine and Wrightson, *Whickham*, pp. 329–44; see also, for example, Nair, *Highley*, ch. 3.

[15] M. Slater, *Family Life in the Seventeenth Century: The Verneys of Claydon House* (London, 1984), esp. pp. 34–67.   [16] Laslett, *The World We Have Lost – Further Explored*, p. 93.

[17] P. Rushton, 'Property, power and family networks, the problem of disputed marriage in early modern England', *Journal of Family History* 11 (1986), 205–19; Ingram, *Church Courts, Sex and Marriage*, e.g. pp. 127, 140, 200–5; Stone, *Road to Divorce*, pp. 45–7; and Stone, *Broken Lives*. These studies show how near and distant kin, guardians, employers, companions, and various others were all active as 'friends' in advising about the progress of courtship, witnessing exchanges of promises, and generally intervening in helpful and unhelpful ways. 'Friends' are mentioned often in documents concerning marriage and divorce, and it may not be a coincidence that many of the historical studies of 'friends' have been made in these contexts.

examines the importance of 'friends' in negotiating marriages while offering a new anthropological analysis of their role.[18] Namier traces connections of 'friends' in eighteenth-century politics, and Perkin discusses the great importance of 'friends' in many areas of eighteenth-century social and political life.[19] More recently, D'Cruze investigates the role of 'friends' in the context of social and occupational networks among people of 'the middling sort' in late eighteenth-century Colchester, and Hunt examines 'friendship' in the context of financial relationships among middling people more broadly.[20] Scholars have also investigated male and female homosexual friendship.[21] The role of friends in the eighteenth century has also attracted the interest of literary scholars. Their focus, however, has usually been on individually chosen and affective friendship, rather than on the possible contemporary interconnections between friendship, kinship, and patronage.[22]

Evidently, we possess many significant contributions to the study of friendship in eighteenth-century England, and in the early modern period more broadly. What we still lack, however, are detailed case studies that investigate 'friendship' relationships in all their aspects, from 'friendship' among kin to other ties of friendship and patronage. It is also important to examine not only ideas about friendship, but also interpersonal relationships between real men and women in the past. The role of friendship in the lives of ordinary people, however, is particularly hard to gauge, and a historical study that focuses on them can offer a particular contribution.[23]

[18] O'Hara, 'Ruled by my friends'. See also my previous discussion of 'friends' and 'friendship': Tadmor, '"Family" and "friend" in *Pamela*'.

[19] Namier, *The Structure of Politics*; Perkin, *Origins of Modern English Society*, pp. 45–51. Perkin's description is extremely good in depicting the richness, instrumentality, and moral significance of such relationships.

[20] D'Cruze, 'The middling sort in eighteenth-century Colchester', and p. 189 on 'friends'; Hunt, *The Middling Sort*, ch. 1, and see the reference to 'friends' on p. 23 and n. 4.

[21] See, for example, E. Donoghue, *Passions Between Women: British Lesbian Culture, 1668–1801* (London, 1993); A. Bray, 'Homosexuality and the signs of male friendship in Elizabethan England', *History Workshop Journal* 29 (1990), 1–19.

[22] See, for example, J. Todd, *Women's Friendship in Literature* (New York, 1980); R. A. Sharp, *Friendship and Literature: Spirit and Form* (Durham, 1986); D. Robinson, 'Unravelling the "cord which ties good men to good men": male friendship in Richardson's novels', in M. A. Doody (ed.), *Samuel Richardson: Tercentenary Essays* (Cambridge, 1989), pp. 167–87. Donoghue notes the possibility of an overlap of friendship and kinship and also discusses the friendship between Sarah and Henry Fielding. Her main emphasis, however, is on friendship as a sentimental relationship: Donoghue, 'Male–female friendship and English fiction in the mid-eighteenth century', esp. pp. 10–11, 59–100. A broad discussion of friendship, however, can be found in L. Hutson, *The Usurer's Daughter: Male Friendship and Fictions of Women in Sixteenth-Century England* (New York, 1994).

[23] Macfarlane's path-breaking analysis of Ralph Josselin's diary is still a rare example of a detailed study of friendship at both the individual and general levels. But although Macfarlane notes the historical concept of 'friends' as kin, his actual analysis in this study

The aim of this and the following chapters, then, is to provide such specific, yet conceptually broad analyses. Friendship relationships, this book suggests, were major social relationships in eighteenth-century England, and they merit a detailed investigation. But it is essential to explore them while taking account of the fact that 'friendship' could comprise a very broad spectrum of relationships.

Let us turn, then, to a series of case-studies concerning 'friendship'. The main focus of this and the following chapter is once more the eighteenth-century shopkeeper and diarist, Thomas Turner. We shall investigate his ties with his 'friends', his ideas about friendship, the role of 'friends' in his life and in the lives of others with whom he was connected. We will use the case of Turner and his 'friends' not only to study particular dynamics of 'friendship', but also to address broader issues regarding the significance of 'friendship' in eighteenth-century society and culture. In order to do this, however, we shall supplement our main source – the diary of Thomas Turner – with many other personal, administrative, and legal records. Chapter 6 will examine specifically the political friendships in Turner's world. Finally, we shall complement these analyses with a study of ideas about friendship and representations of friendship in prescriptive and literary texts.

From the methodological point of view, we shall continue to focus on eighteenth-century language usages. The aim here, too, is to avoid categorical anachronism. Friendship relationships might be studied with the aid of various approaches: philosophy, sociology, anthropology, psychology, and literature are the main fields that provide useful tools for examining friendship. Focusing on Turner, we could thus proceed to study his friendships in terms of their social functions, their ethics, their psychological dynamics, or symbolic representations. Whichever approach we would choose, however, we would no doubt have to decide whom we should count as Turner's 'friends'. For instance, should we count his village companions as 'friends'? Are we to regard his fellow tradesmen as 'friends'? Will we include his relatives in the analysis? If so, which relatives shall we choose? Or perhaps we should simply rely on our intuition and discuss as 'friends' only those who seem to us to merit the title 'Turner's friends'? Our previous analyses of concepts of household, family, and kinship – and our knowledge of the range of relationships encapsulated in the eighteenth century under the category of 'friends' – alert us to the pitfalls of misguided intuition. Let us, then, take once more a deductive approach. Rather than decide in advance who could be the friends of a man such as Thomas Turner, or whom might he have defined

is overshadowed by the fact that he prejudges the identity of 'friends' as non-kin, and of kin as separate from 'friends'.

as his 'friend', let us begin by examining those people and groups who were actually recognised by Turner as his 'friends'. The basic question that will guide us in the remaining part of this chapter, then, is very simple: who were Turner's friends? All other questions follow from it. What sort of friends were they? What sort of relationships did he have with them? And what can these relationships tell us about the significance of friendship and kinship in eighteenth-century society and culture more broadly?

Who were Thomas Turner's friends?

Thomas Turner lived in a small village. Hardly a day passed without his recording some interaction with people from his neighbourhood. Holidays and workdays, weddings and funerals were all spent in close contact with them. Turner was also a responsible and trustworthy member of his local community: he was not only appointed to a succession of parish offices, but his neighbours also displayed their trust in him by asking his help and advice in their personal affairs. At the same time, Turner's livelihood was built upon dealings within his locality. People from East Hoathly and from neighbouring villages bought at his shop. If they were good customers, if they happened to buy a large amount, or if Turner simply enjoyed their company, they could be invited to tea, or even to share Turner's midday dinner. Both business and social life continued in the evenings, as many people called at Turner's house to settle business, exchange news, smoke a pipe, or read aloud in company.

Some people in Thomas Turner's local circle were more closely connected to him than others. People in East Hoathly exchanged hospitality with one another, and Thomas and Peggy Turner were invited to rounds of festive dinners often meeting with the same couples: the rector and his wife, the village butcher and his wife, the tallow chandler and his wife, the blacksmith and his wife, some farmers and their wives, and various others.[24] Master and Dame Durrant, the blacksmith and his wife, were among the neighbours with whom Turner had particularly close ties. He spent much time at their house and during Peggy Turner's long illness the Durrants were very kind and helpful.[25] Some of Turner's social inferiors were also socially close to him. As we saw in the first chapter, these included faithful servants and former servants, as well as some of their kin, who were not only employed by Turner, but also shared his domestic and social life. Lastly, Thomas Turner also had close personal companions in the village. Thomas Davy the shoemaker, for example, was the

---

[24] Some of these people were roughly Turner's equals, others, such as the rector and the steward of the Duke of Newcastle, were his superiors both socially and financially.
[25] Turner, *Diary*, ed. Vaisey, p. 330.

same age as Thomas Turner, and in the early years of the diary the two spent much time together talking and drinking, reading aloud, playing cards, visiting, and doing business.[26] So did the butcher's son, Joseph Fuller, junior, six months younger than Turner.[27] Thomas Turner also had many ties beyond his immediate locality. He travelled much in the near neighbourhood transacting business, settling parish affairs, visiting and socialising. His relatives and acquaintances were spread through towns and villages in Sussex and Kent.[28] His business even brought him into contact with places further away: he had regular connections with tradesmen in London, and his direct suppliers were situated as far away as Manchester.[29] But in important ways Thomas Turner could be seen as an ordinary middling eighteenth-century man: he was a member of a small and familiar rural community, in which most of his daily exchanges took place. A present-day observer could think of such a community with yearning and nostalgia, the cosy opposite of modern mass society. One might even be tempted to say that Thomas Turner lived among friends. But who were the people whom Thomas Turner counted as his friends?

When one examines Turner's diary, looking for the people he described as 'my friends', it becomes clear that Turner did not count his neighbours as 'friends'. None of the local couples with whom he dined and made merry – and with whom he had so many other exchanges – were referred to by him in his diary as 'friends'. Nor were his close neighbours, such as Master Joseph and Dame Durrant, in whose house he spent so much time and from whom he received much help. Nor were his close peers and companions in the village referred to by him in his diary as his 'friends'.[30] Of course, the fact that Turner did not mention these people as 'friends' should not be taken to mean that he did not care for them, or that they were unimportant in his life. On the contrary, at least some of these people were so closely connected to Turner that he probably took for granted their presence in his life, and therefore found no reason to discuss his relationship with them in his diary. But it could also be that Turner did not count his neighbours and everyday companions as his

---

[26] See *ibid.*, pp. 329–30. He is described as 'Turner's best friend' during the early years of the diary. See also Turner's warm sentiments towards him, Thomas Turner, Diary, 3 Feb. 1757.

[27] Turner, *Diary*, ed. Vaisey, pp. 331–2.

[28] This kinship network may resemble those studied by Mitson as 'dynastic families': Mitson, 'The significance of kinship networks'. See also Lord, 'Communities of common interest'; Wrightson, 'Postscript', in Wrightson and Levine, *Poverty and Piety*, pp. 187–97.

[29] Turner, *Diary*, ed. Vaisey, Appendix C, pp. 340–6.

[30] With the important exception of the occasional ironic usages, such as those made in relation to Joseph Fuller (Thomas Turner, Diary, 15 Jan., 1 Apr. 1765). The naming of Thomas Durrant as a 'friend' on 17 Oct. 1764 is also an exception, see n. 195 below.

'friends' because 'friendship' was to him a special and different relationship.[31]

On a close examination, it appears that Thomas Turner was both sparing and precise in his usage of the epithet 'friend'. If we examine all the people to whom he referred in his diary as 'friends', we discover some recurring features. In order to be counted as a 'friend' by Thomas Turner, a person needed to have one or more of the following qualifications. This person could be (1) one of Thomas Turner's relations; (2) his wife; (3) a person with whom he had a close intellectual or devotional affinity; (4) a trusty tradesman with whom he had special business contacts; (5) his tenant or landlord; (6) an officer of the excise. The seventh and last category of 'friends' that Thomas Turner mentioned in his diary included a more general group of people. These were the supporters of the Whig interest in the locality, especially the supporters of the Duke of Newcastle.[32]

As we shall see, Turner's relationships with all these 'friends' were important in his life, whether in terms of individual interaction or in terms of broader social networks. I suggest that these relationships were also important in terms of their broader moral values and that they were significant in forming a contemporary social order. This chapter thus proceeds to examine Turner's notions of 'friendship' and the significance of different 'friends' in his life, starting with his kin. Turner's relationships with his 'friends' were also dynamic, and this chapter will attempt to trace some significant changes in them over time, and with regard to life-course changes. Subsequent sections deal with Turner's wife, and his select 'friends'. It should be emphasised, however, that although for the sake of the analysis these groups of 'friends' are dealt with separately, they actually had many characteristics in common and they contributed together to forming the wide spectrum of 'friendship' ties in Turner's life. Some of these common characteristics will become evident in the course of the following discussion, others will be discussed in the conclusion to this chapter.

---

[31] Compare, for example, C. I. Cohen and H. Rajkowski, 'What's in a friend? Substantive and theoretical issues', *The Gerontologist* 22 (1982), 261–6. They found that elderly people, residing in hotels, were more likely to name those contacts outside the hotel as 'friends', despite the fact that they were seen less frequently, and despite the fact that they also had intimate multiplex relationships with many people in the hotel defined as 'non-friends'. At the same time, 17 per cent of the outside 'friends' were also defined as 'not important', and with 46 per cent of them intimate thoughts were not shared.
[32] See below, ch. 6.

Related friends

Thomas Turner used the terms 'friends' and 'relations' as references to kin. For example, when he complained in his diary 'living so near *my Friends* is I think a very great disadvantage', he was probably referring to his mother and siblings who lived in the neighbouring village.[33] On this occasion he was even considering moving elsewhere to get further away from them. Contrary to Turner's complaint, however, his relationships with his related 'friends' also had some distinct advantages. As we shall see, Turner's related 'friends' formed a close network of sentimental and instrumental exchange. The language of 'friendship' served Turner throughout the years to designate kin, set expectations, negotiate exchanges, and express hardships. This was a dynamic language, used over time, in the context of active relationships and through life-course changes.

Two related 'friends' who were particularly significant in Thomas Turner's life were his father and mother. Thomas's father, John Turner died before the start of the diary and the diary includes only few direct references to him. Years later, however, Thomas Turner described the loss that he suffered in his father's death, naming him not only as 'the best of parents', but also as a '*Friend and Brother*'.[34] This formulaic eulogy was perhaps particularly apt in Turner's case not only because he was, as we shall see, a favoured son and heir, but also because it could be that unlike so many other youths in his time, he never left home for a formal period of apprenticeship, but was rather taught his trade as a shopkeeper at home by his mother, and by his brother-tradesman, his father. It is clear that Turner was employed at one time as a servant in Lewes.[35] But whereas we have evidence of the apprenticeships of a number of his relations and companions, including Turner's own records of periods of service undertaken by his brothers,[36] there is no record of his own apprenticeship either in his diary, or in other family papers, or in other formal registers which I have been able to check. One possible interpretation is that Turner actually had not had a period of formal apprenticeship, but was rather taught the art of shopkeeping at home and was then sent for an additional period of service in Lewes.

Mrs Elizabeth Turner, Thomas Turner's mother, was another import-

---

[33] Thomas Turner, Diary, 16 Sept. 1757.
[34] See ESRO, SAS/SM 210, also reprinted in Turner, *Diary*, ed. Turner, under the title 'Notes on Family History'.
[35] See his own evidence, Thomas Turner, Diary, 12 Sept. 1762. Vaisey suggests that he may have also been to school there, Turner, *Diary*, ed. Vaisey, pp. xviii–xix.
[36] The absence of any reference to Turner's own apprenticeship in ESRO, SAS/SM 210, is intriguing, for in this document he noted the schooling, training, or employment of his siblings and wives.

ant 'friend'. When Thomas's father died, he left his house and shop in the village of Framfield, where he and his wife lived, to his wife during her lifetime; after her death they were to pass to the eldest son and heir of this marriage, Thomas.[37] Thus, until her death in April 1759 Elizabeth Turner featured in her son's chronicles as an able tradeswoman and an impressive matriarch, who not only ran the Framfield house and shop but also kept together a complex web of dependants, relations, and acquaintances. As time went by, however, the possibility arose that Elizabeth should be 'leaving of trading'.[38] Whether the idea of retirement was hers or her son's remains unknown. What is clear is that at some stage Thomas actually made plans for taking over the management of the Framfield shop, and even made an offer to one Charles Diggens to become his partner.[39] This plan did not materialise and Elizabeth Turner continued in her shop and Thomas in his. The cooperation between the Framfield house and shop and the house and shop in East Hoathly, however, remained close and probably became yet closer, with Thomas Turner taking upon himself much travelling and dealing on his mother's behalf. At various times when he travelled to meet tradesmen, he settled his mother's business as well, and he even made orders to suppliers in London for both shops. He went to Framfield time and again, dined, visited, and performed many services for his mother. His wife contributed her labour, and his younger brother, Moses, assisted in the business of both shops.[40] Expressive relationships among friends are sometimes

[37] John Turner's Will, ESRO, W/SM D9, f. 233. Having made various bequests, he also left his remaining personal estate to be divided equally between his wife and his son Thomas, after discharge of debt. Thomas Turner was admitted to the property as a customary tenant on 25 Oct. 1753, subject to his mother's 'Estate or Interest' in it: ESRO, ADA 118, ff. 13, 49–51. See also n. 57 below.

[38] Thomas Turner, Diary, 15 Mar. 1756; see also 26, 30 Oct. 1756. This may have been connected with the fact that in the previous year Elizabeth Turner was ill.

[39] Thomas Turner, Diary, 28 Mar., 2 Apr. 1756. See also the plan that Turner should move to Framfield: *ibid.*, 22 Apr. 1756. Later he tried to make other deals with other tradesmen. Various negotiations concerning the taking over of the East Hoathly and Framfield shops were held in Oct. to Dec. 1756, and see also 10–11 Mar. 1757. One might guess that the coldness with which Thomas Turner was received by his 'friends' and his bitter argument with his mother on 22 Feb. 1756, may have been related to the question of the shop's management. It is likely that for Thomas Turner one of the attractions of moving to Framfield was that in addition to looking after his paternal estate, he would have enjoyed the custom of a bigger village. In Archbishop Wake's visitation to Framfield in 1717, 102 families were counted, compared with 40 counted in East Hoathly in a visitation in 1724: *Chichester Diocesan Surveys, 1686 and 1724*, ed. W. K. Ford, Sussex Record Society, vol. 78 (Lewes, 1994), pp. 229–30 for Framfield and p. 168 for East Hoathly.

[40] See, for example, various exchanges on 1, 15, 19, 27, 30 Mar., 11 July, 5, 15, 28 Aug. 1755, 1, 12, 14, 18, 20, 27, 28, 30 Mar., 2, 22, 29 Apr., 7, 18, 27 May, 7 June 1756. See also some detailed accounts that demonstrate the richness of these relationships: on 9 June Thomas sent his maid to Framfield for some eggs, and on 11 June she went once more. On 19 June Moses came to stand the shop for Thomas. On 20 June he went with him to visit Thomas's father-in-law. On 2 July the maid went to Framfield again and on 3 July Moses stood the shop for Thomas. On 4 July Mrs Turner came to visit (after a long time when

described as opposed to instrumental relationships.[41] In the case of the Turner 'friends', we can see that affective friendship relationships were increasingly tied with instrumental and occupational relationships. At times it seemed that these related 'friends' simply pooled their labour and resources, and then redistributed them to their mutual advantage. Some studies also propose an opposition between economic individualism and close familial cooperation among parents, married children, and adult siblings, while presenting early modern England as a society in which individualism prevailed.[42] However, in this case it is also clear that individualism and close familial cooperation were not mutually exclusive.

she had not been to East Hoathly). On 5 July Thomas walked to Framfield, dealt with his mother's shop, and also received from her a payment for the mare that he and his mother had bought jointly. On 11 July he took his nephew to his mother's. On 16 July he went to Framfield to help with the haying (for some time Thomas and his mother had the use of a farm jointly: see 9 Jan. 1758); on that day he also dined with his mother and balanced accounts with her on the purchase and carriage of cheese. He continued haying on 19 and 21 July. On 28 July Moses came to East Hoathly, Thomas went to Framfield to borrow sugar from his mother, and also took his nephew from her house. On 29 July he paid the gardener at Halland on his and his mother's account. On 30 July he rode to Framfield to borrow more sugar. On 2 Aug. he bought wool for his mother and on 6 Aug. he walked to Framfield to dine with her. On 7 Aug. he went to Lewes to borrow money for his mother from a local attorney. On 8 Aug. Thomas's mother, brother, and his younger brother's master came to visit and went to church together. On 14 Aug. Moses stood the shop for Thomas and on 26 Aug. the two brothers worked together packing and weighing their mother's wool. A few months later: on 3 Dec. Thomas balanced accounts with his mother for various debts and purchases. On 11 Dec. he made further negotiations regarding his mother's shop. On 31 Dec. he went to Framfield again to balance accounts. He promised his mother to 'serve a funeral' for her on 1 Jan. 1757, but on that evening he received a letter from his sister informing him that the funeral had been postponed. On 2 Jan. he and his wife worked in the evening tying 'favours' for the funeral, and on the following day he went to Framfield and served the funeral for his mother. See also, for example, 26 Dec. 1757, 1, 4, 9, 12 Jan. 1758, etc. For accounts in London, see esp. 21 Mar. 1759.

[41] E. G. Wolf, 'Kinship, friendship and patron–client relations in complex societies', in M. Banton (ed.), *The Social Anthropology of Complex Societies* (London, 1968), pp. 1–22, and esp. p. 10; cf. J. Pitt-Rivers, 'The kith and kin', in J. Goody (ed.), *The Character of Kinship* (Cambridge, 1973), pp. 89–105. Note also the distinction between friendship and kinship. See also Tadmor, '"Family" and "friend" in *Pamela*', esp. pp. 300–1. Relationships between material interests and familial relationships are also explored in Medick and Sabean, *Interest and Emotion*. See also discussion above, ch. 1, p. 28.

[42] Macfarlane argues that from the thirteenth century the majority of ordinary people in England were 'rampant individualists, highly mobile, both geographically and socially, economically "rational", market oriented and acquisitive, ego-centred in kinship and social life'. He also argues against the possibility that groups of siblings or parents and married children in early modern England, who did not share the same household, might still have been acting as joint or extended economic and social units in terms of owner- ship, production, consumption, or operational cooperation: see *Individualism*, esp. pp. 74–5, 82, 88, and the quotation in this note on p. 163; Macfarlane, 'The myth of the peasantry', esp. 341, 344–5, 347; Macfarlane, *Marriage and Love in England*, pp. 42, and esp. 98–102. In the case of the Turners the extended or joint family was in part a basic unit of ownership. Though it was not the basic unit of production or consumption, the case of the Turners also reveals operational and productive cooperation among separate family households. Such a realm of exchange, I suggest, can be obscured by an overly dichotomous presentation of 'individualism' versus 'familism'.

As we can see, individual and familial enterprises were closely linked among the Turner 'friends', and familial cooperation did not necessarily negate individual economic action, or a desire for individual gain.[43] A mixture of individualism and familial cooperation is also evident in the ways in which particular transactions among the Turners were carried out. Instrumental exchanges among the Turner 'friends' were conducted on the whole in a spirit of generosity, but they were also calculated with great care. Labour and hospitality were liberally exchanged, cash and kind were a different matter. Transactions could thus range from the spontaneous and casual to formal and contractual agreements. On 28 July 1756, for example, Thomas Turner recorded borrowing sixpence-worth of sugar from his mother. Two days later he recorded buying for her twopence-worth of walnuts.[44] Nor did he refrain from making a profit on such transactions: a pair of sheets bought by Thomas for 10s, for instance, was sold to his mother at 10s 6d.[45] Turner's diary provides a written record of many similar transactions, and he probably kept other records in other account books that did not survive. Besides transactions documented in writing, these 'friends' also made formal contractual agreements. On 16 July 1756, for example, when Turner and his mother balanced their accounts, as they did regularly and methodically, he received from her a note of hand payable on demand and charged her interest at the rate of 4 per cent per annum.[46] Various financial transactions between Thomas and his siblings were also reckoned with exactness to pennies and half-pennies, and sometimes transcribed in contractual notes of hand. When Thomas Turner forgave his 'friends' their debts to him, which he did very generously at least on two occasions, he also recorded the amounts forfeited.[47]

Cooperation bred tension. However affective, the relationships among these related 'friends' were not always amicable. Thomas Turner's diary contains many accounts of altercations with his kin, primarily with his mother. At one time she became so suspicious of his handling of her affairs that, according to Turner's evidence, she did not trust him with even some remnants of cloth, for fear he might trim them.[48] It appears

---

[43] As Mascuch explains on the basis of his study of autobiographies from 1600 to 1750, familial considerations were also used to justify and explain economic enterprise: Mascuch, 'Social mobility and middling self-identity. See also M. Mascuch, *Origins of the Individualist Self: Autobiography and Self-Identity in England, 1591–1791* (Cambridge, 1997).

[44] On this occasion he also borrowed some sugar and sold his mother half a gallon of blackcurrants.   [45] Thomas Turner, Diary, 27, 30 Mar. 1755.

[46] He also noted the sums still owed to him, which were not calculated in this account. For Turner's accounts with his mother, see also e.g. *ibid.*, 3 Apr. 1754, 21 Feb., 30 Mar. 1755, 26 Aug. 1756.

[47] *Ibid.*, 22 Feb. 1756, 8 Mar. 1765.

that their mother's anxiety affected Turner's siblings, who at some point took her side and treated Thomas coldly. Thomas Turner's assistance to his kin, as well as his discontent with them, was expressed in the diary using the language of 'friendship'. In a typical entry from 22 February 1756, for example, he wrote:

> my Mother & I had a great many Words or at least my mother had with me. what *my Friends* would have with me I know not . . . how happy could I be would *my friends* let but a free & Sincere Communication of *Friendship* once more be open'd between us & wch has of Late been shut up.[49]

The language of 'friendship' thus served Thomas Turner both for designating relationships with kin, and for proposing expectations. At the same time, this language heightened the importance of instrumentality in 'friendship'. At the heart of this 'friendship' relationship was a notion of 'service'. 'Service', in Turner's terms, could extend from general concern to very substantial help. Ideally, the service should be rendered to promote the interest of the 'friend', rather than one's own; but since friendship was supposed to be mutual, the idea was also that one should not expect a 'friend' to render a service that would be damaging to the other 'friend'.[50] Lastly, the idea was also that friendship should be acknowledged with gratitude, if not actually reciprocated. Thus, for example, after an argument with his mother Turner complained of his 'friends' and protested strongly: 'I have always done to the utmost of my power to *serve them.*'[51] He then repeated once more his 'service' to them, asserting his regard for their 'interests', and implying his own disinterestedness: 'I can with justice to my self and all mankind say I have *their Interest* intirely at Heart and never think my self more happy than in *serving them.*'[52] On another occasion Turner blamed the same 'friends' for taking his services for granted, while rendering him none. This lack of mutuality was attributed to the self-interest of his 'friends': 'I should be willing to lend them [my friends] all the assistance that is in my power', he said, 'but they seem to study nothing but *self-interest*, or if they have no design to take advantage, it turns out very much to my disadvantage.'[53] Significantly,

---

[48] *Ibid.*, 4 Jan. 1758. On 4 July 1756, for example, Turner also noted that his mother came to visit him for the first time in seventeen or eighteen months.

[49] *Ibid.*, 22 Feb. 1756. However, see also at a later date: 'hardly any Friend in the World that can or Will be a Friend to me but many of my Relations quite the Reverse': *ibid.*, 30 Oct. 1762.

[50] See also Muldrew, discussion of 'interest' in *The Economy of Obligation*, esp. p. 140.

[51] Thomas Turner, Diary, 22 Feb. 1756.

[52] *Ibid.* The specific 'service' mentioned here was acquitting his mother of a 'book-debt' of forty pounds, which he hoped he would never have to press, thus presumably helping not only her but also his siblings who lived in her house.

[53] *Ibid.*, 16 Sept. 1757.

many of Thomas Turner's references to his relations, in which he named
them as 'friends', were actually made in the context of negative expressions, registering disappointment.[54]
Dynamics over time, however, were also important. When Thomas
Turner's mother died, a different chord was struck. Discontent with
'friends' and frustrated expectations gave way to mourning their departure – at least for a while. After their mother's funeral, when the Turner
siblings and other kin gathered in the house at Framfield, Thomas Turner
wrote: 'We are now left as it were with out any Head, quite Mother &
Fatherless and it seems just as if we was now a going to turn out in a Wild
World *without any Friends*.'[55] Nonetheless the 'services' between Thomas
Turner and the rest of his related 'friends' continued. After their mother's
death they remained geographically near and instrumentally connected.
Thomas Turner sometimes felt hampered by these commitments to his
'friends'. He feared that if they accumulated debts they might also sink
him, particularly if his own business was slow. '[M]y affairs are so connected with *my Friends* that I know not how to Extricate my self out of my
trouble', he complained.[56] It is therefore important to try to clarify here
what these complex connections entailed.

Important connections among Thomas Turner and his 'friends' were
set contractually. One crucial set of connections can be traced back to the
terms of the wills of Thomas Turner's parents. John Turner, Thomas's
father, was married twice, and Elizabeth, Thomas's mother, was his
second wife. After Thomas, the couple had three more children: Moses,
Sarah, and Richard. John Turner also had three children by his first wife,
who were considerably older. John Turner's obligations to both sets of
children were reflected in his will. John held the tenancy of a farm in Kent.
At his death he charged the farm with various payments to his offspring
by his first marriage, including his eldest son, daughter, and grandchild.
He also charged it with another sum that was to be divided equally among
his four children by Elizabeth: Thomas, Moses, Richard, and Sarah.[57]

[54] See also above, ch. 4. The point has been made that the language of kinship, with its
moral implications, was also used to negotiate frustration and disappointment.
[55] Thomas Turner, Diary, 5 Apr. 1759.
[56] *Ibid.*, 18 Sept. 1760; 'I am so Embarrass'd in my affairs what with my Friends and
together with the debts due on my Trade': *ibid.*, 16 Dec. 1761. See also his references to
'family connections': 'I am so embarrass'd in my Family Connections that I hardly know
how to act with the most prudence'; at another time he also felt 'Confin'd and limited
with family Connections', *ibid.*, 31 July, 11 Nov. 1761.
[57] ESRO, W/SM D9, f. 233; CKS, U908 T158. This will was preceded by other legal
agreements in which John Turner made some similar arrangements. In 1734 he bound
himself with an indenture and a bond to promise his wife Elizabeth a widow's annuity of
£12 (to be taken from the proceeds of the Kentish farm) and her children equal shares in a
bequest of £300. A subsequent receipt dated 1745 indicates that he gave his eldest son by
his first marriage, John Jun., an advance to the amount of £50, one third of his future

Elizabeth made some similar arrangements in her will. She made a small bequest to her husband's daughter and grandson by his first marriage, and then left the farm's tenancy to be held in common by her own four children.[58] In addition to the farm in Kent, John Turner also left the house and shop in Framfield to Elizabeth's use during her lifetime, and after her death they were to pass to her eldest son, Thomas. However, this property was also charged with an annuity to one of John Turner's sons by his first marriage. On 20 April 1759, after his mother's will had been opened, Thomas Turner described in his diary some of its provisions and then added hopefully: 'Oh! may The God of all mercy pour down his blessings upon my Brothers and Sister as also upon my self, that we may live in peace and unity amongst our selves.'[59] This was probably a genuine wish, for their parents' wills postulated binding ties among the Turners for many years to come.

It is clear that these familial contracts, namely, the two wills, commanded the Turners' respect. This may have been assisted by the fact that John Turner's will contained some stipulations against default of payment.[60] The formal sanction of probation, however, was evidently not very important in the eyes of the Turners. The contents of the wills were known and served to guide familial policy, as documented in Thomas Turner's diary, but it was only in 1777 – twenty-five years after John Turner's death and eighteen years after the death of Elizabeth – that the two wills were finally proven.[61] The way in which the Turners managed their affairs also reveals that, as long as there was friendly understanding, there was also room for flexibility and interpretation of even the strictest legal contracts. Many of the provisions of the parents' wills were indeed carried out meticulously,[62] but others were not. Most importantly,

legacy. In 1753 John Jun. acknowledged the receipt of his full legacy and renounced any further claims against Thomas Turner: see the indenture dated 1 May 1734; a bond dated 18 May 1734; a receipt dated 26 Oct. 1745; a release dated 1 May 1753, all held among the title deeds of 'Little Buckhurst', Kent, CKS, U908 T158.

[58] This, however, was subject to annuities to Elizabeth, her husband's daughter from his first marriage, and her son Philip: CKS, U908 T158; ESRO, W/SM D9, f. 236. Elizabeth Turner's will was written on 19 Oct. 1754. Thomas Turner was admitted to the property only on 28 Aug. 1764, as he records in his diary; see also Turner, *Diary*, ed. Vaisey, p. 301, and n. 26.

[59] See also Thomas Turner's earlier reference to the provisions made for Philip Turner in his father's will: Thomas Turner, Diary, 15 Feb. 1757.

[60] John Turner authorised the beneficiaries of the Kentish property to enter it in case of a default of payment and seize its profits until their debts were satisfied; he made the same stipulation with regard to William's £4 annuity, charged to the Framfield property.

[61] John Turner died in 1752 and Elizabeth in 1759; their wills were proved on 28 Aug. 1777. John Turner's will was proved by Thomas Turner. The wills were probably proved in order to enable Thomas Turner's sale of the farm in 1777. By 1777, however, he had acquired his siblings' shares.

[62] For example, on 14 Feb. 1760 Thomas Turner balanced accounts with his siblings over

Thomas Turner's rights in his paternal estate were not fully realised. During the years of the diary, and probably for many years later, the Turners seem to have managed their affairs with the understanding that the Framfield house and shop were a communal family base, as well as Thomas Turner's property: familial cooperation and individual possession were thus once more linked inextricably. As long as Thomas's mother was alive, the house and shop in Framfield were managed by her, in accordance with her life-interest in the property indicated in her husband's will, but after her death both were taken over not by Thomas, but by his brother Moses.[63] Thomas's sister Sarah probably continued to live in the house, and the house continued to serve as a meeting place for others of Thomas's kin. Thomas Turner acknowledged his brother's status as the holder of the Framfield house by promptly changing his references to it from '*my mother's*', as he had previously called it, to '*my brother's*': already on the day of his mother's funeral, after he returned from Framfield we find him reporting that he had 'dined *at my Brothers*'.[64] Thomas Turner remained a tenant in East Hoathly, where, during the years of the diary, he owned neither house, nor shop.[65] In the land tax register of 1785 he was still listed as the owner of the Framfield property, while Moses Turner was listed as its occupier.[66]

Thomas Turner's exact reasons for sharing his inherited estate with his kin remain unknown: perhaps he was no longer interested in the Framfield property for himself, perhaps he was moved by generosity and affection towards his siblings, and perhaps he was also compensated in

the farm's rent and Philip Turner's upkeep, and then handed his siblings notes of hand payable on demand for their share. At that time Thomas Turner also realised that he had calculated the sum mistakenly and detracted 10s 1/2d from each share. See also Thomas Turner, Diary, 21 Feb. 1761.

[63] Moses Turner proposed 'keeping forward the Shop' and Thomas Turner evidently accepted his proposal, *ibid.*, 1 May 1759. The inventory of the shop and its goods taken on that day was made for both Thomas and Moses Turner.

[64] *Ibid.*, 5 Apr. 1759. This is an interesting example not only because it signals that the management of the Framfield property had changed hands, but also because it separates Turner's '*family at home*' from 'his brother's', and both from his kin. The '*Family at home*' which stayed in East Hoathly and dined on the remains of Sunday's dinner included on that occasion Thomas Turner's wife, Peggy, and a servant-maid. (It may have been that Peggy Turner's illness had conveniently prevented her from attending her mother-in-law's funeral.) Those listed among the 'company' at 'my brother's' included Thomas's brothers Moses and Richard, sister Sarah, half-brothers John and William, and six aunts, uncles, and cousins.

[65] Just after the diary ends, Turner bought the premises of the shop from Francis Weller Jr: ESRO, A2327 1/4/5, f. 9; Turner, *Diary*, ed. Vaisey, p. 339. See also copyhold listings in East Hoathly, 1764–86, and lists of East Hoathly proprietors, 'Notes listing the landholding in East Hoathly', the 'Worcester material', Thomas Turner Papers, Manuscripts, and Archives, Yale University Library.

[66] *East Sussex Land Tax, 1785*, ed. R. Davey, Sussex Record Society, vol. 77 (Lewes, 1991), p. 84, and see also pp. 111–12.

other ways. To his younger brother Moses, however, he proved a kind friend and patron. Moses Turner was a tailor by trade and his transition to sole shopkeeping may not have been so easy.[67] There was a time when Thomas doubted his brother's abilities 'in regard to trade', expressing his concern that Moses would not do well and consequently that he himself would be ruined.[68] Indeed, Thomas continued to direct to Moses orders for tailoring work: even orders on behalf of East Hoathly parish found their way to Moses Turner at Framfield, and were then recorded neatly in Thomas's own hand among the East Hoathly parish overseers' accounts.[69] However, Moses proved to be not only a capable tradesman but also a grateful and obliging brother. Thus, by serving as a 'friend' to Moses, Thomas Turner eventually served himself. Time after time Moses came to East Hoathly 'to stand the shop' in his elder brother's absence.[70] In fact, Thomas Turner's successful management of his many affairs in the years after his wife's death was probably partly owed to the fact that he had a capable and trusty brother to rely on. The relationship between the elder and younger brothers thus continued to be very close and it may not be a coincidence that when Moses eventually married, he named his eldest surviving daughter 'Thomisin'.[71]

To his younger brother Richard, too, Thomas Turner was a conscientious friend and patron. He probably had a hand in arranging his apprenticeship; when it ended he witnessed the formal expiry of the indentures and settled financial affairs with Richard's master.[72] He then made fur-

---

[67] Moses Turner, born on 29 June 1733, was apprenticed to Mr Isaac Hook, a tailor at Lewes on 26 Mar. 1749, for seven years: R. Garraway Rice, *Sussex Apprentices and Masters, 1710–1752*, Sussex Record Society, vol. 28 (1922) (London, 1924), p. 193. As Thomas Turner recorded, his apprenticeship ended on 5 Apr. 1754: ESRO, SAS/SM 210. See also Turner, *Diary*, ed. Turner, p. 107; Turner, *The Diary of a Georgian Shopkeeper*, p. 83. One of Thomas's brothers suffered at least at some point from very bad eyesight and was once even described as being almost blind. If this was Moses, as I believe it was, the need to relieve him from his occupation as a tailor was no doubt pressing (although he evidently continued to accept tailoring work while also being a shopkeeper): see Thomas Turner, Diary, 2–7 May, 1, 11, 18 July, 11 Aug. 1757. The bill paid by Thomas Turner on account of Moses's treatment by Dr Snelling suggests that the 'brother' suffering from eye problems was Moses: *ibid.*, 7–8 Sept. 1757.

[68] 'I am afraid my Brother at Framfield will not do well and I am so deeply Concern'd that should he do Ill I must be entirely ruin'd': Thomas Turner, Diary, 10, 17 Apr. 1760.

[69] East Hoathly Overseers' Account Book, ESRO, PAR 378/31/1/1, e.g. f. 33. See also a bill for Moses Turner for making clothes, Apr. 1762–Feb. 1763, filed together with other East Hoathly overseers' papers: ESRO, AMS 4841/10.

[70] On these occasions he dined at his brother's table and sometimes shared his bed.

[71] Moses Turner was married in 1772. Thomisin was baptised on 13 Apr. 1785, see ESRO, Baptism Index.

[72] Richard's master was Thomas Turner's former servant, see above, ch. 1, p. 30. See Thomas Turner, Diary, 1 Jan. 1761. On this occasion he returned to Richard's master a note of hand which he had kept in trust and saw the cancellation of another note.

ther arrangements and agreed with one of his personal friends and suppliers in Lewes to take Richard as a servant in his shop. The terms of
Richard's service were all negotiated by Thomas, whereas Richard displayed his trust in his elder brother by depositing in his hands his payment
from his apprenticeship years with 'no Note or any thing to show for it'.[73]
Once Richard Turner became a servant at Lewes, the brothers had many
opportunities to meet, and it seems that at this point they mixed together
in the same circle of fellow-tradesman who did business in this county
town, exchanged visits, and frequented together the town's public
houses. When this term of service ended, Thomas Turner took his
brother to his own house to work in his own shop.

Thomas Turner thus served as his younger brother's faithful friend. It
was because of their fraternal friendship that he was also willing to
tolerate behaviour from Richard that he would probably not have accepted from a non-related 'friend', let alone an ordinary journeyman. A few
weeks after Richard's arrival at Thomas's house, he returned home 'Very
much in Liquor', having spent every farthing of money in his pocket.[74] On
this occasion he also fell down and 'had the Misfortune to Dislocate the
Great Bone of the arm'.[75] Some weeks later Richard was evidently well
enough to set off on another 'Wild Ramble': this time two people had to
go and fetch him back.[76] Only one month passed and Thomas reported in
his diary wryly: 'My Brother out upon the Wild Order again to day.'[77]
'The Trouble I have with *my Relations*' complained Thomas, 'Makes me
quite insane.'[78] It may have been the case that Thomas's approaching
nuptials gave him the happy excuse to ask his brother to go away. The
fraternal friendship, however, continued. Some years later Richard
Turner died in his elder brother's house.

The role of Thomas Turner's sister Sarah (Sally) in this kinship-based
'friendship' network is harder to detect. It is likely that whenever Thomas
went to visit his mother's house – and later his brother's – he met his sister
there too. It is also likely that whenever he complained about his 'friends'
and 'relations', his bitter words were also directed at her. But as he usually

---

[73] *Ibid.*, 1 Jan. 1761.
[74] *Ibid.*, 25 Jan. 1765. When Richard, as a young apprentice, came to visit Thomas, Thomas
was actually pleased to note that he had 'seemingly being become a Very Sober Prudent
young Fellow'. Although he did criticise his brother for coming to visit him at church
time: see 12 Dec. 1762. Nonetheless, it is important to remember that Richard also
continued to enjoy his brother's trust: Thomas let him handle affairs in his shop, collect
valuable debts and bills, and he even took him as a companion when he went courting.   [75] *Ibid.*, 25 Jan. 1765.
[76] [In] the afternoon my Brother Set of upon a Wild Ramble', *ibid.*, 12–13 Mar. 1765. On the
following day Richard was 'Quite asham'd'.
[77] *Ibid.*, 11 Apr. 1765.
[78] *Ibid.*, 25 Jan. 1765. He also blamed himself and 'his Own Folly'.

described households by naming them after their householders, and also used inclusive terms such as 'friends' and 'relations' for designating kin, Sally's presence remains elusive.[79] Nonetheless, when Sally came to East Hoathly she clearly felt at home. In January 1764, for example, she was not only staying with her elder brother but was also 'keeping house' for him.[80] In November she came one evening, stayed for over a week, and also spent time socialising with neighbours in the village.[81] At the start of the following year, when she was ill, Thomas made special trips to visit her.[82] Sarah is also mentioned in the diary in relation to financial affairs, conveying money from Moses to Thomas and handling family and trade bills.

Thomas Turner's relationships with his half-siblings were not as multi-layered as with his full brothers. The age gap between them was also significant. Nonetheless, there was a durable 'friendship' between them. They exchanged visits and many 'services'.[83] Thomas Turner had a hand in settling affairs between William and his master.[84] The connection between Thomas Turner and his half-brother William is also demonstrated by the fact that when William made his will he not only asked Thomas to write it for him, but also made him his executor and left him

[79] Sarah was not a frequent visitor in Turner's house. Whereas male and female servants were often sent from East Hoathly to Framfield and back, and the Turner brothers travelled back and forth freely, their women-folk did not travel much, and when they did they were usually accompanied by men. Nonetheless, it is likely that Sarah's role in this kinship-based 'friendship' network is not duly represented by the existing evidence. It was probably she who kept Moses's house, and it may have been her presence in the house that also freed Moses to go to East Hoathly when needed and assist Thomas.

[80] See *ibid.*, 17 Jan. 1764. She arrived on 15 Jan. accompanied by her brother, probably Moses.

[81] She came on 9 Nov., and on 18 Nov. brother Moses came to fetch her.

[82] See *ibid.*, 27 Jan., 3, 17 Feb. 1765. On 26 Jan. Thomas Turner received a letter telling him that his sister 'kept her Chamber'. On the following day he went to visit her.

[83] Thomas visited his elder brother John in Tunbridge Wells and was visited by him. The two also met at the house in Framfield: *ibid.*, e.g. 10, 28 July, 14–15 Aug. 1756, 11 Jan. 1757. William also made visits to Framfield and to Thomas Turner in East Hoathly: see e.g. *ibid.* 7 Apr. 1754, 6 Apr., 28 Aug., 26 Dec. 1755, 14 Mar., 14 May, 6–8 June 1756, 13 Feb., 11 Apr. 1757, 12 Mar., 7 May, 1 Oct., 13 Dec. 1758. Records concerning John Turner's children by his first marriage can be found in CKS, Speldhurst Parish Register, 1700–38, P344/1/3, ff. 17, 19, 30. Elizabeth was baptised on 31 Dec. 1718, William on 25 Mar. 1721, and John (born 3 Jan. 1716, ESRO SAS/SM 210) was confirmed at Tunbridge by the Bishop of Rochester on 24 July 1733.

[84] William's master Mr Hill came to Turner's house 'to Settle my Brother Will. Turners Accts': Thomas Turner, Diary, 4 Apr. 1754. On the following Saturday Thomas, his wife, and his wife's sister walked to meet William and Mr Hill at Framfield.

money and books.[85] It is doubtful whether Thomas Turner had any active relationship with his half-sister Elizabeth (Bett) during the years of the diary:[86] in a document written by him at least a decade after the end of the diary, she was described as 'a vagabond'.[87] But although she seems to have disappeared from Thomas's life, she remained involved in it through her illegitimate son, Philip Turner.[88] Philip Turner was also provided for in John Turner's will, and he was cared for at various times by a number of his relations and friends.[89] He lived with his step-grandmother at Framfield, then joined Thomas's house and 'family', and finally he was placed as Moses Turner's apprentice. In the case of Philip, cooperation was beneficial to all 'friends', as it allowed them to keep Philip's maintenance allowance in the family and also use him partly as a child-servant.[90]

[85] *Ibid.*, 13 Dec. 1758. William's connection with his other half-siblings was also evident in his will. After naming his brother, sister, and nephew and making his main bequests, he divided part of his estate between Moses, Richard, and Sarah, and gave them the reversion of the main part. See also Turner's letter to his son, reporting the burial of William at Framfield: 'Your Uncle William Was bro[t] in a Herst last Fryday to be Inter'd at Framfield', Thomas Turner to his son Philip, 18 Nov. 1789, 'Special Files', Thomas Turner Papers, Yale University Library.

[86] In 1738, when Elizabeth was twenty years old and Thomas Turner was ten, she was apprenticed to a mantuamaker in Kent for the duration of two years: Garraway Rice, *Sussex Apprentices and Masters*, p. 193. As the register records, she was apprenticed to Mary Birsey of Westerham, Kent, for £9.9s. Her whereabouts in subsequent years are unclear. In 1754, when Thomas Turner's mother made her will, Elizabeth was mentioned as 'wife of Archibald Blare', but Thomas Turner makes no mention of this in his diary: ESRO, W/SM D9, f. 236; Turner, *Diary*, ed. Vaisey, Appendix A. Elizabeth Turner was left an annuity of 50s, to be paid quarterly from the proceeds of the farm in Kent, but there seems to be no evidence in Turner's diary of its payment to her. Thomas Turner's detachment from Elizabeth was sometimes also manifested linguistically. His half-brothers were referred to by him in his diary as 'brothers', although he sometimes distinguished them by naming them by their Christian name and surname; but he referred to Elizabeth as '*Sister in law*', and '*half Sister*', thus manifesting his distance from her as a sibling: see Thomas Turner, Diary, 20 Apr. 1759, 26 May 1764.

[87] ESRO, SAS/SM 210. It may be significant that, when William Turner left Elizabeth some money in his will, he made the careful provision that it should be hers 'if demanded in 2 Years': Thomas Turner, Diary, 13 Dec. 1758. In the following year Elizabeth was left six pounds in her step-mother's will. This money was to go to her 'if she be living', see *ibid.*, 20 Apr. 1759.

[88] Philip was baptised on 13 Mar. 1749: ESRO, Baptism Index.

[89] See Thomas Turner, Diary, 20 Apr. 1759. He was promised an annuity of five pounds for the first fourteen years of his life, and then ten additional pounds 'to place him out Apprentice to some Trade'. During his apprenticeship he was to have fifteen shillings a year for his clothes. As he was a minor, the discharge of these sums was left to the discretion of Thomas Turner's mother and Philip's step-grandmother, Elizabeth Turner. Like so many of these provisions, the money for Philip's upbringing was to come from the proceeds of the farm in Kent: John Turner's will, ESRO, W/SM D9, f. 233. Thomas Turner referred to Philip as '(the Boy We had the Care of) as also his maintainance, according to the Will of my Father': Thomas Turner, Diary, 26 May 1764.

[90] To poor Philip, however, this apprenticeship was not beneficial. On 26 May 1764, at the age of fifteen, he died at Framfield of scarlet fever. On 8 Mar. 1765 Thomas Turner went to Framfield to settle 'all acc[t] relating to Philip'. He and Moses 'did not make a particular

In addition, Thomas Turner took into his 'family' the son of his elder half-brother John, who was burdened with many children. When Peggy Turner was ill, John's daughter came to live in the house and tend her. Thomas's help to his brother John's family occasioned one of his periodic complaints of unreciprocated 'services'. On Thursday 5 May 1757 John's wife arrived at Framfield and presumably visited Mrs Elizabeth Turner, her step-mother-in-law, but by the Saturday she had still not come to see Thomas in East Hoathly, nor sent a word of greeting, nor asked Thomas or any of his household to come and see her, and that despite the fact that her son had been staying with Thomas since the previous July. Thomas Turner protested about his disinterested 'service' to his '*relations*', saying that he never thought himself more happy than '*a Serving*' them, although this left him 'greatly injured and, I may say impoverished'.[91] He tried to console himself that their 'Natural Affection' must bear sway, and their ill usage must have surely proceeded from acting without thought.[92]

Thus Thomas Turner's network of related 'friends' endured many years and many trials. Husbands and wives, children and step-children, siblings and half-siblings cooperated together. Their relationships were affective and sentimental, but, throughout, they were also heavily instrumental. They held property in common. They made careful accounts in their day-to-day dealings, but they also transferred and re-allocated funds with considerations of mutual, as well as personal benefit. Significantly, many of the obligations among the Turner 'friends' were also contractually enshrined, the main contracts being the parents' wills which served to divide property but also to perpetuate financial obligations among the next generation of Turner siblings. The weightiness of these wills in the eyes of all parties concerned is evident from the fact that so many of their provisions were executed while the wills themselves remained officially unproven. However, the ways in which the Turners managed their affairs also shows that legal contracts could be mitigated by broad interpretations and informal agreements. This combination of formal obligations

Balance', and Thomas used the opportunity to make Moses a generous present of twelve pounds. Thus, even on this last occasion Philip's allowance helped to subsidise Moses and Sarah's establishment at Framfield. It should be noted, however, that when Philip's maintenance costs exceeded his annuity, as they did by 16s 6d in 1760, the extra cost was probably absorbed by the Turner siblings: Thomas Turner, Diary, 14 Feb. 1760. The possible affective ties among Thomas Turner and Philip are unknown, however, and they may have been stronger than the spare diary records regarding Philip reveal. One possibly significant piece of evidence is that Turner named his third child 'Philip'. The eldest, Margaret, was probably named after Thomas's first wife, Peggy. The second, Peter, was given the same name as the only son of that marriage who died in infancy. The third was named Philip.

[91] *Ibid.* 7 May 1757. The boy, however, was sent for from Framfield.
[92] *Ibid.*

and informal understanding also contributed to the making of an enduring 'friendship' among the Turners.

As we have seen, in the case of this network of related 'friends' individualism and familial solidarity also went hand in hand, and many of the
members of this network were engaged in both familial cooperation and a
quest for personal gain. These combined qualities were also manifested in
times of need. Each of the Turners expected themselves and their
'friends' to maintain self-reliance as much as possible. Even the most
needy among them did not fall as complete charges upon the rest. But
again and again, if the need arose, they were given help. An ageing parent,
such as Mrs Elizabeth Turner, received assistance from all her children. A
sick woman, such as Peggy Turner, was cared for by her and her husband's relations. A lonely widower, such as Thomas Turner, received
significant help from his siblings. An elder brother with numerous
children, such as John Turner, was given occasional support, whereas
every attempt was made to equip younger and financially disadvantaged
brothers, such as Moses and Richard Turner, with the means to make an
independent existence. Even the illegitimate son of a 'vagabond', Philip
Turner, was provided by his 'friends' with a safety-net and a chance for
the future. That is not to say that relationships among these 'friends' were
always amicable and harmonious: far from it. As we saw, Thomas
Turner's diary contains rich evidence of familial altercations and disputes. It is also significant that most of Turner's references to his 'friends'
were in fact made in the context of expressing frustrated expectations.
Ties could even be severed, as the case of Thomas's half-sister Elizabeth
clearly shows. But notions of family duty and affection probably helped
the Turners to remain 'friends'. And indeed, they had many opportunities to see that there is more to be gained by agreement than by strife.

When Thomas Turner married, conventions of kinship recognition as
well as norms of familial duty and affection probably encouraged him to
add his wife's kin to his network of related 'friends'. Thomas Turner
detested his wife's mother, whom he thought was 'the very Picture of Ill
nature',[93] but he remained dutiful to her nonetheless. His relationships
with his wife's father and siblings were warm.[94] He exchanged many visits
with his in-laws, including visits which he and Peggy and various mem-

---

[93] *Ibid.*, 27 June 1756.
[94] For instance, in the summer of 1754 Peggy's sister came to visit and also contributed her
labour, making a feather bed for Joseph Fuller: *ibid.*, 27, 30 July, 1 Aug. 1754. See also, for
example, 22, 28, 29 Nov. 1755, 6–7 Mar. 1756, etc. In 1764, for example, 'Bro. Sam' still
came to Turner (by now a widower), and dined with his 'Family': *ibid.*, 4 May 1764. Note
that there were also various multiple connections. For example, on one day Peggy's sister,
her father, Thomas's brother Moses, and George Beard (Thomas Turner's former
servant and the master of his brother Richard) all came to visit and dined with Thomas
Turner: *ibid.*, 20 Oct. 1755.

bers of the Slater family made separately. He did business with his father-in-law and also carried out business on his behalf.[95] He reflected on him positively in his diary: clearly, the two men were fond of each other and had some common interests. Peggy's father also made the couple various gifts.[96] When Peggy Turner was ill, her mother came to East Hoathly to tend her. After Peggy's death, Thomas remained in touch with his in-laws, still naming them 'father', 'mother', and 'brother'.[97] It is therefore not surprising that, when he was disappointed in them, he expressed his disappointment using his formulaic complaint about his *'friends'*. On Wednesday 21 June 1758 Peggy Turner left to visit her father's house, and was supposed to return on the following Friday, accompanied by her brother. They did not return as planned, and by Saturday Thomas felt entirely abandoned by his selfish 'friends':

Prodigious uneasy to think my Wife did not come home according to her appointment wch was last night, Neither for my Bro. to come over as he promis'd. It quite astonishes me to see how I am as it were deserted by *all my Friends* . . . sometimes I think I must be a Prodigy that all my relations in general seem to be so indifferent to me, But when I come to take a more nearer View I can find amongst the greatest Part of their Behaviour some thing of *self Interest* intermixed with it.[98]

More distant relations could also be numbered as 'friends'. Such was the case of Thomas Turner's *'friend & Couzin'*, Charles Hill,[99] the son of one of Thomas Turner's maternal aunts.[100] In the early years of the diary Charles Hill served as a surgeon on board the *Monarch* (or *Monarque*), where he witnessed the travails of Admiral Byng, the scapegoat for the loss of Minorca whose court-martial and execution aroused great public interest. Thomas Turner and his cousin therefore probably did not see each other for a number years. However, Thomas Turner's continuing interest in his cousin is demonstrated by the fact that as soon as a letter

[95] On 20 June 1756, for example, he did a business deal with him. On 21 Mar. 1759 he balanced Mr Slater's accounts, which he had settled for him in London.

[96] On 24 Jan. 1756, for example, Thomas Turner lent his father-in-law a volume of plays. When the volume was returned, it was accompanied by a gift of 'Speer rib': *ibid.*, 29 Feb. 1756. On 27 June 1756 Thomas and his 'father Slater' balanced accounts and Slater added 20*s* to Thomas's bill as if it were a part of the account, and unknown to his wife. During Peggy's long illness he also contributed some money towards the great cost of her medical care.

[97] See, for example, *ibid.*, 11 Jan. 1764: 'my Father Slater Came to see me in the Even . . .'.

[98] *Ibid.*, 24 June 1758. Peggy Turner went to see her sister, who was very ill. Sam Slater finally brought her back that day.

[99] *Ibid.*, 18 June, 19 Jan. 1761. He was also named at various times as 'couzin Hill', 'my old friend and acquaintance', Mr Charles Hill, or Dr Hill.

[100] This was conveyed to me kindly by Roger Davey. Charles Hill's father was referred to by Turner as 'uncle', see for example *ibid.*, 16 Apr. 1758, or simply as 'Mr Hill'. Connections were evidently also kept with him and Thomas Turner's mother. On Sunday 7 Apr. 1754, for example, Mr Hill visited Mrs Turner in Framfield together with his servant William Turner, who was also Elizabeth Turner's step-son.

from Charles Hill arrived at Framfield, a messenger was sent to East
Hoathly to inform Turner of the event, at which point he made special
arrangements to walk to Framfield on the same afternoon to read the
letter.[101]

Like other familial 'friendships', the relationship between Thomas
Turner and Charles Hill also had instrumental and contractual aspects,
and these developed over time. Charles Hill's branch of the family was
originally more prosperous than Thomas Turner's. Whereas Thomas's
brother Moses was apprenticed to a tailor for the sum of £20, Charles Hill
was apprenticed to a surgeon for the substantial sum of £50.[102] Indeed
Thomas's half-brother William worked as a servant to Charles Hill's
father. Charles Hill also seemed to mix in better company than Thomas:
significantly, on the occasions that he met his cousin's acquaintances,
Thomas described them as 'gentlemen', a title that he did not use lightly.[103] At times he also added to Charles Hill's name the epithet 'respected': after Charles Hill's service on board the *Monarch* ended, for example,
Thomas wrote in his diary: '*my respected friend & Couzin* Charles Hill
Came to see me & Staid all night'.[104] However Charles Hill lived above his
means, and, before long, he needed the help of his more humble friend
and cousin. An initial loan of six pounds, which Thomas gave to Charles
Hill in 1761, grew to twenty, and, by 1764, reached sixty.[105] Thomas
Turner had to take measures to secure himself against a future loss. When
Charles Hill first borrowed money from Thomas, he gave him his note of
hand, but as the debt increased Charles Hill's father added his security.[106]
Thomas Turner also charged interest on the loan. But in this case, too,
formal obligations were entwined with an informal understanding. In the
course of time, Charles Hill got married, and Thomas agreed to keep the
matter of the debt between them unknown to Charles Hill's wife. Thus,

[101] *Ibid.*, 13 Feb. 1757. On an earlier occasion, when Hill was making his way to Portsmouth
to depart on the *Monarch*, he passed by East Hoathly, presumably to bid farewell.
Thomas was then summoned immediately and he and his sister rushed to Framfield to
spend forty minutes with their cousin, before he set out on his way: *ibid.*, 21 May 1756.
Later on, Turner was probably also very pleased to have through his cousin a first-hand
account of the affair of Admiral Byng, one of the most controversial affairs of his time. It
could also be that having a relation on board the *Monarch* served to excite his interest in
this affair: see his writing on the affair of Admiral Byng on 29 July, 4 Dec. 1756, 13 Feb.,
16 Mar. 1757. In addition, Thomas Turner may have also shared with his cousin an
interest in medicine and medical prescriptions. One of the prescriptions collected by him
was for weakness of sight, taken from 'the Bristol amusement', by Dr Hill: medical
prescriptions collected by Turner, mostly undated, in Special Files, Thomas Turner
Papers, Manuscripts and Archives, Yale University Library.
[102] Garraway Rice, *Sussex Apprentices and Masters*, pp. 193, 94.
[103] Thomas Turner, Diary, 14 Feb. 1762. See also 26–7 Apr. 1764.
[104] *Ibid.*, 19 Jan. 1761.
[105] See *ibid.*, 10 Mar. 1761, 5 Nov. 1763, when Thomas Turner balanced accounts with '*my
Friend Hill*'.   [106] *Ibid.*, 20 Jan., 10 Mar. 1761.

for example, on 10 March 1761 he sent a bill to his cousin under cover to another person. By April 1764 he decided it was time to go to his cousin's house and discuss the affair with him. By that time he had already accumulated some resentment against his cousin, as can be seen from the following poignant usage of the term 'friend': 'In the Morn I Set out for Yalden to see my old acquaintance & Cuz (*and I ought to have Reason as Well to Say Worthy Friend*) . . .'.[107]

Charles Hill did not pay his debt. Moreover, he gave Thomas Turner yet another opportunity to mourn the wickedness of the ungrateful.[108] On 29 April 1764, when Thomas prepared to leave his cousin's house, he was presented to his great surprise with charges of maintenance for his horse. 'Now this is what I Could not have Once thought would be So', he exclaimed in his diary, and then noted that whenever Charles Hill was in East Hoathly, he had always received entertainment both for himself and horse, and that despite the fact that Thomas, too, could have used the excuse that he had no stable. 'Oh ingratitude, Ingratitude', lamented Thomas Turner, 'thou Common but hateful Vice a Vice which in my Oppinion Clouds all our Other Virtues, and I think no man Guilty of it in a higher degree than Mr Hill.'[109]

Thomas Turner thus used the language of 'friendship' throughout the years in relation to his kin. This language of 'friendship' proposed a powerful fusion of familial sentiments and familial instrumentality. Expectations of 'service', preferably disinterested 'service', were proposed even when actually frustrated. The related 'friend' was thus not merely a person linked by blood and marriage, but one with whom one was presumed to have an *active* relationship. These relationships were a matter of both obligation and choice.[110] Actions usually entailed at least some measure of personal volition, but they were also understood within a broader framework of recognised duties.[111] It is important to remember, however, that these relationships, however powerful, were often far from harmonious. As we have seen, the language of 'friendship' was used by Thomas Turner to express and negotiate his disappointment in kin.

On the whole, as is evident elsewhere in this book, the case of the Turners shows that 'friendship' among kin failed to conform to commonplace dichotomous descriptions. These relationships were both sentimental and instrumental; both contractual and informal; both sentimental and contractual. In many cases it even appeared that these

---

[107] *Ibid.*, 26 Apr. 1764.
[108] On 27 Apr. he gave Thomas Turner a bond of £60, bearing interest at 5 per cent per annum. Mr Hill then paid Thomas Turner £1 2s 6d interest due to the day. The bond was witnessed by one Mr Pope, Jr, a tradesman in Maidstone with whom Turner also had a business connection.   [109] *Ibid.*, 29 Apr. 1764.
[110] Issa, 'Obligation and choice'.   [111] See also Cressy, *Coming Over*, p. 274.

apparently disparate properties actually sustained one another. Sentimental ties among the Turners, for example, were instrumentally expressed. They were also contractually expressed. But whereas contractual obligations among the Turners were both common and highly respected, they could also be partly fulfilled, partly supplemented, and partly replaced by other agreements. Finally, much as the sentimental bonds among the Turners were important, they were not a necessary condition for the endurance of 'friendship'. Formal contracts and notions of duty also ensured the continuation of 'friendship' above and beyond many personal sentiments of like and dislike.

Friendship in marriage

Among Thomas Turner's 'friends', his wife Peggy had a cardinal role. Over the years Turner used the language of friendship not only to reflect on his marriage, but also to negotiate some very difficult experiences.

> for I married if I know my own mind with nothing in View but intirely to make my Wife & Self happy and to live in a Course of Virtue & Religion & to be a mutal [sic] help and Assistance to each other. I was neither Instigated to marry by avarice ambition, nor Lust. no, nor was I promped [sic] to it by anything only *the Pure and desirable Sake of Friendship*.[112]

These words communicate Thomas Turner's reflections on his marriage. They also echo widely current contemporary idioms about marriage as a moral relationship, and a relationship of friendship. Thomas Turner's feelings towards his wife were intimate, and his diary, in which he wrote his feelings, was a private document. But the language in which he expressed his feelings – as we have noticed in this book in other contexts – was often neither private, nor very intimate: it contained many formulaic usages, and it was often very similar to the language of the sermon, the novel, and the conduct book. Turner would probably have agreed with Samuel Richardson's words that '*wives and husbands are, or should be, friends*'.[113] He would probably have also approved of the sentiments expressed in the contemporary treatise by 'Philogamus', that 'friendship is the most pure and true when it has marriage for its foundation'; for 'a prudent and amiable Wife can make the cares of the World sit easy . . . She is a Man's best companion in prosperity and his only Friend in Adversity.'[114] Certainly, he knew the biblical words of praise for the

---

[112] Thomas Turner, Diary, 1 Jan. 1756.
[113] Richardson, *Pamela*, ed. Sabor, p. 469. Italics in the original. See also the detailed discussion of ideas of marriage and friendship, below, ch. 7.
[114] Philogamus, *Marriage Defended, or, the Ladies Protected* (London, 1741), p. 44. See especially the discussion of friendship in marriage in Jeremy Taylor's work, below, pp. 242–3.

'virtuous woman', a treasure to her husband: wise and charitable, fully trustworthy and widely respected, 'who looketh well to the ways of her household, and eateth not the bread of idleness'.[115] Using expressions such as these, he constructed his own thoughts concerning his marriage in terms of 'friendship'. This friendship was seen to be cemented by tender feelings, mutual religious sentiments, shared notions of duty, and, last but not least, by great appreciation of Peggy Turner's skills in housewifery.

The marriage of Thomas and Peggy Turner lends further substance to the growing understanding among historians of the family that the line between a union of interests and a love-match is not always easily drawn. Between the high-born daughter, disposed of by parents and guardians to a man she hardly knew, and the instinctive conviction of love at first sight, lay a broad grey area in which both sentiment and prudence interplayed.[116] The marriage of Thomas and Peggy Turner belonged to this intermediary zone. Thomas Turner was probably fond of his wife's appearance: years later he described her lovingly as 'remarkably Sweet & Cleanly in her Person'.[117] In social and economic terms, he and she were well suited. When they met, Thomas was either a journeyman or a young village shopkeeper. He was religious and sociable, well read, well connected, and very eager to succeed in trade. Peggy Slater was four years younger. Originally a farmer's daughter, she had become a household servant (a phase termed by historians as 'life-cycle service').[118] She, too, was religious, sociable, educated, and extremely hard-working.[119]

---

[115] Proverbs, 31: 11–31. These words were also used, for example, in Robert Wilkinson's wedding sermon, 'Conjugal duty', pp. 13–17, cited in A. Clark, *The Working Life of Women in the Seventeenth Century*, ed. A. L. Erickson (London 1992; 1st edn 1919), pp. 39–40.

[116] Stone has most famously drawn the distinction between interest and love in marriage, while presenting a developmental process in which marriage in England underwent a transition between the sixteenth and eighteenth centuries, from interests to rising affection and 'romantic love'. Importantly, however, Stone also emphasises the role of friendship in marriage, particularly from the seventeenth century. Others, such as Martin Ingram and Peter Earle, describe measured deliberations weighing both sentiments and interests and other considerations concerning compatibility: Stone, *The Family, Sex and Marriage*; Ingram, *Church Courts, Sex and Marriage*; Earle, *The Making of the English Middle Class*, ch. 7; Cressy, *Birth, Marriage and Death*, esp. ch. 10; Wrightson, 'The family in early modern England', pp. 16–17. See also Macfarlane's discussion on friendship in marriage and many references to friendship in marriage in Macfarlane, *Marriage and Love*, esp. chs. 8, 9.

[117] Thomas Turner, Diary, 23 June 1761.

[118] In a later document Turner recorded that she 'lived with' Mrs Pellet, at Lewes, see ESRO, SAS/SM 210. The phrase 'to live with' probably referred to a service relationships, cf. 'mary martin Came to live with me at 30s a year', Thomas Turner, Diary, 25 Mar. 1754. 'Mrs Pellet' may have been a member of the Pellat family, a family of wealthy Lewes merchants.

[119] According to her husband's testimony, Peggy had 'a Chearful tho' religious turn of mind'. Indeed, she could enjoy both a good sermon and a heart-breaking romance: Thomas Turner, Diary, 23 June 1761.

Thomas Turner's reflections, quoted above, show that he prided himself that this well-suited match was not contracted as a result of any economic or social pressures, but was entirely a matter of personal choice: 'I married if I know my own mind with nothing in View but intirely to make my Wife & Self happy.' At the same time, he was proud that he did not base his marriage on the fleeting lure of sexual desire. Rather, it was '*the Pure and desirable Sake of Friendship*' that prompted him to unite with his wife in a bond of virtue, religion, and mutual comfort, a mixture of sensibility and sense.

Despite their compatibility, the marriage of Thomas and Peggy Turner was not always happy. The couple knew bitter arguments; indeed, the lines quoted at the start of this section were written in the aftermath of one of their worst disputes.[120] The language of friendship thus served Thomas Turner not only for reflecting on his marriage, but it also provided him with a moral framework for negotiating his own difficulties with his wife. Indeed, Turner protested that his marriage was based on 'friendship', and expressed the hope that his wife would surely see that his actions, too, must be 'Convincing proofs of *Love and Friendship*'. Eventually, he even 'almost made as it were a resolution to make a Sepparation', settle his affairs, and part '*in Friendship*'.[121] A friendly separation did not occur. But during most of her married life, Peggy Turner received little praise from her husband's pen. Besides obvious expressions of discontent, he was usually simply silent.

In retrospect it is possible to suggest that Thomas Turner's expressions of disagreement with his wife were the dark side of a very deep emotional attachment. His silences in his diary, too, can be interpreted in more than one way. At times they may have been a sign that there was no special news to recount, or even that all was going well; at times they may have been a sign of repressed anger, emotional pain, or resignation. Indeed, if there was unhappiness in Peggy and Thomas Turner's marriage, it was not only because of personal differences. Since her pregnancy and the death of her baby Peggy had never fully regained her health. Although she continued to work hard in the house and the shop, she became increas-

---

[120] Thomas Turner complained about his wife's temper, whereas he, alas, was too fond of drink. On his third wedding anniversary, for example, he wrote a sad account: 'doubtless Many have been the disputes which have happened between my Wife and my Self during the time'. He then mentioned specifically 'the many Animositys & desensions which have been almost incessantly continued & fermented between us & our Friends from almost the very day of our Marriage': *ibid.*, 15 Oct. 1756. Indeed, spoiling his relationships with his related 'friends' was one of Turner's complaints against his wife. Two years later, he conceded that his wife enjoyed 'but little pleasure of her life in the Marriage State', however he protested that he was only 'to[o] careful' of her, attributing her problems to ill health: *ibid.*, 6 June 1758.
[121] *Ibid.*, 1 Jan. 1756.

ingly debilitated, no doubt suffering from great pain. When Thomas
Turner began to realise that his wife's illness was likely to be terminal, he
resorted once more to the language of friendship. Once more, this language provided him with the verbal and conceptual idioms for dealing
with emotional distress. This time it was his dread of his forthcoming loss:
'oh how do I tremble at the thought of loosing *so valuable a friend and
Companion*'.[122] Using formulaic idioms, he pictured his marriage once
more as a union of true friendship, '*Friendships more Exalted tye*', a tie of
'nature & of Love', not 'built on passions Lust'.[123] He was also aware that
with the loss of his wife he would be deprived of the last most intimately
related friend: 'Oh! how Mellancholy a time it is quite destitute of Father
or Mother and am in all probability like to loose my Wife the only *friend* I
believe I have now in this World and the alone Center of my Worldly
Happiness.'[124] Lastly, he also expressed his great esteem of his wife,
describing her with a mixture of popular aphorisms and biblical para-
phrases, drawn from the book of Proverbs: 'a Virtuous & prudent Wife,
an inestimable Treasure, a Treasure more Valuable than peruvian mines
or all the Shining Gems of the East'.[125]

When Peggy Turner died, Thomas Turner formulated his experience
yet again using the language of friendship. This time, the familiar idioms
gave an air of solemn ritual to his grief. On 23 June 1761 he wrote: 'About
50 m[inutes] p[ast] 1 it Pleas'd Almighty God to take from me by Beloved
Wife . . . In her I have lost a *Sincere Friend* & Virtuous Wife, a Prudent &
good OEconomist in her Family, and a Very Valuable Companion.'[126]
Lamentations of lost friendship were also combined with a growing
retrospective appreciation of Peggy's housekeeping. However good his
servants were, Thomas Turner was well aware of the difference between

---

[122] *Ibid.*, 1 Feb. 1761. See also 'ah! mellancholly situation My Wife Extremely Ill, quite
alone, almost & trade Very dead, but still what is this to the prospect of Looseing my
intimate, my familiar & sincere friend': *ibid.*, 18 Feb. 1761.

[123] *Ibid.*, 22 Jan. 1761.

[124] *Ibid.*, 3 Oct. 1760. On 14 June 1761, when Peggy Turner was lying on her deathbed,
Thomas Turner also accused both himself and his related 'friends': 'what it is owing to I
Cannot tell. whether from my Own unhappy Temper or that of *my friends and relations*,
but in this my day of trouble they seem to stand aloof and as it were staring at me like a
Stranger'.

[125] *Ibid.*, 1 Feb. 1761. See also Proverbs 31: 10ff: 'Who can find a virtuous woman? for her
price is far above rubies.' See also his descriptions of her as a 'treasure', e.g. 5, 20 June
1761.

[126] After a few days he lamented once again the loss of his dear friend: 'I am now destitute of
a Friend to converse with or even *a sincere friend* on whom I can rely for advice, now I
have lost the dear, dear Partner of my Soul': Thomas Turner, Diary, 27 June 1761. In
this case Thomas Turner also emphasised that he never concealed from his wife 'the
most minutest Circumstance' of his affairs, even when his mind was 'overloaded with
trouble', thus emphasising a joint personal and business confidence, or perhaps recognising their bad times together.

their management of his household affairs, and his wife's 'good OEconomy'.[127] In the following quotation he complained about the state of his domestic affairs, as well as the loss of his wife's friendship. This passage highlights furthermore the connection between Turner's language of friendship and contemporary prototypes of the good housekeeper and virtuous wife:

but yet when I reflect how Regular and Compos'd my mind then was as well as the governm[en]t of my Domestic affairs and compare them with my present Situation how Can I be other wise than Uneasy. then had I a Sincere and inviolable *Friend* whose Company made home agreeable and to whom I could impart the most secret and inmost receses of mind and receive Comfort if in the Power of Nature to give it & by whose prudent and discrete OEeconomy my Family affairs where govern'd with the greatest frugality and regularity, but now my mind has lost that Calm and naught but Tempest Resides there. No *Friend* or agreable Companion to sooth the anxiety of my mind, or with whom I can spend an hour in Sacred *Friendship*.[128]

As time went by, the eulogies of lost friendship became a recurring motif in Thomas Turner's diary. Formulaic idioms of friendship combined again and again with notions of personal bereavement. The following quotation presents a typical example of these recurring lamentations:

Oh! Mellancholly Time how does the Ideas of that Valuable Woman my Wife Constantly present themselves to my mind One in who I enjoy'd almost Every thing this World can afford to make life happy, a Valuable and truely sincere *Friend* and a most agreable Companion and a Virtuous, loving and indulgent Wife.[129]

These repeated laments for a lost friend might lead us to imagine that after his wife's death Turner retreated to a more reclusive form of life. Such was not the case. While the language of friendship served Turner to express feelings of loss and loneliness in the years following the death of his wife, it cannot be understood as any straightforward representation of his social experience. Contrary to what Turner's words conveyed, in any practical terms he was hardly ever socially isolated. After his wife's death, he continued to lead a very active life surrounded with many neighbours, relations, clients, servants, and friends. In fact, it sometimes seems that the more socially active he was, the more he used the language of friendship to imagine his life with his wife as a time of blissful calm. The

[127] See *ibid.*, 10 Nov. 1761: 'and who can describe the difference between the good OEconomy of my Wife in the Prudent management of her affairs and what I now by sad Experience find and yet I believe few have more honest & truer servants'. See also *ibid.*, 13 Sept. 1764: 'I have now no One Friend in the World to whom I can trust the management of my affairs To, Even my serv^t wh^{ch} bares the Character of an Excelent One is defective in a Proper care and what is beyond all that Seriousness of Temper & pious behaviour.'   [128] *Ibid.*, 10 Nov. 1763.
[129] *Ibid.*, 21 Aug. 1762. See also, for example, 15, 17 July, 13, 16 Sept., 10 Nov. 1761, 22 Feb., 12 Apr., 16 June 1762, etc.

conjunction of Turner's laments, and his continuing – if not increased – participation in a range of social networks, thus emphasises the importance of analysing discourse within the context of social action. The first day of February 1764, for example, was a full day. One neighbour stayed over and slept in Turner's house. Another female neighbour came to buy in the shop and stayed and drank tea, and yet another neighbour sent Turner a gift of a few sausages and some pork bones. In the evening the village shoemaker came to the house and played cards. After all this social interaction, Turner wrote 'my Tumultuous mind! What's all the World without a Friend!' Similarly, 21 to 23 February 1764 were full of events, including a journey to Newhaven in company with a close male friend, and a dinner in company with another close friend. One friend then stayed with Turner overnight and took part of his bed. In the same two days Turner also received help from his brother, who came to stand the shop for him, as well as from the loyal former maidservant, Mary Martin. After interacting with so many individuals and receiving so much assistance and support, Turner still exclaimed in his diary: 'Oh! how unpleasant is my Present Situation. What's life without a Sincere Friend and when that valuable thing happens in a Wife how Great the Blessing.'[130]

It seems that in the course of time these lamentations of friendship had become for Thomas Turner a ritualised pattern of remembrance and even a form of moral discipline. Often written at weekends, sometimes in a neat hand that seems to have been copied, they demonstrate that he had not forgotten his wife, and that in the midst of his busy life he still appreciated both her and simple domestic pleasures. This may be the reason why Thomas Turner's image of his calm life with his wife was invoked particularly forcefully at times when his current social life resulted in heavy drinking. On 18 January 1765, for example, he declared his abhorrence of drinking, but he then apologised that 'having no company at home agreable ... when I do Get Out my Spirits are So Elated that reason is quite dethron'd'. A few weeks later he lamented in a very neat hand the loss of friendship, his wife, and calmness of mind altogether.

I have I dare Say no *friend* in the World that I could confide in with the firm assurance of Fidelity and upon the Whole I may with the most Strictest Truth Say I know not what it has been to have one minutes True pleasure Since I lost my Wife for When I am in possession of my reason I am always reflecting upon the Pleasure I then Enjoy'd in a calm, Sedate & regular course of Life. Every thing Serene & home of all places was the Most delightful & pleasant and particularly So if no One but my Wife & Self together But now alas! I am all Tempest & Storm Within.[131]

Thus, in the course of the years the commonplace idioms of marriage and friendship were used by Thomas Turner as his most personal idioms,

[130] *Ibid.*, 23 Feb. 1764. [131] *Ibid.*, 7 Feb. 1765.

repeated again and again in his diary. The language of friendship helped Turner to construct his understanding of his marriage. At times, it lent his sentiments an air of solidity and virtue, presenting personal experience in the pattern of well-known truths. Many times, this language may have also helped him to negotiate painful emotions, to express the inexpressible, and to ritualise grief. Eventually, the language of friendship acquired in his diary the force of a formula of remembrance. At this stage, it served not only to convey Turner's moral understanding of his marriage, but also the weight of his memories of his life with his wife.

Thomas Turner's select friends

All in all, the number of persons whom Turner mentioned in his diary as his 'friends' – and who were not among his kin – amounts to sixteen. All of them were male, most were probably about the same age as Thomas Turner, most lived outside of East Hoathly but nearly all of them lived in Sussex. Four 'friends' were fellow-tradesmen in neighbouring towns and villages, three were officers of the excise, two were victuallers (one of them both a victualler and a brewer and also an excise officer), one was a schoolmaster, and another was a schoolmaster who became an excise officer. (At various times both schoolmasters also rented Thomas Turner a warehouse.) The surgeon who treated Peggy Turner in her long illness was also numbered as a 'friend', as was the sub-tenant who rented the farm in Kent whose tenancy was held jointly by the Turner siblings. The list of people named by Turner as 'friends' also included an odd-jobs labourer, occasionally in receipt of poor relief, to whom Turner extended his friendship and patronage, and a former pupil who also performed many errands and who became a close companion (as well as an assistant to an excise officer). Lastly, there was a small number of men to whom the epithet 'friend' seems to have been applied ironically, such as Mr Robson, the headborough of Laughton, whom Thomas Turner threatened with prosecution over some parish affair,[132] and Mr Joseph Fuller, named 'my worthy friend', who cheated Thomas Turner when buying a horse.[133]

In the case of these 'friendship' relationships, too, dynamic changes over time were extremely important. From around the time of Peggy's

---

[132] *Ibid.*, 1 Mar. 1757.

[133] *Ibid.*, 27 June 1757. Thomas Turner asked Joseph Fuller's help '*as a friend*' in buying a certain horse, but Fuller bought that horse for himself, and then offered to resell it to Turner at a higher price. He moreover laughed at Turner 'and counted it as a piece of wit and a sharp look-out for a man to serve himself when he can and his neighbour next'. Significantly, Turner's condemnation reverses the formulaic expressions of service among friends. He also denounced Fuller's behaviour as dishonest and contrary to religion. It remains unclear, however, whether this was Joseph Fuller Junior or Senior.

illness, Thomas Turner's references to 'friends', made in his diary, increased dramatically; after her death they appear as regular usages. It seems that during the difficult time of his wife's illness Thomas Turner reached a new understanding of the value of friendship and the importance of select friends in his life. Thus, although nearly all the people whom he mentioned in his diary as 'friends' had been known to him for years, the pattern of distinguishing them as 'friends' only became evident from around the summer and autumn of 1760. Around that time Turner began to give up hope that his wife would ever recover,[134] and some of the visitors who came to the house to see him, and possibly to comfort him, were named by him as 'friends'. Mr George Richardson was the first to receive this appellation consistently. By 1760 Turner and Richardson had already known each other for a long time.[135] As early as 28 September 1755 Thomas Turner lent George Richardson a copy of Young's *Night Thoughts*, and on 20 May 1756 he heard from him of the outbreak of the Seven Years War. From around the summer and the autumn of 1760, however, Richardson's visits became more frequent, and when Thomas Turner recorded them he started describing him using terms such as '*my Friend*', '*my good friend*', '*my Worthy Friend*', '*my quondam friend*', and '*my Old Friend*'.[136] When Peggy Turner died, George Richardson came immediately to console Thomas Turner and advise him.[137] George Richardson and Thomas Turner's friendship was thus based on personal intimacy and some shared interests in literature and current affairs, but they also had other important connections. Richardson was a tradesman in Lewes, where Thomas Turner's main suppliers were also located and where Thomas Turner himself had worked as a servant. Later Richardson set up his own shop in the small town of Steyning: at that stage he asked Thomas Turner to be his agent in appraising the new shop and its goods.[138]

George Richardson was one of a number of fellow-tradesmen, professional men, and office-holders with whom Thomas Turner was

[134] See e.g. *ibid.*, 3 Oct. 1760: '[I] am in all probability like to loose my Wife.' See also 'my Wife Poor Creature, most prodigious Ill . . . I have now no prospect of her recovery': *ibid.*, 20 Nov. 1760.

[135] He may have been George Richardson of Godstone, Surrey, who was apprenticed to James Waller of Allfriston, Sussex, mercer, on 22 May 1738, for the period of seven years, Garraway Rice, *Sussex Apprentices and Masters*, p. 158.

[136] See, for example, Thomas Turner, Diary, 9, 17 Aug., 5 Oct., 23 Nov. 1760, 2 Jan., 6–7 Sept. 1761, 26 Apr. 1762. On Friday 7 Jan. 1763 he was called 'my Old Friend and Very intimate acquaintance'.   [137] *Ibid.*, 23, 24 June, 6–7 Sept. 1761.

[138] 'I set out for Steyning in order to appraize a Shop of goods belonging to the Wid. Foreman and now taken by my friend Geo. Richardson . . .'; 'ab[t] 20 m[inutes] p[ast] 10 We began appraize the Goods: /Viz/, Mr John Balcombe of Angmering in behalf of Mrs Foreman and my Self in behalf of *my Friend Geo. Richardson*', *ibid.*, 20–1 Sept. 1761.

connected both personally and occupationally. As this study attempts to show, Turner's circle of select 'friends' formed a small but impressive regional network of men of the 'middling sort': literate and capable men, pillars of their communities, bound together in long-lasting connections of friendship and trade. Thomas Turner's relationships with these 'friends' were typified by trust, some shared intellectual and spiritual interests, as well as shared business interests. These relationships also led to mutual transactions and exchanges. Lastly, if Thomas Turner was an active member of his community, serving in a range of public offices, so it seems were at least some of his 'friends'.[139]

Such, for example, was Thomas Turner's 'friend', the shopkeeper John Breeden of Pevensey.[140] John Breeden was a year younger than Thomas Turner.[141] In 1745, at the age of fifteen, he entered the Corporation of Pevensey as a freeman.[142] At the age of seventeen he was mentioned as an occupier of a tenement in the town.[143] At the age of twenty-nine he obtained for the first time a Sacrament Certificate, attesting that he had taken the Sacrament according to the rites of the Church of England and denied transubstantiation, a prerequisite for bearing public office.[144] In future years he had occasions to repeat this avowal.[145] In 1768, at the age of thirty-eight, for example, he was the Bailiff of the Town and Liberty of Pevensey.[146] His strong position in his local community is also evident in

---

[139] See also at this point: D. Eastwood, *Government and Community in the Provinces, 1700–1870* (London, 1997), esp. chs. 2 and 3, and references there; Langford, *Public Life and the Propertied Englishman*, esp. ch. 4.

[140] His name was also spelled as 'Bredon', 'Breden', 'Bredin', 'Breaden'.

[141] He was probably 'John Breden', son of William and Sarah, baptised in Pevensey on 8 Feb. 1730, ESRO, Baptism Index.

[142] Pevensey Corporation Records, Appendix II: Rolls of Pevensey Freemen, ESRO, PEV 385/m.10, 11 Oct. 1745.

[143] Counterpart lease for forty years, Pevensey Corporation Properties: Leases and Related Documents, 10 July 1747, ESRO, PEV 546. See also a counterpart lease for eleven years to 'John Breden of Pevensey, shopkeeper and one of the jurats', at the annual rent of £18 10s, as well as an annual payment of £5 per acre for any land converted to tillage, 22 Jan. 1771, ESRO, PEV 548. See also the counterpart lease to John Breden Sn. of Pevensey, shopkeeper, at the annual rent of 1s, 5 Oct. 1790, ESRO, PEV 566. John Breeden, Jun., possibly his son, is mentioned as a shopkeeper of Pevensey in a counterpart lease for forty years, 27 Jan. 1787, ESRO, PEV 563.

[144] Appendix I: Detailed list of Sacrament Certificates issued in Pevensey (nos. 285–381), 7 Oct. 1759, ESRO, PEV 299. This was necessary for the bearing of public office to attest that the bearer was neither a dissenter, nor a Catholic. Other necessary oaths were the oaths of allegiance and supremacy, required from 1673 by the Test Act (25 Chas.II c.2), and the oath of abjuration (13 & 14 Will. III (1701) c. 6). In this document he is listed as 'John Bredon Shopkeeper'.

[145] Sacrament Certificates, Pevensey, 26 Oct. 1760, ESRO, PEV 302; 27 Dec. 1761, ESRO, PEV 320; 20 Oct. 1765, ESRO, PEV 344; 23 Oct. 1768, ESRO, PEV 349; 18 Oct. 1772, ESRO, PEV 356; 6 Oct. 1776, ESRO, PEV 360; 7 Oct. 1781, ESRO, PEV 366.

[146] Sacrament Certificates, Pevensey, 23 Oct. 1768, ESRO, PEV 349. So he was in 1781, ESRO, PEV 366.

the fact that in some registers the title 'Esq.' was added to his name.[147] Like Thomas Turner, John Breeden was considered trusty and capable enough to be appointed as a collector of the land and window tax.[148] He held this position probably until his late fifties or early sixties. His prosperity is evident from the fact that in 1774, when the window tax was collected, nineteen 'lights' were counted in his house, taxed at the rate of £1 11s 6d.[149] For the land tax of 1778 his house was assessed at £6 0s 3d.[150] In his will he was titled 'Gent.'.[151]

Thomas Turner clearly thought highly of John Breeden and valued him greatly as a friend. During the years he mentioned him in his diary as '*my Friend*', '*my Esteem'd Friend*', '*my Worthy Friend*', and even '*my Old acquaintance & Very Worthy Friend*'.[152] When Turner wished to look for a new shop, it was to John Breeden that he turned for advice and help.[153] When his mother died, he asked John Breeden to come and take an inventory of her stock-in-trade.[154] Thomas Turner also deposited in the hands of Breeden the delicate task of finding a housekeeper, giving him full power to bargain with the prospective servant 'as if it were his own affair'.[155] Their friendship evidently continued in the years after the diary ended: in 1771 John Breeden stood as godfather to Thomas Turner's son Frederick.[156]

Another close 'friend' and fellow-tradesman was John Madgwick of

---

[147] Sacrament Certificates, Pevensey, 27 Dec. 1761, ESRO, PEV 320; 23 Oct. 1768, ESRO, PEV 349. However he continued to be described as 'shopkeeper'.

[148] See, for example, a receipt for land tax payment for the year 1776 signed by 'John Breeden Collector', ESRO, Archive of the Plumley Family, PLU 6/32. See also similar receipts for May 1777 in ESRO, PLU 6/33, 35; Nov. 1778, ESRO, PLU 6/37, 39, 40. See receipts for the collection of quit-rent by J. Breeden for 1777, ESRO, PLU 6/34; 1778, ESRO, PLU 6/36; 1779, ESRO, PLU 6/38.

[149] An assessment made on 'the Houses & Windows and Lights' in the Liberty of Pevensey, 5 Apr. 1774, ESRO, PEV 1385.

[150] Land tax records, 1778, ESRO, PEV 1387.

[151] The will of John Breden, Gent., 1796, ESRO, Lewes Archdeaconry Wills Register W/A67, f. 211. See also the will of George Breden, Mercer, 1743, ESRO, W/A56, f. 316.

[152] He was the next after George Richardson to appear in the diary bearing the title 'friend' consistently. See, for example, Thomas Turner, Diary, 4, 6, 24, 26 May, 29 Aug. 1761, 15 May 1762, 26 Oct. 1764. On 1 Jan. 1763 he was called 'my Intimate acquaintance and Very Worthy Friend'. As in the case of George Richardson, however, their close relationship started earlier.

[153] *Ibid.*, 16, 28 Sept. 1757.

[154] *Ibid.*, 30 Apr.–3 May 1759. During the appraisal John Breeden stayed and lodged in Thomas Turner's house and also socialised with him, his siblings, and other neighbours. On 4 May he continued on his way to a fair.

[155] *Ibid.*, 26 May 1761. Cooperation and trust existed between them in less weighty matters as well. On 15 May 1762, for example, John Breeden called at Thomas Turner's house on his way to London, paid him a debt of £2 18s 0d and continued to London riding on Thomas Turner's horse, leaving his own horse behind.

[156] Baptised 8 Dec. 1771, died 7 Nov. 1774, SAS/SM 210; Turner, *Diary*, ed. Vaisey, Appendix A. On Godparenthood in Tudor and Stuart England, see Cressy, *Birth, Marriage and Death*, esp. pp. 149–72.

Lewes. No doubt of a higher social standing, he came from a family of gentlemen and he married a gentleman's daughter; however, he was also described both in his marriage settlement and his will as a mercer.[157] Thomas Turner described John Madgwick as '*my Friend*' and '*my Very Worthy acquaintance*'.[158] John Madgwick was one of Thomas Turner's main suppliers in Lewes.[159] Thomas Turner not only bought many goods from his shop but also used him as a banker for disposing of large sums of cash that it was unsafe to keep and carry. On 27 July 1761, for example, he traded £70 in cash for a bill from John Madgwick. Thomas Turner often met John Madgwick when he went to Lewes on business and also dined with him and lodged in his house; sometimes John Madgwick called in at East Hoathly and dined with Thomas Turner. John Madgwick was one of the 'sponsors' of Thomas Turner's first son, Peter.[160] Thomas Turner arranged for his younger brother Richard to work as a servant in John Madgwick's shop, and later took into his house and shop John Madgwick's own shop assistant, Henry Dodson. John Madgwick, like John Breeden, was also a prominent citizen. In 1761, for example, he was chosen as headborough of the town and borough of Lewes.[161]

The language of 'friendship' thus served Thomas Turner to distinguish men such as George Richardson, John Breeden, and John Madgwick. It signalled his special relationships with them and manifested his sense of esteem. Thomas Turner had many acquaintances, but *these* were people whom he was pleased to distinguish as 'friends'. Lastly, in the case of Thomas Turner's select 'friends', as in so many of his other relationships, sentimental and sociable ties were very closely entwined with instrumental and business ties.[162] Some similar connections were evident also in the case of other select friends, such as Thomas Tipper, a brewer and innkeeper from Newhaven, Thomas Scrace (or Scrase), a substantial victualler from Lewes (who will be discussed in greater detail below), the

---

[157] A settlement for the marriage of John Madgwick and Dorothy Tourle, 10 Apr. 1754, Documents relating to the Tourle family of Lewes, 1708–1878, ESRO, AMS 2134ᵇ. See also the will of Thomas Tourll sen., yeo., 20 May 1723, ESRO, AMS 2134ᵃ. John Madgwick's own will, dated 22 Feb. 1765, was proved on 17 Dec. 1779: probate of the will of John Madgwick of Lewes, Mercer, ESRO, AMS 2140. Among other provisions, he left his wife £50 p.a., a portion of £1,000 each to two daughters, £16 p.a. to his daughters for maintenance until they were twenty-one, and the same to one son up to the age of twelve, when he was to be sent to boarding-school.
[158] Thomas Turner, Diary, 19 Feb. 1762, 4 Mar., 4 May 1764.
[159] He lived in the parish of All Saints, Lewes, where six of his eight children were baptised: ESRO, Baptism Index.
[160] ESRO, SAS/SM 210. Peter was born on 19 Aug. 1754 and died on 16 Jan. 1755.
[161] *The Town Book of Lewes, 1702–1837*, ed. V. Smith, Sussex Record Society (Lewes, 1972–3), p. 51.
[162] On the structure of credit networks and their sociable side see Muldrew, *The Economy of Obligation*, esp. chs. 4–5.

surgeon John Snelling of Alfriston, and Francis Elless, who replaced Turner as the schoolmaster of East Hoathly.[163] These 'friends', too, were attached to Turner in personal and business ties, which included many reciprocal visits, the purchase of goods, renting and hiring, lending and borrowing. In the cases of Scrace and Snelling, friendship was tightened by ties of godparenthood: Thomas Scrace was one of the 'sponsors' of Thomas Turner's son Peter, and Snelling stood as sponsor to Turner's son Michael.[164] With his 'Worthy Friend' Thomas Tipper, Turner had business ties as well as social ties and intellectual affinity.[165] On the evening of Tuesday 14 September 1762, for example, Tipper introduced Turner to a recently published book, reading to him aloud, as Turner reported 'Part of a I know not what to call it But Tristram Shandy'. They probably also shared an interest in medicine and medical prescriptions.[166] With Francis Elless, Turner had a long-standing relationship which ranged from playing cricket to learning together the art of surveying.[167] This relationship was also instrumental: Turner rented a warehouse from Elless,[168] and lent him money, charging him interest against a note of hand.[169] In the course of the years Elless gained the title 'my Old and Worthy Friend'.[170] Turner also expressed his particular appreciation

---

[163] Thomas Turner, Diary, 15 May, 1756. He moved from there to Alfriston and then to Uckfield.

[164] Michael Turner, a mercer, born 29 Apr. 1773, buried 13 July 1810: ESRO, SAS/SM 210; Turner, *Diary*, ed. Vaisey, Appendix A, p. 325. Although by 16 July 1762 Thomas Turner mentioned Dr Snelling as 'my Worthy Friend and Old Acquaintance', in earlier years he complained about his bad temper and ingratitude, Thomas Turner, Diary, 29 Dec. 1755, 11 Oct. 1756. After Peggy Turner's death there were also rumours that Dr Snelling had 'Castrated' her and thereby caused her death: *ibid.*, 1 July, 8 Oct. 1761.

[165] Thomas Turner, Diary, 3 Nov. 1764. See also, for example, meetings with 'my friend' on 15 May, 27 June, 1 July, 24, 26 Aug. 1764, etc. He was also named as an 'acquaintance'. Thomas Tipper died in 1785, aged fifty-four. In his will he was described as an innholder, and his goods were estimated as being worth under £1,000: the Will of Thomas Tipper, Innholder of Newhaven, 1785, ESRO, Lewes Archdeaconry Wills Register W/A65, f. 60. His tombstone, on which it says that he 'knew immortal Hudibras by heart' is illustrated in *SCM* 12 (1938), p. 179, referred to in Turner, *Diary*, ed. Vaisey, p. 258. See also the notice of Tipper's death on 14 May 1785, printed in Brighton, in Thomas Turner Papers, Manuscripts and Archives, Yale University Library.

[166] Turner's interest in medicine is evident in his diary, and also in the prescriptions collected by him kept in 'Special Files': Thomas Turner Papers, Manuscripts and Archives, Yale University Library. Among them is a letter by Tipper of 15 Aug. 1769, which includes a prescription and a promise to come soon to Hoathly to wait on Mrs Turner.   [167] For example, Thomas Turner, Diary, 16 Feb., 18 July 1758.

[168] *Ibid.*, 9 Jan. 1758. Part of Turner's rent was balanced against Elless's debt to Turner for the school's 'Tables, forms &.', as well as his future credit with Turner.

[169] *Ibid.*, 2 Feb. 1764. He did this, as he explained, as the debt was 'Pretty long Time Standing'. See also 21 Feb. 1765.

[170] *Ibid.*, 29 Sept. 1764. See also *ibid.*, 7 Apr., 25 July, 30 Sept. 1764; see also 'old acquaintance', *ibid.*, 30 Mar. 1765.

of Elless's genteel manner, which combined 'the greatest politeness imaginable' and 'the Greatest Freedom & *Friendship*'.[171] On one occasion he explained explicitly why Elless won his esteem. His words show that in the case of this select 'friend', too, 'friendship' was understood not only as a sociable and instrumental relationship but also as a moral sentiment.

I think my *Friend* Mr Elless is as agreable Companion as any amongst my acquaintance he being Sober and Virtuous, and a man of a Great deal of Good Sense and Endu'd with Good Nature and has Improv'd his Natural Parts with a great deal of use ful Learning.[172]

Thus, as we see, besides being sociable and moral, Thomas Turner's select friendships were also useful. These combined qualities were particularly evident in Thomas Turner's friendship with officers of the excise. Thomas Turner was always on good terms with excise officers of his acquaintance. When a resident excise officer in East Hoathly was replaced, Turner kept in touch with the outgoing officer and welcomed warmly the new man. When the Supervisor of the Excise came to East Hoathly, he not only stayed at Turner's house but also shared his bed.[173] One possible reason why Thomas Turner sought the company of excise officers was that they, like him, were educated, with good literacy and numeracy skills.[174] Thomas Turner and excise officers may also have shared other values, such as the importance of maintaining a reputation for honesty and ideas of the common good (remember that Thomas Turner himself bore many public offices). Excise officers were also relatively well travelled, and Turner may have been interested in them for that reason.[175] However, as a shopkeeper Turner had other reasons for cultivating ties with excise officers. He dealt with many taxed goods, such as coffee, tea, chocolate, spirits, tobacco, and hops. He also bought and sold confiscated goods, particularly brandy caught from smugglers at the shore. Having good connections with excise officers was therefore very important for him, and although fraternisation between excise officers and traders was strongly discouraged by the excise authorities and could lead to the officer's removal, excise officers became Thomas Turner's close acquaintances and 'friends'.[176] Such a 'friend' was Mr George Banister, officer of the excise and Thomas Turner's next-door neighbour. Turner played cricket with him, went with him to the horse races, bought spirits from him and feasted with him on confiscated brandy. He was also

[171] *Ibid.*, 12 Apr. 1764.   [172] *Ibid.*, 29 Sept. 1764.   [173] *Ibid.*, 10 Feb. 1764.
[174] See J. Brewer, *The Sinews of Power: War, Money and the English State* (London, Boston, Sydney, and Wellington, 1989), esp. pp. 101–14.
[175] As Brewer explains, the Excise offered a highly mobile career for its officers.
[176] Brewer, *Sinews of Power*, p. 110. See also Turner, *Diary*, ed. Vaisey, e.g. 25 May 1759, 3 June 1762, pp. 249, 338.

godfather to Banister's daughter,[177] gave evidence on his behalf when
Banister breached the peace in a neighbourly dispute,[178] and sat with him
as a juror.[179] Mr Tipper, Thomas Turner's 'worthy friend', was also an
officer of the excise. At the time when he met Thomas Turner and read to
him from *Tristram Shandy*, he was actually staying in East Hoathly in his
capacity as an excise officer during the hop harvest.[180] Another 'friend'
who became an excise officer was Mr John Long. He, too, was an
educated man. In 1760 he came to East Hoathly as a schoolmaster (at
which point Thomas Turner also rented from him a warehouse),[181] and
he soon became one of Thomas Turner's close companions. In time he
also acquired the title '*my Friend*'.[182] In 1761 Thomas Turner signed a
bond to the value of £200 as a security for John Long's service as an excise
officer during the hop harvest.[183] In 1764 John Long undertook instruction to join the excise as a permanent officer; however, he died in Novem-
ber of that year. Thomas Turner reported his death in his diary naming
him as '*my old acquaintance and Worthy Friend*'.[184]

These select 'friends' were people in whom Thomas Turner trusted,
for whom he felt special regard, and of whose acquaintance he was
particularly proud, either because they were reputable businessmen, or
because they were particularly cultivated, or both.[185] In the case of the
select 'friends', as in the case of other 'friends', the language of friendship
posed moral expectations. Thomas Turner clearly enjoyed the company
of his select 'friends'; however, he saw friendship as a moral relationship
and expected his 'friends' to be honest, virtuous, and godfearing people; if
they were sober and moderate, he applauded them all the more. Reciprocity and fair-dealing were always important, and Turner was quick to
detect selfishness and ingratitude. In addition, he valued his friends'
education and was eager to benefit from an intellectual exchange. Looking at this array of select 'friends', it seems that the only one who was not
judged by very high standards was George Banister, a short-tempered and
sometimes rowdy man, but it might be that being an excise officer and a
next-door neighbour compensated for his lack of gravity.

---

[177] Thomas Turner, Diary, 10 July 1763. He was surprised, however, that the girl was simply
baptised as 'Molly'.   [178] *Ibid.*, 7, 9 Feb. 1764.   [179] *Ibid.*, 10 Nov. 1764.
[180] See Turner, *Diary*, ed. Vaisey, p. 258.
[181] Thomas Turner, Diary, 12 Jan. 1760; see also 9 Jan. 1758.
[182] *Ibid.*, 14 Feb., 11 Mar. 1764. He was also referred to as 'my late Customer', 13 Feb. 1764,
and 'my Old Acquaintance', 8 June 1764.
[183] *Ibid.*, 1 Sept. 1761. See Turner, *Diary*, ed. Vaisey, pp. 233–4.
[184] Thomas Turner, Diary, 1 Nov. 1764. John Long died of smallpox which he contracted as
a result of inoculation. Another excise officer with whom Thomas Turner was closely
connected was Mr Lawrence Thornton, however he was only named as 'old acquaintance' and never acquired the higher status of 'friend'.
[185] See also Muldrew, *The Economy of Obligation*, esp. ch. 5.

As the language of 'friendship' was used to present expectations, it could also be inverted to express criticism. Such an inversion was seen above when Thomas Turner expressed his disapproval of his cousin and friend Mr Hill, referring to him as 'my Old acquaintance & Cuz (and I ought to have Reason as Well to Say *Worthy Friend*)'.[186] In a similar way Mr Tucker was degraded from the title '*my Friend*', to the description 'my foolish and drunken visitant', and later 'my Old and I wish I could Say Worthy acquaintance Mr Tucker'.[187] On another occasion Turner used the language of 'friendship' ironically, accusing himself that 'like a *true Friend* and bold Hearty Fellow', he left Mr Peter Adams in the middle of a brawl and, while Adams came to his help, he made his escape riding on Adams's horse.[188]

From a social and economic point of view, Thomas Turner's select 'friends' formed a regional network of men of 'the middling sort'. This network included tradesmen and shopkeepers, schoolmasters, victuallers, one surgeon, and a number of office holders. A number of Thomas Turner's 'friends' (including himself) were enterprising, ambitious, and eventually upwardly mobile. During the years of the diary, some of the 'friends' were clearly more affluent than others: John Madgwick, for example, was richer than Thomas Turner or Francis Elless. But, significantly, they were all fully literate. Some, not necessarily the wealthiest, were very interested in the world of books. One could almost say that literacy was a precondition for being counted among Thomas Turner's select 'friends': indeed, he was so engaged in various activities relating to writing and reading that it is hard to imagine him contracting a close friendship with a person who could have no access to these aspects of his life. Lastly, these 'middling sort of men' in Thomas Turner's network of 'friends' were active members of their communities. Nearly all of them bore public offices and served both their parishes and the Crown as churchwardens, jurors, tax collectors, excise officers, etc.

Thomas Turner's relationships with these 'friends' were both personal and instrumental. These 'friends' also negotiated many contractual agreements, from terms for the fulfilment of work to formal bills and notes of hand. Indeed many of these select 'friends' were initially a part of the broader social and economic milieu in which Thomas Turner con-

---

[186] Thomas Turner, Diary, 26 Apr. 1764.
[187] *Ibid.*, 21 June 1761, 26 Feb. 1764, but see also 'my friend', 4–5 Nov. 1764. See also Thomas Turner's criticism of 'My Friend Joseph Fuller' who is 'too Fruit ful in his invention to Contrive Some Way to Get a little liquor or a Pipe or Two of Tobacco': *ibid.*, 1 Apr. 1765. This was probably Joseph Fuller, Jun. See also, however, Turner's reference to Joseph Fuller, Jun. who brought his 'most intimate Friends (or at least acquaintance) a little Treat', brandy: *ibid.*, 15 Jan. 1765.
[188] *Ibid.*, 8 June 1756. On that occasion Turner was also very drunk.

ducted his business. In addition, Turner's notion of 'friendship' as a moral sentiment was so closely connected to notions of trust that it is easy to see how his personal and business relationships could intertwine. Among Turner's 'friends', the select 'friends' are probably those who come nearest to Julian Pitt-Rivers's definition: 'all friendship must be both sentimental in inspiration and instrumental in effects'.[189] The balance between sentiments and interests, however, could vary from relationship to relationship, and over time. Thomas Tipper, for example, was probably better liked and more respected by Thomas Turner than George Banister, the sociable and rowdy excise officer and next-door neighbour, with whom it was very prudent for Turner to maintain friendly ties. In the case of Thomas Tipper, it is also evident that the instrumental aspect of their friendship increased over time. For example, as the 'friendship' developed, Turner asked Tipper's help in bringing to court a delicate case of insolvency.[190] Another related characteristic of this network of 'friends' was that its 'friendship' relationships cut through boundaries that many would now understand as 'private' and 'public' spheres.[191] When one examines Turner's relationships with his select 'friends', it is in fact very hard to know when private affairs end, and public matters start. Thomas Turner's interactions with his select 'friends' spanned a wide range of activities, including dining, conversing, drinking, striking deals, balancing accounts, performing public duties, reading aloud, playing cricket, fishing, watching horse-races, etc. Significantly, many of these diverse activities could take place in the context of single meetings. In terms of their locations, too, the interactions among the 'friends' could take place both in 'private' and in 'public': at home, in the market-place, at the public house, the race course, or in a formal meeting of state officers. This leads to the last characteristic of this network, namely, that it was a male network. Such relationships of 'friendship', combining personal and intellectual affinity, business, sports, and public service inevitably left women behind. From a practical

---

[189] Pitt-Rivers, 'The kith and kin', p. 97.
[190] The insolvency case concerned Thomas Turner's neighbour, the alehouse keeper John Jones. Mr Neatby, a Southwark distiller, was a creditor of John Jones, and as he no longer trusted John Jones to pay him his bond on the sum of £32 10s 0d, he agreed instead to take possession of Jones's house and ale-house. Being an acquaintance of Thomas Turner, Neatby asked Turner to represent him in the actual surrender at the court baron. Thomas Turner explains his refusal obliquely only saying: 'I could not attend Court my Self.' My understanding is that he did not want to act directly against his old neighbour. Thomas Turner's solution was to turn to Thomas Tipper and ask him to act for Mr Neatby as 'suppos'd attorney', which Tipper did: see especially Thomas Turner, Diary, 21 Oct. 1762.
[191] This follows Habermas's famous distinction: J. Habermas, *The Structural Transformation of the Public Sphere: An Inquiry into a Category of Bourgeois Society*, trans. T. Burger with the assistance of F. Lawrence (Cambridge, 1989).

point of view, too, it would probably have been very difficult for Thomas Turner to have regular private meetings with women, as he had with his male 'friends', without arousing great suspicion and gossip. It is also doubtful whether a virtuous woman, whose 'friendship' Thomas Turner could esteem, would have agreed to engage in many private meetings, unless this was in the context of serious courtship.[192] On the two or three occasions when Turner happened to drink tea with a neighbour's servant-maid, an *'Old acquaintance'* from his days in Lewes, he was aware that he was providing 'a most delicious and Savory morsel for the Gossiping Part of my Neighbours to Chew & Band about from House to House'.[193] Indeed, at this point he invoked an entire social universe to witness his innocence:

I can assure you, my good *Friends, Neighbours, acquaintance, intimates, Gossips, Lovers, Haters, Foes, Farters, Friskers, Cuckolds and all the other sorts of Christians of what name or denomination so ever* that there has not one Word of Courting yet Pass'd between us or Ever will.[194]

Clearly, Thomas Turner had to reach beyond his immediate locality to establish for himself his network of select 'friends'. His trade interests and intellectual curiosity could not have found satisfaction in East Hoathly alone. His public duties, too, took him beyond his parish. East Hoathly was undoubtedly an important junction in Turner's map of 'friends': some of them even lived there at some point in their lives and established their relationships with Thomas Turner. However, the county town, Lewes, was also a very important junction. Thomas Turner probably met some of his 'friends' while he was still a servant in Lewes, and during the years he and his 'friends' had many meetings in Lewes's public houses, in individual people's houses, or around the horse-racing course. Fairs were also useful for giving Thomas Turner and his friends opportunities to meet, and Turner and his 'friends' had many specially planned visits. By and large, however, Thomas Turner's select 'friends' were not the same people with whom he interacted in his day-to-day neighbourly contacts.

A notable exception is Turner's *'worthy friend'* Samuel Jenner.[195] Sam

---

[192] Such private meetings did indeed take place between Thomas Turner and his intended wife, Mary (Molly) Hicks.

[193] Thomas Turner, Diary, 17 Sept. 1762; see also 12 Sept. 1762. At that time they were 'almost Next door Neighbour', though, as Turner explains, there was 'nought of Love' between them.   [194] *Ibid.*, 17 Sept. 1762.

[195] Another exception is Thomas Durrant, a neighbour's son, eight years younger than Turner and his former pupil (*ibid.*, 30 Jan., 27 Feb. 1755). By 17 Oct. 1764 Turner described him as a 'friend', as Thomas Durrant came to visit him together with Joseph Fuller. However, by that time the two had behind them nearly a decade of numerous exchanges and close companionship. Over these years young Thomas was employed by his neighbour to perform many errands and services in both personal and parish affairs. He accompanied him when Turner went to collect debts, and was taken by him as a

Jenner was an East Hoathlian and could hardly be counted among 'the middling sort'. He was a poor man, and in the years of the diary he even received parish help. After Peggy Turner's death, Sam Jenner was often employed by Turner. He worked in his house and shop, did gardening work for him, brewed cider, went on errands, accompanied him on journeys, and kept his servant company when Thomas Turner was away (Thomas Turner's servant-maid usually did not stay alone in the house for full days, and particularly not overnight).[196] However Thomas Turner also enjoyed Jenner's company and often invited him to dine with him and not only to sleep in his house, but also to take part of his bed. The two socialised together, and in company with others, talking, drinking, reading, and playing cards. In the course of time, Sam Jenner acquired the titles *'my friend'* and *'my Worthy Friend'*.[197]

Sam Jenner's relationship with Thomas Turner had much in common with other relationships which Turner had with local East Hoathly companions and occasional employees. What made their relationship different, however, was that Thomas Turner sincerely esteemed Sam Jenner as a man of virtue, learning, and good sense. This moral and intellectual affinity introduced equality into their otherwise unequal relationship, and it was probably this that enabled Jenner to be counted as Turner's 'friend'. Thomas Turner's neighbours indeed wondered why he spent so much time with Sam Jenner, as Thomas Turner reported in his diary. However he explained that 'I have always found him a Very Sincere Friend a Worthy & [*sic*] Man, a learned and agreable Companion, a Sincere & good Christian.'[198]

companion on business trips. He also socialised with him and enjoyed together with him various sporting activities. By 1761 Turner displayed his faith in his young companion by signing, together with Thomas Durrant's father, a bond of surety to the value of two hundred pounds guaranteeing young Durrant's good behaviour as an assistant to the excise officer during the hop harvest. In the subsequent years Durrant also socialised increasingly with a number of other of Turner's select 'friends'. For example, Thomas Turner went to visit Mr Tipper together with Thomas Durrant, naming him 'our Friend Tipper' (*ibid.*, 26 Aug. 1764). On 10 Nov. 1764 Thomas Durrant also took his place alongside Thomas Turner as a coroner's juror. It seems that in this case long-term personal companionship, linked with many exchanges and services, had matured over the years, and was cemented by trust. Thus, this long-standing tie of neighbourhood companionship was eventually distinguished as 'friendship'. For Thomas Durrant, see also Turner, *Diary*, ed. Vaisey, p. 330.

[196] On Monday 12 Mar. 1763, for example, Sam Jenner did gardening work for Thomas Turner all day. He also worked for him on 15–17 Mar., and on 22–3 Mar., and at the start of Apr. On 10 Apr. he kept Turner's servant company while Turner was away. On 13 Apr. he went to Framfield and delivered a parcel for Turner. See brewing cider on 25 May 1765.

[197] *Ibid.*, 20 Feb. 1764. See also 'my Friend', e.g. 2 Oct., 26 Dec. 1763, 19, 21, 25 Feb. 1764, etc. See 'my old and worthy acquaintance': *ibid.*, 25 Dec. 1763. Sam Jenner celebrated that Christmas together with Thomas Turner and the Marchant family.

[198] *Ibid.*, 23 Mar. 1764; see also 9 Mar. 1764.

The other side of Thomas Turner's 'friendship' with Sam Jenner was the exchange of patronage and services. In addition to companionship and edifying conversations, Sam Jenner gained through his friendship with Thomas Turner numerous hot meals and evenings by a warm fire. Who knows whether he could have provided such conveniences for himself. Thomas Turner, on his side, benefited from Jenner's free labour. As Turner noted in his diary when explaining their friendship, Jenner 'oft times does my Gardening &c for nothing', and is, generally, 'at any Time willing to do any business for me, and that without any Gratuity'.[199] Thomas Turner's patronage of his poor friend was also evident when it came to the distribution of alms. On St Thomas's day, a few days before Christmas, Thomas Turner used to give charity – one penny and a draught of ale – to about thirty paupers in his parish, among them Sam Jenner.[200] Thomas Turner also gave alms to his friend whilst acting on behalf of his parish. On 7 February 1762, for example, he, together with two other parish officers, gave Jenner the sum of three shillings.[201] The same happened in 1763 and 1764.[202] These particular donations were given out of the interest on a sum of one hundred pounds, bequeathed to East Hoathly, and the individual doles were divided 'in such manner and to such Persons as the minister & Church Warden for the time being shall think Proper'.[203] Although we have no reason to suspect that Sam Jenner was not genuinely poor, it might be that his close association with Turner was helpful in making him eligible for this desirable charity.[204]

Thomas Turner's network of select 'friends', traced among flourishing middling men in mid-eighteenth-century Sussex, thus even stretched down to the level of the village poor. One last case of vertically connected friendship which should be mentioned here is Thomas Turner's friendship towards his maidservant Sarah (Sally) Waller. In this case, too, service and patronage led to the formation of 'friendship' ties. However in this case it was clearly also restricted and one-sided: Turner did not mention Sally Waller as his 'friend', although he served as a 'friend' to

[199] Ibid., 9, 23 Mar. 1764.
[200] See ibid., 21 Dec. 1756, 22 Dec. 1760, 21 Dec. 1762, 21 Dec. 1763.
[201] Among the other recipients on this occasion we find names that recur in Thomas Turner's diary as occasional employees and in relation to parish affairs: Richard Prall, 3s; Widow Cornwell, 2s; John Durrant, 4s; Richard Vinal, 3s; Will Elphick, 5s: ibid., 7 Feb. 1762.   [202] Ibid., 13 Feb. 1763, 11 Mar. 1764.   [203] Ibid., 7 Feb. 1762.
[204] Although Sam Jenner received these charitable gifts from the parish, his name does not appear among the regular recipients of poor relief during those years: ESRO, PAR 378/31/1/1. Thomas Turner's own account for provisions supplied to the parish in 1762, to the sum of £10 7s 81/2d can be found in ESRO, PAR 378/31/1/1, f. 10. It is also interesting to note that this parish book seems to have been written almost entirely in Thomas Turner's own hand, with the exception of signatures by JPs and vestry members, as well as the line 'when the sun rises in the morning it is time to' written seven times on ibid., f. 51.

her.[205] Sally Waller, aged twenty, was employed by Thomas Turner as his housekeeper. Her service did not last long: fourteen months, compared to the years served by Mary Martin and Hannah Marchant. On 15 August 1762 she left Thomas Turner in order to keep the house of her uncle, a widower with two children. As she went away, Thomas Turner was careful to note in his diary that 'her leaving my Service was as (She protested) without any dislike or the least reason for dislike and Contrary to her inclinations and the most Earnest Persuasions of her *Friends*'.[206] The identity of these 'friends' remains unknown. But only a week or two after she had left, Sally received enough testimony of her uncle's ill usage of her to make her write a secret letter to Thomas Turner, begging him to condescend and come and meet her, 'as She was destitute of any *Friend* to Consult or advise with'.[207] Thomas Turner's 'friendship' to Sally Waller did not extend as far as to ask her to resume her service, as she had hoped. Nonetheless she remained in touch, borrowed money from Turner and even paid him visits together with her lover. When they married on 19 September 1764, Turner commented ironically on the penniless match. The case of Sally Waller thus shows how service ties could translate into patronage, in which the former employer acted as the former servant's 'friend': Thomas Turner was probably a senior select 'friend' for Sally Waller, but the relationship was not mutual. Nor was it very close, because although Thomas Turner was evidently fascinated by Sally Waller, he did not think very highly of her fickle choice of lovers and employers.[208] Turner's awareness of his neighbours' gossip, moreover, as well as his protestations of his own innocence in his dealings with Sally Waller, all show how delicate it was for a single man such as he, who cared greatly about his reputation, to conduct a 'friendship' relationship with a single and apparently lively young woman such as Sally Waller.

Conclusion

Studies by modern social scientists define friendship as a voluntary relationship, often among peers, and essentially among non-kin: 'emotionally close, proximate, frequently seen, non work or non kin-relationships'.[209]

---

[205] She was probably Sarah, daughter of James and Grace Waller of Alfriston, christened 9 Feb. 1741, ESRO, Baptism Index.   [206] Thomas Turner, Diary, 15 Aug. 1762.
[207] *Ibid.*, 5 Sept. 1762.
[208] Conventionally associating folly and female beauty, he commented after her visit 'What pitty it is that the most beautiful of the Creation is so fickle & unconstant': *ibid.*, 7 May 1763.
[209] See the *International Encyclopedia of the Social Sciences*, vol. VI, s.v. 'friend', esp. p. 12; Blieszner and Adams, *Adult Friendship*, p. 41; R. G. Adams 'Conceptual and methodological issues in studying friendships of older adults', in Adams and Blieszner (eds.), *Older Adult Friendship*, esp. pp. 20–3.

Our study of 'friendship' in eighteenth-century England highlights how historically and culturally specific such modern definitions of 'friendship' are. Had we employed them for analysing Thomas Turner's network of 'friends', we would have inevitably misrepresented it. Clearly, an eighteenth-century man such as Turner had a strong notion of friendship freely chosen among peers, but his idea of 'friendship' as a social relationship was far broader, as was his network of 'friends'.

For an eighteenth-century individual such as Turner, one of the most important characteristics of 'friendship' was that it straddled what we would now term familial and non-familial relationships. That is not to say that the status of people as kin and non-kin was of little importance for Turner – far from it. Nonetheless, Turner had a broadly recognised category of 'friends' that could include kin and non-kin. Indeed, as we saw, his most significant relationships were both expressed and negotiated in terms of 'friendship'. Thomas Turner did not use the term 'friend' lightly. Many of the people with whom he had regular contact did not receive from him the epithet 'friend'. But a careful analysis of Turner's personal diary has shown that there was a group of people, whom Turner designated as 'friends', and who were also closely bound to him in ties of sympathy, loyalty, mutual interest, and many reciprocal exchanges and 'services'. These friends included Turner's wife, near and distant relations, as well as select associates and companions. As we shall see in the next chapter, ties of 'friendship' also extended to include Turner's political connections.

The range of Turner's 'friends' was thus broad and his relationships with particular 'friends' was multi-faceted. But Turner's relationships with his spectrum of 'friends' also manifested some shared characteristics. One important characteristic of these 'friendship' relationships was that they were affective and sentimental. Such were his 'friendships' with his wife, with many of his related 'friends', and with many of his 'select friends'. As we shall see in the next chapter, he may even have been somehow sentimentally attached to his grand neighbour, the Duke of Newcastle. At the same time, however, different 'friendship' relationships were also instrumental. Indeed, instrumental exchanges characterised Thomas Turner's relationships with all his 'friends', related and non-related. Thomas Turner and his 'friends' worked together and for each other, lent and borrowed money and goods, bought and sold to and from each other, recommended themselves to other 'friends', and exchanged many other 'favours' and 'services'. This combination of sentimentality and instrumentality is also similar to that found above in the analysis of the household-family relationships: sentimentality and instrumentality often went hand in hand, and often the nearer the connection, the more the relationships were also manifested in instrumental terms.

Many 'friendship' ties also had contractual aspects and manifestations, from the marriage contract that bound together Thomas Turner and his wife, to binding provisions made in the Turner family wills, and on to the numerous bonds and notes of hand exchanged between Turner and his 'friends'. In this respect, too, we find similarity to the household-family relationships. Lastly, many 'friendship' relationships also had an occupational dimension. Thomas Turner and his wife were linked together occupationally, as were his parents, siblings, and many other 'friends'. Turner thus had manifold relationships with many of his 'friends'. His brother Moses, for example, was a related 'friend', a fellow-tradesman, a close companion, and, as we shall see, probably also a political ally. Thomas Turner's 'friend' John Madgwick was also a fellow-tradesman, a close companion, a political ally, and was linked to Thomas Turner's kin by ties of godparenthood and by occupational and domestic relationships.

Thomas Turner's relationships with all his 'friends' cannot therefore be adequately described by any clear sets of dichotomous terms. They included kin and non-kin. They were nearly always both useful and expressive. They could be informal and spontaneous, but they were often also manifested in contractual ties. They were very often linked to occupational ties. They could be conducted according to individual choice, and to prescribed obligations and duties. They could take place in spheres which we would now describe as both 'private' and 'public'.

Thus, the friendship connections, which formed many of the pivotal axes in Thomas Turner's social relationships, were complex and many-sided. The fact that they were so, however, was seen by Turner and his friends as a distinct virtue. This was because 'friendship' was understood as a moral and reciprocal relationship. The moral duty of 'friends' was to stand by each other, and, if necessary, 'serve' each other as best they could, and in as many ways as possible (including ways that may seem to us now to crisscross hopelessly the boundaries of 'private' and 'public', such as personal relationships in business and civil service). Such 'services' should ideally have been rendered in a disinterested manner; however, it was wrong to ask for a 'service' that would be injurious to the 'friend'. Requests for 'favours' and 'services' were therefore seen as positive opportunities for proving 'friendship': these were opportunities for displaying 'acts of friendship', presenting 'marks' and 'tokens' of friendship, and obliging the 'friend' in further reciprocal exchanges. Edward Gibbon declared that one of the main purposes of obtaining a seat in Parliament is 'to employ the weight and consideration it gives *in the service of one's friends*': scholars have noted his words while discussing the importance of 'services' among 'friends' in eighteenth-century political and social life.[210] We can now see that very similar notions of service also prevailed in the humble sphere of Thomas Turner.

Of course, the moral expectations of 'friendship' were not always fulfilled. In the case of Thomas Turner, they seem to have failed particularly in the case of the related 'friends', about whom he complained habitually, accusing them of both selfishness and coldness. But although expectations of 'friendship' could be frustrated, it is important to realise that they still reveal a model of 'friendship'. The fact that Turner complained so much about the selfishness and coldness with which he was treated by his related 'friends' shows that he expected his 'friends' to be supportive, considerate, and warm. In other ways, too, appreciation of 'friends' was guided by moral principles. As we saw, it was important for Turner that his 'friends' were honest, godfearing, literate, and, hopefully, also sober people.

Ties of 'friendship' were thus extremely important in forming the social order in which Thomas Turner lived. Historians discuss the social order of early modern England in terms of 'sorts', 'ranks', or 'classes'.[211] As this analysis has shown, 'friendship', too, had a role in the making of the social order in eighteenth-century England, and in mediating relationships within it. Kin and non-kin were bound as 'friends' in many transactions: sentiments, 'services', and obligations were regularly exchanged among them. Such 'friendship' relationships were very important in fusing relationships among peers. For people of 'the middling sort' such as Turner and his 'friends', 'friendship' relationships were indeed crucial, for it was along the lines of 'friendship' that these people mobilised many of their social and economic interests, thus forming regional networks well beyond their immediate neighbourhoods. But 'friendship' relationships were also extremely important in forging unequal relationships.[212] As we have seen, relationships of patronage and dependence were also under-

---

[210] *Private Letters of Edward Gibbon (1753–94)* ed. R. E. Porthero (1896), vol. I, pp. 23–4; quoted in Namier, *The Structure of Politics*, p. 18; discussed in Perkin, *Origins of Modern English Society*, p. 45. My understanding at this point is similar to Perkin's.

[211] See, for example, the following discussions of the social order in early modern England: Laslett, *The World We Have Lost*, esp. ch. 2; L. Stone, 'Social mobility in England, 1500–1700', *P&P* 33 (1966), 16–55; Thompson, 'Patricians and plebs'; Earle, *The Making of the English Middle Class*; Corfield (ed.), *Language, History and Class*, esp. introduction and chapters by Wrightson and Corfield; K. Wrightson, 'Sorts of people in Tudor and Stuart England', in Barry and Brooks (eds.), *The Middling Sort of People*, pp. 28–51; See also Barry, 'Introduction', in Barry and Brooks (eds.), *The Middling Sort of People*, pp. 1–27, and further references there.

[212] Arguably, even 'friendship' with peers could be segmented into specific moments in which individuals stood in unequal positions in relation to each other and requested 'services' and 'favours'. But repeated reciprocity could serve as an equaliser in these relationships.

stood in terms of 'friendship', from John Turner's position as a 'friend' to his son Thomas, to Thomas Turner's position as a 'friend' to the pauper Sam Jenner.

Lastly, while friendship forged powerful cohesive bonds in eighteenth-century England, it was also divisive. Alongside the 'friends' there were always 'enemies' and 'strangers', or simply 'neighbours', who did not partake of the bonds of 'friendship'. As we saw, Thomas Turner excluded systematically from his circle of 'friends' nearly all his neighbours and associates with whom he interacted on a daily basis. And whereas he was in some ways very successful in negotiating 'friendship' ties, he also discovered again and again that estrangement among 'friends' was painful to bear. Indeed, however powerful, 'friendship' relationships were always dynamic relationships that needed cultivation. There was always the danger that they might be damaged by distance, disagreement, or disappointment. 'Friendship' relationships also tended to be so multi-faceted that there were a great many ways in which they could go wrong. Thus, at the same time as they served to forge a social order in eighteenth-century England, 'friendship' relationships also brought about a dynamics of anxiety and conflict.

6 Political friends

On 8 February 1756 Thomas Turner wrote in his diary rules for a new regimen. At home, in company, or abroad he promised never to drink more than four glasses: one to toast the King's health, the second to the royal family, the third to '*all Friends*', and the fourth to the pleasure of the company. The reader familiar with eighteenth-century expressions can guess what sort of connections Thomas Turner may have had in mind when he wrote about '*all Friends*': these may have been the political connections in his locality. Indeed, these were no mean connections. Sussex and its small boroughs were among the main power-bases of Thomas Pelham-Holles, First Duke of Newcastle and one of the most powerful men of his time who, during the years of the diary, served as First Lord of the Treasury, and then as Lord Privy Seal.[1] Thomas Turner's village of East Hoathly was situated in very near proximity to the Duke of Newcastle's Sussex seat at Halland House.[2] Moreover, as the next pages will reveal, many of Turner's neighbours, fellow-tradesmen, acquaintances, and 'friends' were linked directly to the Duke of Newcastle's interest, and were among his active supporters. But how did eighteenth-century politics impinge upon the life of a middling and provincial eighteenth-century man such as Thomas Turner? What were the ramifications of concepts and practices of friendship in this context?

The strands of the Duke of Newcastle's interest, famously explored by Sir Lewis Namier, certainly reached the humble sphere of Thomas Turner.[3] Indeed, they spread even more deeply and densely than Namier suggests. Events around the 1761 general election in Sussex and Lewes – as well as other events in Thomas Turner's milieu – demonstrate how Turner's world was strongly connected with the political sphere of his time, and particularly with the Pelham interest.

---

[1] He was First Lord of the Treasury from 1754 to 1756 and 1757 to 1762, and Lord Privy Seal from 1765 to 1766.

[2] The Duke was also the lord of Laughton Manor to which Turner's village belonged.

[3] Namier, *The Structure of Politics*; L. B. Namier, *England in the Age of the American Revolution* (London, 1961; 1st edn 1930).

In comparison with some other mid-eighteenth-century elections, the general election of 1761 in Turner's locality was a low-key event. The main opposition in Sussex and Lewes consisted of Mr George Medley, a wealthy gentleman who wished to stand for the county, and Mr John Fuller, who threatened to stand for Lewes, but eventually their opposition was not pressed to the poll.[4] Nonetheless, the Duke's 'friends' had to labour for their success. Medley and Fuller relied on a small but determined core of 'independents', who did not wish to submerge themselves in the Duke of Newcastle's powerful interest. Their opposition was vociferous, and in some cases alarmingly effective. J. A. Phillips has shown that, contrary to the Namierite interpretation, the independent opposition was active in Lewes elections despite aristocratic patronage. The effect of patronage, however, is seen to be especially significant under the influence of the first Duke of Newcastle.[5] The case of the 1761 election highlights the fact that even behind an uncontested election, apparently swayed by aristocratic patronage, there could be a political battle.[6]

[4] L. B. Namier and J. Brooke, *The History of Parliament: The House of Commons, 1754–1790*, 3 vols. (London, 1964), vol. III, pp. 127–8 for Medley, and vol. I, pp. 393–5 for Lewes. Medley also had an interest in Steyning, where he stood with very little success, and in Seaford, where he presented a real threat and where he was elected in 1768: see *ibid.*, vol. I, pp. 454–7. John Fuller Esq. was MP for Tregony (1754–61), and had also received £1,455 from the secret service funds: *ibid.*, vol. II, p. 476. Namier and Brooke suggest to identify him as John, son of Joseph Fuller and his wife Mary of East Hoathly, in which case he would have been the son of Thomas Turner's near neighbour, Mr Joseph Fuller, a butcher, who died in 1762 with an evaluated estate of £152 19s 7d: Thomas Turner, Diary, 2 Apr. 1762. However, John, son of Joseph and Mary Fuller of East Hoathly, was most probably a butcher in Lewes, mentioned in Turner's diary. See also Turner, *Diary*, ed. Vaisey, pp. 331–2; see also a reference to John Fuller, a butcher, in 'Tradesmen usually employed by his Grace the Duke of Newcastle', Newcastle Papers, BL Add. MS 33,059, f. 75. Brent identifies John Fuller as a Wealden landowner: C. Brent, *Georgian Lewes, 1714–1830* (Lewes, 1993), p. 179.

[5] This active 'inhabitant' and scot and lot borough was too open and difficult to control. It had a continuous current of independence, directed against the Pelham family, and also often associated with religious dissent. As Phillips explains, however, the effect of these independent interests was limited in 1761, and probably longer, as 'the Duke of Newcastle possessed an unquestioned "interest" in Lewes until his death in 1768'. Lewes voters 'complied with his wishes as a rule, but only conditionally', particularly after 1761: see J. A. Phillips, *Electoral Behaviour in Unreformed England, 1761–1802: Plumpers, Splitters and Straighters* (Princeton, 1982), and the specific points made on pp. 43, 48, 83. See also J. A. Phillips, 'The structure of electoral politics in unreformed England', *Journal of British Studies* 19 (1979), 76–100; W. B. Mills, *Parliamentary History of the Borough of Lewes: 1795–1885* (London, 1908); F. O'Gorman, 'Electoral deference in "unreformed" England, 1760–1832', *Journal of Modern History* 56 (1984), 391–429; F. O'Gorman, *Voters, Patrons and Parties: The Unreformed Electoral System of Hanoverian England, 1734–1832* (Oxford, 1989), and especially e.g. pp. 48–50, 272, 350; Brent, *Georgian Lewes*, pp. 170–82.

[6] Indeed, Phillips also suggests that the level of popular political participation in England's boroughs may be considerably understated by the figures on contested elections, as 'contests frequently were fought up to, yet short of, a poll': Phillips, *Electoral Behaviour*, p. 72; see also N. Rogers, 'The middling sort in eighteenth-century politics', in Barry and Brooks (eds.), *The Middling Sort of People*, pp. 168–70.

The Duke of Newcastle's campaign was conducted in the language of 'friendship'. The Duke and his supporters referred to themselves as 'friends', and to their opponents as 'the opposition', or even 'the enemy'. In terms of their rank, the Duke's 'friends' were extremely diverse. They included aristocrats, gentlemen, professional men, tradesmen, artisans, farmers, and others. In the case of these 'friends', too, notions of 'service' were extremely important. The 'friends' served the Duke in various ways, not least by casting their votes in his favour and fighting the opposition, whereas the Duke served as a powerful 'friend', procuring jobs and positions for his supporters, extending financial assistance in times of hardship, offering hospitality, and patronising a wide range of businesses, churches, and other institutions.

The Sussex election was scheduled for Monday 6 April 1761, and it was to be preceded by the election in the boroughs. By 15 January 1761 gentlemen of the county assembled in a 'great Meeting' in Lewes and declared themselves for the Duke of Newcastle's interest.[7] In due course active 'friends' of the Duke canvassed the town.[8] Votes were solicited publicly as a 'favour' and a 'mark of obligation', and support was duly thanked as a 'mark of regard' and 'esteem'.[9] It was important not to offend electors by neglecting to ask for their support;[10] however sanctions for disobliging could be severe. 'If it could be of any service I would turn him out of his House', suggested a local magistrate, one of the Duke of Newcastle's 'friends', as he reported to the Duke that one of his own tenants, whom he hoped to put at the Duke's service, might vote for the opposition, as he had been 'so much employed' by Mr Medley.[11] Indeed, at that time the opposition was also busy spreading its influence. Mr

---

[7] See W. Michell to T. H[urdis], 15 Jan. 1761, Newcastle Papers, BL Add. MS 32,917, ff. 341–4. This was also when the nominations for the county election were made and when the Quarter Sessions opened: *Sussex Advertiser, or Lewes Journal*, 29 Dec. 1760, and see also 12, 19, 20 Jan. 1761. For the two candidates, Thomas Pelham and John Butler, see Namier and Brooke, *House of Commons*, vol. II, p. 166, vol. III, pp. 258–9; for Sussex, see *ibid.*, vol. I, p. 388.

[8] See the reference to Luke Spence Esq. and others who had gone 'round the Town': Luke Spence to the Duke of Newcastle, 9 Mar. 1761, Newcastle Papers, BL Add. MS 32,920, f. 25.

[9] See the advertisements by the candidates for Sussex in the *Sussex Advertiser*, e.g. 20 Jan., 2 Feb., 6 Mar. 1761, and thanks on 6, 20 Apr. 1761.

[10] Thus, when one elector was not at home when the supporters of the Duke's interest canvassed the town, it was said that he 'seemed to think himself slighted in not having been since spoke to': BL Add. MS 32,920, f. 25. Indeed, it may well have been the case that Mr Medley's opposition to the Duke was also fuelled by the fact that he felt slighted by the Duke: O'Gorman, *Voters, Patrons and Parties*, pp. 120–1.

[11] BL Add. MS 32,920, f. 25. The ejection, however, would have taken place only after the election. Another elector gave his word to vote for the Duke's candidates, and 'under that promise' was 'treated' to the rental of a house. This voter was a publican who had business bespoke by Mr Medley, but he gave his word that no 'favour' from Medley 'shall any ways influence his Vote'.

Medley and Mr Fuller went 'Round the Town to beg the Favour of their Votes', and their supporters met in a local coffee house and in public houses in town.[12] Some loyal 'friends' (among them one of the two constables and returning officers for Lewes) reported with concern the presence of up to forty Lewes electors at one of the opposition's gatherings. 'We beg that this may not alarm his Grace', they wrote to one of the Duke's closest supporters, as forty voters could amount to nearly a quarter of the borough electorate.[13] 'Be assur'd, good S^r We Remain His Graces *Friends*', they subscribed.[14]

By 17 March success seemed near enough. The Duke was pleased that 'Mr Medley has resigned the County'. He hoped that his loyal 'friend' in Lewes, the attorney Mr Rideout, to whom the letter was addressed, 'will soon oblige Mr Fuller to do the same at Lewes'.[15] Indeed, by that time '107 *staunch Friends*' had made a 'noble appearance' for the Duke in Lewes.[16] Nor did the Duke fear the opposition's design to create a rift between him and one of his candidates for Lewes: '*our Friendship and*

[12] T. Best, W. Young, and H. Verall to the Revd Mr Hurdis, 'Wednesday Morn two oth Clock', undated, stamped 12 Mar. 1761, Newcastle Papers, BL Add. MS 32,920, f. 111. According to this letter, the campaign was held jointly, while Mr Medley was asking for support for the County and Mr Fuller for Lewes. According to another report written on 12 Mar. by the Duke's 'friend' Mr Rideout, Mr Medley was no longer a candidate for the county at that stage but was only asking support for Mr Fuller (with the aim of also splitting the votes of the Duke's supporters). Mr Rideout also noted that a 'deluge of strong beer had been poured forth by Mr Medley and Mr Fuller', but that it was received with 'so much Coolness by the Mob that they could hardly find People to take it away': R. Rideout to Dr Chandler, 12 Mar. 1761, Newcastle Papers, BL Add. MS 32,920, f. 143. See also W. Michell to the Duke of Newcastle, 7 Mar. 1761, Newcastle Papers, BL Add. MS 32,918, f. 506.

[13] BL Add. MS 32,920, f. 111. In 1768 the electorate numbered 177 men, 153 of whom actually polled. In the preceding contested election 156 electors polled: *A Poll Taken by Tho. Friend and James Reeve, Constables of the Borough of Lewes* (London, 1734); *A Poll Taken by Samuel Ollive and Thomas Scrace, Constables of the Borough of Lewes* (Lewes, 1768); see also the *Town Book of Lewes*, pp. 50–1. One of these 'friends', Henry Verrall, was the proprietor of the Whig coffee house, situated in Newcastle House in Lewes: W. H. Godfrey, 'Seatholders of St. Michael's Church, Lewes in 1753 & 1803 with their dwelling houses', *SNQ* 1 (1927), 177; P. Lucas, 'The Verrall family of Lewes', *SAC* 58 (1961), 99–101; see also various accounts relating to the rental of the coffee house, BL Add. MS 33,166 ff. 14, 62, 70.

[14] BL Add. MS 32,920, f. 111. This letter was sent to the Revd Mr Hurdis at Newcastle House in Lincoln's Inn Fields. Reports were also sent to one of the Lewes MPs and to the Duke's agent Mr Michell, then campaigning at Seaford.

[15] The Duke of Newcastle to R. Rideout, 17 Mar. 1761, Newcastle Papers, BL Add. MS 32,920, ff. 280–2.

[16] As these 'friends' are discussed in the context of the Lewes election, and the Duke congratulates his agent on his dealing with 'Our Lewes Affair', I take it that this is a reference to Lewes electors: BL Add. MS 32,920, f. 280. The Duke was aware, however, that, as Mr Medley had given up his campaign for the county, he might direct his attention to Lewes, and that therefore 'care should be taken about Lewis': The Duke of Newcastle to W. Michell, 17 Mar. 1761, Newcastle Papers, BL Add. MS 32,920, ff. 383–4. See also 'State of Lewes Borough', Mar. 1761, Newcastle Papers, BL Add. MS 33,059, ff. 17–20.

Union are so sincere, and so solidly connected for any such attempt as that to succeed', he said.[17] He thus devised a plan to come to his seat at Halland House two days before the county election. This would give him an ideal opportunity to thank his 'friends' for their support, display his bounty, and make a powerful appearance with his legion of 'friends' in order both to strengthen them and deter any remaining opposition. He explained his plan to Mr Rideout in the following words.

I am too old to canvass. Fifty years canvass is enough; But I intend to come to the County Election to attend, and thank *my Friends* in the County. I propose to be at Harland on Saturday the 4th april, to desire the Company of all the Gentleman at Lewes, and in the Neighbourhood, to dine with me at Haland on Sunday, and I shall come to Lewes with *my Friends in the East* [i.e. the Eastern Division of the County of Sussex], who I hope will breakfast at Haland on Monday Morning, to be present at the Election, where I hope the Nobility, Gentry, and Clergy, will be so good as to come, to show every body the Credit and Strength we should have had if the opposition had gone on.[18]

However, there was still room for further campaigning and there could always be unpleasant surprises. Mr Medley's opposition was gathering force in the nearby borough of Seaford, and the Duke's 'friends' reported that he and his men were 'upon the watch continually to get at *our Friends*'.[19] Mr Fuller proved slow to step down.[20] The concerned 'friends' in Lewes now spied on a meeting in a local public house that defined itself as 'the Independent Club', and planned future action. One of them actually sat at the meeting and produced a list of the participants. 'We humbly hope this Intelligence may not hurt our neighbours', said the 'friends', as they sent the list of the participants 'on the other Side' to the Duke.[21] 'Your Grace's presence will be necessary the day before the election', urged two other 'friends'.[22] Evidently, the original plan had to

---

[17] BL Add. MS 32,920, f. 281. For Mr Sergison, see also Namier and Brooke, *House of Commons*, vol. III, pp. 421–2. Mr Sergison served as MP for Lewes from 1747 to 1766. Originally one of the Duke's opponents, he reached an agreement with him and was returned as his candidate.

[18] *Ibid.*, f. 281. 'I dont propose to be either at the Lewes, or Seaford Election', he declared. 'My best compliments to all my good Friends', he added.

[19] Already in Jan. 1761, when it was rumoured that Medley was about to present an opposition at Seaford, the Duke's agent Mr Michell warned that he might meet with support. By mid-Feb. this 'strong opposition' was discussed in the local newspaper, as Mr Medley's mill at Friston was burned down. Eventually, the Duke's most active 'friends' in Sussex and Lewes had to go to Seaford more than once to confront Medley: e.g. BL Add. MS 32,918, ff. 505–6; Lord Gage, J. Peachy, and others to the Duke of Newcastle, 21 Mar. 1761, Newcastle Papers, BL Add. MS 32,920, f. 416; see also *Sussex Advertiser*, 16 Feb. 1761; Namier and Brooke, *House of Commons*, vol. I, p. 454.

[20] Three days before the Lewes election his name was still advertised in the local newspaper as a candidate: *Sussex Advertiser*, 23 Mar. 1761.

[21] T. Best, W. Young, and H. Verrall to the Duke of Newcastle, 'half past Eleven Oth Clock', 18 Mar. 1761, Newcastle Papers, BL Add. MS 32,919, f. 461.

[22] W. Michell and R. Yeates to the Duke of Newcastle, 22 Mar. 1761, Newcastle Papers, BL Add. MS 32,920, f. 472.

be rethought. The Duke would come to Halland sooner. He would attend the Lewes election. The great gathering at Halland would take place as planned, but its impact would now be more necessary than originally deemed by the Duke.

The Duke's orders were soon carried out. Invitations were written, and letters of acceptance started to arrive.[23] Mr Christopher Coates, the Duke's agent at Halland House and Thomas Turner's neighbour, who features prominently in the diary, was busy managing the operation. In a letter of 30 March he informed the Duke of its progress: he listed acceptances, as well as the names of local gentlemen who were in charge of raising the support of their parishes.[24] In consequence, Thomas Turner, the local shopkeeper, was also busy. He arranged for his former servant Mary Martin to come for a few days and help in the shop. Brother Moses also came to help.[25] On 2 April he went down to Halland three times, supplying goods. On 3 April he went there four times, in addition to rushing to Lewes especially to buy some expensive lump sugar for Halland. On 4 April he wrote 'To and fro at Halland all day'.

On Sunday 5 April the gathering took place. This great gathering at Halland, as Thomas Turner described it, numbered five or six hundred participants. Thomas Turner spent nearly the entire day there, as did his brother.[26] In the evening he came home together with one of the guests, a Captain Lamb, who lodged at Thomas Turner's house, 'there being not beds enough at Halland', as Thomas Turner explained. He may have been connected to Mr Lamb of Rye, whose name appears in Mr Coates's letter among the acceptances, and who on another occasion was thanked warmly by the Duke as '*my friend Mr Lamb*', who succeeded so well to tie Rye in a 'steady attachment to the Whig case and to my family'.[27] Thomas Turner was later rewarded for his services not only by the considerable

[23] See Sir Whistler Webster to the Duke of Newcastle, 28 Mar. 1761, Newcastle Papers, BL Add. MS 32,921, f. 142; J. Boyes to the Duke of Newcastle, 29 Mar. 1761, Newcastle Papers, BL Add. MS 32,921, f. 162; The Duke of Newcastle to Mr Rose Fuller, 29 Mar., 1761, Newcastle Papers, BL Add. MS 32,921, f. 222. As Thomas Turner reports, the Duke arrived at Halland on 27 Mar.: 'In the Even the Duke of Newcastle came to Hall^d from the election at Lewes': Thomas Turner, Diary, 27 Mar. 1761.
[24] C. Coates to the Duke of Newcastle, 30 Mar. 1761, Newcastle Papers, BL Add. MS 32,921, f. 179.   [25] Thomas Turner, Diary, 2 Apr. 1761.
[26] 'This day there was a Public Day at Halland where I believe there was 5 or 6 Hund. People. At Halland almost all day': *ibid.*
[27] Quoted in D. J. Hope-Wallace, 'Eighteenth-century election methods', *SCM* 6 (1932), 698. See also Namier, *England in the Age of the American Revolution*, pp. 407, 410, 412, Lamb and others in the Exchequer of Rye lost their positions in 1763 when so many of the Duke of Newcastle's 'friends' were removed from office. He was described in the list prepared for the Duke as 'a very good Officer, Many Years an Officer, under My Lord Hardwicke when His Lordship was Lord Chancellor': 'List of Persons to be removed and appointed', 23 Jan. 1763, Newcastle Papers, BL Add. MS 32,946, f. 181.

sum of £11 16s 3d, paid in cash, but by a present of a shoulder of lamb sent to him from Halland.[28] Thomas Turner thus numbered among the cohorts of the Duke of Newcastle's 'friends', who participated in demonstrating the extent of the Pelham interest in Sussex before the general election of 1761. Turner's participation in political life, as evident on this occasion, is suggestive all the more in view of the fact that he probably lacked the property qualifications that would have enabled him to vote in his county. His brother, too, was most probably not enfranchised.[29] But it seems that as an active tradesman and a respectable parishioner Turner both wanted – and perhaps was also expected – to demonstrate allegiance to this powerful connection of political 'friends'.[30]

Indeed, the influence of the Duke of Newcastle and his connection of 'friends' was felt in Turner's locality well beyond election years, and beyond the circle of the electorate. The impact of the Duke and his vast estate was felt in East Hoathly in everyday life. Furthermore, at this local level the Duke of Newcastle's 'friendship' was both mediated and reinforced by a local power-axis.[31] Thomas Porter, the influential rector of East Hoathly and an active landowner and farmer in his own right, who is mentioned so often in Thomas Turner's diary, was married to Mary, the only daughter of Mr Coates, the Duke's agent at Halland.[32] Thomas

[28] Thomas Turner, Diary, 6, 21 Apr. 1761.
[29] After 1753 Thomas Turner was a customary tenant in Framfield, Sussex. In East Hoathly he was at that time only a copyholder's sub-tenant. As Langford explains, following the Oxfordshire election of 1754, an act had been instituted that prohibited copyholders from assuming the electoral right of forty-shilling freeholders. This meant that Thomas Turner could not vote in 1761. For the Turners' Framfield property, see Framfield Manor Books, ESRO, ADA 117, ff. 24–5, ESRO ADA 118, ff. 13, 49–51; *East Sussex Land Tax, 1785*, pp. 84, 111–12; Turner, *Diary*, ed. Vaisey, p. 339. See also Laughton Manor Book, ESRO, A2327/1/4/5, f. 9. For copyholders' franchise, see P. Langford, *A Polite and Commercial People: England 1727–1783* (Oxford, 1989), p. 718; Langford, *Public Life and the Propertied Englishman*, pp. 69, 278–80.
[30] As O'Gorman explains, eighteenth-century elections were 'communal events' that included non-electors as well, and they were also a part of a long-term dialogue between the patron or patrons and the community: O'Gorman, *Voters, Patrons and Parties*, e.g. pp. 385–9.   [31] See also above, ch. 3, pp. 82–9.
[32] Thomas Porter was instituted to the rectory of East Hoathly after his brother, Richard Porter, resigned it in his favour: E. H. W. Dunkin, 'Contributions towards the ecclesiastical history of the deanery of South Malling in the county of Sussex', *SAC* 26 (1875), 71; Turner, *Diary*, ed. Vaisey, p. 336. The patron of the benefice was in fact Lord Abergavenny. 'Lord Bergavenny' was already mentioned in 1605 as the patron, and the Earl of Abergavenny was still mentioned as patron in 1835: W. C. Renshaw, 'Some clergy of the Archdeaconry of Lewes and South Malling Deanery', *SAC* 55 (1912), p. 238; T. W. Horsfield, *The History, Antiquities and Topography of the County of Sussex*, 2 vols. (Lewes, 1835), vol. I, p. 359. From 1754 to 1761 Lord Abergavenny was Lord Lieutenant of Sussex and a supporter of the Pelham interest (see also Turner, *Diary*, ed. Vaisey, p. 156 and note there). Mr Coates also enjoyed the Duke's patronage in other ways, for he was also appointed by him as Commissioner of Hawkers and Pedlars in Sussex. In 1762–3 he was

Porter knew the Duke of Newcastle and sought favours from him. Specifically, he wanted the Duke to recommend him to an additional living, which he hoped to hold in plurality with East Hoathly. He thus wrote a number of petitions to the Duke to this effect, promising him that 'if I shou'd be so happy as to succeed in this affair the favour shall always be acknowledg'd'.[33] His request was supported by a separate petition from Mrs Coates (herself a familiar figure from Thomas Turner's diary).[34] The first of the petitions was sent in 1754, and by February 1757 Thomas Porter was finally about to succeed to a second living in Ripe.[35] It is therefore not surprising that we find him listed in the Duke of Newcastle's papers among the supporters of his interest who attended the 'great Meeting' in Lewes on 15 January 1761, when the Pelhamite nominations for the County election were also made.[36]

The Coates–Porter axis brought power-relations into many every day exchanges in Thomas Turner's life. When Thomas Turner refused to buy Mr Coates's wool at an inflated price, Mr Coates retaliated by taking away from him valuable orders from Halland.[37] Mrs Porter, too, demanded that Thomas Turner should sell her raisins without profit, whereas Mr Porter 'huff'd' him over the sale of a cheese.[38] On these occasions Thomas Turner stood his ground. At other times he conceded. He was critical about big social gatherings at which alcohol was consumed in large quantities, but he found himself nonetheless going to a drunken gathering at Halland, so as not to 'disoblige Mr Coates'.[39] He had to swallow his pride when Mrs Porter treated him in an imperious manner, as if she were 'more of a Turk or infidel than a Christian, and I an abject slave'.[40] Nor did he probably disclose to Mr Porter his real opinion

removed from this office, together with many of the Duke's 'friends': Namier, *England in the Age of the American Revolution*, pp. 408, 410–12, and references to Mr Coates there; 'List of Persons to be removed and appointed', BL Add. MS 32,946, f. 182.

[33] See Thomas Porter first petition: T. Porter to the Duke of Newcastle, 24 June 1755, Newcastle Papers, BL Add. MS 32,856, f. 185. See also his petitions: T. Porter to the Duke of Newcastle, 23 Aug. 1755, Newcastle Papers, BL Add. MS 32,858, f. 269; T. Porter to the Duke of Newcastle, Newcastle Papers, 20 Aug. 1756, BL Add. MS 32,866, f. 500, from which the above quotation is taken.

[34] M. Coates to the Duke of Newcastle, 26 Oct. 1754, Newcastle Papers, BL Add. MS 32,737, f. 216. The petition includes also a reference to the Duke's previous favour to Mrs Coates's nephew.

[35] T. Porter to the Duke of Newcastle, 10 Feb. 1757, Newcastle Papers, BL Add. MS 32,870, f. 173. This was his living in Ripe, Sussex, which was later taken over by his own son-in-law.

[36] 15 Jan. 1761, BL Add. MS 32,917, f. 344; *Sussex Advertiser*, 29 Dec. 1760, 12, 19 Jan. 1761.   [37] Thomas Turner, Diary, 1, 8 Aug. 1755.

[38] *Ibid.*, 19 Mar. 1757. Thomas Porter 'huff'd' Thomas Turner for not taking back a whole cheese, which had been ordered especially for him and which he had also taken home and kept for a while: *ibid.*, 26 June 1758.   [39] *Ibid.*, 30 June 1758.

[40] *Ibid.*, 20 May 1757.

about his meanness and ruthlessness in some business and parish affairs,[41] his critical thoughts concerning plurality in church benefices,[42] nor
tell him to his face that he had heard him preach the same sermon seven
times 'with Very little or any alteration'.[43] On all these occasions Turner
probably revealed his discontent to his diary alone. In his business dealings, in parish affairs, and in social life he cooperated again and again with
Mr Coates, Mr Porter, and their wives, and they cooperated with him.
When he had to choose a godmother for his son Frederick, he chose Mrs
Mary Porter, daughter of Mr Coates.[44]

Other actions and deeds performed by Thomas Turner further indicate
that he knew his way around the beneficial networks of 'friendship' and
patronage and had the agility to use them to advantage. As a parish
officer, he received from the rector of East Hoathly donations made to
pay for repairs in the East Hoathly parish church: one was from the rector
himself, another was from the Duke of Newcastle.[45] However as a shopkeeper he charged his parish for pulpit cloth and fittings, provided by
himself: items such as 'Brass Turn Buckles', 'Fringe and Tassels' and
'Silk and thread' raised the bill to £12 8s 3/4d.[46] Putting on once again the
parish officer's hat, he recorded the charge in the parish overseers' account book.[47] He wrote a petition to the Duke of Newcastle for one of his
old acquaintances, one Master Diggens, asking to promote Diggens's son
to the position of a 'Supervisor', presumably a supervisor in the excise.[48]

[41] One particular affair of a village pauper who absconded from East Hoathly, leaving his
family chargeable to the parish, occasioned some bitter reflections. Turner complained
about 'many of the richest & leading men of our parish' who prefer to employ 'certificate
men' rather than pay decent wages to local labourers, and who then, moreover, try to
punish them harshly. When this pauper finally returned to East Hoathly, the harsh policy
towards him was suggested at the parish vestry by Mr Coates, Mr Porter, and another
substantial farmer, Mr French: see *ibid.*, 20 Oct. 1756, 11 Dec. 1761. On another occasion
Turner served as a witness in a transaction in which Porter bought from another
parishioner, Mr Burges, the bulk of his land to the value of £900, while maintaining a
right of first refusal on the rest. Turner thought Burges was 'not equally qualify'd with Mr
Porter to make a bargain', but nonetheless he remained silent and signed as a witness,
alongside the village butcher Mr Fuller: *ibid.*, 16 Apr. 1761; see also comments on Porter's
meanness: 10 Aug. 1756, 25 Feb. 1758.

[42] See his thoughts following some reading on this matter: *ibid.*, 19 June 1762.

[43] *Ibid.*, 22 May 1763.

[44] He was born on 8 Dec. 1771: ESRO, SAS/SM 210; Turner, *Diary*, ed. Turner, p. 110.
This was the first of Turner's sons by this name. It is also worth noting that one of
Thomas Turner's neighbours in East Hoathly, Mrs Atkins, was the widow of the Duke of
Newcastle's former steward at Halland. This connection, too, was strengthened by
godparenthood, as Mrs Atkins became godmother to Thomas Turner's first daughter
Margaret.

[45] Thomas Turner, *Diary*, 23 Apr. 1763. He then lent the money to a local farmer to incur
interest for the parish.

[46] See a bill by Thomas Turner 'on Acct of the Church', 13 Nov. 1762, ESRO, AMS 5841/9.

[47] East Hoathly Overseers' Account Book, ESRO, PAR 378/31/1/1, 7 Apr. 1763.

[48] Thomas Turner, *Diary*, 13 Nov. 1759. On 21 Nov. 1757 Turner also wrote a petition in

He himself went to Lewes to Mr William Michell, the Duke's agent and one of his main *'friends'* in town (who was also very active in the 1761 election) to ask 'the favour to serve the nails' for a new building that was then being built by the Duke.[49]

When Thomas Turner went to Lewes, he found himself once more surrounded by a dense network of political *'friendship'*. When we examine Thomas Turner's acquaintances and fellow-tradesmen in Lewes, we discover that many of them, too, were linked directly to the Duke of Newcastle. Such, for example, was Mr Thomas Friend, a wool merchant and the owner of a public house named the *White Horse*.[50] It was he who served as constable and returning officer in Lewes in the bitterly contested election of 1734, when he managed to obtain a sufficient number of 'good' votes, and disqualify enough 'bad' votes to ensure victory for the Duke.[51] In subsequent years he continued to serve as one of the Duke's loyal 'friends' in town, as can be seen from the Duke of Newcastle's correspondence.[52] Thomas Turner promised Thomas Friend to give him

the name of the widow Mrs Virgoe, addressed to Mrs Medley, the wife of George Medley who was to become the Duke's 'enemy' in 1760–1. Mrs Virgoe owned a butcher's shop which was about to re-open under a new management, and in the petition she asked Mrs Medley to renew her custom to the shop. On 4 Nov. 1757 Turner was dissuaded by George Verrall from approaching Mrs Medley on Mrs Virgoe's behalf, but evidently he later changed his mind.

[49] *Ibid.*, 5 June 1762. The meeting of the court baron for the manor of Laughton at Whitesmith, 24 May 1764, attended by both Mr Michell and Thomas Turner, is mentioned in both Turner's diary and the Duke of Newcastle's correspondence: W. Michell to R. Turner, 13 May 1764, Newcastle Papers, BL Add. MS 32,958, f. 415. Mr Michell had also been appointed by Newcastle as Treasurer of the Salt Office, an office that he lost in 1762–3 together with many of the Duke's loyal 'friends'. At this stage he was described as 'an attorney' and 'a borough agent for the D. of N', 'known loved by all the gentlemen in Sussex', and 'many Years Under Sheriff': BL Add. MS 32,946, f. 185, and see also R. Rideout to the Duke of Newcastle, 29 Jan. 1763, *ibid.*, f. 226; BL Add. MS 38,334, ff. 214–16, quoted in Namier, *England in the Age of the American Revolution*, p. 412. Turner's expertise in the ways of patronage and trade was later communicated by him to his son Philip, then a servant to a tradesman at Brighton: 'If the Duke of York is at Brighton and Mr Kirby [Philip's master] has the Honour to Serve Him I believe a French Man of the name of Longe or something like it is his Head Cook, Clerk of the Kitchen, House Steward etc. who I understand has great influence with the Duke and is a good Sort of man, I would recommend it to you to ingratiate your Self unto his favour by Civility, Complaisance and good manners.' He then supplies him with further information about Longe, acquired by another acquaintance who was 'Hand and Glove' with Mr Longe when he was Cook to the Earl of Ashburnham, while telling Philip that his information is 'to your Self alone': Thomas Turner to his son Philip, 24 July 1789, 'Special Files', Thomas Turner Papers, Yale University Library.   [50] See Brent, *Georgian Lewes*, p. 33.

[51] *A Poll Taken by Tho. Friend and James Reeve*, and see especially the fiercely disputed cases on pp. 8–16. The two constables and returning officers were elected annually by the town residents at the court leet held alternately by the Dukes of Dorset and Norfolk and Lord Abergavenny. The Duke of Newcastle referred to this particular electoral victory as won by 'having the officer', i.e. the returning officer: Namier and Brooke, *House of Commons*, vol. I, 'Sussex', p. 336; see also Phillips, *Electoral Behaviour*, p. 105.

[52] Thomas Friend's letters to the Duke, sometimes written together with other 'friends' and

'the Prefference before another' in buying his own wool, and he used him as a banker.[53] The *White Horse*, owned by Friend, was the Lewes public house which Turner frequented most regularly to drink, dine, stay the night, meet many acquaintances, and do business.[54] Various members of the Verrall family were also among Thomas Turner's familiar acquaintances in Lewes, and they, too, numbered among the Duke's 'friends' in town. Such, for example, were the brothers Edward, George, and William Verrall. Edward Verrall was a bookseller and printer, and also served as a justice's clerk at Lewes. George Verrall was an auctioneer and a supplier of soap, and William, formerly a servant in the Duke of Newcastle's kitchens, became the master of the *White Hart*, a large inn situated at the heart of Lewes.[55] Thomas Turner had dealings with all of them. He met Edward Verrall on parish and business matters,[56] he did business and socialised with George Verrall,[57] and the *White Hart* was a local inn he knew well. The Duke of Newcastle also had many dealings with the

activists, present the Duke with many requests to release pressed sailors, remove billeted soldiers, appoint 'friends' to offices, promote others, assist relations, etc. In one petition, for instance, Friend and others ask the Duke for an appointment in the excise for a man 'who was always a steady *Friend*' and 'who serv'd your Grace at several elections in the Borough of Lewes': A petition by T. Friend and others on behalf of A. Gann, 30 Sept. 1746, Newcastle Papers, BL Add. MS 32,708, f. 391. Interestingly, in another letter Friend informed the Duke that he had heard from Mr Coates at Halland that a local farm was about to become vacant, and he proposed it should be given to his nephew: T. Friend to the Duke of Newcastle, 26 Oct. 1751, Newcastle Papers, BL Add. MS 32,725, f. 353. For letters and petitions signed by Friend, see also: A petition by publicans in Lewes asking to remove a company of soldiers, 1744, Newcastle Papers, BL Add. MS 32,704, f. 22; T. Friend to the Duke of Newcastle, 11 Aug. 1761, Newcastle Papers, BL Add. MS 32,926, f. 380. Thomas Friend and other 'friends' evidently felt confident enough of the Duke's favour that they allowed themselves to write to him, presenting themselves as '*your Graces sincere and Hearty Friends*', in order to inform him that his agent in Lewes was disliked by too many people in town, implying that it would be best if he were replaced: A. Morris, T. Friend, and others to the Duke of Newcastle, 3 Nov. 1740, Newcastle Papers, BL Add. MS 32,695, f. 371.

[53] Thomas Turner, Diary, 13 Aug. 1755. See also, for example, *ibid.*, 9 Apr. 1754: 'Sent Geo: Ottway two Bills drawn by Friend . . . £10, 0, 0 on my mother's account.'

[54] See, for example, *ibid.*, 10, 11 May, 7 Aug. 1756, 24 Feb., 30 Mar., 14 June 1757, etc.

[55] In 1759 William Verrall published a cookery book, entitled *A Complete System of Cookery, in which is Set Forth a Variety of Genuine Recipts, Collected from Several Years Experience under the Celebrated Mr De St. Clouet, Sometimes Since Cook to his Grace the Duke of Newcastle* . . . (Lewes, 1759): see Lucas, 'The Verrall family', 104–6. In the *Sussex Advertiser*, 22 Jan. 1759, the book is advertised as being 'shortly in the press'. The subscription offered is five shillings. The subscription was taken by Edward Verrall the printer, and William's brother.

[56] See, e.g. Thomas Turner, Diary, 14 Feb., 3, 31 July 1756, 3 Sept. 1757, 9 July 1758. He also read the local newspaper owned and printed by him, the *Sussex Advertiser*.

[57] Thomas Turner, Diary, 13–14 Feb., 5, 8 June 1756, 12 Aug. 1757, 18 Dec., 1 Apr. 1761, etc.

Verrall family.[58] He acted as their patron, obtained commissions for them, extended to them his help over many years, and relied on their political cooperation and 'friendship'.[59] And, of course, when Thomas Turner had to settle legal or administrative matters, which he occasionally had to do for himself and for his parish, he resorted once more to the Duke's 'friends'. Such, for example, was Luke Spence Esq., a Justice of the Peace and a staunch '*friend*' of the Duke of Newcastle, to whom Turner turned often on parish matters and in whose house Mary (Molly) Hicks, Thomas Turner's second wife, was employed as a servant. Luke Spence's correspondence with the Duke of Newcastle is saturated with the language of 'friendship', and before the 1761 election we find him canvassing and raising votes for the Duke among his own tenants.[60] Such a 'friend' was also Mr Rideout the attorney, the Duke's supporter and loyal 'friend', mentioned above, who was probably also the Turner family lawyer, who drew up and witnessed the wills of Thomas Turner's parents,[61] and whom Turner continued to use for borrowing a large sum of

[58] See Lucas, 'The Verrall family', 91–131, and many references there to the Duke of Newcastle's correspondence.
[59] See, for example, a petition by E. Verrall to the Duke of Newcastle, 24 Feb. 1746, Newcastle Papers, BL Add. MS 32,710, f. 236; E. Verrall to the Duke of Newcastle, 16 Feb. 1758, Newcastle Papers, BL Add. MS 32,877, f. 46. In another petition, written not long before the 1761 election E. Verrall asked the Duke for a position as a 'surveyor of the Windows', assuring him that 'I can be well recommended by all your Grace's *Friends* as a fit object for your Grace's benevolence': E. Verrall to the Duke of Newcastle, 19 July 1760, Newcastle Papers, BL Add. MS 32,908, f. 381. At another time he thanks the Duke for obtaining for his son a commission as a supervisor of the window tax: E. Verrall to the Duke of Newcastle, 20 Aug. 1763, Newcastle Papers, BL Add. MS 32,969, f. 133. See also, for example, a joint petition by the Verralls on behalf of 'their brother Manfield', who failed in trade: S., E., H., W. Verrall and others to the Duke of Newcastle, 13 Mar. 1756, Newcastle Papers, BL Add. MS 32,863, f. 278. See also W. Verrall to the Duke of Newcastle, 4 Apr. 1756, Newcastle Papers, BL Add. MS 32,864, f. 271; C. Verrall to the Duke of Newcastle, 26 Dec. 1760, Newcastle Papers, BL Add. MS 32,916, f. 340.
[60] Indeed it was he who suggested that he evict his tenant in the above quoted example as a 'service' to the Duke, p. 218. See the letters exchanged between Luke Spence and the Duke of Newcastle: Luke Spence to the Duke of Newcastle, 15 Aug. 1747, Newcastle Papers, BL Add. MS 32,712, f. 388; Luke Spence to the Duke of Newcastle, 24 Mar. 1748, Newcastle Papers, BL Add. MS 32,718, f. 137; Luke Spence to the Duke of Newcastle, 7 Aug. 1749, Newcastle Papers, BL Add. MS 32,719, f. 15; Luke Spence to the Duke of Newcastle, 27 Oct. 1753, Newcastle Papers, BL Add. MS 32,733, f. 152; the Duke of Newcastle to Luke Spence, 16 Jan. 1757, Newcastle Papers, BL Add. MS 32,870, f. 56; Luke Spence to the Duke of Newcastle, 18 Jan. 1757, Newcastle Papers, BL Add. MS 32,870, f. 68; Luke Spence to the Duke of Newcastle, 1 Sept. 1759, Newcastle Papers, BL Add. MS 32,895, f. 111; Luke Spence to the Duke of Newcastle, 24 Dec. 1759, Newcastle Papers, BL Add. MS 32,900, f. 302; Luke Spence to the Duke of Newcastle, 6 Oct 1760, Newcastle Papers, BL Add. MS 32,912, f. 419; Luke Spence to the Duke of Newcastle, 27 Oct. 1760, Newcastle Papers, BL Add. MS 32,913, f. 386; BL Add. MS 32,920, f. 25; Luke Spence to the Duke of Newcastle, 29 Sept. 1761, Newcastle Papers, BL Add. MS 32,928, f. 428.
[61] The will of John Turner, ESRO, W/SM D9 ff., 233–5; the will of Elizabeth Turner, *ibid.*, ff. 236–7.

money on his mother's account,[62] for receiving advice about a personal debtor,[63] and for examining the putative father of a bastard on behalf of East Hoathly parish.[64]

Further links to the Duke of Newcastle can also be traced among Thomas Turner's select 'friends'. John Madgwick, one of Thomas Turner's 'friends' and main suppliers in Lewes also signed his name on a petition addressed to the Duke of Newcastle.[65] In October 1761 we find him bearing the position of headborough of Lewes.[66] However among Thomas Turner's 'friends', the one most involved in politics was probably the victualler Thomas Scrace. Thomas Scrace was described by Thomas Turner as an '*Old Friend*'.[67] When in Lewes, Turner often met Scrace and also dined, drank, and socialised with him in the company of other 'friends' and tradesmen, whereas Scrace visited Turner in East Hoathly. The two also had business connections: Turner supplied Scrace with provisions, and the credit relations between them extended over years and were settled in cash and kind.[68] As in the case of other 'friends', this 'friendship', too, was linked to godparenthood. Thomas Scrace was one of the 'sponsors' of Thomas Turner's son Peter.[69]

In 1761, just as the election was pending, Thomas Scrace took over the management of the *White Hart*.[70] William Verrall, one of the Verrall brothers mentioned above, did not do very well in his business. Although he had inherited from his father a commodious and well-furnished inn, which offered not only fine food and drink but also dozens of bedsteads and halters for one hundred and twenty horses, he fell into debt.[71] One of his main creditors was his brother, George Verrall the auctioneer. By January 1761 Mr Rideout tried to reach a transaction with William Verrall on behalf of the Duke of Newcastle to leave his house and

---

[62] Thomas Turner, Diary, 7 Aug. 1756. The sum borrowed was forty pounds.
[63] *Ibid.*, 22 May, 30 Mar. 1758.   [64] *Ibid.*, 23 Feb. 1763.
[65] Among the names in this petition we also find Henry Verrall, one of the brothers of the Verrall family, and Thomas Scrace, discussed below. This interesting petition was written in favour of Sir Francis Poole, the son of the former local MP and one of the Duke's relations who had served his interest in town for many years: see a petition to the Duke of Newcastle in favour of Sir Francis Poole, 12 Aug. 1765, BL Add. MS 32,969, f. 92.   [66] *Town Book of Lewes*, p. 51.
[67] Thomas Turner, Diary, 5 May 1762. See Scrace's advertisement in Brent, *Georgian Lewes*, p. 16.
[68] For example, on 21 Jan. 1760 Scrace and Turner settled accounts. Scrace owed Turner for fabric bought in 1759 and butter bought in 1758, whereas Turner owed Scrace for one wig bought for himself and two for his brother William. The balance of £2 9s 4d was paid in cash by Scrace, but the debt for 104 pounds of butter, supplied by Turner in 1759, remained outstanding: Thomas Turner, Diary, 21 Jan. 1760. See also accounts and meetings with Scrace: *ibid.*, 28 Feb., 5, 12 Mar., 14 July 1758, 20 Nov. 1759, 26 Feb. 1760, etc.   [69] ESRO, SAS/SM 210.
[70] Brent, *Georgian Lewes*, pp. 16–17. I am grateful to Colin Brent for discussing this matter with me.   [71] *Ibid.*; Lucas, 'The Verrall family', 106.

business.[72] Poor William Verrall expressed the hope that 'my Ld Duke would not have him out of his House on so short a notice without doing something for him to keep him from starving',[73] but by February an advertisement appeared in the local newspaper, the *Sussex Advertiser, or Lewes Journal* (owned by William's brother, Edward Verrall), announcing the sale of 'all the Household Furniture, Plates, Linens, Brewing Utensils and Several Post Chariots, Chaise and Harness, of William Verrall'.[74] By the end of March 1761 William Verrall was dead.[75] With the approaching election, however, business at the *White Hart* had to continue as usual, and Thomas Scrace therefore no doubt had to take over its management in as smooth a manner as possible. Indeed the management of the *White Hart* had political implications. The *White Hart* was more than just an inn, it was the headquarters of Lewes's political life, and of the political life of East Sussex more broadly. That is where the Quarter Sessions for the Eastern Division of Sussex were opened, where the county electors met to nominate candidates, where electioneering campaigns were held, and where, eventually, the polling station for the county was located.[76] The Duke of Newcastle therefore had an interest in the management of the *White Hart*, all the more so as the *White Hart* was directly tied to his own connection: the house in which the *White Hart* was located belonged to the Pelham family, and in the previous century it had served as the Pelham townhouse.[77]

---

[72] W. Michell to the Duke of Newcastle, 22 Jan. 1761, Newcastle Papers, BL Add. MS 32,918, f. 12. In this letter of 22 Jan. 1761, Michell, the Duke's agent and 'friend' referred to Rideout's transaction with William Verrall, whom he described as 'a very odd man'.

[73] *Ibid.* On this occasion the agent could not extract from him a promise to leave the house, but he emphasised that William ought to comply if he expected any 'Favour from his Grace'. The Duke kindly recommended William Verrall as a keeper of the house of correction for the county. As this appointment was pending, however, William was declared bankrupt and was no longer eligible for the appointment: Lucas, 'The Verrall family', 106, and G. Hammond to the Duke of Newcastle, 12 Mar. 1762, BL Add. MS 32,920, f. 133, also referred to there.

[74] *Sussex Advertiser*, 22 Feb. 1761. The sale was scheduled for 2 Mar.

[75] He was buried at St Michael's, Lewes, on 26 Mar. Administration of his goods was granted on 30 Nov. 1761 to his brother George Verrall, a creditor, his widow renouncing: quoted in Lucas, 'The Verrall family', 106.

[76] See, for example, notices in the *Sussex Advertiser* for a meeting at the *White Hart* of 'The Gentlemen, Clergy and Freeholders of the County of Sussex' to nominate candidates for the election, 29 Dec. 1760, 12 Jan. 1761. See notices in the *Sussex Advertiser* for the opening of the Quarter Sessions for the Eastern Part of Sussex at the *White Hart*, 29 Sept., 6 Oct. 1760, 12 Jan., 23, and 30 Mar. 1761. See also the notice for 'election for the Knights of the Shire, at the White Hart in this Town', Monday, 5 Apr. 1761. See also the reference to Mr Poole, JP, who summoned Peter Adams, the putative father of a bastard, to appear before him at the *White Hart*: Thomas Turner, Diary, 24 July 1756.

[77] *SNQ* 12 (1948–9), 'Notes', p. 63. The Duke of Newcastle appointed Richard Verrall, the father of the Verrall brothers mentioned above, as the master of the *White Hart*, where he served until his death in 1737. Richard ('Dick') Verrall is mentioned frequently in the

Thus, ties of 'friendship' crossed social ranks: from 1761 onwards we find Mr Scrace, Thomas Turner's *'friend'*, also listed in the Duke of Newcastle's correspondence alongside the Duke's *'friends'*. In March 1761 he may have been among those who advised the Duke to appear in person to make the greatest impact against the opposition.[78] Prior to the election of 1763 the Duke invited his supporters to supper at the *White Hart*.[79] In the general election of 1768 Scrace appeared in the weighty position of constable and returning officer for the town and borough of Lewes.[80] Then, however, he failed in his mission. In the confusion that dominated this election, he and his fellow returning officer failed to control the electors, and even to cast their own votes.[81] Thus Thomas

Pelham Correspondence and accounts, providing 'election entertainment' etc.: Lucas, 'The Verrall family', 92. See also references to accounts by William Verrall from 1738 onwards for supplying dinners and suppers at Pelham House on visits of the Duke there, or other important occasions: *ibid.*, p. 105.

[78] BL Add. MS 32,920, f. 472. The reference here is to a 'Mr Scrase'. Thomas Scrace is also listed among the Duke's supporters in BL Add. MS 33,059, ff. 17–20.

[79] Duke of Newcastle to Mr Hurdis and Mr Michell, 15 Feb. 1763, BL Add. MS 32,947, f. 10, written probably in the Duke's own hand. The election was held on 21 Feb. In the same year a Mr Scrace is consulted with in relation to affairs in Lewes: Mr Michell to the Duke of Newcastle, 11 June 1763, Newcastle Papers, BL Add. MS 32,949, f.94.

[80] *A Poll Taken by Samuel Ollive and Thomas Scrace.* See also the *Town Book of Lewes*, pp. 55–6. The Duke's expectations from the constables and returning officers for Lewes are evident in his instructions from 1739: they were to report the names of his supporters, the names of possible supporters for the opposition, and even suggest the means by which doubtful voters could be secured and individual voters could be 'got off' from the other side: Considerations Relating to the Town of Lewes, 1739, Newcastle Papers, BL Add. MS 33,058, ff. 389–90.

[81] The confusion was due to the fact that the Duke decided to replace his candidate, Colonel Hay, shortly before the election. By the time he informed the town of his decision, Hay had already canvassed Lewes, accompanied by the two constables, and assured the electors that he was acting on the Duke's orders. Voters' promises made to Hay were hard to break, and eventually Hay was also elected with the independents' support. The two constables abstained. The furious Duke devised plans to punish Lewes by giving notice to all his tenants to leave their houses, stopping orders from tradesmen, and withdrawing his concern for 'the Interest and Emoliement' of the town. But he then decided to show his benevolence by forgiving all those who admitted their error. Wisely, he had the affair concluded before the Lewes Races. Letters from around the time of the races show that Scrace remained in favour: the Duke gave personal instructions to provide entertainment during the races at the *White Hart*, and Mr Pelham of Stanmer, the Duke's cousin and heir, assured him that he had gone in person to see 'Harry Verrall & Scrace of the White Hart, and settl'd everything with them for the first Day of the Races, and the Ball, they seem quite satisfied'. See, e.g., the Duke's promise to recommend Hay to Lewes: the Duke of Newcastle to Mr West, 20 Feb. 1768, Newcastle Papers, BL Add. MS 32,988, f. 389. See the Duke's letter announcing his candidates: the Duke of Newcastle to the inhabitants of Lewes, 1 Mar. 1768, Newcastle Papers, BL Add. MS 32,989, f. 3. For Mr Hay's canvassing, see e.g. W. Michell to J. Jewelle, 1 Mar. 1768, Newcastle Papers, BL Add. MS 32,989, f. 11, T. Miller to the Duke of Newcastle, 1 Mar. 1768, Newcastle Papers, BL Add. MS 32,989, f. 13. and also T. Miller to the Duke of Newcastle, 4 Mar. 1768, Newcastle Papers, BL Add. MS 32,989, f. 33. See the above quotations in the Duke of Newcastle to A. Baley, 6 June 1768, Newcastle Papers, BL

Scrace had a hand in bringing about the Duke's loss of one of the valuable seats for Lewes. But by that time the Duke was old and frail and not the political force he once had been. Despite his initial plans to punish the town, he forgave the people of Lewes magnanimously.[82] He died before that year was out. Thomas Scrace, however, continued to thrive and enjoy the patronage of the Pelham family. He ran the *White Hart* until 1791. In the land tax register of 1785 he was listed as an occupier of a house in Lewes with the substantial rental value of £21 p.a. as well as two stables belonging to John Pelham Esq., a brook, and lands to the total rental value of £33 15s p.a.[83]

With this dense local network in mind, the reader of Thomas Turner's diary is tempted to speculate about the political significance of some of Thomas Turner's actions. Various actions, which initially appear inconspicuous and ordinary can now be seen in a different light. Focusing once more on the 1761 Lewes election, for example, let us examine Turner's movements. Most of the time before the election Turner worked in and around East Hoathly, but on two occasions he went to Lewes. On 9 February he dined with John Madgwick and drank tea with George Verrall; on 21 February he dined with John Madgwick and then called upon George Verrall and Thomas Scrace.[84] On both occasions he returned home 'not sober'. When he recorded these journeys, Turner did not say a word about politics. All he mentioned were the people he met, the business he transacted, the contents of his meals, and regrets about his drinking too much. In the light of the present analysis, however, we

Add. MS 32,990, f. 165, and T. Pelham of Stanmer to the Duke of Newcastle, 15 July 1768, Newcastle Papers, BL Add. MS 32,990, f. 309. See other references to the *White Hart* and the *Star* in the Duke of Newcastle to the Duke of Richmond, 31 July 1768, Newcastle Papers, BL Add. MS 32,990, f. 360; Duke of Richmond to the Duke of Newcastle, 5 Aug. 1768, Newcastle Papers, BL Add. MS 32,990, f. 385; T. Hurdis to the Rt Hon. Mr Pelham, 7 Aug. 1768, Newcastle Papers, BL Add. MS 32,990, f. 393; T. Pelham to the Duke of Newcastle, 14 Aug. 1768, Newcastle Papers, BL Add. MS 32,990, f. 433. Namier and Brooke trace the Duke's incoherent behaviour to his illness: Namier and Brooke, *House of Commons*, vol. I, p. 394; see also Brent, *Georgian Lewes*, pp. 181–2.

[82] See memoranda relating to Lewes, July 1768, Newcastle Papers, BL Add. MS 33,059, ff. 81–6, and esp. 85–6. See also account paid to Thomas Scrace at the *White Hart*, Newcastle Papers, BL Add. MS 33,059, f. 92; a bill by Thomas Scrace of the *White Hart*, 1780, Newcastle Papers, BL Add. MS 33,059, f. 104.

[83] *East Sussex Land Tax, 1785*, pp. 139, 142. By his death on 31 Mar. 1792, however, he was in financial difficulties: see a notice of Thomas Scrace's death intestate and his estate passing to his creditors: ESRO, Archdeaconry of Lewes Administrations, B20/181. Interestingly, Thomas Scrace's daughter Mary married into the Verrall family, thus further cementing political and business connections with kinship ties: Lucas, 'The Verrall family', 128.

[84] See also Thomas Turner, Diary, 14 Feb., 1 Apr. 1761, when he also settled accounts with George Verrall.

can speculate on the possible political significance of these meetings in Lewes. It seems very likely that on both occasions Thomas Turner was at least exposed to the contemporary political scene – if he was not actually involved in it. Such visits to the county town, so near the time of a general election, in company with politically identifiable people and possibly in politically identifiable places, must have brought Thomas Turner in close touch with the current events and with the heavily politicised local scene. It may have even been the case that his excessive drinking on these occasions – with George Verrall and Thomas Scrace and possibly at the *White Hart* – was linked to the electioneering campaign.

Scholars who have studied Thomas Turner's diary are struck by the ways in which politics is so little discussed in the diary.[85] In the light of present work, however, it seems that Turner's silence about politics reveals not his unawareness of it, but his acceptance of its widespread presence. Indeed the political dimension of life in his locality may have been so obvious for Turner that he found no reason to explain it in his diary. For example, Thomas Turner's use of the *White Hart*, a public house so clearly associated with the Pelham interest, and his close relationship with its proprietor helps the present-day reader to place Thomas Turner on the contemporary political map, all the more so when compared to his neglect of the *Star*, the public house associated with the independent interest in Lewes. However, this political identification was probably so obvious for Turner that he simply did not mention it in his diary.

But while Thomas Turner was bound within networks of political 'friendship', he did not always approve of the workings of patronage and connections, at least theoretically. On 17 February 1758, after a general fast and humiliation day dedicated to the British forces at war, he wrote in his diary pious sentiments expressing his disapproval of 'private Interest and connection of *Friends*'. These meditations, which associate political 'friendship' with immorality, national weakness, and particularly weakness in the face of France, have a suspiciously anti-Pelhamite resonance and echo the terms of patriotic opposition to Whig oligarchy.[86]

---

[85] J. B. Priestley, 'Introduction', in Turner, *Diary*, ed. Turner; D. K. Worcester, Jun., *The Life and Times of Thomas Turner of East Hoathly*, *Undergraduate Prize Essays*, vol. IV (Oxford and New Haven, 1948), pp. 21, 41–2; Vaisey, 'Introduction', in Turner, *Diary*, ed. Vaisey, pp. xvii–xviii.

[86] See, for example, Q. R. D. Skinner, 'The principles and practice of opposition: the case of Bolingbroke versus Walpole', in N. McKendrick (ed.), *Historical Perspectives: Studies in English Thought and Society in Honour of J. H. Plumb* (London, 1974), pp. 93–128; J. Brewer, *Party Ideology and Popular Politics at the Accession of George III* (Cambridge, 1976); L. Colley, *In Defiance of Oligarchy: The Tory Party 1714–60* (Cambridge, 1982).

Oh! may Religion once more rear up her head in this wicked and impious nation and triumph over Vice and immorality! . . . then (and not till then) will will [sic] all private Interest and connection of *Friends* give way and become subordinate to the love of their King and Country. what then might not the sons of Britain expect but that the Forces of the Proud Gaul so fond of Universal Monarchy would give way as they did once to an Edward and an Henry.

Some of Turner's reading material also contained political criticism. For example, on 13 July 1763 he recorded his favourable impressions after reading 'several Political Papers call'd the North Briton', written by John Wilkes, 'for the Writing of wch he has been committed to the Tower, and procured his release by a Writ of Habeas Corpus. I really think they breath forth Such a Spirit of Liberty', Turner said. Clearly, he thought well of Wilkes's journal and believed it was 'an Extreme good Pap[r]'.[87] Other reading material included less obvious but still poignant points of criticism directed against aristocratic ministers and their corrupt 'friend-ship'. Turner was particularly struck by a part of Smollett's *Peregrine Pickle*, which recounts the disintegration of 'friendship' due to the treach-erous behaviour of an aristocratic minister during an election campaign. The 'prudent apophthegm' which he thought worth copying into his diary on this occasion included the following:

Self accusation very often dissolves the closest friendship: a man conscious of his own indiscretion, is implacably offended at the rectitude of his Com-panion's conduct, which he Considers as an insult upon his failings, never to be forgiven . . . [88]

general profession is a necessary armour worn by all State ministers in their own defence, against the importunity of those whom they will not *befriend* and would not disoblige.[89]

Thomas Turner had not only general reservations about mighty minis-ters and their political 'friendship', but he also had particular reservations about the Duke of Newcastle. In particular, he disapproved of the 'lux-ury' fostered by the Duke, and this was linked closely to his patriotic and religious sentiments and his sense of social justice. For example, when preparations were made for a large gathering at Halland in 1759, Turner denounced this display of 'Luxury and intemperance'. He also saw the gathering, which was to take place on a Sunday, as a profanity of the

---

[87] Thomas Turner, Diary, 13 July 1763. He also objected to the Hardwicke Marriage Act, which he saw as contrary to the laws of God: *ibid.*, 11 Jan. 1758. He firmly believed in the innocence of Admiral Byng, and criticised the 'Treacherous or Simple ministers' or the lords of the Admiralty who had planned his voyage. He also believed the naval attack on St Malo did not justify the effort: *ibid.*, 4 Dec. 1756, 16 Mar. 1757, 19 June, 1758.

[88] T. Smollett, *The Adventures of Peregrine Pickle* (1751), 2 vols. (London, 1904), vol. II, ch. XC, p. 271; see Thomas Turner, Diary, 12 Feb. 1755.

[89] Smollett, *Peregrine Pickle*, vol. II, ch. XCI, p. 281; see Thomas Turner, Diary, 12 Feb. 1755.

Sabbath and a mockery of the industrious poor, whose needs could have been relieved by the bounty.[90] That 'luxury and debauchery' were set loose with the approbation of 'almost the next man to the King' was to him doubly objectionable.[91] Turner's national sentiments were also wounded by the fact that the Duke employed so many French cooks.[92] Indeed, his political repertoire included various patriotic comments in favour of 'our happy Constitution' and 'our holy religion', and against French 'Slavery' and 'Popery'.[93] When assessing such sentiments, however, it is important to take account of the genre of the personal diary and the gaps between Turner's ideas and actions. Whereas obvious political details were deemed self-evident by Turner to the degree that he did not mention them in his diary, he used his diary also to record sentiments that he did not necessarily own in public, and that moreover bore no necessary relation to other social actions. We have seen this complexity in Turner's treatment of his powerful neighbours, Mr Coates and Mr Porter. The same is true of his attitude to the Duke of Newcastle. Turner's criticism of the Duke of Newcastle may have been a case of brave defiance and independent thinking. But it may also have been a sort of counterpart to Turner's outward deference towards the Duke and his people. Turner's criticism of the Duke's luxury was also invariably linked to remorse about his own drunkenness. Such sentiments expressed in Thomas Turner's diary are not easy to interpret, and that is why it is all the more important to judge them against social action. It is certainly very significant that Thomas Turner was critical about the Duke's gatherings. But it is also significant that he was present, that he revealed enough knowledge of the political scene to recognise the distinguished guests, that he drank together with the rest of the crowd, and probably also joined with them in their toasts and cheering.

Lastly, the way in which Thomas Turner was attached to his grand neighbour is evident from his description of his funeral in 1768. This was written, significantly, after he had stopped keeping his regular diary.[94]

[90] Thomas Turner, Diary, 1 Aug. 1759, and see also 5 Aug. 1759 in Turner, *Diary*, ed. Vaisey. Turner firmly believed that 'God giveth the victory', and thus 'to Him should thanks and praises be returned' for success in war. National joy, rightly justified by the taking of Quebec, for example, should therefore have been expressed according to Turner by charitable support of the industrious poor, rather than by vanity and luxury, profanity and irreligion: Thomas Turner, Diary, 23 Oct. 1759.

[91] 5 Aug. 1759 in Turner, *Diary*, ed. Vaisey.   [92] *Ibid.*; see also 3 Aug. 1758.

[93] *Ibid.*, 29 Feb. 1756. At this time a French invasion was feared. See also, for example, his patriotic sentiments in *ibid.*, 16 Feb., 15 Oct. 1759.

[94] The first documentation of the Turner collection includes an eyewitness account of the stately funeral of the Duke of Newcastle, interred in his family vault at Laughton on 18 Nov. 1768: Blencowe and Lower, 'Extracts from the diary of a Sussex tradesman', 219–20. This description of Newcastle's funeral is also quoted in an article by L. B. Smith in *SCM* 4 (1930), 372. However, I have been unable to locate this particular document. It

Turner described the achievements placed on the Duke's various houses, including 'Newcastle House, Clearmont House, Halland House and Bishopstone House'. He then reported how the funeral procession was followed by 'his Grace's tenants and principal inhabitants of East Hothly and Laughton', riding two by two, on horseback; presumably, he included himself among these loyal followers who accompanied the once-powerful Duke on his last journey.

Thus, Thomas Turner's world was surrounded with webs of political 'friendship'. Far from being an 'eighteenth-century non-entity' and a political 'nobody' - as J. B. Priestley described Turner in his introduction to the 1925 edition of diary extracts - we can now see that Turner was situated at the heart of a very active Whig constituency, and that he was clearly aware of its political connections of 'friends'.[95] As this chapter has shown, the powerful interest of the Duke of Newcastle bore on the life of a middling and provincial man such as Turner not only on important occasions, such as parliamentary elections, but also in everyday life. In Turner's locality, to use Wrightson's key phrase, 'the politics of the parish' was strongly linked to state politics.[96] Furthermore, politics was also important for a man such as Turner for both he, and many of his 'friends', belonged to the growing number of people of 'the middling sort', who cared about national, religious, and moral issues, who could read a growing number of widely circulated newspapers and other publications, who moved around, and who could engage in political discussions at venues such as coffee houses, public houses, societies, and clubs.[97] It is political life at this level that also was expressed increasingly from the middle decades of the eighteenth century in growing waves of activism, radicalism, patriotism, and populism.

Political life in a mid-eighteenth-century locality such as Turner's was therefore far from stagnant.[98] The engagement with politics on the part of middling men clearly also existed beyond the heightened scene of

may have been lost. I would like to take this opportunity to thank the archivists in East Sussex Record Office and the Librarians in Yale University Library who helped me in this search.

[95] Priestley, 'Introduction', in Turner, *Diary*, ed. Turner, p. vi.
[96] K. Wrightson, 'The politics of the parish in early modern England', in Griffiths, Fox, and Hindle (eds.), *The Experience of Authority*, pp. 10–46, and esp. pp. 25–31 on 'The politics of reformation and state formation'.
[97] See especially J. Brewer, 'Commercialization and politics', in McKendrick, Brewer, and Plumb (eds.), *The Birth of a Consumer Society*, pp. 197–262; Brewer, *Party Ideology and Popular Politics at the Accession of George III*.
[98] See also, for example, J. H. Plumb, 'Political man', in J. L. Clifford (ed.), *Man Versus Society in Eighteenth-Century Britain: Six Points of View* (Cambridge, 1968), pp. 1–21; Phillips, *Electoral Behaviour*; Colley, *In Defiance of Oligarchy*; O'Gorman, 'Electoral deference'; O'Gorman, *Voters, Patrons and Parties*; Langford, *Public Life and the Propertied Englishman*; Rogers, 'The middling sort in eighteenth-century politics'.

parliamentary elections, and beyond the boundaries of the electorate. But, however active this political scene was, it is important to realise that political brokerage in Turner's society was also negotiated along active networks of 'friendship'. It is at this point that the history of the family can help to illumine some of the key issues in mid-eighteenth-century political history. We have seen in the previous chapter that Turner was very circumspect in his use of the epithet 'friend'. He did not use the term lightly, and he knew well the difference between 'friends' and ordinary companions, acquaintances, and neighbours. But if there was a sense in which the term 'friend' acquired for Turner a sweeping meaning, it was the political sense. Political connections created in Thomas Turner's locality broad yet compelling interest groups of 'friends'. It was, more-over, difficult to escape from their grasp, for they were also closely interlinked with many other ties of kinship, affection, neighbourliness, and trade.

Political relationships, such as membership in the Duke of Newcastle's interest and the pleasure of his patronage, were thus negotiated and understood in terms of 'friendship'. Indeed, the language of 'friendship' served to introduce an element of sentiment and reciprocity into these patently unequal and utilitarian relationships. But the strands of 'friend-ship' spread both widely and deeply. By following connections of 'friendship', we can trace our way from the prime minister of England to Thomas Turner, and from him to a wide circle of 'friends', and even down to the level of the village poor. In all these ways – in forging both horizontal and vertical relationships, and indeed dynamic relationships – friendship was an essential component in forming the eighteenth-century social order.

7   Ideas about friendship and the constructions of friendship in literary texts

Introduction

The broad spectrum of 'friendship' relationships, which were seen in the previous chapters to have played such an important role in the life of an eighteenth-century individual such as Thomas Turner and in the lives of so many people around him, also played an important role in contemporary cultural production. There were novels, essays, sermons, and diverse other literary texts which were preoccupied with friendship both directly and indirectly. For instance, Elizabeth Singer Rowe's *Friendship in Death*, first published in 1728, was one of the most popular works in the eighteenth century, printed in twenty-six editions by 1790.[1] Sarah Fielding's *The Adventures of David Simple, Containing an Account of his Travels Through the Cities of London and Westminster in Search of a Real Friend*, first published in 1744, also continued to be reprinted until the end of the eighteenth century.[2] Other well-known works such *Joseph Andrews*,[3] *Peregrine Pickle*,[4] *Clarissa*,[5] or *The Vicar of Wakefield*[6] presented a range of friendship relationships, explored interactions among friends, praised good friendship – and condemned false and evil friends.

It is not surprising that such literary texts were preoccupied with the issue of friendship. As we have seen in the previous chapters, in seventeenth- and eighteenth-century England friendship encompassed a broad and extremely important spectrum of relationships, including kinship relationships, sociable relationships, occupational relationships, and even political connections and patronage. There can, therefore, be little wonder that literary works also dwelled upon such ties. A related reason why notions of 'friendship' attracted the attention of writers and thinkers in seventeenth- and eighteenth-century England, however, was that friend-

---

[1] Raven, *British Fiction*, p. 64.   [2] *Ibid.*, p. 90.
[3] H. Fielding, *Joseph Andrews* (1742), ed. R. F. Brissenden (Harmondsworth, 1978).
[4] Smollett, *Peregrine Pickle*.   [5] Richardson, *Clarissa*.
[6] O. Goldsmith, *The Vicar of Wakefield* (1766), ed. S. Coote (Harmondsworth, 1982).

ship was also perplexing, for it entailed a range of ideas that were so difficult to explain and prescribe in any consistent manner. By the seventeenth century, scholars who wished to write about friendship had to accommodate not only a broad and potentially conflicting range of friendship relationships that they could identify around them, but also a complex yet distinguished intellectual tradition of works on friendship. Three important landmarks also particularly worth noting in this context are Aristotle's threefold division of friendship into useful, pleasant, and virtuous friendship,[7] Cicero's *De Amicitia*,[8] and Christian notions of friendship as formulated most influentially by St Thomas Aquinas.[9] Whereas Aristotle defined perfect friendship as 'the friendship of those who are good, and similar in their goodness . . . For these people each alike wish good for the other *qua* good, and they are good in themselves',[10] and Cicero defined it as 'a complete sympathy in all matters of importance, plus goodwill and affection',[11] Aquinas saw clearly the tension between such exclusive sentiments, and Christian notions of universal charity. For the sake of God, he argued, a man should not limit his love to his friends, but love his neighbour and fellow-man. Furthermore, while Aquinas agreed that it is meritorious to love a friend, he contended that it is still more meritorious to love an enemy, for a friend is easily loved whereas an enemy is loved with labour, and a friend can be loved for himself whereas an enemy can only be loved for God's sake.[12]

Early modern thinkers, who did not wish to repudiate these Classical and Christian traditions, and who also wished to discuss friendship in a way that bore some relation to their familiar social reality had, therefore, to make great efforts to reconcile conflicting notions of friendship. How can friends be loved in a way that is both universally Christian and selective? And how can friendship be described as selective, while so many friendships are obviously predicated upon existing kinship relationships? How can friends be loved both for their virtue, and for their usefulness? And what happens if non-selected 'friends', such as parents, other patrons, or siblings, are useful but not virtuous? How can love between friends be mutual, while also being restricted by proper notions of deference and duty, as befits the ranks and degrees of the friends concerned? And can select friendship exist among women, or between

---

[7] Aristotle, *The Ethics of Aristotle*, trans. J. A. K. Thomson, revised trans. H. Tredennick (London, 1976), Book VIII, 1–13, and especially 3 and 4; Book IX, 3, 8.

[8] Marcus Tullius Cicero, 'On friendship', in *On Old Age and On Friendship*, trans. F. O. Copley (Ann Arbor, 1972).

[9] See especially St Thomas Aquinas, *Summa Theologiae*, vol. 34, trans. R. J. Batten (London, 1975), 2a 2ae Q. 23, 'The nature of charity', First Article; 2a 2ae Q. 25, 'The object of charity', First Article; 2a 2ae Q. 25, First, Fourth, Sixth and Eighth Article, etc.

[10] Aristotle, *Ethics*, trans. Thomson, Book VIII: 3, p. 263.

[11] Cicero, 'On friendship', VI 20, p. 54.   [12] Aquinas, *Summa Theologiae*, 2a 2ae Q. 25.

men and women, or can it exist only between men? And if the latter is the case, how, then, can friendship be described as Christian and universal?

When a seventeenth-century thinker such as Jeremy Taylor, for example, came to examine the idea of friendship, he had to turn his mind to questions such as these. His treatise, *The Measures and Offices of Friendship*, published in 1662, indeed presented an attempt to negotiate and accommodate contradictory notions of friendship.[13] The work of this leading churchman and casuistic thinker was influential in its time,[14] and it continued to be admired in the eighteenth century. Samuel Richardson, for example, was clearly familiar with Taylor's work, as his references to Taylor's treatises in his correspondence and in his novel *Clarissa* indicate.[15] More than a century later, George Eliot still says of her heroine, Dorothea Brooke, that she 'knew many passages' of Taylor 'by heart'.[16] It is therefore worth examining in some detail how a thinker such as Taylor negotiated different notions of 'friendship'. Having investigated ideas about friendship at this intellectual level, we shall next see how historical notions of friendship were employed in the construction of two popular eighteenth-century novels: Eliza Haywood's *The History of Miss Betsy Thoughtless* and Samuel Richardson's *Clarissa*.

The measures and offices of friendship

At the start of his treatise on *The Measures and Offices of Friendship* Jeremy Taylor presents a religious dilemma, emphasising the tension between universal charity and exclusive friendship: 'how far a Dear and a perfect friendship is authoriz'd by the principles of Christianity?'[17] Initially, his answer follows Aquinas's line. He asserts the universality of Christian charity,[18] and notes, moreover, that the word 'friendship' does not appear in the New Testament even once: this is seen as a possible indication that

[13] J. Taylor, *The Measures and Offices of Friendship* (1662), ed. Travis Du Priest, Scholars Facsimile and Reprints (New York, 1984). Taylor followed other Christian humanists, such as Bacon, Montaigne, and the author of *The Whole Duty of Man*, in combining classical and Christian traditions of friendship with views of the social world around him. He was also writing with particular reference to questions raised by Katherine Phillips: see Du Priest's 'Introduction' to Taylor, *Measures and Offices of Friendship*, pp. iii–xiv, and references there.

[14] In the seventeenth century the word 'casuistic' had not yet acquired its pejorative sense.

[15] See the references to Taylor: Richardson, *Clarissa*, pp. 1001–2, and note for L313 on p. 1521. This is a significant reference to Clarissa's rape, death, and funeral. Clarissa also meditates on Taylor's words in her distress. Additionally, Richardson mentioned Taylor in his correspondence. For a discussion of these and other references see T. Keymer, *Richardson's Clarissa and the Eighteenth-Century Reader* (Cambridge, 1992).

[16] George Eliot, *Middlemarch* (1871–2), ed. W. J. Harvey (Harmondsworth, 1994), p. 8.

[17] Taylor, *Measures and Offices of Friendship*, p. 7.

[18] E.g. 'Christian Charity is Friendship to all the world', *ibid.*, p. 10.

friendship was not among the imperatives of ancient Christianity.[19] But next Taylor presents a more modified view. 'Universal Friendship', he argues, 'must be *limited* because *we are so.*'[20] Using a metaphor drawn from a familiar contemporary reality, Taylor explains that when men contract friendship they 'inclose the Commons',[21] and limit to two or three friends that which originally has been intended for all, like the air, the rivers, and the strands of the seas. Though from a Christian point of view this limitation of charity is regrettable, it is in fact inevitable, and indeed natural.[22]

But although universal charity is restricted by human limitations, and thus turned into a lesser form of friendship, friendship remains, according to Taylor, a virtuous and noble sentiment. The great value that Taylor places on friendship is evident, for example, in his following description of its merits:

Friendship is the allay of our sorrows, the ease of our passions, the discharge of our oppressions, the sanctuary to our calamities, the counsellor of our doubts, the clarity of our minds, the emission of our thoughts, the exercise and improvement of what we meditate.[23]

While glorifying friendship, these words also highlight another modifying compromise that Taylor strives to present. Taylor's praises of friendship bind together the spiritual and the practical. Allaying sorrows, relieving doubts, discharging passions, etc., are 'measures and offices of friendship' which can be understood in both spiritual and practical terms. In other passages in his treatise Taylor expresses this view more explicitly. As opposed to Aristotle, who rates virtuous friendship as the most meritorious, pleasant friendship as second to it, and useful friendship as the most inferior, Taylor sees friendship as a unity of all three – merit, pleasure, and usefulness: 'that which in friendship is most *pleasing* and most *useful*, is also most *reasonable* and most *true*'.[24] Having claimed that, Taylor goes one step further and argues that usefulness is actually a test for proving merit: 'although I love my friend because he is worthy, yet he is not worthy if he can do no good'.[25] '[T]hose friendships must needs be most perfect, where the friends can be most useful.'[26]

Bearing in mind the social roles of friends in seventeenth- and eighteenth-century England, discussed in previous chapters,[27] one is able to

---

[19] *Ibid.*, pp. 7–8.   [20] *Ibid.*, p. 19. Italics in the original.   [21] *Ibid.*, p. 11.

[22] Relying on Cicero, Taylor observes that nature has also made friendships, societies, relations, and endearments. Christianity has indeed released humanity from the constraints of enclosed friendship, and has re-introduced the principle of universal charity; however, the implication of Taylor's argument remains that friendship, and hence the limitation of universal charity, are also in accord with nature: *ibid.*, pp. 10–12.

[23] *Ibid.*, p. 29.   [24] *Ibid.*, p. 6. Italics in the original.   [25] *Ibid.*, p. 29.   [26] *Ibid.*, p. 32.

[27] See above, chapters 4, 5, and 6.

understand the sort of meritorious utility that Jeremy Taylor had in mind. The 'friend' that Taylor depicts is not necessarily a person with whom one engages in abstract philosophical discussions,[28] nor is it necessarily a friend alongside whom one fights together on the battlefield, like many of the great friends in the Greek and Roman tradition. Nor is it a holy friend who lives ascetically for the love of God. Rather, this is a dependable friend who can give useful advice, who can support one's cause, who can be trusted in financial matters and offer financial assistance when necessary, who can serve as a trustee to one's children, and who can stand as a witness.[29] In short, Taylor's ideal friend is an active and useful individual, who performs many of the 'offices' that social historians of early modern England have identified while investigating wills, debt and credit relations, or litigation concerning marriage, separation, and divorce, and which we have also been able to trace in our study so far.

The good friend, according to Taylor, should thus be virtuous, wise, merciful, true and honest, open and ingenuous, however also tenacious of a secret. At the same time, this friend should be rich, and free with his money. Lastly, this friend should also be close at hand so that all these good things could be enjoyed.[30] There is no sense, says Taylor, in wasting 'the Bravery of friendship' on impertinent people who may only become burdens to their families.[31] Those who are neither virtuous nor useful are simply not fit to serve as friends: a fool cannot give good counsel, a beggar can give no relief, a pitiless person will not be sympathetic, a stranger cannot show the right conduct, a tattler cannot keep a secret, a covetous person cannot be trusted with a child's fortune, and a false person cannot be trusted as a witness.[32]

This takes us to the next point over which Taylor tries to offer yet another accommodating view, namely, the issue of choice. According to Taylor, the principle of choice is very important for contracting friendship: 'He is not my friend till I have chosen him, or loved him.'[33] Moreover, the most beloved, useful, and virtuous friends should only be chosen with great care. But how can that be reconciled with the familiar social reality, in which relatives, who usually cannot be chosen, serve so often as one's 'friends'? The answer at this point goes back to the nature of the sentiments of friendship, as well as to the somewhat contractual nature of friendship among kin. The most excellent, virtuous, and useful friendships, explains Taylor, are contracted by nature;[34] therefore, one will do well to choose as a friend a person whose friendship has already been naturally contracted: 'by nature such friendships are contracted,

---

[28] Indeed Taylor despises empty 'contemplation and noise' among friends: *Measures and Offices of Friendship*, p. 93.   [29] See especially *ibid.*, pp. 32–3.   [30] *Ibid.*, p. 33.
[31] *Ibid.*, p. 31.   [32] *Ibid.*, pp. 32–3.   [33] *Ibid.*, p. 35.   [34] *Ibid.*, pp. 62–3.

without which we cannot live, and be educated, or be well, or be at all'.[35] The greatest natural friendship is said to exist between parents and children.[36] Next to it is 'the society and dearnesse of Brothers and Sisters'.[37] Thus, in the case of the related 'friends', 'choice' can be exercised by means of confirmation, as a ratifying contract is made amongst those very persons whose friendship has been established by nature. Another way of exercising choice in the case of related friends is by elimination, namely, by avoiding (or indeed also possibly dissolving) a contract, and thus dismissing redundant kin from the circle of friends. For example, if a brother is 'a fool or a vitious person',[38] one can choose not to develop the existing relationship with him into friendship, and only to allow him the 'pity and fair provisions, and assistances' he deserves.[39] 'Negative choice' can also be the effect of physical distance and long separation. For example, Taylor explains that when parents and children live far apart, their love might dwindle, and their relationship might be supported by only 'fame and duty, by customes and religion', not by active friendship.[40] Thus, according to Taylor, both moral and practical considerations should guide individuals in 'choosing' their friends from amongst those natural friends whom they already have. This argument lends prescriptive justification to what was, as we have seen, a familiar reality, in which some of the most important friendships were among kin, but in which people were also selective in their relationships with kin.

Choice, according to Taylor, is exercised more decisively when friendship is formed entirely by contract. Taylor ranks the fully contractual friendship as second to natural friendship.[41] Its merits, however, can be equally high, and, in some senses, higher, because of the great importance of the marriage contract. The marriage contract unites virtue, usefulness and pleasure all at once. 'A Husband and Wife are the best friends',[42]

[35] *Ibid.*, p. 64.
[36] *Ibid.*, p. 64. 'In this scence, that of Parents and Children is the greatest, which indeed is begun in nature.'
[37] *Ibid.*, p. 68. Taylor's advice to prefer an old friend to a new might also be seen to apply primarily in the case of parents. Compare 'The duty and love to Parents must not yield to . . . any new friendships' (*ibid.*, p. 67) and 'When all things else are equal, preferre an old friend before a new', *ibid.*, p. 106, italics in the original.   [38] *Ibid.*, pp. 73–4.
[39] *Ibid.*, p. 74. Indeed, Taylor maintains that, all things being equal, a '*friend-Brother* is better than a *friend-stranger*'. However, he also notes that there are friends who are better than brothers, and he quotes the words of Solomon '*Better is a neighbour that is near, than a Brother that is far off*', Proverbs 27:10, Taylor, *Measures and Offices of Friendship*, pp. 70, 74–5. The italics in this note are in the original.
[40] See, for example, *ibid.*, pp. 65, 68ff.
[41] 'Some friendships are made by *nature*, some by *contract*, and some by *interest*, and some by *souls*. And in proportion to these wayes of Uniting, so the friendships are greater or less, vertuous or natural, profitable or holy, or all this together': *ibid.*, pp. 62–3. Italics in the original.   [42] *Ibid.*, p. 81.

affirms Taylor, and he quotes the words of the Scriptures: 'a man must leave father and mother, and cleave to his Wife'.[43] Indeed, marriage is such a high form of friendship that it serves as a paradigm for all friendships, which should all be '*Marriages* of the soul, and of fortunes and interests, and counsels'.[44]

... the marriage is the Queen of friendships, in which there is a communication of all that can be communicated by friendship: and it being made sacred by vows and love, by bodies and souls, by interest and custome, by religion and by laws, by common counsels and common fortunes; it is the principal in the kind of friendship, and the measure of all the rest.[45]

As can be understood from Taylor's depiction of friendship in marriage, he sees women as perfectly able to contract and maintain friendship relationships. Taylor indeed declares that he differs from those morose 'Cynics' who would not admit the female sex 'into the community of a noble friendship'.[46] In addition, Taylor rejects the argument that women cannot be friends because they are imperfect, for men are also imperfect, and friendship as a relationship is rooted in human imperfection.[47] Thus, Taylor argues that 'a woman can love as passionately, and converse as pleasantly, and retain a secret as faithfully, and be useful in her proper ministeries, and she can die for her friend as well as the bravest Roman Knight'.[48] In particular, Taylor asserts, 'Wives have been the best friends in the world.'[49] Nonetheless, Taylor has reservations about women's friendship. Women are not capable 'of all those excellencies by which men can oblige the world',[50] and therefore women's friendships do not always stand well the important test of usefulness: a woman is 'not so good a counsellor as a wise man, and cannot so well defend my honour; nor dispose of reliefs and assistances, if she be under the power of another'.[51] Thus, here, too, Taylor reaches a pragmatic compromise, '[a] man is the best friend in trouble, but a woman may be equal to him in the dayes of joy'.[52]

This takes us to the last point at which Taylor presents an accommodating view of friendship, namely, the issue of inequality among friends. According to Taylor, inequality among friends is certainly an impediment. For example, in the final section of his treatise concerning right conduct among friends, Taylor declares that if a person gives advice to a friend, this person should also give the friend freedom either to follow the advice, or not: 'He that gives advice to his friend, *& exacts obedience* to it,

[43] *Ibid.*, p. 82.   [44] *Ibid.*, p. 83. Italics in the original.   [45] *Ibid.*, p. 80.   [46] *Ibid.*, pp. 94–5.
[47] *Ibid.*, pp. 98–9.   [48] *Ibid.*, p. 96.   [49] *Ibid.*, p. 95.   [50] *Ibid.*, p. 96.
[51] The latter point applies especially to married women whose property rights are restricted by coverture: *ibid.*, p. 96.
[52] *Ibid.*, p. 97. See also p. 98: 'a woman can as well increase our comforts, but cannot so well lessen our sorrows'.

does not the kindness and ingenuity of a friend, but the office and pertnesse of a School-master.'[53] Inequality also forms an impediment in friendship among near relatives. Indeed, the main problem that Taylor identifies in the friendship between parents and children is that it is not equal, as 'there is too much authority on one side, and too much fear on the other, to make equal friendships'.[54] The lack of equality is especially problematic in the case of the relation between children and their parents, to the degree that that relation is described as 'not properly friendship, but gratitude and interest, and religion'; if that relationship becomes friendship, it is due to an exercise of choice, and as a result of the merit of the parties concerned and their spending time together in close association.[55] However, throughout his treatise, a degree of inequality among friends is also taken by Taylor for granted, if not seen as distinctly commendable. The ideal friend, who is rich, socially influential, and possibly financially supportive, can also be superior in terms of degree and rank. The noble friendship between a husband and his virtuous and obedient wife is inevitably unequal; so might be the friendship between an elder and younger brother. Taylor's advice about the right conduct among friends, in issues such as receiving and giving admonition and material gifts, also implies that at least some measure of inequality among friends is either taken by him for granted, or seen as meritorious.[56]

Thus, in all these ways, Jeremy Taylor tries to 'square the circle', or, perhaps, one should better say 'square the triangle', as his treatise strives to bring together three different conceptions of friendship: a Christian view of friendship, a classical view of friendship, and, last but not least, contemporary practices and norms of friendship, which Taylor was no doubt able to recognise in the social world around him. According to this compromise, friendship emerges as a relationship that exists among near relations, spouses, and very carefully selected non-related individuals. Its aims are 'charity in society', as well as 'material comforts & noble treatments and usages'.[57] This relationship is both natural and contractual, chosen and determined, equal and hierarchical. It is thoroughly practical, and unashamedly instrumental, whilst striving to satisfy principles of virtue and religion. Taylor's treatise, in which this modified view of friendship is presented, is a testimony to his eloquence: it requires great argumentative skills to bring together these conflicting views. It is important to realise, however, that it is only because we have been able to identify in previous chapters social practices and norms of friendship, current in seventeenth- and eighteenth-century England, and especially the close association between friendship, kinship, and patronage, that we

[53] *Ibid.*, pp. 104–5. Italics in the original.   [54] *Ibid.*, p. 66.   [55] *Ibid.*, p. 65.
[56] *Ibid.*, pp. 104–5, 107–8.   [57] *Ibid.*, p. 93.

could trace these notions in Jeremy Taylor's treatise. Without this social-historical notion of friendship, we would have seen only two sides of Taylor's triangle, and we would, therefore, hardly have been able to comprehend the full intellectual undertaking of his treatise.

The friends of Miss Betsy Thoughtless

Concepts of friendship continued to be manifested in eighteenth-century texts. In the remaining part of this chapter we shall investigate the ways in which concepts of friendship were manifested in eighteenth-century literary texts. We shall first examine a relatively simple case, Eliza Haywood's novel *The History of Miss Betsy Thoughtless*, in order to see how contemporary concepts of friendship were used in constructing the plot and characters of a popular mid-eighteenth-century novel. We shall then proceed to a more complex case, in which conflicting notions of friendship were the making of a tragedy, Samuel Richardson's *Clarissa*.

The History of Miss Betsy Thoughtless is a novel about conduct; it is therefore also inevitably a novel about 'friends'. Characters in this novel interact with 'friends', and their conduct is examined in the context of these interactions. At the first and most basic level, then, friendship relationships form an essential part of the social landscape of this novel. The main network of 'friends' can be traced around the heroine, Miss Betsy Thoughtless. This network includes a broad spectrum of 'friendship' relationships: friendship and patronage, kinship-based 'friendship', select 'friendship', sociable 'friendship', and even political 'friendship'. When her father dies, soon after the start of the novel, Betsy is placed under the care of 'friends': 'I have, indeed, no parent to direct, and but few *faithful friends* to guide me through the perplexing labyrinth of life', is how she describes her situation at one point.[58] Two of her most faithful 'friends', appointed as guardians by her dying father, are Sir Ralph Trusty, a near neighbour in the country, and Mr Goodman, a wealthy merchant in the city of London, 'both of them gentlemen of unquestionable integrity, and with whom he had preserved a *long and uninterrupted friendship*'.[59] Lady Trusty, Sir Ralph Trusty's wife, also numbers among Betsy's faithful friends. This 'most dear, and truly valuable *friend*', formerly a friend of Betsy's mother,[60] is regarded by Betsy as a 'second mother'.[61] Clearly all these 'friends' are senior to Betsy in terms of their

---

[58] Haywood, *Betsy Thoughtless*, p. 184.   [59] *Ibid.*, p. 9.

[60] 'There had been a great intimacy and *friendship* between her [Lady Trusty] and the mother of Miss Betsy', *ibid.*, pp. 11, 273.

[61] *Ibid.*, pp. 273, 491–2. Importantly, the wife of the other guardian, Mr Goodman, is not one of Betsy's loyal 'friends'.

age, their wealth, and their social standing. Furthermore, their 'friend-ship' towards her forms a continuation of previous friendships, contrac-ted with Betsy's parents. These trans-generational friendships provide both Betsy and the novel with a framework of social support and moral virtues. These 'friends' manage Betsy's fortune, take care to improve it, accommodate her in their houses, supervise (or at least try to supervise) the procedure of her courtships, and give her general advice and help. Even their reproofs are administered as '*marks of the friendship*'.[62] Betsy, in turn, acknowledges with gratitude their kind friendship and sincere care of her 'interests'. See, for example, the way in which she and her younger brother, who is also placed under the care of these 'friends', refer to the guardian Mr Goodman: 'the long experienced *friend* of our family',[63] 'so honest and worthy a *friend*',[64] 'a very dear *friend*',[65] 'so sincere and valuable a *friend*',[66] and 'so good a *friend*', etc.[67]

In addition, Betsy's main 'friends' include her nearest relations, her two brothers. For example, when her thoughtless behaviour brings shame upon her 'friends', her elder brother admonishes Betsy: 'O what eternal plagues . . . has the vanity of this girl brought upon *all her friends!*'[68] But although the brothers number among Betsy's 'friends', usages employed in describing their relationship also present their relation in a way that suggests a distinction between kinship and 'friendship'. For example, when Francis writes to Miss Betsy, he subscribes himself 'your very affectionate *friend, and brother*',[69] and Betsy signs 'being, my dear brother, by *friendship* as well as by *blood*, most affectionately yours'.[70] These usages reveal notions of friendship similar to those examined in Taylor's treatise: the friendship among these siblings is seen to be rooted in both nature, and choice, as it confirms existing ties of blood and natural affection. As Lady Trusty says when she encourages Betsy's visit to her brother, 'the natural affection between brothers and sisters could not be too much cultivated'.[71]

Miss Betsy's 'friends' also include select 'friends' and companions, from the virtuous Miss Mable to the promiscuous Miss Forward, whose relationships with Betsy are discussed below. Some of her relationships with former suitors also change from love to 'friendship'. For example, Mr Saving, a former lover, still has '*friendly regard*' to Miss Betsy's honour and peace.[72] In addition, Betsy has occasional sociable 'friends'. For

---

[62] *Ibid.*, p. 447.   [63] *Ibid.*, p. 97.   [64] *Ibid.*, p. 273.   [65] *Ibid.*, p. 302.
[66] *Ibid.*, p. 303.   [67] *Ibid.*, p. 308.   [68] *Ibid.*, p. 399.   [69] *Ibid.*, p. 177.
[70] *Ibid.*, p. 58, and see also 'natural affection' on pp. 40, 60, 312.
[71] *Ibid.*, p. 40. See also 'natural affection', on p. 312. Similar usages have been observed in Thomas Turner's diary.
[72] *Ibid.*, p. 167. His advice is said to be given 'not by a lover, but a friend', *ibid.*, p. 168. See also the case of the disappointed Mr Trueworth, *ibid.*, p. 283.

example, after a meeting with Mr Saving, she is said to visit a '*friend*': 'Miss Betsy, after having taken leave of Mr Saving, went to the apartment of *her friend*; where she staid supper.'[73]

The range of 'friendship' relationships, connected to Betsy, also includes political patronage. Betsy's husband, Mr Munden, has a distinguished 'friend' and patron, Lord ****, whom he regards as the '*best of friends*'.[74] He is said to have an 'interest' with this 'friend', and is dependent on him for the receipt of 'favour' or 'a gift', whose exact nature remains unknown but it is clear that it has financial value.[75] Lastly, Betsy also serves as a kind 'friend' and patron to others. She and her friend Miss Mable act as '*worthy friends*' towards the poor woman whom they employ for starching and making up their fine linen.[76] They stand as godmothers to this woman's daughter, and take care of her after her mother's death.

The heroine of this novel thus makes her way amidst a dense network of 'friendship' relationships. These are, as we can see, relationships whose meanings and aims can be well located in contemporary social and cultural contexts. Other characters in the novel also have 'friendship' networks. For example, a vital network of 'friends' is centred around Betsy's guardian, Mr Goodman. He is, of course, linked to Betsy's main network of 'friends': Betsy's father is described as his '*deceased friend*',[77] and he is also mentioned as a 'friend' of the fellow-guardian Sir Ralph Trusty.[78] In addition, however, Goodman has an independent network of 'friends', which includes a number of fellow-tradesmen and professional city men. This network of 'friends' shares some similar features with Thomas Turner's network of select 'friends', studied above. Both the fictional city merchant and the humble village shopkeeper have long-standing relationships with a circle of select and trusty business associates and personal companions, with whom they have many important exchanges.

Goodman's network of select 'friends', and the exchanges that take place with its members are in fact extremely important for the construction of this novel's characters and plot. Goodman's network of 'friends' serves as a reservoir of useful characters, who are incorporated into the plot in the course of the novel. Three suitors, whose relationships with Betsy supply the material for important episodes are introduced as either Goodman's 'friends', or as sons of his 'friends'. They include young Mr Saving and his father, young Mr Staple and his father, and Captain

---

[73] *Ibid.*, p. 173. This 'friend' is also mentioned on p. 168, where she is described as 'an acquaintance'. [74] *Ibid.*, p. 517. [75] *Ibid.*, pp. 499, 517–18.
[76] *Ibid.*, pp. 219–20. [77] *Ibid.*, p. 10. [78] *Ibid.*, p. 37.

Hysom.[79] Another character who makes his appearance from among Goodman's 'friends' is the post-office clerk, who intercepts Betsy's let-ters;[80] so does the trusty lawyer, described as Goodman's 'acquaintance of a long standing and a *very good friend*'.[81] Goodman's 'friends' thus appear in the novel performing many important tasks: they introduce characters to one another and initiate courtships, advise to end these courtships, dispose of characters by shipping them overseas, provide financial means, make legal arrangements, and so on. In short, they perform many of the deeds that both propel the plot, and provide it with a backdrop of plausible social, economic, and amicable interactions.

In addition, Goodman's 'friends' also supply the novel with an enduring framework of social relationships, including, indeed, financial relation-ships. A number of Goodman's 'friends' (as can also be seen in the above quoted examples) are mentioned explicitly as '*old* friends', or friends of '*long standing*'. These long-term friendships, tested by years of trust, form a background against which other, and more transient rela-tionships can appear and disappear. It is significant that these long-standing friendships are maintained by a character who is himself a paragon of kindness and honesty, as his name, 'Mr Goodman', testifies. Good and enduring inter-personal ties and fair-dealing are thus seen to correspond to broader notions of virtue and common well-being. Indeed, by the end of the novel, Goodman's friendships prove their lasting merit by becoming trans-generational. When Mr Goodman dies, his 'friend-ship' network is taken over by his heir, young Goodman, who continues to maintain the same circle of 'friends': Sir Ralph Trusty and his wife, the two Mr Thoughtlesses, the faithful lawyer, and others.[82] And when young Goodman finally succeeds to transport to Jamaica the evil Lady Mellasin and her daughter Flora, it is not only his own well-being that his 'friends' celebrate, but the country's well-being and the triumph of virtue: '*All Mr Goodman's friends* congratulated him on the service he had done his country, in ridding it of the three persons who . . . were capable of doing the greatest mischiefs to the more innocent and unwary.'[83]

Whilst serving all these important purposes and performing all these roles, Goodman and his network of 'friends' also serve to locate the novel in the bustling London scene. Wealthy merchants, lawyers, civil servants, and urban office-holders could have been identified by contemporary readers as part of the busy life of the metropolis, whether they had

---

[79] See young Saving, son of Alderman Saving, the '*old friend*': *ibid.*, pp. 27, 29; another suitor, Mr Staple, is also brought in as the son of a man with whom Goodman 'had lived in *a long friendship*': *ibid.*, p. 135; Captain Hysom is yet another suitor who is introduced to both Betsy and the plot as Mr Goodman's '*friend*': *ibid.*, pp. 106–10.

[80] *Ibid.*, p. 29.

[81] *Ibid.*, p. 236. He is also the man 'who had transacted all the business he [Mr Goodman] had'.   [82] *Ibid.*, pp. 475, 483, 486.   [83] *Ibid.*, p. 486.

personal experience of it or not. Goodman's network of select 'friends' and business companions could have also added to the novel's credibility, because readers may have been able to recognise the resemblance between this network and other 'friendship' networks, which they may have been able see around them, or even experience in their own lives. Readers such as Thomas Turner, or his wife, for example, could have probably recognised the familiar patterns of Goodman's 'friendship' relationships with little difficulty.

Characters in *The History of Miss Betsy Thoughtless* are thus surrounded by 'friendship' networks, and, in turn, these networks have an essential role in constructing the novel's characters and plot. In addition, notions of 'friendship' are also explored in this novel as an important theme. There are central episodes in the novel devoted explicitly to examining notions of friendship. Most importantly, Betsy's thoughtlessness causes constant friction between conflicting notions of friendship. She keeps company with 'giddy creatures', for whom she can have no real affection, and feels uninterested in the company of serious persons, whose virtue she loves and respects. Her most mistaken friendship is contracted with Miss Forward. An eighteenth-century reader of this novel could have probably identified the ominous nature of Miss Betsy and Miss Forward's friendship from its very beginning. The two become friends at boarding-school, away from parental care. There Miss Forward, true to her proverbial name, turns her younger friend into her confidant and accomplice in the secret of an 'amorous intrigue'.[84] When Betsy leaves school and goes to London, the relationship stops, but it is renewed when Miss Forward arrives in London and asks to see Miss Betsy. She is, by now, a desolate creature. Having given birth to an illegitimate child, who died soon after the birth, she is abandoned by her lover and banished forever from her father's favour. 'How sweet are the consolations of a sincere friend!', exclaims the narrator, when Miss Betsy arrives to comfort Miss Forward. From this point onwards, their relationship proceeds as a series of fiascos, which gives ample scope for demonstrating Miss Betsy's thoughtless conduct. She is not only careless enough about her own reputation to renew an acquaintance with a fallen woman, but she proceeds to accept uncritically Miss Forward's unlikely explanation that she is now maintained by a distant, and hitherto unknown 'kinsman' (as we have seen in a previous chapter, this opaque kinship term is very useful in this context for creating irony).[85] She then makes a public appearance alongside Miss Forward, sharing with her a box in the theatre, to the

---

[84] *Ibid.*, pp. 4–6. The implication is also that such relationships would have been more difficult to contract under parental care.

[85] See above, ch. 4, p. 129. Of course, he is no kinsman. Rather, he is a Jew, whose mistress she has become.

amazement and shock of the whole fashionable world. Subsequently, she accompanies her to a private dinner, in company with two strange men. On this occasion she makes the further mistake of staying out past midnight. When she foolishly agrees to ride home in a coach together with one of the strange men, instead of travelling home singly in a chair, she is nearly raped, because by that stage her companion has no reason to suspect that she, unlike Miss Forward, is not 'a woman of the town'.[86]

Throughout these episodes, the extent of Betsy's thoughtlessness is further aggravated by the fact that she rejects all warnings about Miss Forward's character, and the merit of her friendship with her. Most notably, Mr Trueworth advises Betsy that '*Friendships* begun in childhood . . . ought to be continued or broke off, according as the parties persevere in innocence, or degenerate into vice and infamy', and she scorns his advice.[87] Betsy's friendship with Miss Forward thus proceeds as a model of an inappropriate and badly conducted female friendship. Its only point of merit is that it proves Betsy to be genuinely virtuous. She is too innocent to recognise the full gravity of Miss Forward's situation, and she remains honest despite her corrupting influence. Her relationship with Miss Forward demonstrates her own loyalty and generosity. See, for example, her staunch, though misplaced, support of her friend as she refuses to hear what she believes is slanderous gossip against Miss Forward: 'I love Miss Forward, and neither know, nor will believe, any ill of her. Whenever I am convinced that she is unworthy *my of [sic] friendship*, it must be by her own actions, not by the report of others.'[88] Eventually, Betsy realises the mistaken nature of her friendship with Miss Forward. She acknowledges her own folly, and blames Miss Forward for misleading her: 'If you had retained the least spark of generosity or good-will towards me, you would rather have avoided than coveted my company.'[89] Poor Miss Forward now also changes her tone: 'I have long since rendered myself unworthy of your *friendship* – it is solely your compassion and charity that I now implore.'[90]

In contrast to this bad friendship, the friendship between Miss Betsy and Miss Mable presents a model of virtuous female friendship. When Betsy becomes a repentant and respectable married woman, she reaches the stage in her development at which she can partake in a virtuous friendship. Her renewed friendship with the worthy Miss Mable, now Lady Loveit, is described as a model of all that is good, as can be seen from the following quotation:

Mrs Munden was extremely rejoiced at the opportunity of renewing her acquaintance with this lady; . . . They had always loved each other – there was a great parity

---

[86] *Ibid.*, p. 210.   [87] *Ibid.*, p. 203.   [88] *Ibid.*, p. 203.   [89] *Ibid.*, p. 214.   [90] *Ibid.*, p. 442.

of sentiment and principle between them; and as nothing but their different ways of thinking, in point of conduct towards the men, had hindered them from becoming *inseparable friends*, that bar being removed by Mrs Munden's change of temper . . . no other remained to keep them from communicating their thoughts with the utmost freedom to each other.[91]

Conflicting notions of friendship are also examined with regard to political friendship. Lord ****, Mr Munden's 'best friend', takes advantage of Munden's dependency and tries to seduce his wife Betsy. This episode is constructed in the language of friendship, harping on the tensions between moral and instrumental friendship, and indeed also on the wide currency of political friendship, as investigated in the previous chapter. When Betsy is assaulted by Lord ****, she resists by pointing out to him the discrepancy between his declared 'friendship' to her husband, and his behaviour towards her: 'this is not language with which the wife of him you are pleased to call *your friend* could expect to be entertained', she says.[92] The lord's reply removes all pretences to virtue from this instrumental 'friendship': 'ought *my friendship* for the husband to render me insensible to the beauties of the wife? . . . be assured, my angel, that in blessing me you fix the happiness of your husband, and establish his future fortune in the world'. He assures Betsy that 'some husbands, and those of the first rank, too' have 'consented to the complaisance of their wives in this point' in order '*to oblige a friend*'.[93] When Mr Munden is told of the affair, he refuses to believe his wife: 'I am certain my lord has too much *friendship* for me to offer any rudeness to you', he says.[94] But Betsy answers poignantly in words that question both the virtue and the instrumentality of this 'friendship': 'Be not too certain . . . of the *friendship* of that base great man.'[95]

When one examines the novel's interaction, however, it appears that the point at which 'friends' become most active is in matters concerning courtship and marriage. Like present-day historians, who emphasise the importance of the 'multilateral consent' of 'friends' in spouse-selection, so this novel asserts that proper courtship can only be conducted with the knowledge and consent of '*friends on both sides*'.[96] A model courtship, in which a worthy gentleman and a young and virtuous gentlewoman make their way towards a happy marriage under the guidance of 'friends', can be found in a nutshell in the case of Miss Harriot and Mr Trueworth. Mr Trueworth becomes acquainted with the lovely Miss Harriot through Sir

[91] *Ibid.*, p. 525. [92] *Ibid.*, p. 511. [93] *Ibid.*, p. 511. [94] *Ibid.*, p. 517.
[95] *Ibid.*, p. 517.
[96] See Ingram, *Church Courts, Sex and Marriage*, pp. 134–42, and esp. p. 142; Wrightson, 'The family in early modern England', pp. 16–17. See also 'the treaty [had] been concluded after all was agreed upon by *the friends on both sides*', Richardson, *Pamela*, ed. Sabor, p. 488.

Bazil, Harriot's elder brother and his own 'old friend'. Sir Bazil is well acquainted with the great advantages of Trueworth's 'family and fortune'. Once he learns from Trueworth of his sentiments towards his sister, he takes it upon himself to promote the match.[97] He acts as a double 'friend' to both his sister and his friend and takes the matter further to his married sister. She is also convinced by the great advantages of the alliance, and she proceeds to persuade Miss Harriot to accept it.[98] Harriot has full confidence in the sincerity of these two 'friends' and their assiduous care for her 'interest and happiness'. A modest and virtuous young woman, she allows herself to be guided by them. The following lines present a model scene of female consent to marriage, as well as submission to 'friends'. Miss Harriot remains silent for a considerable time, but at last she replies, 'in a low and hesitating voice, that she would be guided by her *friends*, who, she was perfectly convinced, had her interest at heart, and knew much better than herself what conduct she ought to observe'.[99]

At this critical moment, Harriot expresses her consent by declaring her submission to her 'friends'. A similar formulaic form of acceptance has been noted by social historians, investigating legal cases concerning marriage.[100] Only later does the reader learn that 'it was with pleasure' that Harriot has yielded to 'the persuasions of her *friends*' in favour of Trueworth's love.[101] Modesty prevents her from owning her sentiments openly until the actual marriage is near. This perfect courtship then leads to a perfect marriage, in which 'two persons of virtue, honour, and good sense', are 'by love and law united', 'bound by duty and inclination to promote each other's happiness'.[102]

Many episodes in *The History of Miss Betsy Thoughtless* should be understood with this model courtship in mind, and many twists in the plot occur when the correct procedure is not maintained. Things go wrong, for example, when different 'friends' intercede at the same time to introduce different suitors to the same woman. For example, while her brother Francis engages Betsy to be courted by one man, her guardian Mr Goodman gives permission for courtship to another.[103] Contrary to the

---

[97] *Betsy Thoughtless*, p. 333.
[98] When Harriot makes some faint protest, she explains to her that 'she might, perhaps, never have so good an offer, and could not possibly have a better; therefore advised her not to slip the present opportunity': *ibid.*, p. 340.   [99] *Ibid.*
[100] O'Hara, 'Ruled by my friends'.   [101] *Betsy Thoughtless*, p. 369.   [102] *Ibid.*, p. 344.
[103] This is Mr Staple, the son of his old friend. As soon as Goodman realises the situation, he tries to dissuade Staple from courting Betsy, but he intervenes too late: see, e.g., *ibid.*, pp. 153–5. The man introduced by Francis Thoughtless is Mr Trueworth. This relationship takes place before Trueworth meets and marries Miss Harriot, and it ends in heartbreak. Structurally, however, it is remarkably similar to Trueworth and Harriot's courtship. Francis introduces Betsy to his 'worthy friend' Trueworth, and after spending

rules of good conduct, Betsy encourages both. In the end, she also loses both, but not before she damages her reputation, embarrasses her 'friends', and causes her two suitors to risk their lives in a duel. The dangers are greater when the proper procedure is not maintained because the 'friends' fail to investigate the suitability of prospective partners, or because they neglect to keep an open eye on the courtship's development. The peril is greatest, however, if the courtship procedure is mediated by a false 'friend'. The most wrongly conducted courtship takes place in this novel when Betsy is introduced to a prospective suitor not by a trusty 'friend', but by her mantua-maker (dressmaker). This mediating 'friend', ominously called 'Mrs Modely', introduces Betsy to a man who bears the name of 'Sir Frederick Fineer'. When she introduces Sir Frederick, Modely actually uses the correct formulae of reference: she assures Betsy, as if on the basis of her personal knowledge, that Sir Frederick comes of an ancient county family and has 'a great estate in possession, and another in reversion'. She then adds that he is next in kin to a coronet, and keeps company with nothing but lords and dukes.[104] Betsy is foolish enough to accept this inflated description; nor does she suspect Sir Frederick's ludicrous letters. Following her brother's all-too-brief and superficial inquiry, she protests that Sir Frederick has been introduced to her by a person who is well familiar with his excellent circumstances. But Sir Frederick is really an outcast servant. Knowing Betsy is an orphan, he tries to make his fortune by trapping her into marriage. Although she happily encourages the courtship, Betsy is not so careless as to dispose of herself in marriage without the approbation of 'friends'. When the false Sir Frederick presses her to marry him, she refers him to her brothers. The impostor is startled to hear that Betsy has brothers,[105] and he tries to lure her into a romantic scheme:[106] 'I made a vow', he says, 'never to marry any woman, how dear soever she might be to me, that would not assure me of her love, by flying privately with me to the altar, *without consulting friends*, or asking advice but her own soft desires.' 'Let us haste, then, to tie the blissful knot, and surprize *our friends* with a marriage they

some time with Betsy in company Trueworth duly falls in love with her. When he confesses his love, Francis decides to forward the match: *ibid.*, pp. 118, 123, 154. He takes matters further and appeals to other senior 'friends', Mr Goodman, in whose house Betsy lives, and the guardian's wife Lady Trusty, and he asks them, too, to espouse the cause of Mr Trueworth: *ibid.*, p. 260. This, for example, is how he writes to Mr Goodman. After listing Trueworth's merits, and assuring the guardian of his wealth, descent, and honourable intentions, he concludes: 'I therefore entreat you, Sir, as the long experienced *friend* of our family, to forward this match, both by your advice, and whatever else is in your power', *ibid.*, p. 97.   [104] *Ibid.*, p. 291.   [105] *Ibid.*, p. 356.

[106] *Ibid.*, pp. 375–6. He explains to her that it is only because of 'sordid interest' and 'the persuasion of friends' that 'so many jarring pairs' are 'united in the sacred yoke of matrimony'.

little dreamt of.'[107] This extreme speech in defiance of 'friends' and in favour of clandestine marriage finally arouses Betsy's suspicion, and she writes a letter to Mrs Modely asking her to inform Sir Frederick that she will not engage in any clandestine correspondence with him. The next development occurs when Mrs Modely hurries to Betsy and asks her to come and see Sir Frederick, who is lying on his deathbed and only wants to marry Betsy and leave her his fortune before he breathes his last breath. A surgeon and a parson hasten Betsy to pronounce the marriage vows, at which point Sir Frederick leaps out of bed, perfectly healthy, and embraces his new wife. On the verge of utter ruin, Betsy is rescued by Mr Trueworth, who bursts open the door with his sword drawn in his hand.[108]

These dramatic events illustrate vividly the importance of trusty 'friends' for maintaining the right conduct of courtship and marriage. Had Betsy and her 'friends' followed the correct procedure, many of these fateful events would not have happened. Betsy would have allowed herself to be guided only by the advice of real 'friends', and would not have engaged in a private correspondence with a strange man, whereas the 'friends' would have taken better care in inquiring after her suitors and observing their courtships of her. This episode also warns young women against the great danger that might await them from fortune-hunters. This danger, it seems, is seen to be particularly great in London. In the big capital, in which there are so many people, many of them migrants, recently arrived from many different places, one is all the more dependent upon 'friends' to verify who is true and who is false. In view of the demographic history of migration to London, this literary depiction makes sense. One in six individuals at that time, as Wrigley has established, had personal experience of life in the metropolis at some point in his or her life.[109] As Brodsky Elliot has found out, young women who came to London as migrants also experienced greater difficulties in finding suitable husbands, compared to those native London girls who enjoyed the support of a local network of relatives and friends; as a rule, the latter tended to marry at a considerably younger age than the newcomers.[110] Stories about fortune-hunters, heiress snatchers, clandestine marriages, and similar such scandals were also common in the contemporary press. It is therefore not surprising that this novel relates to such phenomena, and it is significant that it presents the reliance on trusty 'friends' as the formula for safe conduct in metropolitan life.

The mediating role of 'friends' in matters of courtship and marriage is

---

[107] *Ibid.*, p. 376.   [108] *Ibid.*, pp. 388–92.
[109] Wrigley, 'A simple model of London's importance', 49.
[110] Brodsky Elliot, 'Single women in the London marriage market'.

seen as so important that characters can be presented as having 'friends' even if these 'friends' actually remain invisible. For example, when a young linen draper wishes to marry Miss Flora, it is said that 'he got *a friend* to intercede with Lady Mellasin [Flora's mother] for leave to pay his respects to her daughter'.[111] This 'friend's' identity remains unknown. But the fact that this 'friend' is mentioned nonetheless, as a trusty mediator, serves as a proof of the young man's respectability and serious intentions. The opacity of the term 'friend', examined above in our discussion of the language of kinship, allows for this usage, as it enables a character to be simply referred to as a 'friend' without disclosing any further details about him or her. The most interesting case of invisible 'friends' can be found in the context of one of the major characters of the novel, Mr Trueworth. Mr Trueworth is presented as having a network of supporting 'friends', and they are invoked at two crucial points: when he initiates his courtship with Betsy, and when he decides to end it.[112] But if one examines the novel closely, it remains unclear who these 'friends' of Trueworth might be. The reader is told at some point that Trueworth has an aunt, who is his only relation in London. After he separates from Betsy, he also meets his old friend Sir Bazil and renews his friendship with him. But during his affair with Betsy, no 'friends' of his are actually mentioned. Furthermore, to the extent that his kin are referred to in the novel, the implication seems to be that Trueworth is remarkably independent. Although he is said to be a descendant of an ancient family, his ownership of a large estate suggests that his father, at least, is no longer alive.[113] The advantage of his having a small universe of kin is also intimated when it is said that he is unencumbered with 'poor relations', and it is further suggested by the fact that he is said to have no debts and mortgages, which to a contemporary reader might indicate that he has no younger siblings or family widows for whom to provide.[114] Thus, Trueworth is presented as a free agent, blissfully independent of imposing 'friends'. The way in which his anonymous 'friends' are nonetheless

---

[111] *Betsy Thoughtless*, p. 157.

[112] When he first wishes to court Miss Betsy, he declares his serious intentions by invoking his 'friends': 'my friends have, for these six months past, been teazing me to think of marriage, and several proposals have been made to me on that score; but never till I saw the amiable Miss Betsy, did I behold the face for whom I would exchange my liberty', he says to Betsy's brother: *ibid.*, p. 63. When he is bitterly disappointed by Betsy and decides to 'break his acquaintance' with her, his 'friends' surface once again, support his decision and offer him consolation and advice. He decides to return to the country and bids his '*friends*' goodbye: *ibid.*, p. 256. However his friends, some of whom had entertained severe doubts as to Betsy's reputation, console him, and persuade him to stay and enjoy the pleasures of the town: *ibid.*, p. 283, see also p. 276.

[113] See the discussion in chapter 3 above on Trueworth's 'family' and lineage: pp. 93–5.

[114] *Betsy Thoughtless*, p. 64.

invoked at the crucial points in his courtship shows that what is more important than the details about these 'friends' is the assurance of their existence and support. A good character such as Trueworth is assumed to be backed by a phalanx of trusty 'friends', even if they themselves remain largely invisible.

Following the same logic, few situations in this novel are presented as more grim than being left entirely 'friendless'; this is all the more the case for a poor young woman in the city of London. The story of Miss Forward provides a sad example of what might happen to a young woman, who has lost her virtue and has therefore also been banished by her 'friends'. Indeed, Miss Forward has relatives and potential 'friends' living: she has a father, a stepmother, and one aunt, who are mentioned in the novel. But they refuse to help her, and therefore, to all intents and purposes, she is '*friendless*'. The main road open before her leads to prostitution. The topos of the friendless young woman is indeed a familiar one in eighteenth-century literature. Samuel Richardson's Pamela, for example, dreads the prospect of becoming 'friendless'.[115] Conversely, Fanny Hill starts her downfall as a 'friendless' woman in London.[116]

When Betsy's marriage is finally contracted, her whole network of 'friends' is put into action. After Betsy exposes herself to so many risks, and tests the patience of her 'friends' in so many ways, they have no choice but to try to secure her honour in marriage. The wheels are set in motion when Mr Munden arrives on the scene. Once the 'friends' gather forces to sanction and promote his courtship, affairs soon reach a point where it is very hard to retract with honour.[117] Despite Betsy's delaying tactics, all her 'friends' act together to seal the match.[118] The repeated phrase in this context, '*all her friends*',[119] emphasises the unanimity and pressure of the whole 'friends' network. Betsy has no choice but to accept. Note the similarities between the scene of her acceptance, quoted below, and Harriot's acceptance, quoted above. Betsy, too, expresses her consent by making the formulaic declaration of submission to '*friends*'.

---

[115] See Tadmor, '"Family" and "friend" in *Pamela*', p. 300.
[116] 'I was now left an unhappy friendless orphan'; 'Left thus alone, absolutely destitute and friendless': J. Cleland, *Memoirs of A Woman of Pleasure* (1748–9; first legal edn, 1963), ed. P. Sabor (Oxford, 1985), pp. 2, 5.
[117] See above, p. 97, on how Betsy realises that she has come to the point at which she must marry 'any man that was of a good family and had an estate': *Betsy Thoughtless*, p. 383. The point of no return arrives when Mr Munden's financial circumstances are investigated by Betsy's brother, and found satisfactory.
[118] As Betsy understands that she has 'gone too far with Mr Munden to be able to go back with honour', she tries to play for time. Her delaying technique consists of trying to obtain as 'multilateral' a consent as possible. She now wishes to have '*the approbation of as many of my friends as possible* in a thing of so much consequence to my future peace', as she explains. See *ibid.*, p. 425; see also p. 447.   [119] *Ibid.*, pp. 451, 456, 457.

'You will marry him, then?' . . . 'Yes . . . ' answered Miss Betsy; and added, though not without some hesitation, 'Since my marriage is a thing so much desired by those to whose will I shall always be ready to submit . . . ' She said no more, but hung down her head.[120]

This formula in which young women express their consent to marriage by declaring their willingness 'to be guided by their friends' is more than just a ritualised form of acceptance, however; it is also the undertaking of a mutual obligation. As the woman obliges her 'friends' by placing herself under their guidance, so should they remain obliged to her, and give her their guidance and assistance if the marriage fails. Indeed, kin and 'friends' were very active in cases of marital breakdown, and without the protection and assistance of 'friends' it was virtually impossible at that time for a woman to make legal arrangements for separation and divorce.[121] Thus, the last point at which Betsy's network of 'friends' is activated to its full capacity is when her marriage breaks down. Throughout the collapse of her marriage, Betsy's conduct is carefully constructed to present her and her decisions in as justified a light as possible. For example, she demonstrates not only her regard for her husband's honour, but also her prudent management of the household accounts.[122] Her reformed behaviour as a wife is presented, in other words, as beyond reproach. Nor does she despair of her marriage without an active attempt to save it. When Betsy's relationship with her husband reaches crisis point, she turns to her former guardian, who suggests that Betsy's *'friends* should take upon them to interpose in the affair'.[123] A reconciliation is obtained, but unfortunately it does not last long. When Mr Munden brings home his French mistress, to live under the same roof with his wife, she has sufficient ground for leaving him. Before she takes any fatal steps, however, she secures the support of her 'friends':

She would not . . . do anything precipitately; it was not sufficient, she thought, that she should be justified to herself, she was willing also to be justified in the opinion of *her friends*:[124]

Betsy is assured of the continuing *'friendship and protection'* of her 'friends', especially her elder brother, who agrees to take her into his

---

[120] *Ibid.*, p. 447. Her guardian's wife, Lady Trusty, further tries to assure Betsy: 'I flatter Myself [Mr Munden] has every qualification to make you happy, and to shew that your *friends*, in advising you to marry him, have not misled your choice': *ibid.*, pp. 457–8.
[121] Stone, *Road to Divorce*.
[122] The narrator takes care to assure the reader that Mr Munden 'had, indeed, a treasure in her beyond what he could ever have imagined, or *her friends*, from her former behaviour, had any reason to have expected': *Betsy Thoughtless*, p. 461. Compare, for example, Turner's formulaic depiction of his wife as a 'treasure', above, ch. 5, pp. 192–3, 195.
[123] *Ibid.*, pp. 474–5.   [124] *Ibid.*, p. 552.

house and 'family'.[125] Taking with her no more than a few personal belongings (so that she could not be blamed for stealing her husband's goods), she escapes to her brother's, leaving her husband the following note:

> [I] fly for ever from your ill-usage, and once more put myself under *the protection of my friends*, to whom I also shall commit the care of settling with you the terms of your separation.[126]

Removing herself from her husband's care and placing herself under the 'protection' of her 'friends' is in fact the only transitional step that Betsy performs as her own agent. From this point onwards, her 'friends' take up her cause.[127] Mr Munden does not agree to a legal separation, but fortunately he dies before causing much further damage. He leaves Betsy a well-provided widow. Not long passes before Betsy is able to be reunited with her old suitor, Mr Trueworth, who by now has also become a young widower.

'Friendship' relationships are thus explored in *The History of Miss Betsy Thoughtless* both implicitly and explicitly. As we have seen, this novel includes developed 'friendship' networks and many 'friendship' relationships, which are essential in the construction of the novel's characters and plot. In addition, friendship is examined in this novel as an important theme. *The History of Miss Betsy Thoughtless* is a novel about conduct, and in this context the heroine's relationships with 'friends' are especially important. The first and longest part of the novel deals with Betsy's thoughtless conduct. This faulty conduct is demonstrated by her association with bad 'friends', her rejection of good 'friends', and the many aggravations that she causes to her related and senior 'friends'. The latter are thus led to orchestrate her marriage to Mr Munden. Betsy's marriage is personally unhappy but socially correct. It thus gives scope for Betsy to demonstrate her good conduct as a wife and as a housekeeper. By this stage she also becomes better integrated within her network of 'friends', and when her marriage breaks down she enjoys their well-earned support. Finally, in her last phase, Betsy's moral reformation is both demonstrated and rewarded by a triumph of love and friendship. She is reunited with Mr Trueworth in a marriage based on friendship and love, gratitude and esteem.[128] Moreover, she and Mr

---

[125] '[he] had approved her conduct in regard to her unfaithful husband – had assured her of the continuance of his *friendship and protection*': *ibid.*, p. 556, and see also p. 562. See also above, pp. 48–51.   [126] *Ibid.*, p. 556.

[127] See, for example, *ibid.*, pp. 556, 557, 562, 565.

[128] See expressions in *ibid.*, pp. 410, 568, 574. See also Lady Trusty's words: 'there is more true felicity in the sincere and tender friendship of one man of honour, than in all the flattering pretensions of a thousand coxcombs', *ibid.*, p. 179, and compare p. 249.

Trueworth together reproduce a new and durable trans-generational 'friendship' network. Remember that during the bulk of the novel Betsy's main 'friends' are not chosen by her, but assigned to her by her parents, whether as guardians or as kin. But the multiple 'friendship' ties between Betsy and Mr Trueworth, and their 'worthy friends' Sir Bazil and Lady Loveit, resemble those contracted in the previous generation between Betsy's parents and Sir Ralph and Lady Trusty. These selective, affective, sociable, but also extremely useful relationships finally confirm Betsy's integration into her society, and ensure the future continuation of harmony and good order.

This broad scope of 'friendship' relationships, the numerous roles of 'friends', and the multiple meanings of interactions among 'friends' – all these could not have been identified, let alone investigated, without reading this text against the history of its time. It is only through a historical reading that we, as later scholars, are able to reconstruct concepts which to contemporary readers would have been self-evident. For example, the roles of 'friends' as guardians and trustees, the important mediation of 'friends' in matters of courtship and marriage, or the prescriptive duty to obtain their blessing and consent were basic concepts, which were a part of an eighteenth-century reader's frame of reference. These concepts were embedded in the social vocabulary of the time. They were articulated among the members of a contemporary 'language community', as discussed in previous chapters in this book, and they were manifested and explored in contemporary texts. Bearing all this in mind, let us turn to *Clarissa*.

Who are Clarissa's friends?

When a present-day reader of *Clarissa* is faced with the question, 'who are Clarissa's friends?', the first name that comes to mind is that of Clarissa's intimate friend, Anna Howe. Clarissa's friendship with Anna Howe has indeed received the attention of literary scholars, as a devoted and sentimental friendship between two women. This, for example, is how it is discussed sensitively by Janet Todd.[129] But if one takes further account of historical notions of friendship, such as instrumental 'friendship' and 'friendship' among kin, which, as we have seen, were manifested so strongly in the language and culture of the time, a different view can be suggested. As the present analysis attempts to show, Clarissa's 'friends' include first and foremost her near relations: her father and mother, her brother and sister, her uncles, aunt, and cousins. The identity of these

---

[129] Todd, *Women's Friendship in Literature*, pp. 9–68. For a discussion of male friendship, see Robinson, 'Unravelling the "cord which ties good men to good men"', pp. 167–87.

characters as 'friends', and their conduct as 'friends', underlie the dynamics of many important interactions in the novel. Moreover, it is only in relation to this type of kinship-based 'friendship' that the significance of Clarissa's changing relationship with her select friends, and most importantly with Anna Howe, can be fully understood.

The identity of Clarissa's relations as her 'friends' is expressed in the language of the novel. At times they are referred to as her 'best' or 'natural' friends,[130] and most frequently they are simply referred to as her 'friends'.[131] See, for example, the following account of a meeting of Clarissa's 'friends', and the plans suggested for their future assembly:

My aunt . . . has just left me. She came to tell me the result of *my friends'* deliberations about me. It is this.

Next Wednesday morning they are all to be assembled: to wit, my father, mother, my uncles, herself, and my uncle Hervey; my brother and sister of course; my good Mrs Norton is likewise to be admitted.[132]

It is clear from this example that Clarissa's nearest kin – her parents, siblings, uncles, and aunt – are numbered among her 'friends'. The only non-related individual who is admitted to this gathering of 'friends' is the gentlewoman Mrs Norton, Clarissa's old and beloved nurse.[133] All these 'friends' are also senior to Clarissa in terms of their age and their familial status. Clarissa's circle of 'friends' thus also consists of those persons to whom she, as a daughter and a young woman, owes duty, obedience, and respect. The following quotations proceed to present a brief but typical selection, to prove further the wide currency of the term 'friend' in the novel as referring to Clarissa's kin.

my friends (my papa and uncles, however, if not my brother and sister) begin to think that I have been treated unkindly.[134]

your brother has a *view* in discrediting you with *all your friends*, with your uncles in particular.[135]

the gentle treatment of *all my friends*, my mamma's particularly.[136]

all my friends are below . . . There are two doors to *my* parlour . . . As I entered at one, *my friends* hurried out at the other. I saw just the gown of my sister, the last who slid away. My uncle Antony went out with them.[137]

---

[130] See, e.g., *Clarissa*, pp. 939, 1413.
[131] The term 'relation' is often mentioned in this novel in similar ways, including usages such as 'principal relations' and 'near relations'.
[132] Clarissa Harlowe to Anna Howe: *ibid.*, p. 346.
[133] Another non-related person is Dr Lewin, who remains 'at hand' to conduct the marriage ceremony. Dr Lewin is described as 'a divine of great piety and learning, to whom Miss Clarissa Harlowe owed much of her improvement': *ibid.*, 'The principal characters', p. 38.   [134] Clarissa Harlowe to Anna Howe: *ibid.*, p. 55.
[135] *Ibid.*, p. 180. Italics for 'view' in the original.   [136] *Ibid.*, p. 192
[137] *Ibid.*, pp. 302–3. Italics for 'All' and 'my' in the original.

But, in the troubled world of *Clarissa*, friendship does not follow its proper course. Contemporary norms, which prescribe the correct conduct among 'friends', as analysed above, are clearly evident in *Clarissa* as well. But unfortunately these norms are not maintained: rather, they serve as a yardstick for gauging the failure of Clarissa's 'friends'. Two important processes unfold in the course of this tragedy. The first is the betrayal of friendship. The second, which follows from it, is the dislocation of friendship. Though it is impossible in this context to offer a comprehensive discussion of these processes, it is possible to outline them. The betrayal of friendship starts from the very beginning of the novel, when Clarissa's relations betray her by failing to act as her trustworthy 'friends'. Following the conventional pattern, they act as intermediaries in arranging her courtship and marriage. But they betray their cause by procuring for her two unsuitable suitors, Mr Lovelace, and Mr Solmes. Mr Lovelace presents a splendid match in terms of his birth, his wealth, and his personal accomplishments; not, however, in terms of his 'character', for he is an infamous libertine. The 'friends' should have been more wary of him as a match for any virtuous young woman, let alone the devout Clarissa.[138] In offering him as a suitor to Clarissa, they thus show their reasonable desire to promote the rank and wealth of a daughter of the family, but also their own undue regard for important considerations of religion and merit. After a conflict with Clarissa's brother, the 'friends' withdraw their approbation of Mr Lovelace and 'espouse the cause' of Mr Solmes. Mr Solmes is suitably wealthy, and he also has the advantage of being a near neighbour in the country. Though his ancestry is not very impressive, he is nonetheless not a total 'upstart', as the angry Clarissa claims.[139] But Mr Solmes's repulsive appearance offers a poor match for

[138] Mr Lovelace first enters the scene as a suitor to Clarissa's elder sister Arabella, but as he discovers his preference for Clarissa he is allowed to court her.

[139] He comes from a lesser branch of a local gentry family, and he has been brought up as the heir to his wealthy though uncouth uncle, Sir Oliver. He has been chosen by his uncle Sir Oliver in preference to other relations with an equal claim to Sir Oliver's favour. For Mr Solmes and his social status, see *ibid.*, pp. 81, 101, 153, 156, 224. Clarissa's family background is often underestimated, and thought of mistakenly as 'bourgeois'. But although the proud Lovelace says that Harlowe Place, like Versailles, has 'sprung up from a dunghill within every elderly person's remembrance' (*ibid.*, p. 161), his derogation does not amount to a reliable social description. Clarissa believes her family is 'no inconsiderable or upstart one' (*ibid.*, p. 77), and she is right. On her father's side, Clarissa has behind her at least four or five generations of landed wealth. Clarissa's grandfather has already been in possession of a substantial landed estate, as well as a collection of family pictures and plate 'of two-three generations standing' (p. 194). On her mother's side, Clarissa is a descendant of the aristocracy: her mother is a noblewoman born, the heiress of a viscount (*ibid.*, p. 132). From the point of view of status, therefore, Solmes is not entirely unworthy of Clarissa, although she could have expected a more illustrious match. See also Tadmor, 'Dimensions of inequality among siblings in eighteenth-century novels', esp. p. 317 and notes there.

the young and beautiful Clarissa. Most importantly, Solmes is patently inferior to Clarissa in terms of his 'breeding' and moral sentiments. In addition, he also has an ulterior motive for wishing to marry Clarissa: her independent landed estate, bequeathed to her by her grandfather, which is conveniently situated between two of his own estates and, if united, would greatly increase their value.[140] The 'friends' should have known that a coarse and avaricious country gentleman such as Mr Solmes would never make a suitable husband whom Clarissa could respect. Thus, in his case, too, they err in their judgement. 'It is very unhappy, my dear, since *your friends* will have you marry, that such a merit as yours should be addressed by a succession of worthless creatures', says Anna Howe to Clarissa. 'That these presumers appear not in this very unworthy light to some of *your friends* is because their defects are not so striking to them as to others', she explains.[141]

Having offered these inappropriate suitors to Clarissa, the 'friends' proceed to negotiate the terms of her marriage to Mr Solmes with a view to their own best interests, rather than to Clarissa's. Different 'friends' have different selfish considerations. For example, Clarissa's brother, James Harlowe Junior, hopes to recover by this alliance some of the fortune that was lost to him when Clarissa was made an heiress by her grandfather.[142] He arranges with Mr Solmes an exchange of estates, which would bring him financial gain and political influence in his county. He also stands to gain from Clarissa's union with Solmes in case of their premature death.[143] Clarissa's uncle, Mr Antony Harlowe, regards Mr Solmes as a 'select friend', and he has business ties with him.[144] Arabella, Clarissa's sister, is bitterly envious of her younger and better-loved sister, and she delights in inflicting misery on her. Clarissa expresses her disappointment of these considerations of her 'friends': 'I now take up my pen, to lay before you the inducements and motives which *my friends* have to espouse so earnestly the address of this Mr Solmes', she writes to Anna Howe. 'Indeed it concerns me not a little *that my friends* could be brought to encourage such offers on *such* motives.'[145]

Though improperly motivated, the negotiations for Clarissa's marriage

---

[140] See *Clarissa*, pp. 81, 101, 153, 156, 224.   [141] *Ibid.*, p. 84.
[142] He also wishes to contradict the uncles' plans of making Clarissa their heiress: *ibid.*, pp. 77–8, 295, 310. Cousin Morden's promise to settle his wealth on Clarissa if he dies unmarried and without children can be found in *ibid.*, p. 1289, and see also p. 1279. 'This little siren is in a fair way to *out-uncle* as well as *out grandfather* us both', is an expression of Clarissa's siblings' fear. See Tadmor, 'Dimensions of inequality among siblings in eighteenth-century novels', esp. pp. 316–17, and notes there, and see C. Hill, 'Clarissa Harlowe and her times', in C. Hill, *Puritanism and Revolution: Studies in Interpretation of the English Revolution of the Seventeenth Century* (London, 1958), pp. 367–94.
[143] *Clarissa*, pp. 81, 101.   [144] See also 'particular friend', e.g. *ibid.*, pp. 61, 150.
[145] *Ibid.*, pp. 76, 81. Italics for 'such' in the original.

are conducted nonetheless in the language of 'friendship'. Clarissa uses the language of 'friendship' to try and convince her 'friends' of their responsibility towards her: '*my friends* . . . desire to see me married to one I *cannot* love . . . I must say, I thought *my friends* put a higher value upon me', she says.[146] She also uses the language of 'friendship' to move her 'friends' in her favour by stirring their compassion: 'my dearest Bella, my sister, my *friend*, my companion, my adviser', she implores her sister at one point.[147] Taking a firm step, she addresses herself to Mr Solmes, and reminds him that it is her 'friends'' consent that he has obtained, not hers: 'You addressed yourself to *my friends*. Your proposals were approved of by them; approved of without consulting me . . . '.[148] At the same time, she dutifully prevents Mr Lovelace from continuing his addresses to her: 'he is to expect no favour from me, against *the approbation of my friends*', she declares, using the familiar formula, analysed above.[149] However, Clarissa's brother uses the same formula of 'friendship' to extract his sister's compliance: 'show your readiness, in one point at least, *to oblige your friends*', he says.[150] His usage is poignant, not only because it belittles the sacrifice required of Clarissa, but also because his own friendly concerns are by now extremely suspect.[151] Clarissa tries her best to oblige. 'I would, if I could, oblige all *my friends* – But will it be *just*, will it be honest to marry a man I cannot endure?', she asks.[152] Finally, she consents to an interview with Mr Solmes 'purely as an act of duty, to show *my friends* that I will comply with their commands as far as I can'.[153]

When used in different situations, and by different speakers, the language of 'friendship' thus invokes different notions and obligations. It also exposes the tension embedded in many situations. As we can see from the above examples, the language of 'friendship' is used by Clarissa as an expressive (though unfortunately mostly ineffectual) idiom of communication. It enables her to make demands, to implore, to insist on mutuality, and even to oppose her 'friends', whilst still declaring her duty to them as her 'friends'. In doing all this, moreover, she also demonstrates her good sense of decorum: she is well aware of the right conduct in matters of courtship and marriage, and even in difficult circumstances she strives to maintain it. But when used by other characters, such as James

---

[146] *Ibid.*, pp. 151–2. Italics for 'cannot' in the original.   [147] *Ibid.*, p. 139.
[148] *Ibid.*, p. 159. She adds: 'I write, sir, to demand of you the peace of mind you have robbed me of: to demand of you the love of so many *dear friends*, of which you have deprived me.'
[149] *Ibid.*, p. 99.
[150] *Ibid.*, p. 234; see also *ibid.*, p. 61: 'he affects to rally me, and not to believe it possible that one so dutiful and so discreet as his sister Clary can resolve to *disoblige all her friends*'.
[151] 'Is it such a mighty matter for a young lady to give up her own inclination *to oblige her friends*?', Mrs Howe adds her pressure: *ibid.*, p. 245.
[152] *Ibid.*, p. 139. Italics for 'just' and 'honest' in the original.   [153] *Ibid.*, p. 289.

Harlowe Junior, the language of 'friendship' often conveys a sense of bitter irony. It draws attention to the disloyalty and coercion of the 'friends', and it exposes all the more Clarissa's growing loneliness. As the tragedy proceeds, Clarissa, who has always presented in her behaviour a model of affectionate and dutiful submission, is indeed driven by her 'friends' to a point at which she cannot but refuse them. Nothing would please her more than to return to a position in which she, once again, could be guided by her 'friends', but that is made impossible because of their betrayal of their 'friendship'.

All these recurring usages demonstrate again and again the wide currency of the language of 'friendship' in *Clarissa*. They also demonstrate the wide currency of the language of 'friendship' in the contemporary language more broadly: indeed, some of these usages, as we can see, are coined in formulaic expressions that can be traced through different texts. The social and moral norms of 'friendship' contained in these formulae were no doubt familiar to Richardson and his original readership. In addition to encapsulating many of the tragic tensions of *Clarissa*, the conventional language of 'friendship' thus also provides the readers of this novel with signposts for interpretation. As it derives its impact from a well-known cultural repertoire of expectations and norms, the language of 'friendship' invites the reader to reflect on the ways in which Clarissa's 'friends' behave and perform their roles as 'friends', on the ways in which she acts by them, and on the tensions and conflicts embedded in different commitments of 'friendship'.

Gradually, the growing rift between Clarissa and her 'friends' leads to their withdrawal of 'friendship'. 'I have not a friend in my sister', Clarissa recognises sadly.[154] 'I have in *you* a *brother*, but not a *friend*', she says to her brother.[155] 'Let me invoke your returning kindness, my *only brother*! And give me cause, I beseech you, to call you my *compassionating friend*', she begs him.[156] 'You must not expect an advocate or even a *friend* in me', declares Clarissa's uncle.[157] Anna Howe finally denounces the betrayal of Clarissa's relations by refusing to name them any more as her '*friends*'. '[Y]our *relations*', she calls them, and adds '*friends* no more will I call them, unworthy they are even of the *other* name!'[158] Kinship relationships have thus been divested of well-wishing friendship.

---

[154] *Ibid.*, p. 113.   [155] *Ibid.*, p. 137. Italics for 'you' in the original.
[156] *Ibid.*, p. 138. Italics in the original. 'You are sure of a friend, as well as a brother, if it be not your own fault', he answers in return, *ibid.*, p. 138.   [157] *Ibid.*, p. 158.
[158] *Ibid.*, p. 133. Italics for 'friends' and 'other' in the original. Her declaration continues to resonate in the novel. 'I must own that my friends are very severe', says Clarissa at a later stage to Anna Howe. 'You, my dear, would not call them my *friends*, you said long ago; but my relations: indeed I cannot call them my *relations*, I think!': *ibid.*, p. 1194. Italics in the original.

Thus Clarissa is left 'friendless': 'all your friends made your enemies' is how Anna Howe describes Clarissa's situation.[159] This state of 'friend-lessness', as we have already seen above, was a familiar topos in eight-eenth-century literature, and a very dangerous situation. The greatest danger is that the friendless woman might find herself – whether willingly or inadvertently – an object of improper protection. Clarissa's state as a 'friendless' woman is materialised most acutely when she is snatched by Mr Lovelace from her father's house. She thus not only loses her rela-tions' support, but she is also thrown into the 'protection' of a false and treacherous 'friend'. 'She has not one friend in town', says Mr Belford.[160] 'She has *not a single friend* to stand by her.'[161] 'Now tell me, sir, has not this lady lost *all the friends she had in the world* for your sake?', he asks Mr Lovelace.[162] '[D]espised and forsaken by all her friends', is how Clarissa describes her own situation.[163] A 'poor creature made *friendless*' by Mr Lovelace's cruel art.[164] 'Indeed I am afraid nothing but her being at the last extremity of all will make her father, and her uncles, and her *other friends*, forgive her', says Clarissa's mother.[165] She is sadly wrong. Not even the greatest extremity returns Clarissa to her 'natural friends'.

Alongside the betrayal of 'friendship', another process takes place: the dislocation of 'friendship'. As Clarissa is cast off by her 'natural friends', chosen friends seek to take their place. In doing so, however, they not only fail to save Clarissa, but they remind both Clarissa and the reader that she is bereft of those friends for whose friendship she yearns, and whose friendship she really needs. The dislocation of friendship is evident in Clarissa's relationship with Anna Howe. Clarissa treasures her friendship with Anna Howe, but however dear, this select friendship cannot console her for the loss of her 'natural friends'. 'I am deserted of every friend but Miss Howe', she says. In calling her 'my best, my dearest, my *only friend!*', she thus expresses not only a singular sentimental bond between two women, as Janet Todd points out, but also the absence of those who should have been her best friends.[166]

As Clarissa's troubles increase, dislocation encroaches increasingly into her friendship with Anna Howe. When Clarissa is persecuted by her relations, Anna Howe supports her by praising the bond of their chosen friendship, whilst belittling her unworthy 'friends'. Her words at this point sound as a direct paraphrase of one of Jeremy Taylor's maxims from his treatise on friendship: 'a brother may *not* be a *friend*: but a *friend* will be

[159] *Ibid.*, p. 1138.   [160] *Ibid.*, p. 605.   [161] *Ibid.*, p. 1188.   [162] *Ibid.*, p. 1028.
[163] *Ibid.*, p. 1301.   [164] *Ibid.*, p. 985.   [165] *Ibid.*, p. 1156.
[166] *Ibid.*, p. 974. See also, for example, 'my only friend': *ibid.*, p. 1088; 'my best friend': *ibid.*,
p. 1115; 'sister of my heart', *ibid.*, p. 1415; 'the only friend I have in the world', *ibid.*,
p. 1070.

always a brother'.[167] One of the sharpest manifestations of dislocated 'friendship' takes place when Clarissa sends to Anna Howe Lovelace's proposals of marriage. At long last, Mr Lovelace makes Clarissa formal proposals for a marriage settlement. According to the convention, those should be inspected by her 'friends'. But who, at this stage, might these 'friends' be? To whom can Clarissa turn? First, as Anna Howe suggests, she must turn to herself: 'as your evil destiny has thrown you out of all other protection and mediation, you must be father, mother, uncle to yourself, and enter upon the requisite points for yourself'.[168] Contrary to the social convention, and contrary to Clarissa's own sense of female modesty, she thus has to conduct with Mr Lovelace her own settlement negotiations. Having done that, she then turns to Anna Howe, and sends the proposals to her. At this point Anna Howe, Clarissa's select friend, has to act as a senior 'friend', and examine the marriage proposals. Mr Lovelace's openness at this point, in agreeing to the inspection of the proposals, is, at one level, a proof of his serious intentions: he at least appears to follow the correct procedure, referring the proposals to the considerations of the nearest available 'friends'.[169] But this scene at which a dangerous villain offers a weighty document, such as marriage proposals, for the consideration of two young and inexperienced females, is actually a travesty of the proper conduct. It only highlights Clarissa's position as a 'friendless' woman, and emphasises how impossible it is at this stage to follow the correct procedure of consideration by senior 'friends'.

But although she leans on her beloved friend and draws great strength from her friendship, Clarissa is nonetheless aware of the boundaries of their select friendship, and she makes every effort not to dislocate it much further. Significantly, she is very careful about incurring financial obligations to her friend. When she is imprisoned for debt, she declares that 'she had no friends' and 'would trouble nobody'.[170] A strong manifestation of her *'pure friendship'* with Anna Howe at this point is her refusal to turn to her for financial assistance, in order not to embarrass Anna before her mother, and not to give '*a selfish appearance to a friendship that was above all*

[167] *Ibid.*, p. 212. Italics in the original. See S. Richardson, *A Collection of Moral and Instructive Sentiments, Maxims and Cautious Reflections* (London, 1745), p. 126. Compare Taylor, *The Measures and Offices of Friendship*, p. 76: 'A Brother does not always make a friend, but a friend ever makes a Brother.' As we saw above, Samuel Richardson was indeed familiar with Taylor's work. *Clarissa* includes references to works by Taylor, and it is therefore possible that this maxim was adapted from Taylor's treatise.
[168] *Clarissa*, p. 588. See also Clarissa's usage of these words, *ibid.*, p. 590.
[169] Indeed, when Mr Lovelace makes Clarissa his proposals, he specifies explicitly: 'you may communicate this paper to Miss Howe, who may consult any of *her friends*': *ibid.*, p. 596. But of course, neither Anna Howe nor her own 'friends' are the proper 'friend' to be consulted in this matter.   [170] *Ibid.*, p. 1054.

sordid alloys'.[171] This last phrase echoes later in the novel, when Clarissa, shortly before her death, reflects on her noble friendship with Anna Howe, and looks forward to its most unalloyed manifestation in eternal life.[172]

Another friend whose relationship with Clarissa is rooted in dislocation is Mr Belford, who becomes Clarissa's 'warm friend'.[173] He, indeed, is doubly dislocated, for he not only takes upon himself various tasks which should have been preformed by Clarissa's related 'friends', or which should have been unnecessary had they performed their roles properly, but he also defects from among the ranks of Mr Lovelace's 'friends'. 'Are you not that man's *friend*?', Clarissa asks him. 'I am not a friend, madam, to his vile actions to the *most excellent of women*', he replies.[174] 'Permit me to observe that here you are without *one natural friend*', he says. 'My life and my fortune', he declares, 'are devoted to your service.'[175] Later Belford is described by Mrs Smith as 'the *best friend* she has had', a usage that once again recalls the absence of her 'best and natural friends', as well as the betrayal of Belford's best friend, Lovelace.[176]

Indeed, even Mr Lovelace's related 'friends' gather to offer their 'friendship' to Clarissa. In the following letter, for example, Mr Lovelace's uncle, aunts, and cousins recognise Clarissa's betrayal by her related 'friends' and the evil done to her by their kinsman, and they offer her their material support:

> and as you labour under the unhappy effects of your *friends'* displeasure, which may subject you to inconveniences, his lordship and Lady Sarah and Lady Betty beg of you to accept for your life, or at least till you are admitted to enjoy your own estate, of one hundred guineas *per* quarter . . . and do not, dearest madam, we all beseech your, do not think you are beholden for this token . . . to *the friends of this vile man*; for he has not one friend left among us.[177]

But according to the moral parameters of the novel, such alternative protection, which derives from dislocated 'friendship', can lead to no good. Clarissa expresses this expectation when she says: 'Oh, my dear! What risks may poor giddy girls run when they *throw themselves out of the protection of their natural friends*, and into the wide world?'[178] 'I might appear to you a giddy creature who had *run away from her true and natural*

---

[171] *Ibid.*, p. 1062.   [172] *Ibid.*, p. 1348.   [173] *Ibid.*, p. 1088.
[174] *Ibid.*, p. 1070. Italics in the original. See also 'to the friend of my *destroyer* will I not owe an obligation': *ibid.*, p. 1066.
[175] *Ibid.*, p. 1102. See also Mr Wyerley's letter, p. 1267: 'while your friends (not looking upon you in the just light I do) persecute and banish you . . . while you are destitute of protection . . . I pride myself, I say, to stand forth and offer my fortune, and my life, at your devotion.'   [176] *Ibid.*, p. 1350.   [177] Only the first italics are mine: *ibid.*, p. 1181.
[178] *Ibid.*, p. 1005. At another occasion, however, she affirms: 'I was not a young giddy creature who had run away from her friends': *ibid.*, p. 388.

friends, and who therefore ought to take the consequence of the lot she had drawn', she explains to Mr Belford.[179] The keyword 'protection' is significant in this context, as it emphasises a woman's need for a senior 'friend' to stand by her and act in her name. We have encountered it in *The History of Miss Betsy Thoughtless*: when Betsy escapes from the legal care of her husband, she '*throws herself upon the protection*' of her elder brother, who takes it upon himself to act on her behalf as a 'friend'. But unlike Betsy, Clarissa has no faithful 'natural friend' who can legitimately uphold her cause against her other relations.[180] She receives offers to 'throw herself upon the protection' of Mr Lovelace and his 'friends', but these are unseemly, if not positively dishonourable.[181] Their consequences are also grim. The fact that Clarissa has been willing at all to consider Lovelace's offers provides him with the opportunity to abduct her.[182] Later her brief and misguided trust in the 'protection' of the two imposters, 'Lady Betty' and 'Miss Montague', leads to her rape.[183]

Clarissa is thus caught tragically between the obligations and constraints implicit in different and at times conflicting notions of 'friendship'. Although her natural 'friends' have betrayed and rejected her, their 'friendship' remains irreplaceable, and Clarissa yearns for it. Her relationships with select friends can hardly be enhanced without transgressing her obligations to 'related friends', and without violating boundaries of virtue and decorum. Far from being a true friend, someone who can lay claim to becoming a related friend as Clarissa's husband, Lovelace proves to be her worst enemy. Following this utter dislocation of friendship, after her rape many of Clarissa's struggles are characterised by her desire to remain reserved and independent. Isolated within a small circle of admirers and 'select friends', she awaits her death.

[179] *Ibid.*, p. 1079.

[180] Captain Morden, Clarissa's only relation who might have defended her cause both as her cousin and her trustee, is unavailable when Clarissa needs him most. He finally makes his appearance towards the end of the novel.

[181] See, for example, Clarissa's reactions: 'what would the world conclude would be the end ... were I *to throw myself into the protection of his friends?*': *ibid.*, p. 170 (italics for 'his' in the original). 'I cannot bear the thoughts of *throwing myself upon the protection of his friends*', she says: *ibid.*, p. 327.

[182] Once that happens, she soon discovers that instead of a protector she has gained a ruthless jailer. See, for example, *ibid.*, p. 900: 'since I am a prisoner as I find, in the vilest of houses, and have not a *friend* to *protect* or save me, what thou intendst shall become of the remnant of a life not worth the keeping?' she asks Lovelace in despair. A 'poor young creature whom he ought to have protected; and whom he had first deprived of all other protection', is how she describes herself to Belford, *ibid.*, p. 1079. Even anonymous protection is now better than his: 'I will *throw myself* into the first open house I can find; and beg *protection* till I can get a coach, or a lodging in some honest family', Clarissa says desperately, as she tries to make her escape: *ibid.*, p. 918.

[183] 'I began to reproach myself that I had not at first thrown myself into their protection', Clarissa says as they gain her trust: *ibid.*, p. 1005.

As we can now see, historical notions of friendship are crucial for understanding Samuel Richardson's *Clarissa*: they underlie the social universe of the novel and the dynamics of the plot. The language of 'friendship' serves to expose the social world of *Clarissa*, in which practices of friendship have gone awry. The most basic level at which these concepts are manifested, however, is no doubt the level of the novel's vocabulary. Clearly, if we do not understand the historical meanings of words such as 'friend' and 'friendship', we are bound to read this novel in an anachronistic and at times inaccurate manner. For example, we must be able to tell that when Clarissa refers collectively to her 'friends', she nearly always refers to her parents, uncles, aunt, and siblings, not to Anna Howe, or to any of the other chosen friends and supporters she gathers in the course of the novel.

Beyond understanding the language, historical notions of 'friendship' are also important in reading the plot of *Clarissa*. These concepts of friendship give us a key for tracing some of the fundamental dynamics in the plot, such as the gradual betrayal of 'friendship', and the related dislocation of 'friendship', briefly examined here. Once again, it is important to stress that this understanding was shared by eighteenth-century readers of this novel, as well as by its author. There is little doubt that eighteenth-century readers were familiar with the social world – and the cultural vocabulary – examined here: that they knew, for example, that before contracting a marriage, it is advisable to seek the approbation and consent of 'friends', and that the most important of these friends are parents and guardians. And there is also no doubt that in constructing this novel, and in anticipating its interpretations, Richardson had these norms and obligations of 'friendship' in mind. Recurring usages, and indeed also recurring phrases about 'friendship', which, as we have seen, resonate throughout the novel, were employed by him skilfully as signposts for interpretation.

Not only are historical concepts of 'friendship' important for understanding literary texts but, at the same time, literary texts such as *Clarissa* and *The History of Miss Betsy Thoughtless* illumine social and cultural phenomena. This is not because the plots of these novels are necessarily 'representative', but because they employ a rich array of social and cultural concepts, embedded, as we have seen, most importantly in their language. There is also an advantage in the sheer volume of examples that a large novel such as *Clarissa* provides. Lastly, the rich narratives of these novels present us with a range of concepts of 'friendship', which constantly interact and reflect on one another in ways that are very difficult to find in many other texts.

Conclusion

Historical notions of 'friendship' underlie the three texts discussed here. An attempt to reconcile classical and Christian ideas about friendship with contemporary notions and practices of 'friendship' stands at the heart of Taylor's treatise. As we saw, Taylor uses his best argumentative skills to combine selfless charity and disinterested *amicitia* with the instrumental kinship-based friendship and patronage prevalent in his own social and cultural environment. In *The History of Miss Betsy Thoughtless*, similar social norms and expectations of 'friendship' are also discussed explicitly. But, and even more importantly, they are also used implicitly in the construction of the characters and the plot. Characters are surrounded by 'friends', and are also constructed as 'friends'. The actions of characters *vis-à-vis* 'friends', too, are essential for the progress of the novel. The same applies to *Clarissa*. But in this latter novel, betrayed friendship, dislocated friendship, and conflicting notions and obligations of friendship are the making of a tragedy.

Beyond all this, as we saw, historical notions of 'friendship' are deeply embedded in the language of these texts. In addition to recognising the similar vocabulary of 'friendship' in these three texts, we were also able to trace in them recurring conventional and formulaic usages. For example, the importance of obtaining the 'consent of friends' in matters of courtship and marriage, the importance of women's guidance by 'friends', their need to 'throw themselves on the protection of friends' in cases of trouble, and the dangers of 'friendlessness' – all these were seen to be familiar notions, manifested in recurring verbal usages, which we have been able to trace in both novels, as well as in some other texts.

Lastly, the fact that the language of these texts contains so many social and cultural norms of 'friendship' also provides grounds for reflecting on matters of friendship. Whilst employing the language of 'friendship', these texts reflect upon its expectations and norms. All these texts, as we saw, are engaged actively, and indeed often consciously, in exploring different notions and obligations of 'friendship', and in examining and testing them against each other. There is even evidence of conscious borrowing among members of the same 'language community', as we saw in Richardson's references to Jeremy Taylor. Furthermore, since many of these notions of friendship are embedded in familiar and formulaic usages, they are also employed by the authors in directing the reader's interpretation: they create a sense of irony, they invite textual and intertextual comparisons, they draw attention to conflicting notions and obligations, or they simply signal to the reader that here are practices and norms of 'friendship' that deserve attention, observation, and thought. In their verbal construction, in their social construction, and in their moral observations, these texts thus present us with vibrant and dense explorations of historical notions and practices of 'friendship'.

Conclusion

This book has attempted to examine some historical concepts of the family. Central to the project has been the exploration of the household-family. When people in the eighteenth century spoke or wrote about 'families', they certainly could have had in mind groups of kin living together, or separately, as in present-day usages. They could also have had in mind significant notions of lineage and ancestry. But more often, what they had in mind was a household unit, which could comprise related and non-related dependants living together under the authority of a householder: it might include a spouse, children, other relations, servants and apprentices, boarders, sojourners, or only some of these. This concept of the family was thus flexible and permeable, for it could accommodate diverse family members and many changes over time. But as we have seen, 'family' units such as these also formed structured frameworks, with some well-understood roles and relationships. Important contractual relationships, occupational and instrumental relationships, affective relationships, and indeed kinship relationships existed within households, and these were also construed and represented in 'familial' terms. Accordingly, when people in the eighteenth century moved in and out of households (which they did often as servants, apprentices, spouses, wards, boarders, lodgers, or even long-term guests), their actions were often understood in terms of the household-family, its roles and relationships. Similarly, acts of transgression and defiance of authority could also be understood in terms of the structural and relational framework of the household-family.

Units defined in the eighteenth century as 'families' thus certainly included kin, but they were not necessarily exclusively comprised of kin, and there were also 'families' which included no kin at all. Another important set of relationships that included kinship ties, but also extended beyond them, were 'friendship' relationships. Near and distant kin in the eighteenth century acted as 'friends', as well as non-related employers, patrons, neighbours, and intimate personal companions. Such 'friends' exchanged views, obligations, 'services', and many 'favours'. These, indeed, were often the most significant relationships in an individual's life. We saw that, among men of 'the middling sort', 'friendship' networks even formed vital regional networks, reflected, not least, in trade links, intellectual exchanges, local government, and political activism. 'Friendship' relationships such as these formed powerful cohesive bonds within the eighteenth-century social order. At the same time, such relationships often also introduced a dynamic of anxiety and conflict. There were always 'enemies', 'strangers', and simply 'neighbours' who did not participate in the 'friendship' relationships. People also did not always approve of what their 'friends' said or did, and different 'friends' made competing demands. In fact, the 'friendship' relationships were so multi-faceted that there were endless ways in which they could go wrong. Just as the language of 'friendship' was used effectively to express affinity and mobilise support, so was it also used to negotiate tension and disaffection.

The 'family' and 'friendship' relationships thus constituted two important forms of social alignment in eighteenth-century England: the one often centred around households, the other often extended through different households. In both types of alignment, kinship ties were highly important. But neither the 'familial' nor 'friendship' alignments corresponded precisely to any ties of blood and marriage, and both contained historically specific norms and relationships.

It was the focus on the nuclear family as the prototype of household and family relationships, and the anachronistic demarcation of familial and non-familial relationships, I suggest, that has led historians to overlook the significance of historical alignments such as these. Taking Stone's chronology, for example, we would have expected the nuclear family to be overwhelmingly manifested in our evidence, for, according to Stone, nuclear family patterns have been propagated by literate middling individuals, like members of our 'language community', since the seventeenth century. The effectiveness of 'extended' family relationships would thus also be seen to be in decline. Similarly, according to Laslett, Wrightson, and Houlbrooke we would have expected the nuclear family to be overwhelmingly present in our sources, for according to these historians the nuclear family (as opposed to various forms of the 'extended' family household and as separate from other kinship and domestic relationships) has been typical of ordinary people in England for a very long time indeed. The oppositional and anachronistic terms of this historiographical debate have left little scope for addressing the complex social and familial alignments examined here. Only by extricating ourselves from these terms of debate have we been able to historicise concepts such as 'family' and 'friends' and thus appreciate better their social and cultural significance in the eighteenth century.

If people in the eighteenth century did not focus exclusively on the nuclear family as the prototype of household and family relationships, and if at the same time they valued greatly 'friendship' ties among both kin and non-kin, that is not to say that they had no notions of kinship. On the contrary, our examination of language usages reveals that there were powerful concepts of kinship current in the eighteenth century. But these, too, fit uneasily with commonly used models and categories. Scholars have emphasised the limited extent of English kinship terminology, often presenting it as evidence of a restricted kinship universe and the dominance of the nuclear family. But, as we have seen, there were widely current usages that enabled people in the seventeenth and eighteenth centuries to employ the language of kinship not only to identify existing kin, but also to enlarge considerably their reservoir of recognised kin. The nuclear family itself had a remarkable capacity for internal extension, for 'nuclear family' terms were used regularly to refer to step-relations, half-relations, and a wide range of in-law relations. Such usages led us to question once more the utility of categories such as 'the nuclear family' and 'the extended family', as well as the presently used model for mapping English kinship terminology in the past. Furthermore, there were a number of widely used terms that did not highlight the nuclear family and separate it from other kinship ties, as historians and anthropologists have led us to expect, but actually served to submerge it in broader kinship relationships. There were also terms that did not demarcate clearly any kinship degree; instead, these terms were both inclusive and opaque, properties valued by many speakers in social situations in which they did not want to be specific. There were also overlapping terms in different registers, as well as in regional and colloquial usages, and these further enriched the vocabulary of kinship whilst also preventing it from fitting neatly into any existing descriptive scheme.

Usages such as these, I argue, attest to the vitality of the language of kinship in early modern England. This, indeed, was a powerful language of negotiation. Beyond the prescribed duty to care for spouses and minor children, there were in early modern England few unavoidable obligations regulating relations among kin,[1] but there were nonetheless strong

---

[1] From the legal point of view, parents had the duty to serve as their children's guardians for nurture until the age of fourteen, but only at the level of necessity. They also had the right to dispose of the custody of a child, born or unborn, until the age of twenty-one: Blackstone, *Commentaries of the Laws of England*, vol. I, pp. 446–59, and esp. pp. 453, 461. For the duties of husband and wife, see *ibid.*, pp. 433–45. For the duty to support parents, see *ibid.*, p. 454, and see also above, pp. 109–10.

expectations for consideration, duty, solidarity, and reciprocity among kin.[2] These were negotiated in the language of kinship. All too often, historians have studied the language of kinship by looking mainly for manifestations of what people actually received from each other or did for one another. Equally significant, I suggest, was what they believed they should receive or do: expressions of such expectations, too, were forms of social action. The language of kinship was indeed often a language of disappointment. Expressions of disappointment, nonetheless, reveal significant social norms and cultural expectations.

Powerful as it was, however, the language of kinship was not used in the eighteenth century to apply to relations of blood and marriage only. Like the terms of 'family' and 'friendship', the language of kinship could also be applied to diverse social relations. First, the language of kinship could be applied to such remote and complex relationships that it virtually diffused into the realm of relations among non-kin. Secondly, the language of kinship was so powerful that it was used as a model for diffusing patterns of kinship, not only among relations by blood and marriage but in many areas of life. Various people in positions of authority, for example, received the appellation 'father'. Servants, slaves, and neighbours were named 'uncle' and 'aunt'. Terms such as 'brother' and 'sister' were applied very broadly to express amity in many personal and institutional relationships. There was, indeed, hardly a single kinship term used in the eighteenth century to designate relations by blood and marriage alone.

Thus, by tracing and analysing language usages we have retrieved a rich historical vocabulary of social and familial concepts, and patterns of alignment. English family and kinship patterns were often seen by scholars to be marked by long-term continuity. Focusing on the eighteenth century, *Family and Friends* does not attempt to provide an answer to the question of long-term continuity and change in family history. However, the rich relationships examined here suggest that, as well as patterns of continuity, family ties in England over the past centuries should be seen within the context of significant conceptual and social changes. For example, nuclear family relations, as we have seen, were extremely potent in the eighteenth-century circles studied here. But however potent these relations were, middling people at that time had a plurality of concepts of the family, including a strong and flexible concept of the family as a household that makes it impossible to regard 'the nuclear family' as the abiding organisational and cultural epitome of domestic and familial relationships in seventeenth- and eighteenth-century England. A more

---

[2] For some similar concerns in the context of twentieth-century history see J. Finch, *Family Obligations and Social Change* (Cambridge, 1989).

exclusive and closely defined concept of the family centred around the nuclear core was yet to become dominant. Earlier concepts of the family still remain to be explored. From the point of view of the present, however, it would also seem that a concept of 'the nuclear family', embedded strongly in notions of conjugality, cannot be seen as the definite hallmark of familial 'modernity', nor the ultimate stage of familial development.[3] A related issue concerns notions of kinship. Clearly, the eighteenth-century circles studied here suffered from no paucity in kinship recognition. If the history of the English family is marked at some point by a narrowly focused and well-differentiated universe of recognised kin, then, it would seem that this form of conceptualisation, too, was yet to become dominant. In the society examined here, household and kinship mattered greatly. They were also closely entwined with other, and extremely significant, social and economic ties. However, these relationships were not necessarily either harmonious, or positive. A long-term chronological inquiry, then, might investigate not whether past societies were dominated by 'nuclear' or 'extended' family patterns, for these oppositional terms convey little; but rather, the ways in which concepts of family, friendship, and kinship were understood, and the ways in which vibrant ties among kin, friends, and household members changed, and at some stage also shifted boundaries and narrowed down. Yet that narrowing down might not be the end of the story.

In addition, this book has implications for our understanding of questions beyond the history of the family. One of the aims of *Family and Friends* is to link the analysis of linguistic concepts to the study of textual constructions more broadly. Here we have seen that central concepts of family, friendship, kinship, and patronage were not only widely current in many eighteenth-century texts from different genres, but also served as fundamental building blocks in the construction of literary characters and plots. The analysis of texts thus proved useful for the historical analysis; at the same time, the historical reading of literary texts has led us to offer new readings of popular novels such as *Pamela* and *Clarissa*, as well as of significant prescriptive treatises. Both household-family relationships and the performances of kin and patrons as 'friends' play large and vital roles within these texts. A better understanding of these relationships may forestall some misreading. All too often critics have imposed upon these texts an anachronistic notion of what family and friendship meant in the eighteenth century.

---

[3] See, for example, the treatment of secrets, sexuality, and the family, or the stigma of illegitimacy: Davidoff, Doolittle, Fink, and Holden, *The Family Story*, e.g. pp. 247–51. For the number of divorced or single women today, and the idea of cohabitation as 'partnerhood', see *ibid.*, pp. 266–8, and references there.

When we turn to the historiography of the eighteenth century, we see that the analysis of familial and social ties illumines anew key issues investigated by eighteenth-century historians. For example, our exploration of notions of lineage and ancestry extended beyond a discussion of concepts of familial ancestry and their significance for different social strata, to deal with issues such as the local influence of the aristocracy and reactions to changes in local custom. Here we were able to trace notions of deference and networks of patronage, but we also saw how people of 'the middling sort' voiced criticism and acted with clear considerations of their own interests and merit. Similarly, the analysis of 'friendship' ties has enabled us to address questions in eighteenth-century political history. While investigating 'friendship' ties, we were able to trace political connections from the prime minister of England to ordinary tradesmen and farmers, and on even to the level of the village poor. We witnessed political activism both within and beyond the circles of the electorate in a mid-eighteenth-century county constituency, and in the active constituency of a near-by county town. We saw how such political connections were maintained and mediated at the local level, and how they were negotiated and mobilised with general elections in view. Such connections, often discussed in the context of eighteenth-century high politics, were seen to be significant in local social relations, and they were also seen to be closely linked to relationships of kinship, friendship, and patronage.

Family and Friends has also enabled us to observe closely the ways in which some provincial, rural, and middling men were linked to the eighteenth-century 'public sphere'. Important studies of eighteenth-century England emphasise the role of 'the middling sort' in the urban scene. In 1750, however, 79 per cent of the English population still lived in the countryside, and, while 58 per cent of those were engaged in overwhelmingly commercially oriented agricultural production, 42 per cent were engaged in various forms of manufacture, industry, and service activities.[4] A man such as Thomas Turner belonged to this active rural scene. The case of Turner and his circles thus gives us further insight into the ways in which middling, provincial, and rural men may have participated in the crucial milieu of their time. They sought one another across regional networks and exchanged credit, books, news, ideas, and many favours. Some of them were very interested indeed in expanding their knowledge and in the world of books. However, they also dealt and traded with one another and were active in local administration. If they toured places of interest and historical sites, they also visited country fairs and were very familiar with local public houses. They had links with London, but their

---

[4] Based on E. A. Wrigley, 'Urban growth and agricultural change', in E. A. Wrigley, *People, Cities and Wealth: The Transformation of a Traditional Society* (Oxford, 1987), pp. 168–71.

effective capital was the county town. They were extremely active in 'the politics of the parish',[5] but were also engaged in the politics of the state.

This takes us back to the relationship between family kinship and friendship ties, and economic action. It was the predominance of the small conjugal family household,[6] or indeed an individually and nuclearly oriented family and kinship system more broadly, that was seen to have played a part in promoting in England's precocious economic growth prior to industrialisation.[7] This book suggests that we may also want to direct our attention to the roles of alignments of household, kinship, and friendship in this respect.[8] To judge from the middling people examined here, it would seem that it was not only the independence and mobility associated with the conjugal family household that were so strongly congenial to adaptability or growth,[9] but also cooperation and reciprocity, and successful manoeuvring through close networks of household and kinship, credit and commerce, friendship and patronage, politics and conviviality. If the example of Thomas Turner's milieu illumines economic action, it highlights not only the figure of the individual facing the market, but also men and women enmeshed in dense networks composed of family and household members, friends and kin.[10]

Indeed, *Family and Friends* has argued that the study of concepts of the family is extremely significant for the study of eighteenth-century social, cultural, and economic relations and experiences. The history of eighteenth-century society has not contributed much to arguments about the history of the family. While historians of the family were engaged in debates about the currency of certain familial patterns and continuity and change, central debates in eighteenth-century history concerned issues such as the emergence of a commercial society, relations between patricians and plebs, the rise of the middle class, and the expansion of the public sphere.[11] Paradoxically, it is mainly in some interpretations of eighteenth-century politics that the understanding of familial relations

---

[5] Wrightson, 'The politics of the parish'; Eastwood, *Government and Community in the Provinces, 1700–1870*, ch. 2.   [6] Wrigley, *People, Cities and Wealth*, p. 13.

[7] Macfarlane, *Individualism*, e.g. pp. 196–202, and Macfarlane, *Marriage and Love in England*, e.g. pp. 321–44. See also Macfarlane, *The Culture of Capitalism*.

[8] This may also invite new comparisons with patterns of household and kinship in other societies, both in Europe and beyond it, as arguments on England's unique experience are also linked to observations about comparative household, kinship, and family patterns.

[9] Wrigley, *People, Cities and Wealth*, p. 13.

[10] See also at this point Mascuch, 'Social mobility and middling self-identity'; Muldrew, *The Economy of Obligation*. These issues are investigated in K. Wrightson, *Earthly Necessities: Economic Lives in Early Modern Britain* (New Haven and London, 2000).

[11] Notable exceptions in their contributions to the history of the family are L. Davidoff and C. Hall, *Family Fortunes: Men and Women of the English Middle Class, 1780–1850* (London, 1987); Earle, *The Making of the English Middle Class*; Smail, *The Origins of Middle-Class Culture*; Hunt, *The Middling Sort*.

has informed the understanding of social relations. *Family and Friends* indeed elaborates on this insight. But I hope this book also indicates the many ways in which familial relations were important in the context of social and economic relationships and experiences in the eighteenth century. Labour relations, for instance, were often mediated among 'friends', linked closely to patronage, and negotiated in terms of the household-family and its roles and relationships. Similarly, trade networks and credit relations existed also among 'friends', were bound closely with kinship and patronage, invested in household-families – and were tried and tested in all these contexts. So were circles of religious devotion, intellectual exchange, and ideological commitment. Furthermore, poverty and plenty, migration and removal, war and peace were all experienced and negotiated in relation to ties of 'family', 'friendship', kinship, and patronage. In this sense, *Family and Friends* not only presents a set of closely argued conclusions relating to the historiography of the family, but also proposes new directions which a broader and more connected history of the family might take, and through which it can make a major contribution to our understanding of eighteenth-century history as a whole.

Bibliography

MANUSCRIPT SOURCES

BRITISH LIBRARY, LONDON

Add. MS 32,695; Add. MS 32,704; Add. MS 32,708; Add. MS 32,710;
Add. MS 32,712; Add. MS 32,718; Add. MS 32,719; Add. MS 32,725;
Add. MS 32,733; Add. MS 32,737; Add. MS 32,856; Add. MS 32,858;
Add. MS 32,863; Add. MS 32,864; Add. MS 32,866; Add. MS 32,870;
Add. MS 32,877; Add. MS 32,895; Add. MS 32,900; Add. MS 32,908;
Add. MS 32,912; Add. MS 32,913; Add. MS 32,916; Add. MS 32,917;
Add. MS 32,918; Add. MS 32,919; Add. MS 32,920; Add. MS 32,921;
Add. MS 32,926; Add. MS 32,928; Add. MS 32,946; Add. MS 32,947;
Add. MS 32,949; Add. MS 32,958; Add. MS 32,969; Add. MS 32,988;
Add. MS 32,989; Add. MS 32,990; Add. MS 33,058; Add. MS 33,059;
Add. MS 33,166: Newcastle Papers
Add. MS 4293, ff. 81–2: a letter by Eliza Haywood

CENTRE FOR KENTISH STUDIES, MAIDSTONE

U908 T158: Streatfield MSS
P344/1/1: Speldhurst Parish Book

EAST SUSSEX RECORD OFFICE, LEWES

A2327 1/4/3–5: Laughton Manor Court Books
ADA 117–18: Framfield Manor Court Books
AMS 2134^{a-b}, 2140: Documents Relating to the Tourle Family of Lewes
AMS 5841: Various Accounts by Thomas Turner
AMS 4841/10: East Hoathly Overseers' Papers
B20/181: Archdeaconry of Lewes Administrations
PAR 378/31/1/1: East Hoathly Overseers' Account Book
PEV 299, PEV 302, PEV 320, PEV 344, PEV 349, PEV 356, PEV 360,
    PEV 366, PEV 385, PEV 546, PEV 548, PEV 563, PEV 566, PEV 1385,
    PEV 1387: Records of Pevensey Corporation
PLU 6/32–40: Archive of the Plumley Family of Pevensey
SAS Ha 310: Abraham Baley's Letter Book, 1763–73
SAS/SM 210: Notes on Family History, Thomas Turner

W/SM D9 Register of Wills, South Malling
W/A 56–67, Register of Wills, Archdeaconry of Lewes
East Sussex Baptism Index, 1700–1812

YALE UNIVERSITY LIBRARY, NEW HAVEN

Special Files, Thomas Turner Papers, Manuscripts and Archives: Letters from Thomas Turner to his Children; Medical Prescriptions Collected by Thomas Turner
Thomas Turner Papers, Manuscripts and Archives: Diary of Thomas Turner, 1754–65
Worcester Material, Thomas Turner Papers: Notes Listing the Landholdings in East Hoathly, Chiddingly, and Waldron

PRINTED PRIMARY SOURCES

Anti Pamela: or, Feign'd Innocence Detected (London, 1741)
Aquinas, St Thomas, *Summa Theologiae*, vol. 34, trans. R. J. Batten (London, 1975)
Arbuthnot, J., *An Inquiry into the Connection between the Present Price of Provisions and the Size of Farms* (London, 1773)
Aristotle, *The Ethics of Aristotle*, trans. J. A. K. Thomson, revised trans. H. Tredennick (London, 1976)
Austen, J., *Sense and Sensibility* (1811), ed. T. Tanner (Harmondsworth, 1986)
Pride and Prejudice (1813), ed. J. Kinsley (Oxford, 1989)
Emma (1816), ed. J. Kinsley (Oxford, 1992)
Northanger Abbey (1818), ed. J. Davie (Oxford, 1971)
The Autobiography and Correspondence of Mary Granville, Mrs Delany, ed. Lady Llanover, 3 vols. (London, 1861–2)
Baker, D. E., *Biographia Dramatica, or, Companion to the Play House* (London, 1764)
Blackstone, W., *Commentaries on the Laws of England*, 4 vols. (Oxford, 1770)
Blencowe, R. W., and M. A. Lower, 'Extracts from the diary of a Sussex tradesman, a hundred years ago', *SAC* 11 (London, 1859), 179–220
Blundell, N., *The Great Diurnal of Nicholas Blundell of Little Crosby, Lancashire*, 3 vols. (1720–8), The Record Society of Lancashire and Cheshire 110, 112, 114, ed. J. J. Bayley, transcribed and annotated F. Tyrer (Preston, 1968–72)
Burn, R., *The Justice of the Peace and the Parish Officer*, 4 vols. (14th edn, London, 1780)
Carter, J., *The Scotch Parents: or, the Remarkable Case of John Ramble, Written by Himself (in the Month of February, 1773)* (London, 1773)
Charges to the Grand Jury, 1689–1803, ed. G. Lamoine, Camden Fourth Series, vol. 43 (London, 1992)
Chichester Diocesan Surveys, 1686 and 1724, ed. W. K. Ford, Sussex Record Society, vol. 78 (Lewes, 1994)
Cicero, Marcus Tullius, 'On friendship', in *On Old Age and On Friendship*, trans. F. O. Copley (Ann Arbor, 1972)

Cleland, J., *Memoirs of A Woman of Pleasure* (1748–9; 1st legal edn, 1963), ed. P. Sabor (Oxford, 1985)

The Complete Letter Writer: or, Polite English Secretary (London, 1767)

The Correspondence of Samuel Richardson, ed. A. L. Barbauld, 6 vols. (London, 1804)

The Correspondence of Sir James Clavering, ed. H. T. Dickinson, The Surtees Society (Gateshead, 1967)

Defoe, D., *Moll Flanders* (1722), ed. J. Mitchell (Harmondsworth, 1978)

A Tour Through the Whole Island of Great Britain (London, 1724–6), ed. P. Rogers (Harmondsworth, 1986)

A Tour Through the Whole Island of Great Britain, Sixth Edition with Very Great Additions, Improvements, and Corrections: Which Bring it Down to the End of the Year 1761 (London, 1762)

East Sussex Land Tax, 1785, ed. R. Davey, Sussex Record Society, vol. 77 (Lewes, 1991)

Eliot, George, *Middlemarch* (1871–2), ed. W. J. Harvey (Harmondsworth, 1994)

Evelyn, J., *The Diary of John Evelyn*, ed. E. S. de Beer, 3 vols. (Oxford, 1955)

Fielding, H., *An Apology for the Life of Mrs Shamela Andrews* (1741), ed. J. Hawley (Harmondsworth, 1999), pp. 3–43

Joseph Andrews (1742), ed. R. F. Brissenden (Harmondsworth, 1978)

Tom Jones (1749), ed. R. P. C. Muter (Harmondsworth, 1979)

Fleetwood, W. *The Relative Duties of Parents and Children, Husbands and Wives, Masters and Servants* (London, 1705), Garland Publishing (New York and London, 1985)

The Friendly Society, or a Proposal of a New Way or Method for Securing Houses from any Considerable Loss by Fire, by Way of Subscription and Mutual Contribution (London, 1684)

Friends of the People, Freemasons Tavern, 30 May 1795, At a General Meeting of the Society of the Friends of the People, Associated for the Purpose of Obtaining a Parliamentary Reform, Held this Day (London, 1795)

The Fuller Letters, 1728–1755: Guns, Slaves and Finance, ed. D. Crossley and R. Saville, Sussex Record Society, vol. 76 (Lewes, 1991)

Garraway Rice, R., *Sussex Apprentices and Masters, 1710–1752*, Sussex Record Society, vol. 28 (1922) (London, 1924)

Gawthern, A., *The Diary of Abigail Gawthern of Nottingham, 1751–1810*, ed. A. Hanstock, Thornton Society of Nottinghamshire, Record Series, vol. 33 (Nottingham, 1980)

Godfrey, W. H., 'Seatholders of St. Michael's Church, Lewes in 1753 & 1803 with their dwelling houses', *SNQ* 1 (1927), 176–9

Goldsmith, O., *The Vicar of Wakefield* (1766), ed. S. Coote (Harmondsworth, 1982)

She Stoops to Conquer: Or, The Mistakes of a Night (1773), in *Eighteenth-Century Plays*, ed. R. Quintana (New York, 1952)

Hales, J., *'On The Parish': Recorded Lives of the Poor of Holt and District, 1780–1835*, ed. S. Yaxley (Dereham, 1994)

Hardy, M., *Mary Hardy's Diary*, with introduction by B. Cozens-Hardy, Norfolk Record Society, vol. 37 (Norwich, 1968)

Harrold, E., 'Diary of a Manchester wig maker', *Remains Historical and Literary Connected with the Palatine Counties of Lancaster and Chester*, The Chetham Society, vol. 68 (Manchester, 1866), pp. 172–208

Haywood, E., *Love in Excess* (1719–20), ed. D. Oakleaf (Peterborough, Ontario, 1994)

A Wife to be Lett (London, 1723, 1735)

A Present for a Servant-Maid (Dublin, 1743), facsimile reprint, The Garland series (New York and London, 1985)

The Female Spectator (London, 1745)

The Fortunate Foundlings (3rd edn, London, 1748)

The History of Miss Betsy Thoughtless (1751), Introduction by D. Spender (London and New York, 1986)

Heywood, S., *High Church Politics, Being a Seasonable Appeal to the Friends of the British Constitution against the Practices & Principles of High Churchmen* (London, 1792)

Howard, J., *The State of Prisons in England and Wales, with Preliminary Observations, and an Account of some Foreign Prisons* (Warrington, 1777)

Hughes, A., *The Diary of a Farmer's Wife, 1796–7* (Harmondsworth, 1980)

Josselin, R., *The Diary of Ralph Josselin, 1616–1683*, ed. A. Macfarlane, Records of Social and Economic History, n.s., 3 (Oxford, 1991)

King, G., 'A scheme of the income and expense of the several families of England . . . ', in *Seventeenth-Century Economic Documents*, ed. J. Thirsk and J. P. Cooper (Oxford, 1972), pp. 780–1

A Letter to a Gentleman in the Country, Giving an Account of the Two Insurance Offices, the Fire-Office and Friendly-Society (London, 1684)

Letters from Bath, 1766–67, by the Rev. John Penrose, with an Introduction and Notes by B. Mitchell and H. Penrose (Gloucester, 1983)

Locke, J., *Two Treatises of Government*, ed. M. Goldie (London, 1993)

Madan, M., *Thoughts on Executive Justice, with Respect to our Criminal Laws Particularly on the Circuit* (London, 1785)

Marchant, T., 'The Marchant diary', ed. E. Turner, *SAC* 25 (Lewes, 1873)

Myers Gardiner, J., *History of the Leeds Benevolent or Strangers' Friends Society, 1789–1889* (Leeds, 1890)

Oakes, J., *The Oakes Diaries: Business, Politics and the Family in Bury St. Edmunds, 1778–1827*, ed. J. Fiske, 2 vols. (Woodbridge, 1990–1)

Original Letters of John Locke, Algernon Sidney and Lord Shaftesbury, ed. T. Forster (2nd edn, London 1847; repr. Bristol, 1990)

Paley, R. (ed.), *Justice in Eighteenth-Century Hackney: The Justicing Notebook of Henry Norris and the Hackney Petty Session Book* (London, 1991)

Pamela Censured (London, 1741)

Pepys, S., *The Diary of Samuel Pepys*, ed. R. Latham and W. Matthews, 11 vols. (London, 1970–83)

Philogamus, *Marriage Defended, or, the Ladies Protected* (London, 1741)

Philpot, S., *Essay on the Advantage of a Polite Education Joined with a Learned One* (London, 1747)

A Poll Taken by Tho. Friend and James Reeve, Constables of the Borough of Lewes (London, 1734)

A Poll Taken by Samuel Ollive and Thomas Scrace, Constables of the Borough of Lewes (Lewes, 1768)

The Poll for the Knights of the Shire to Represent the County of Sussex, Taken at Chichester in 1774 . . . (Lewes, 1775)

The Poor Law in Norfolk, 1700–1850: A Collection of Source Material, ed. S. J. Crowley and A. Reid (Norwich, 1983)

Richardson, S., *The Apprentice's Vade Mecum: or Young Man's Pocket-Companion* (London, 1734), ed. A. D. McKillop, The Augustan Reprint Society, publication numbers 169–70 (Los Angeles, 1975)

'An unpublished letter; from Mr Samuel Richardson to his nephew, Thomas Richardson', *Imperial Review: or, London and Dublin Journal* 2 (Aug. 1804), 609–16

Clarissa: or, The History of a Young Lady (London, 1747–8), ed. A. Ross (Harmondsworth, 1985)

A Collection of Moral and Instructive Sentiments, Maxims and Cautious Reflections (London, 1745)

Familiar Letters on Important Occasions, ed. B. W. Down (London, 1928)

Pamela (London, 1740), ed. T. C. D. Eaves and B. D. Kimpel (Boston, 1971)

Pamela (London, 1801), ed. P. Sabor, Introduction by M. A. Doody (Harmondsworth, 1980)

The Paths of Virtue Delineated: or, the History in Miniature of the Celebrated Pamela, Clarissa Harlowe, and Sir Charles Grandison, Familiarized and Adapted to the Capacities of Youths (London, 1756)

Rogers, B., *The Diary of Benjamin Rogers (1727–52)*, ed. C. D. Linnell, Publications of the Bedfordshire Historical Record Society, vol. 30 (Streatley, 1950)

Romains, W., *Friends of the Established Church* (London, 1757)

Rules, Orders & Regulations, of a Friendly Society, Called the British Asurance Society (London, 1795)

Sharp, R., *A Letter to the Public Meeting of the Friends to the Repeal of the Test and Corporation Acts* (London, 1790)

Sheridan, R. B., *The School for Scandal* (1777), in *Four English Comedies*, ed. J. M. Morell (Harmondsworth, 1959)

Smollett, T., *The Adventures of Peregrine Pickle* (1751), 2 vols. (London, 1904)

Stout, W., *The Autobiography of William Stout of Lancaster, 1665–1752*, ed. D. Marshall (Manchester, 1967)

Taylor, J., *The Measures and Offices of Friendship* (1662), ed. Travis Du Priest, Scholars Facsimile and Reprints (New York, 1984)

Thomlinson, J., 'The diary of the Rev. John Thomlinson', in *Six North Country Diaries, The Publications of the Surtees Society*, vol. 118 (Durham, 1910), pp. 64–167

Turner, T., *The Diary of a Georgian Shopkeeper*, a selection by R. W. Blencowe and M. A. Lower, with a preface by F. M. Turner, ed. G. H. Jennings (Oxford, 1979)

The Diary of Thomas Turner of East Hoathly (1754–1765), ed. F. M. Turner, with an introduction by J. B. Priestley (London, 1925)

The Diary of Thomas Turner, 1754–1765, ed. D. Vaisey (Oxford, 1985)

The Town Book of Lewes, 1702–1837, ed. V. Smith, Sussex Record Society (Lewes, 1972–3)

Verney Letters of the Eighteenth Century from the MSS at Claydon House, ed. Margaret Maria, Lady Verney (London, 1930)

Verrall, W., *A Complete System of Cookery, in which is Set Forth a Variety of Genuine Recipts, Collected from Several Years Experience under the Celebrated Mr de St. Clouet, Sometimes Since Cook to his Grace the Duke of Newcastle . . .* (Lewes, 1759)

Weeton, E., *Miss Weeton's Journal of a Governess*, ed. E. Hall, 2 vols. (Oxford, 1936–8; reprinted with a revised epilogue, Oxford, 1969)

Willan, T. S., *An Eighteenth-Century Shopkeeper: Abraham Dent of Kirkby Stephen* (Manchester, 1970), Appendix IV

Withers, J., *The Whigs Vindicated: The Objections that are Commonly Brought against Them Answered, and the Present Ministry Prov'd to be the Best Friends of the Church, the Monarch, the Lasting Peace, and Real Welfare of England* (London, 1715)

Woodforde, J., *Woodforde at Oxford, 1759–76*, ed. W. N. Hargreaves-Mawdsley (Oxford, 1969)

Woodforde, M., 'Mary Woodforde's Book, 1684–1690', in *Woodforde Papers and Diaries*, ed. D. Woodforde (London, 1932), pp. 3–31

Woodforde, N., 'Nancy Woodforde: a diary for the year 1792', in *Woodforde Papers and Diaries*, ed. D. Woodforde (London, 1932), pp. 35–85

BIBLES, CONCORDANCES, AND DICTIONARIES

Bailey, N., *An Universal Etymological English Dictionary* (London, 1721)

Buxtorf, J., *Concordantiae Bibliorum Hebraicae* (Basle, 1632)

The Century Dictionary: An Encyclopedic Lexicon of the English Language, prepared under the superintendence of W. Dwight Whitney, 6 vols. (New York, 1889–91)

The Concise Oxford Dictionary (9th edn, London, New York, Sydney, and Toronto, 1997)

The Coverdale Bible (1535), Introduction by S. L. Greenslade (Folkestone, 1975)

Dictionary of American English on Historical Principles (Oxford, 1938)

The English Dialect Dictionary , ed. J. Wright (New York, 1903)

Holm, J. A., with A. W. Shilling, *Dictionary of Bahamian English* (New York, 1982)

The Holy Bible, Containing the Old and New Testaments with the Apocryphal Book in the Earliest English Versions Made from the Latin Vulgate by John Wycleffe and his Followers, ed. J. Forshall and Sir F. Madden, 2 vols. (Oxford, 1850)

The Holy Bible, Conteyning the Old Testament, and the New: Newly Translated out of the Originall Toungues: & with the Former Translations Diligently Composed and Revised by His Maiesties Special Commandment (London, 1611)

The Holy Bible: New Revised Standard Version: Containing the Old and New Testaments with the Apocryphal/Deuterocanonical Books (London, 1989)

Johnson, S., *Dictionary of the English Language* (London, 1755)

Marbecke, J., *A Concordance, that Is to Saie, a Work Wherein . . . Ye Maie Redely Find Any Worde Conteyned in the Whole Bible* (London, 1550)

The Oxford English Dictionary, 2nd edn, prepared by J. A. Simpson and E. S. C. Weiner (Oxford, 1989)

Torah Nevi'im u-Ketuvim: Biblia Hebraica Stuttgartensia (Stuttgart, 1968)

Tyndale's Old Testament, Being the Pentateuch of 1530, Joshua to 2 Chronicles of 1537 and Jonah, trans. William Tyndale, in a modern spelling edition and with an introduction by D. Daniell (New Haven, 1992)

Wilson, T., *Christian Dictionary* (London, 1612)

NEWSPAPERS AND PERIODICALS

Guardian
Gentleman's Magazine
Monthly Review
Sussex Advertiser, or Lewes Journal

SECONDARY SOURCES

Adams, R. G., 'Conceptual and methodological issues in studying friendships of older adults', in R. G. Adams and R. Blieszner (eds.), *Older Adult Friendship: Structure and Process* (Newbury Park and London, 1989), pp. 17–41

Adams, R. G. and R. Blieszner (eds.), *Older Adult Friendship: Structure and Process* (Newbury Park and London, 1989)

Addy, J., *Death, Money and the Vultures: Inheritance and Avarice, 1660–1750* (London and New York, 1992)

Amussen, S., *An Ordered Society: Gender and Class in Early Modern England* (Oxford, 1988)

Anderson, M., *Family Structure in Nineteenth-Century Lancashire* (Cambridge, 1971)

'What is new about the modern family?', Occasional Papers of the Office of Population Censuses & Surveys, *The Family* 31 (1983), reprinted in M. Drake (ed.), *Time, Family and Community: Perspectives on Family and Community History* (Oxford, 1993), pp. 67–90

Ariès, P., *Centuries of Childhood* (Paris, 1960), trans. R. Baldick (London, 1962)

Armstrong, N., *Desire and Domestic Fiction: A Political History of the Novel* (New York and Oxford, 1989)

Ashton, T. S., *An Eighteenth-Century Industrialist: Peter Stubs of Warrington, 1756–1806* (Manchester, 1961; 1st edn 1939)

Bainham, A., *Children – The Modern Law* (2nd edn, Bristol, 1998)

Ballaster, R., 'Eliza Haywood', in J. Todd (ed.), *Dictionary of British Women Writers* (London, 1989), pp. 322–6

Seductive Forms: Women's Amatory Fiction from 1684–1740 (Oxford and New York, 1992)

Barker, H. and E. Chalus (eds.), *Gender in Eighteenth-Century England: Roles, Representations, Responsibilities* (London, 1997)

Barry, J., 'Bourgeois collectivism? Urban association and middling sort', in J. Barry and C. Brooks (eds.), *The Middling Sort of People: Culture, Society and Politics in England, 1550–1800* (Basingstoke, 1994), pp. 84–112

Barry, J. and C. Brooks (eds.), *The Middling Sort of People: Culture, Society and Politics in England, 1550–1800* (Basingstoke, 1994)

Beckett, J. V., *The Aristocracy in England, 1660–1914* (Oxford, 1986)

Beier, A. L., D. Cannadine, and J. M. Rosenheim (eds.), *The First Modern Society: Essays in English History in Honour of Lawrence Stone* (Cambridge, 1989)

Ben-Amos, I. K., *Adolescence and Youth in Early Modern England* (New Haven and London, 1994)

'Women apprentices in the trades and crafts in early modern Bristol', *Continuity and Change* 6 (1991), 227–52

Berkner, L. K., 'The stem family and the developmental cycle of the peasant household: an eighteenth-century Austrian example', *American Historical Review* 77 (1972), 398–418

'The use and misuse of census data for the historical analysis of family structure', *Journal of Interdisciplinary History* 5 (1975), 721–38

Berry, C. J., *The Idea of Luxury: A Conceptual and Historical Investigation* (Cambridge, 1994)

Blieszner, R. and R. G. Adams, *Adult Friendship* (Newbury Park and London, 1992)

Blouch, C., 'Eliza Haywood and the romance of obscurity', *Studies in English Literature* 31 (1991), 535–52

Bonfield, L., *Marriage Settlements, 1601–1740: The Adoption of the Strict Settlement* (Cambridge, 1983)

'Strict settlement and the family – a differing view', *Economic History Review* 41 (1988), 461–6

Boulton, J., *Neighbourhood and Society: A London Suburb in the Seventeenth Century* (Cambridge, 1987)

Bray, A., 'Homosexuality and the signs of male friendship in Elizabethan England', *History Workshop Journal* 29 (1990), 1–19

Brent, C., *Georgian Lewes, 1714–1830* (Lewes, 1993)

Brewer, J., *Party Ideology and Popular Politics at the Accession of George III* (Cambridge, 1976)

'Commercialization and politics', in N. McKendrick, J. Brewer, and J. H. Plumb (eds.), *The Birth of a Consumer Society: The Commercialization of Eighteenth-Century England* (London, 1982), pp. 197–262

The Sinews of Power: War, Money and the English State (London, Boston, Sydney, and Wellington, 1989)

Brodsky Elliot, V., 'Single women in the London marriage market: age, status and mobility, 1598–1619', in R. B. Outhwaite (ed.), *Marriage and Society: Studies in the Social History of Marriage* (London, 1981), pp. 81–100

'Widows in late Elizabethan London: remarriage, economic opportunity and family orientation', in L. Bonfield and R. M. Smith (eds.), *The World We Have Gained: Essays Presented to Peter Laslett on his 70th Birthday* (Oxford, 1986), pp. 122–54

Brooks, C., 'Apprenticeship, social mobility and the middling sort, 1550–1800', in J. Barry and C. Brooks (eds.), *The Middling Sort of People: Culture, Society and Politics in England, 1550–1800* (Basingstoke, 1994), pp. 52–83

Bushaway, B., *By Rite: Custom, Ceremony and Community in Eighteenth-Century England, 1700–1800* (London, 1982)

Cannon, J., *Aristocratic Century: The Peerage in Eighteenth-Century England* (Cambridge, 1984)

Carter, M., 'Town or urban society? St Ives in Huntingdonshire, 1630–1740', in C. Phythian-Adams (ed.), *Societies, Cultures and Kinship, 1580–1850* (Leicester, 1993), pp. 77–130

Charles, L. and L. Duffin (eds.), *Women and Work in Pre-Industrial England* (London, 1985)

Charles-Edwards, T. M., 'Kinship, status, and the origins of the hide', *P&P* 56 (1972), 3–33

Chaytor, M., 'Household and kinship in Ryton in the late sixteenth and early seventeenth centuries', *History Workshop Journal* 10 (1980), 25–60

Clark, A., *The Working Life of Women in the Seventeenth Century*, ed. A. L. Erickson (London, 1992; 1st edn 1919)

Clark, J. C. D., *English Society, 1688–1832: Ideology, Social Structure and Political Practice during the Ancien Regime* (Cambridge, 1985)

Clark, P., 'The migrant in Kentish towns, 1580–1640', in P. Clark and P. Slack (eds.), *Crisis and Order in English Towns, 1500–1700* (London, 1972), pp. 117–63

English Provincial Society from the Reformation to the Revolution: Religion, Politics and Society in Kent, 1500–1640 (Canterbury, 1977)

'Migration in England during the late seventeenth and early eighteenth centuries', *P&P* 83 (1979), 57–90

'Migrants in the city: the process of social adaptation in English towns', in P. Clark and D. Souden (eds.), *Migration and Society in Early Modern England* (London, 1987), pp. 267–91

Clark, P. and D. Souden (eds.), *Migration and Society in Early Modern England* (London, 1987)

Clay, C., 'Property settlements, financial provisions for the family, and sale of land by the great landowners, 1660–1790', *Journal of British Studies* 21 (1981), 18–38

Cohen, C. I. and H. Rajkowski, 'What's in a friend? Substantive and theoretical issues', *The Gerontologist* 22 (1982), 261–6

Colley, L., *In Defiance of Oligarchy: The Tory Party 1714–60* (Cambridge, 1982)

Britons: Forging the Nation, 1707–1837 (New Haven and London, 1992)

Collinson, P., *The Birthpangs of Protestant England: Religious and Cultural Change in the Sixteenth and Seventeenth Centuries* (Basingstoke, 1988)

Cooper, J. P., 'Patterns of inheritance and settlement by great landowners from the fifteenth to the eighteenth centuries', in J. Goody, J. Thirsk, and E. P. Thompson (eds.), *Family and Inheritance* (Cambridge, 1976), pp. 192–327

Corfield, P. J. (ed.), *Language, History and Class* (Oxford, 1991)

Power and the Professions in Britain (London and New York, 1995)

Crawford, P., 'Attitudes to menstruation in seventeenth-century England', *P&P* 91 (1981), 47–73

Cressy, D., 'Kinship and kin interaction in early modern England', *P&P* 113 (1986), 38–69

Coming Over: Migration and Communication between England and New England in the Seventeenth Century (Cambridge, 1987)

Birth, Marriage and Death: Ritual, Religion and the Life Cycle in Tudor and Stuart England (Oxford, 1997)

Cretney, S. M. and J. M. Masson, *Principles of Family Law* (6th edn, London, 1997)

Davidoff, L., M. Doolittle, J. Fink, and K. Holden, *The Family Story: Blood, Contract and Intimacy, 1830–1960* (London and New York, 1999)

Davidoff, L. and C. Hall, *Family Fortunes: Men and Women of the English Middle Class, 1780–1850* (London, 1987)

Davis, N. Z., 'Ghosts, kin and progeny', *Daedalus* 106 (1977), 87–114

  Fiction in the Archives: Pardon Tales and their Tellers in Sixteenth-Century France (Cambridge, 1988)

D'Cruze, S., 'The middling sort in eighteenth-century Colchester: independence, social relations and the community broker', in J. Barry and C. Brooks (eds.), *The Middling Sort of People: Culture, Society and Politics in England, 1550–1800* (Basingstoke, 1994), pp. 181–207

Derlega, V. J., and B. A. Winstead (eds.), *Friendship and Social Interaction*, Springer Series in Social Psychology (New York, 1986)

Dodgshon, R. A., 'The landholding foundations of the open field system', *P&P* 67 (1975), 3–29

Donoghue, E., *Passions Between Women: British Lesbian Culture, 1668–1801* (London, 1993)

Doody, M. A., *Natural Passion: A Study of the Novels of Samuel Richardson* (Oxford, 1974)

Dunkin, E. H. W., 'Contributions towards the ecclesiastical history of the deanery of South Malling in the county of Sussex', *SAC* 26 (1875), 9–96

Durkheim, E., 'The conjugal family', in E. Durkheim, *On Institutional Analysis*, ed. and trans. M. Traugott (Chicago and London, 1978), pp. 229–39

  'Review on Ferdinand Toennies, *Gemeinschaft und Gesellschaft*', in E. Durkheim, *On Institutional Analysis*, ed. and trans. M. Traugott (Chicago and London, 1978), pp. 115–22

Earle, P., 'The female labour market in London in the late seventeenth and early eighteenth centuries', *Economic History Review* 42 (1989), 328–53

  The Making of the English Middle Class: Business, Society and Family Life in London, 1660–1730 (London, 1989)

  A City Full of People: Men and Women in London, 1650–1750 (London, 1994)

Eastwood, D., *Government and Community in the Provinces, 1700–1870* (London, 1997)

Eaves, T. C. D. and B. D. Kimpel, 'Richardson's revisions of Pamela', *Studies in Bibliography* 20 (1967), 61–88

  Samuel Richardson (Oxford, 1971)

Elder, G. H. Jr, 'Family and lives: some development in life-course studies', in T. K. Hareven and A. Plakans (eds.), *Family History at the Crossroads: A Journal of Family History Reader* (Princeton, 1987), pp. 179–99

Engels, F., *The Origin of the Family, Private Property and the State*, Introduction by M. Barrett (Harmondsworth, 1985; 1st edn 1884)

English, B. and J. Saville, *Strict Settlement: A Guide for Historians* (Hull, 1983)

Erickson, A. L., *Women and Property in Early Modern England* (New York, 1993)

Everitt, A., *Change in the Provinces: The Seventeenth Century* (Leicester, 1969)
  'The English urban inn, 1560–1760', in A. Everitt, *Landscape and Community in England* (London, 1985), pp. 155–208
  'Springs of sensibility: Philip Doddridge of Northampton and the Evangelical tradition', in A. Everitt, *Landscape and Community in England* (London, 1985), pp. 209–45
Eversley, D. E. C., P. Laslett, and E. A. Wrigley, *An Introduction to English Historical Demography from the Sixteenth to the Nineteenth Century* (New York, 1966)
Fildes, V. (ed.), *Women as Mothers in Pre-Industrial England: Essays in Memory of Dorothy McLaren* (London, 1990)
Finch, J., *Family Obligations and Social Change* (Cambridge, 1989)
Firmager, G. M., 'Eliza Haywood: some further light on her background', *N&Q* n.s. 38 (1991), 181–3
Flandrin, J.-L., *Families in Former Times: Kinship, Household and Sexuality* (Paris, 1976), trans. R. Southern (Cambridge, 1979)
Fletcher, A., *A County Community in Peace and War* (London, 1975)
  Gender, Sex and Subordination in England, 1500–1800 (New Haven and London, 1995)
Fox, A., 'Custom, memory and the authority of writing', in P. Griffiths, A. Fox, and S. Hindle (eds.), *The Experience of Authority in Early Modern England* (Basingstoke, 1997), pp. 89–116
Fox, R., *Kinship and Marriage* (Harmondsworth 1984; 1st edn 1967)
Gaskill, M., 'Reporting murder: fiction in the archives in early modern England', *Social History* 23 (1998), 1–30
Gillis, J. R., *For Better or Worse: British Marriages, 1600 to the Present* (New York and Oxford, 1985)
Gittings, C., *Death, Burial, and the Individual in Early Modern England* (London, 1984)
Goldie, M., 'Contextualizing Dryden's Absalom: William Lawrence, the laws of marriage and the case for King Monmouth', in D. B. Hamilton and R. Streier (eds.), *Religion, Literature and Politics in Post-Reformation England, 1540–1688* (Cambridge, 1996), pp. 208–30
Goode, W., *World Revolution and Family Patterns* (London, 1963)
  'The role of the family and industrialization', in R. F. Winch and L. W. Goodman (eds.), *Selected Studies in Marriage and the Family* (3rd edn, New York, 1968; 1st edn 1953), pp. 64–70
Goody, J., 'The evolution of the family', in P. Laslett and R. Wall (eds.), *Household and Family in Past Time: Comparative Studies in the Size and Structure of the Domestic Group Over the Last Three Centuries in England, France, Serbia, Japan and Colonial North America* (Cambridge, 1972), pp. 103–24
  The Development of the Family and Marriage in Europe (Cambridge, 1983)
Goody, J., J. Thirsk, and E. P. Thompson (eds.), *Family and Inheritance* (Cambridge, 1976)
Goose, N., 'Household size and structure in early Stuart Cambridge', *Social History* 5 (1980), 347–85

Gowing, L., *Domestic Dangers: Women, Words and Sex in Early Modern London* (Oxford, 1996)

Grassby, R., 'Love, property and kinship: the courtship of Philip Williams, Levant merchant 1617–50', *Economic History Review* 113 (1998), 335–50

Greenfield, S. M., 'Industrialization and the family in sociological theory', *American Journal of Sociology* 67 (1961), 312–22

Griffiths, P., *Youth and Authority: Formative Experiences in England, 1560–1640* (Oxford, 1996)

Griffiths, P., A. Fox, and S. Hindle (eds.), *The Experience of Authority in Early Modern England* (Basingstoke, 1997)

Habakkuk, H. J., 'Marriage settlements in the eighteenth century', *Transactions of the Royal Historical Society* 32 (1950), 15–30

Habermas, J., *The Structural Transformation of the Public Sphere: An Inquiry into a Category of Bourgeois Society*, trans. T. Burger with the assistance of F. Lawrence (Cambridge, 1989)

Hajnal, J., 'European marriage patterns in perspective', in D. E. Glass and D. E. C. Eversley (eds.), *Population in History: Essays in Historical Demography* (London, 1965), pp. 101–43

Hammel, C. A. and P. Laslett, 'Comparing household structure over time and between cultures', *Comparative Studies in Society and History* 16 (1974), 73–109

Hanawalt, B. A., *The Ties That Bound: Peasant Families in Medieval England* (Oxford, 1986)

Hareven, T. K., 'The family life cycle in historical perspective: a proposal for a developmental approach', in J. Cuisenier and M. Segalen (eds.), *The Family Life Cycle in European Societies* (The Hague, 1977), pp. 339–52

'The dynamics of kin in an industrial community', in J. Demos and S. S. Boocock (eds.), *Turning Points: Historical and Sociological Essays on the Family* (Chicago, 1978), pp. 151–82

'Cycles, courses, and cohorts: reflection on the theoretical and methodological approaches to the historical study of family development', *Journal of Social History* 12 (1978), 97–109

Family Time and Industrial Time (Cambridge, 1982)

'The history of the family and the complexity of social change', *American Historical Review* 91 (1991), 95–124

Hareven, T. K. (ed.), *Transitions: The Family and the Life Course in Historical Perspective* (New York, 1978)

Hareven, T. K. and A. Plakans (eds.), *Family History at the Crossroads: A Journal of Family History Reader* (Princeton, 1987)

Hay D., and N. Rogers, *Eighteenth-Century English Society: Shuttles and Swords* (Oxford, 1977)

Heal, F., *Hospitality in Early Modern England* (Oxford, 1990)

Heal, F. and C. Holmes (eds.), *The Gentry in England and Wales, 1500–1600* (Basingstoke, 1994)

Heinneman, M., 'Eliza Haywood's career in the theatre', *N&Q* n.s. 20 (1973), 9–13

Henry, L., *Manuel de démographie historique* (Paris, 1967)

Hey, D. G., *An English Rural Community: Myddle under the Tudors and the Stuarts* (Leicester, 1974)

Hill, B., *Women, Work and Sexual Politics in Eighteenth-Century England* (London, 1989)

Hill, C., 'Clarissa Harlowe and her times', in C. Hill, *Puritanism and Revolution: Studies in Interpretation of the English Revolution of the Seventeenth Century* (London, 1958), pp. 367–94

Hindle, S., 'Persuasion and protest in the Caddington Common enclosure', *P&P* 158 (1998), 37–78

Hitchcock, T., P. King, and P. Sharpe (eds.), *Chronicling Poverty: The Voices and Strategies of the English Poor, 1640–1840* (Basingstoke, 1997)

Holderness, B. A., 'Credit in English rural society before the nineteenth century, with special reference to the period 1650–1720', *Agricultural History Review* 24 (1976), 97–109

Holmes, G., *Augustan England: Professions, State and Society, 1680–1750* (London, 1982)

Holmes, G. and D. Szechi, *The Age of Oligarchy: Pre-Industrial England, 1722–1783* (London and New York, 1993)

Hont, I. and M. Ignatieff, *Wealth and Virtue: The Shaping of Political Economy in the Scottish Enlightenment* (Cambridge, 1983)

Hope-Wallace, D. J., 'Eighteenth-century election methods', *SCM* 6 (1932), 640–3, 698–70

Hoppit, J., *Risk and Failure in English Business, 1700–1800* (Cambridge, 1987)

Horsfield, T. W., *The History, Antiquities and Topography of the County of Sussex*, 2 vols. (Lewes, 1835)

Houlbrooke, R., *The English Family, 1450–1700* (London, 1984)
  Death, Religion and the Family in England, 1480–1750 (Oxford, 1998)

Houlbrooke, R. (ed.), *Death, Ritual and Bereavement* (London, 1989)

Howell, C., 'Peasant inheritance customs in the Midlands, 1280–1700', in J. Goody, J. Thirsk and E. P. Thompson (eds.), *Family and Inheritance* (Cambridge, 1976), pp. 112–55
  Land, Family and Inheritance in Transition: Kibworth Harcourt (Cambridge, 1983)

Hunt, M., *The Middling Sort: Commerce, Gender and the Family in England, 1680–1780* (Berkeley and Los Angeles, 1996)

Hurwich, J., 'Lineage and kin in the sixteenth-century aristocracy: some comparative evidence on England and Germany', in A. L. Beier, D. Cannadine, and J. M. Rosenheim (eds.), *The First Modern Society: Essays in English History in Honour of Lawrence Stone* (Cambridge, 1989), pp. 33–64

Hutson, L., *The Usurer's Daughter: Male Friendship and Fictions of Women in Sixteenth-Century England* (New York, 1994)

Huxford, J. F., *Arms of Sussex Families* (Southampton, 1982)

Ignatieff, M., *A Just Measure of Pain: The Penitentiary in the Industrial Revolution, 1750–1850* (New York, 1978)

Ingram, M., *Church Courts, Sex and Marriage in England, 1570–1640* (Cambridge, 1987)

The International Encyclopedia of the Social Sciences, 18 vols. (New York, 1968)

James, L. and J. Gjerde, 'Comparative household morphology of stem, joint, and nuclear household systems: Norway, China, and the United States', *Continuity and Change* 1 (1986), 89–111

James, M., 'Two Tudor funerals', in M. James, *Society, Politics and Culture: Studies in Early Modern England* (Cambridge, 1986), pp. 176–87

Jardine, L., *Reading Shakespeare Historically* (London and New York, 1996)

Johnston, J. A., 'Family, kin and community in eight Lincolnshire parishes, 1567–1800', *Rural History* 6 (1995), 179–92

Keymer, T., *Richardson's Clarissa and the Eighteenth-Century Reader* (Cambridge, 1992)

King, P., 'Gleaners, farmers and the failure of legal sanctions in England, 1750–1850', *P&P* 125 (1989), 116–50

'Customary rights and women's earning: the importance of gleaning to the rural labouring poor, 1750–1850', *Economic History Review* 44 (1991), 461–76

'*Edward Thompson's* contribution to eighteenth-century studies: the patrician-plebeian model re-examined', *Social History* 21 (1996), 215–28

Kussmaul, A., *Servants in Husbandry in Early Modern England* (New Haven and London, 1981)

A General View of the Rural Economy of England, 1538–1840 (Cambridge, 1990)

'The pattern of work as the eighteenth century began', in R. Floud and D. McCloskey (eds.), *The Economic History of Britain Since 1700*, 3 vols. (2nd edn, Cambridge, 1994), vol. I, pp. 1–11

Lambarde, F., 'Coats of arms in Sussex churches', part v, *SAC* 71 (1930), 134–70

Lancaster, L., 'Kinship in Anglo-Saxon society', *British Journal of Sociology* 9 (1958), 236–9

Landes, D. S., *Revolution in Time: Clocks and the Making of the Modern World* (Cambridge, Mass., 1983)

Langford, P., *A Polite and Commercial People: England 1727–1783* (Oxford, 1989)

Public Life and the Propertied Englishman, 1689–1798: The Ford Lectures Delivered in the University of Oxford (Oxford, 1991)

Laslett, P., *The World We Have Lost* (New York, 1965)

'Size and structure of the household in England over three centuries', *Population Studies* 23 (1969), 199–223

'Mean household size in England since the sixteenth century', in P. Laslett and R. Wall (eds.), *Household and Family in Past Time: Comparative Studies in the Size and Structure of the Domestic Group Over the Last Three Centuries in England, France, Serbia, Japan and Colonial North America* (Cambridge, 1972), pp. 125–58

'Characteristics of the Western family considered over time', *Journal of Family History* 2 (1977), 89–115

Family Life and Illicit Love in Earlier Generations: Essays in Historical Sociology, (Cambridge, 1977)

'Le cycle familial et le processus de socialization: caractéristiques du schéma occidental considéré dans le temps', in J. Cuisenier and M. Segalen (eds.), *The Family Life Cycle in European Societies* (The Hague, 1977), pp. 317–38

'The family and the collectivity', *Sociology and Social Research* 63 (1979), 432–42

'Family and household as work and kin groups', in R. Wall, J. Robin, and P. Laslett (eds.), *Family Forms in Historic Europe* (Cambridge, 1983), pp. 513–63

The World We Have Lost – Further Explored (Cambridge, 1983)

'The character of familial history, its limitations and the conditions for its proper pursuit', in T. K. Hareven and A. Plakans (eds.), *Family History at the Crossroads: A Journal of Family History Reader* (Princeton, 1987), Appendix, pp. 277–81

'La parenté en chiffres', *Annales: Economies, Sociétés, Civilisations* 43 (1988), 5–24

'Family, kinship and collectivity as systems of support in pre-industrial Europe: a consideration of the "nuclear hardship" hypothesis', *Continuity and Change* 3 (1988), 153–75

Laslett, P. and J. Harrison, 'Clayworth and Cogenhoe', in H. E. Bell and R. L. Ollard (eds.), *Historical Essays, 1600–1750, Presented to David Ogg* (London, 1963), pp. 157–84

Laslett, P. and R. Wall (eds.), *Household and Family in Past Time: Comparative Studies in the Size and Structure of the Domestic Group Over the Last Three Centuries in England, France, Serbia, Japan and Colonial North America* (Cambridge, 1972)

Laurence, A., *Women in England, 1500–1760: A Social History* (London, 1994)

Lawson, J. and H. Silver, *A Social History of Education in England* (London, 1974)

Lees, L. H., *Exiles of Erin: Irish Migrants in Victorian London* (Manchester, 1979)

Levine, D., *Family Formation in an Age of Nascent Capitalism* (New York, 1977)

Reproducing Families: A Political Economy of English Population History (Cambridge, 1987)

Levine, D. and K. Wrightson, *The Making of an Industrial Society: Whickham 1560–1765* (Oxford, 1991)

Lord, E., 'Communities of common interest: the social landscape of south east Surrey, 1750–1850', in C. Phythian-Adams (ed.), *Societies, Cultures and Kinship, 1580–1850* (Leicester, 1993), pp. 131–99

Lucas, P., 'The Verrall family of Lewes', *SAC* 58 (1916), 91–131

Macfarlane, A., *The Family Life of Ralph Josselin: A Seventeenth-Century Clergyman* (Cambridge, 1970)

The Origins of English Individualism: The Family, Property and Social Transition (Oxford, 1978)

'The myth of the peasantry: family, and economy in a northern parish', in R. M. Smith (ed.), *Land, Kinship and Life-Cycle* (Cambridge, 1984), pp. 333–49

Marriage and Love in England, 1300–1840 (Oxford, 1986)

The Culture of Capitalism (Oxford, 1987)

Macfarlane, A., S. Harrison, and C. Jardine, *Reconstructing Historical Communities* (Cambridge, 1977)

McIntosh, M. K., 'Servants and the household unit in an Elizabethan English community', *Journal of Family History* 9 (1984), 3–23

A Community Transformed: The Manor and Liberty of Havering, 1500–1620 (Cambridge, 1991)

McKendrick, N., '"Gentlemen and players" revisited: the gentlemanly ideal, the business ideal and the professional ideal in English literary culture', in N.

McKendrick and R. B. Outhwaite (eds.), *Business Life and Public Policy: Essays in Honour of D. C. Coleman* (Cambridge, 1986), pp. 98–136

McKendrick, N., J. Brewer, and J. H. Plumb (eds.), *The Birth of a Consumer Society: The Commercialization of Eighteenth-Century England* (London, 1982)

McKillop, A. D., *Samuel Richardson, Printer and Novelist* (Chapel Hill, 1936)

Maine, H. S., *Ancient Law: Its Connection with the Early History of Society and Its Relation to Modern Ideas* (London, 1905; 1st edn 1861)

Malcolmson, R. W., *Life and Labour in England, 1700–1780* (London, 1981)

Mascuch, M., 'Social mobility and middling self-identity: the ethos of British autobiographers, 1600–1750', *Social History* 20 (1995), 45–61

Origins of the Individualist Self: Autobiography and Self-Identity in England, 1591–1791 (Cambridge, 1997)

Mayhew, G., 'Life cycle and the family unity in early modern Rye', *Continuity and Change* 6 (1991), 201–26

Medick, H. and D. W. Sabean, *Interest and Emotion: Essays on the Study of Family and Kinship* (Cambridge, 1984)

Mendelson, S. H., 'Debate: the weightiest business', *P&P* 85 (1979), 126–35

Mills, W. B., *Parliamentary History of the Borough of Lewes: 1795–1885* (London, 1908), pp. 24–76

Mitson, A., 'The significance of kinship networks in the seventeenth century: south-west Nottinghamshire', in C. Phythian-Adams (ed.), *Societies, Cultures and Kinship, 1580–1850* (Leicester, 1993), pp. 24–76

Mitterauer, M. and R. Sieder, *The European Family: Patriarchy to Partnership from the Middle Ages to the Present* (Munich, 1977), trans. K. Osterveen and M. Horzinger (Oxford, 1982)

Morgan, E. S., *The Puritan Family: Religion and Domestic Relations in Seventeenth-Century New England* (rev. edn, New York, 1966)

Morgan, L. H., *Systems of Consanguinity and Affinity in the Human Family* (Washington, 1870)

Mui, H.-C. and L. H. Mui, *Shops and Shopkeeping in Eighteenth-Century England* (London and Kingston, 1989)

Muldrew, C., *The Economy of Obligation: The Culture of Credit and Social Relations in Early Modern England* (Basingstoke, 1998)

Murdock, G. P., *Social Structure* (New York, 1949)

Nair, G., *Highley: The Development of a Community 1550–1880* (Oxford, 1988)

Namier, L. B., *The Structure of Politics at the Accession of George III* (London, 1957; 1st edn 1929)

England in the Age of the American Revolution (London, 1961; 1st edn 1930)

Namier, L. B. and J. Brooke, *The History of Parliament: The House of Commons, 1754–1790*, 3 vols. (London, 1964)

Neeson, J., *Commoners: Common Rights, Enclosure and Social Change in England, 1700–1820* (Cambridge, 1993)

Netting, R. McC., R. R. Wilk, and E. J. Arnould (eds.), *Households: Comparative and Historical Studies of the Domestic Group* (Berkeley and Los Angeles, 1984)

Newman Brown, W., 'The receipt of poor relief and the family situation: Aldenham Hertfordshire, 1630–1690', in R. M. Smith (ed.), *Land, Kinship and Life-Cycle* (Cambridge, 1984), pp. 403–22

O'Day, R., *Education and Society, 1500–1800: The Social Foundations of Education in Early Modern England* (London, 1982)
> *The Family and Family Relationships, 1500–1900: England, France and the United States of America* (London, 1994)
Ogburn, W. F., 'Social change and the family', in R. F. Winch and L. W. Goodman (eds.), *Selected Studies in Marriage and the Family* (3rd edn, New York, 1968; 1st edn 1953) pp. 58–63
O'Gorman, F., 'Electoral deference in "unreformed" England, 1760–1832', *Journal of Modern History* 56 (1984), 391–429
> *Voters, Patrons and Parties: The Unreformed Electoral System of Hanoverian England, 1734–1832* (Oxford, 1989)
O'Hara, D., 'Ruled by my friends: aspects of marriage in the diocese of Canterbury *c.* 1540–1570', *Continuity and Change* 6 (1991), 9–41
Ottaway, S., 'Providing for the elderly in eighteenth-century England', *Continuity and Change* 13 (1998), 391–418
Outhwaite, R. B., *Clandestine Marriage in England, 1500–1850* (London, 1995)
Outhwaite, R. B. (ed.), *Marriage and Society: Studies in the Social History of Marriage* (London, 1981)
Parsons, T., 'The kinship system of the contemporary United States', in T. Parsons, *Essays in Social Theory* (rev. edn, New York, 1949; first published in *American Anthropologist*, 1943), pp. 177–98
> 'The social structure of the family', in R. N. Anshen (ed.), *The Family: Its Function and Destiny* (New York, 1959; 1st edn 1949), pp. 241–74
Parsons, T. and R. F. Bales, *Family, Socialization and Interaction Process* (London 1968; 1st edn 1956)
Pedersen, J. C., 'The reform of women's secondary and higher education: institutional change and social values in mid and late Victorian England', *History of Education Quarterly* 19 (1979), 61–91
Pelling, M., 'Apprenticeship, health and social cohesion in early modern London', *History Workshop Journal* 37 (1994), 33–56
Perkin, H., *Origins of Modern English Society, 1780–1880* (London, 1969)
Phillips, J. A., 'The structure of electoral politics in unreformed England', *Journal of British Studies* 19 (1979), 76–100
> *Electoral Behaviour in Unreformed England, 1761–1802: Plumpers, Splitters and Straighters* (Princeton, 1982)
Phillpotts, B., *Kindred and Clan in the Middle Ages and After: A Study in the Sociology of the Teutonic Races* (Cambridge, 1913)
Phythian-Adams, C. (ed.), *Societies, Cultures and Kinship, 1580–1850* (Leicester, 1993)
Pitt-Rivers, J., 'The kith and kin', in J. Goody (ed.), *The Character of Kinship* (Cambridge, 1973), pp. 89–105
Plakans, A., 'Interaction between the household and the kin group in the Eastern European past: posing the problem', in T. K. Hareven and A. Plakans (eds.), *Family History at the Crossroads: A Journal of Family History Reader* (Princeton, 1987), pp. 163–75
Plumb, J. H., 'Political man', in J. L. Clifford (ed.), *Man Versus Society in Eighteenth-Century Britain: Six Points of View* (Cambridge, 1968), pp. 1–21

'The new world of children in eighteenth-century England', in N. McKendrick, J. Brewer, and J. H. Plumb (eds.), *The Birth of a Consumer Society: The Commercialization of Eighteenth-Century England* (London, 1982), pp. 286–315

Pocock, J. G. A., *Virtue, Commerce and History: Essays on Political Thought, Chiefly in the Eighteenth Century* (London, 1985)

Pollock, L., *Forgotten Children: Parent–Child Relations from 1500–1900* (Cambridge, 1983)

'"Teach her to live under obedience": the making of women in the upper ranks of early modern England', *Continuity and Change* 4 (1989), 231–58

'Younger sons in Tudor and Stuart England', *History Today* 39 (1989), 23–9

'Rethinking patriarchy and the family in seventeenth-century England', *Journal of Family History* 23 (1998), 3–27

Porter, R. and S. Tomaselli (eds.), *The Dialectics of Friendship* (London, 1989)

Prior, M., *Fisher Row: Fishermen, Bargemen and Canal Boatmen in Oxford, 1500–1900* (Oxford, 1982)

Rappaport, S., *Worlds Within Worlds: Structures of Life in Sixteenth-Century London* (Cambridge, 1989)

Raven, J., *British Fiction, 1750–1770: A Chronological Check-List of Prose Fiction Printed in Britain and Ireland* (Cranbury, 1987)

Judging New Wealth: Popular Publishing and Responses to Commerce in England, 1750–1800 (Oxford, 1992)

Razi, Z., 'The myth of the immutable English family', *P&P* 140 (1993), 3–44

Reay, B., 'Kinship and neighbourhood in nineteenth-century rural England: the myth of the autonomous nuclear family', *Journal of Family History* 21 (1996), 87–104

Renshaw, W. C., 'Some clergy of the Archdeaconry of Lewes and South Malling Deanery', *SAC* 55 (1912), 220–77

Richetti, J., *Popular Fiction Before Richardson: Narrative Patterns, 1700–1739* (Oxford, 1969)

Robinson, D., 'Unravelling the "cord which ties good men to good men": male friendship in Richardson's novels', in M. A. Doody (ed.), *Samuel Richardson: Tercentenary Essays* (Cambridge, 1989), pp. 167–87

Rogers, N., 'The middling sort in eighteenth-century politics', in J. Barry and C. Brooks (eds.), *The Middling Sort of People: Culture, Society and Politics in England, 1550–1800* (Basingstoke, 1994), pp. 159–80

Rollison, D., *The Local Origins of Modern Society: Gloucestershire, 1500–1800* (London, 1992)

Rosenheim, J., *The Emergence of a Ruling Order: English Landed Society, 1650–1750* (London and New York, 1998)

Rule, J. G., *The Vital Century: England's Developing Economy, 1714–1815* (London and New York, 1992)

Rushton, P., 'Property, power and family networks, the problem of disputed marriage in early modern England', *Journal of Family History* 11 (1986), 205–19

Salzman, L. F., 'Philip Turner', *SNQ* 16 (1963)

Schapera, I., *Kinship Terminology in Jane Austen's Novels*, Royal Anthropological

Institute of Great Britain and Ireland, Occasional Paper no. 33 (London, 1977)

Schochet, G. J., *Patriarchalism in Political Thought* (Oxford, 1973)

Schofield, R. S., 'Age-specific mobility in an eighteenth-century English parish', *Annales de démographie historique* (1970), 261–74

Seaver, P. S., *Wallington's World: A Puritan Artisan in Seventeenth-Century London* (Stanford, 1985)

Segalen, M., *Historical Anthropology of the Family*, trans. J. C. Whitehouse and S. Matthews (Cambridge, 1986)

Sekora, J., *Luxury: The Concept in Western Thought, Eden to Smollett* (Baltimore and London, 1977)

Sharp, R. A., *Friendship and Literature: Spirit and Form* (Durham, 1986)

Sharpe, J. A., *Defamation and Sexual Slander in Early Modern England* (York, 1980)

Early Modern England: A Social History (London, 1987)

Crime in Early Modern England, 1550–1750 (London, 1992)

Sharpe, P., 'Literally spinsters: a new interpretation of local economy and demography in Colyton in the seventeenth and eighteenth centuries', *Economic History Review* 44 (1991), 46–65

Shoemaker, R. B., *Gender in English Society, 1650–1850: The Emergence of Separate Spheres* (London, 1998)

Shorter, E., *The Making of the Modern Family* (London, 1976)

Skedd, S., 'Women teachers and the expansion of girls' schooling in England, c. 1760–1820', in H. Barker and E. Chalus (eds.), *Gender in Eighteenth-Century England: Roles, Representations, Responsibilities* (London, 1997), pp. 101–25

Skinner, Q. R. D., 'The principles and practice of opposition: the case of Bolingbroke versus Walpole', in N. McKendrick (ed.), *Historical Perspectives: Studies in English Thought and Society in Honour of J. H. Plumb* (London, 1974), pp. 93–128

Slack, P., *Poverty and Policy in Tudor and Stuart England* (London and New York, 1988)

Slater, M., 'The weightiest business: marriage in an upper gentry family in seventeenth-century England', *P&P* 72 (1976), 25–54

'Rejoinder', *P&P* 85 (1979), 136–40

Family Life in the Seventeenth Century: The Verneys of Claydon House (London, 1984)

Smail, J., *The Origins of Middle-Class Culture: Halifax, Yorkshire 1660–1780* (Ithaca, 1994)

Smith, L. B., 'The Pelham vault', *SCM* 4 (1930), 370–2

Smith, R. M., 'Some issues concerning families and their property', in R. M. Smith (ed.), *Land, Kinship and Life-Cycle* (Cambridge, 1984), pp. 1–86

(ed.), *Land, Kinship and Life-Cycle* (Cambridge, 1984)

'The structured dependence of the elderly as a recent development: some skeptical historical thoughts', *Ageing and Society* 4 (1984), 409–28

Smith, R. M. and M. Pelling (eds.), *Life, Death and the Elderly: Historical Perspectives* (London, 1994)

Snell, K. D. M., 'Parish registration and the study of labour mobility', *Local Population Studies* 33 (1984), 29–43

Annals of the Labouring Poor: Social Change and Agrarian England, 1660–1900 (Cambridge, 1985)

Souden, D., 'Movers and stayers in family reconstitution populations', *Local Population Studies* 33 (1984), 11–28

Spencer, J., *The Rise of the Woman Novelist: From Aphra Behn to Jane Austen* (Oxford, 1986)

Spring, E., 'The strict settlement: its role in family history', *Economic History Review* 41 (1988), 454–60

Spufford, M., *Contrasting Communities: English Villagers in the Sixteenth and Seventeenth Centuries* (Cambridge, 1974)

Staves, S., *Married Women's Separate Property in England, 1660–1833* (Cambridge, Mass., 1990)

Stone, L., 'Social mobility in England, 1500–1700', *P&P* 33 (1966), 16–55

'The rise of the nuclear family in early modern England: the patriarchal stage', in C. E. Rosenberg (ed.), *The Family in History* (Philadelphia, 1975), pp. 13–57

The Family, Sex and Marriage in England 1500–1800 (Harmondsworth, 1977)

'Spring back', *Albion* 17 (1985), 167–80

Road to Divorce: England 1530–1987 (Oxford, 1992)

Broken Lives: Marriage and Divorce in England 1660–1875 (Oxford, 1995)

Stone, L. and J. C. F. Stone, *An Open Elite? England 1540–1880* (Oxford, 1984)

Suttles, G. D., 'Friendship as a social institution', in G. J. McCall, M. M. McCall, N. K. Denzin, G. D. Suttles, and S. B. Kurth, *Social Relationships* (Chicago, 1970), pp. 95–135

Tadmor, N., '"Family" and "friend" in *Pamela*: a case study in the history of the family in eighteenth-century England', *Social History* 14 (1989), 289–306

'Dimensions of inequality among siblings in eighteenth-century novels: the cases of *Clarissa* and *The History of Miss Betsy Thoughtless*', *Continuity and Change* 7 (1992), 303–33

'The concept of the household-family in eighteenth-century England', *P&P* 151 (1996), 110–40

'In the even my wife read to me: women, reading and household life in the eighteenth century', in J. Raven, H. Small, and N. Tadmor (eds.), *The Practice and Representation of Reading in England* (Cambridge, 1996), pp. 162–74

Taylor, J. S., *Poverty, Migration and Settlement in the Industrial Revolution* (Palo Alto, 1989)

Thomas, K., 'The double standard', *Journal of the History of Ideas* 20 (1959), 195–216

'Age and authority in early modern England', *Proceedings of the British Academy* 62 (1976), 205–48

'Children in early modern England', in G. Avery and J. Briggs (eds.), *Children and their Books: A Celebration of the Work of Iona and Peter Opie* (Oxford, 1989), pp. 45–77

Thompson, E. P., 'Time, work-discipline, and industrial capitalism', *P&P* 38 (1967), 56–97

Customs in Common (London, 1991)

'The patricians and the plebs', in E. P. Thompson, *Customs in Common* (London, 1991), pp. 16–96

Thompson, R., *Mobility and Migration: East Anglia Founders of New England, 1629–1640* (Amherst, Mass., 1994)

Todd, J., *Women's Friendship in Literature* (New York, 1980)

The Sign of Angellica: Women, Writing and Fiction, 1660–1800 (London, 1989)

Toennies, F., *Fundamental Concepts of Sociology (Gemeinschaft und Gesellschaft)*, trans. and supplemented Charles P. Loomis, *American Sociology Series* (1904; 1st edn 1887)

Trumbach, R., *The Rise of the Egalitarian Family: Aristocratic Kinship and Domestic Relations in Eighteenth-Century England* (New York and London, 1978)

Tuck, R., *Natural Rights Theories: Their Origin and Development* (Cambridge, 1979)

Underdown, D. E., *Fire From Heaven: The Life of an English Town in the Seventeenth Century* (London, 1992)

Vann, R. T., 'Wills and the family in an English town: Banbury, 1550–1800', *Journal of Family History* 4 (1979), 346–67

Vickery, A. J., 'Golden age to separate spheres? A review of the categories and chronology of English women's history', *Historical Journal* 36 (1993), 383–414

The Gentleman's Daughter: Women's Life in Georgian England (New Haven and London, 1998)

Wales, T., 'Poverty, poor relief and the life-cycle: some evidence from seventeenth-century Norfolk', in R. M. Smith (ed.), *Land, Kinship and Life-Cycle* (Cambridge, 1984), pp. 351–404

Wall, R., 'Mean household size in England from the printed sources', in P. Laslett and R. Wall (eds.), *Household and Family in Past Time: Comparative Studies in the Size and Structure of the Domestic Group Over the Last Three Centuries in England, France, Serbia, Japan and Colonial North America* (Cambridge, 1972), pp. 159–203

'The age at leaving home', *Journal of Family History* 3 (1978), 181–202

'Regional and temporal variations in English household structure from 1650', in J. Hobcraft and P. Rees (eds.), *Regional Aspects of British Population Growth* (London, 1979), pp. 89–113

'The household: demographic and economic change in England, 1650–1970', in R. Wall, J. Robin and P. Laslett (eds.), *Family Forms in Historic Europe* (Cambridge, 1983), pp. 493–512

'Leaving home and the process of household formation in pre-industrial England', *Continuity and Change* 2 (1987), 77–101

Walter, J., 'A rising of the people – the Oxfordshire rising of 1596', *P&P* 107 (1985), 90–143

Whicher, G. F., *The Life and Romances of Mrs. Eliza Haywood* (New York, 1915)

Wilk, R. R. and R. McC. Netting, 'Households: changing forms and functions', in R. McC. Netting, R. R. Wilk, and E. J. Arnoud (eds.), *Households:*

Comparative and Historical Studies of the Domestic Group (Berkeley and Los Angeles, 1984), pp. 1–28

Williams, R., *Keywords: A Vocabulary of Culture and Society* (London, 1976)

Wilmott, P., 'Kinship and social legislation', *British Journal of Sociology* 9 (1958), 126–42

Winch, R. F. and R. L. Blumberg, 'Social complexity and familial organization', in R. F. Winch and L. W. Goodman (eds.), *Selected Studies in Marriage and the Family* (3rd edn, New York, 1968; 1st edn 1953) pp. 70–92

Wiseman, J. P., 'Friendship: bonds that bind in a voluntary relationship', *Journal of Social and Personal Relationships* 3 (1986), 191–211

Wolf, E. G., 'Kinship, friendship and patron–client relations in complex societies', in M. Banton (ed.), *The Social Anthropology of Complex Societies* (London, 1968), pp. 1–22

Wolfram, S., *In-Laws and Outlaws: Kinship and Marriage in England* (London and Sydney, 1987)

Worcester, D. K. Jun., *The Life and Times of Thomas Turner of East Hoathly*; *Undergraduate Prize Essays*, vol. IV (Oxford and New Haven, 1948)

Wrightson, K., 'Household and kinship in sixteenth-century England', *History Workshop Journal* 12 (1981), 151–8

English Society, 1580–1680 (London, 1982)

'Kinship in an English village: Terling, Essex, 1500–1700', in R. M. Smith (ed.), *Land, Kinship and Life-Cycle* (Cambridge, 1984), pp. 313–32

'The family in early modern England: continuity and change', in S. Taylor, R. Connors, and C. Jones (eds.), *Hanoverian Britain and Empire: Essays in Memory of Philip Lawson* (Woodbridge, 1998), pp. 1–22

'Sorts of people in Tudor and Stuart England', in J. Barry and C. Brooks (eds.), *The Middling Sort of People: Culture, Society and Politics in England, 1550–1800* (Basingstoke, 1994), pp. 28–51

'The politics of the parish in early modern England', in P. Griffiths, A. Fox, and S. Hindle (eds.), *The Experience of Authority in Early Modern England* (Basingstoke, 1997), pp. 10–46

Earthly Necessities: Economic Lives in Early Modern Britain (New Haven and London, 2000)

Wrightson, K. and D. Levine, *Poverty and Piety in an English Village: Terling, 1525–1700* (Oxford, 1995; 1st edn 1979)

Wrigley, E. A., 'Family reconstitution', in D. E. C. Eversley, P. Laslett, and E. A. Wrigley, *An Introduction to English Historical Demography from the Sixteenth to the Nineteenth Century* (New York, 1966), pp. 96–159

'Family limitation in pre-industrial England', *Economic History Review* 19 (1966), 82–109

'A simple model of London's importance in changing English society and economy, 1650–1750', *P&P* 73 (1967), 44–70

Population and History: From the Traditional to the Modern World (London, 1969)

'Reflections on the history of the family', *Daedalus* 106 (1977), 71–85

People, Cities and Wealth: The Transformation of Traditional Society (Oxford, 1987)

'Urban growth and agricultural change', in E. A. Wrigley, *People, Cities and*

Wealth: The Transformation of a Traditional Society (Oxford, 1987), pp. 157–93
Wrigley, E. A. and R. S. Schofield, *The Population History of England, 1541–1871: A Reconstruction* (Cambridge, 1989; 1st edn 1981)
Zomchick, J. P., *Family and the Law in Eighteenth-Century Fiction: The Public Conscience in the Private Sphere* (Cambridge, 1993)

PHD DISSERTATIONS

Brodsky Elliot, V., 'Mobility and marriage in pre-industrial England', unpublished PhD dissertation (Cambridge, 1979)
Donoghue, E., 'Male–female friendship and English fiction in the mid-eighteenth century', unpublished PhD dissertation (Cambridge, 1996)
Issa, C., 'Obligation and choice: aspects of family and kinship in seventeenth-century County Durham', unpublished PhD dissertation (St Andrews, 1987)
Tadmor, N., 'Concepts of the family in five eighteenth-century texts', unpublished PhD dissertation (Cambridge, 1992)

Index

Adams, Peter, 206
adoption, 59, 157, 274n
Alfriston, 203
apprenticeship and apprentices, 30, 35,
    106, 168, 175, 190
  contractual relationships, 27, 57, 58,
    59
  failure, 57, 58, 59, 63
  in households and families, 19, 20, 23,
    39, 45, 53–63, 272
  kinship, 58–9, 108n, 114n, 115, 183, 186
  notions of lineage and ancestry, 89, 91
  notions of time, 63, 64
  untimely termination of contract, 57,
    58
  see also professions and occupations;
    Richardson, Samuel
Aquinas, St Thomas, 238, 239
Aristotle, 238, 240
associational life, 122
  see also societies and clubs
aunts and uncles, 30, 104, 114, 119, 121,
    123, 124, 125, 130, 131, 133, 134, 135,
    138, 140, 144, 147, 150, 151, 152, 155,
    159, 160, 211, 256, 259, 260, 262, 264,
    265, 267, 268, 275
Austen, Jane
  formulaic usages, 68n, 96
  language of kinship, 104, 131–2, 137,
    145, 154
authority, 158, 275
  in household-families, 20, 22, 24, 27, 35,
    42, 43, 50, 54, 272
  see also submission

Baley, Abraham, 87–8
Banister, George, 204–5, 207
Battle, 77, 78–9
Beard, George, 30
Bedfordshire, 52
Ben-Amos, I. K., 115
Bible, 138

Hebrew Bible, 145, 146, 153, 159, 169,
    192–3, 195, 243
  New Testament, 149, 239–40
Blackstone, Sir William, 59n, 130, 160,
    274n
Blundell, Nicholas, 142
boarders, 34, 50
  contractual relationships, 27
  in household-families, 19, 38, 39, 56, 65,
    272
Booker, Gertrude, 144
Breeden, John, 200–1, 202
Bryer, John, 128
Bury St Edmunds, 104, 132, 134, 168
Byng, John, Admiral, 189

Calverley, Mr, 79
Canada, 85
Catholicism and 'popery', 158, 234
charity, 210
  among kin and friends, 124, 126, 128,
    129, 130, 166, 188, 241, 242, 243, 250
  denial of charity and support, 117, 123,
    128, 130
  friendly societies, 168–9
  see also kinship; patronage; Pelham
    family; poverty and poor relief
Chaytor, M., 111–12
children and adolescents, 1, 2, 25, 34–5, 55,
    58, 59n, 104, 112, 114n, 115, 120–1,
    123, 126, 128, 149, 155, 159, 160, 175,
    186, 194, 211, 272, 274
  step-children, 112, 143, 154, 156
  see also apprenticeship and apprentices;
    illegitimacy; life-cycle and life-course;
    parent–child relationships and
    terminology; step-relationships and
    teminology
Cholwich, John, 127
Christian names and surnames, 141–2, 143,
    146, 154, 156, 183
Christianity, 238, 239–40, 270